The Best Test Preparation for the

AP
Italian
Language and Culture Exam

Ellen Valtri Knauer, M.A.
Instructor of French and Italian
West Chester Area School District
West Chester, PA

Research & Education Association
Visit our website at
www.rea.com

Research & Education Association
61 Ethel Road West
Piscataway, New Jersey 08854
E-mail: info@rea.com

The Best Test Preparation for the
AP ITALIAN LANGUAGE AND CULTURE EXAM

Printed in the United States of America

Library of Congress Control Number 2007941757

ISBN-13: 978-0-7386-0214-1
ISBN-10: 0-7386-0214-0

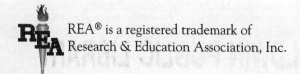

TABLE OF CONTENTS

Detailed Explanations of Answers

FOREWORD

I hope that you will enjoy using this book as much as I have enjoyed writing it. The study of Foreign Languages has been my great joy for more than forty years

I am pleased to offer a new, thorough, and user-friendly study aid to guide you in your preparation for the AP Italian Language and Culture Exam. The drills allow you to concentrate on whatever areas you need to review. The Pre-Exam exercises and three full-length practice tests provide the best possible format to prepare for the actual exam. All answers are explained for you in detail. Complete transcripts are provided for everything you will hear on the audio CDs. All of the recordings were made by native speakers who model authentic accents, pronunciation and intonation.

Work with this book on a regular basis; pace yourself as the exam approaches. If you have a question, you can reach me at this address: *EAKnauer@aol.com*

Coraggio e in bocca al lupo!
Ellen Valtri Knauer

ACKNOWLEDGMENTS

I would like to acknowledge the invaluable help and expertise made available to me at The Language Center, via Mazzini 18, 06059 Todi (Pg) Italy.

Special thanks to these wonderful staff members: Stefania Belli, *titolare*; Federica Vizzotto, vivacious teacher and coordinator; Valentina Tomba, cheerful and indispensable secretary; Giulia Gregori, immersion course manager; and Francesca Granieri, promotional director. To Lilli Caporello, a talented and remarkable young teacher who spent hours going over this manuscript with me, my most sincere and humble grazie. To my wonderful teacher, Eleonora Bracci, for her inspired creativity, cleverness, and the genuine pleasure she took in working on this opera, grazie di cuore. I never had so much fun working so hard in all my life.

I want to extend a special thank you to my former student, David Sanderson, who created the excellent sketches in the picture sequences.

I would also like to thank Diane Goldschmidt, my editor and muse; Filomena Masciantonio Elliott, my colleague and dear friend; Dr. Stefanie Fiore, professor of Italian at Temple Univeristy, for her encouragement and advice; and lastly, my Dad, who always believed in me.

ABOUT OUR AUTHOR

Ellen Knauer earned her B.A. in French Literature at Pennsylvania State University in State College, Pennsylvania. She also studied as an exchange student at the Université de Strasbourg, in Strasbourg, France. She was awarded the Copeland-Andelot Fellowship for graduate study at the University of Delaware, where she earned her M.A. in French Literature. Subsequent coursework at Immaculata College, Saint Joseph's College, West Chester University, and Temple University led to the completion of Pennsylvania teaching certificates in French, German, and Italian. Mrs. Knauer still enjoys taking courses and has accumulated more than 60 post-M.A. graduate credits. She has also published a series of animated lessons for the foreign language classroom in French, German, Italian, and Spanish. She currently teaches French and Italian for the West Chester Area School District, in West Chester, Pennsylvania.

ABOUT RESEARCH & EDUCATION ASSOCIATION

Founded in 1959, Research & Education Association (REA) is dedicated to publishing the finest and most effective educational materials—including software, study guides, and test preps—for students in middle school, high school, college, graduate school, and beyond. REA's test preparation series includes books and software for all academic levels in almost all disciplines. REA publishes test preps for students who have not yet entered high school, as well as high school students preparing to enter college. We invite you to visit us at *www.rea.com* to find out how "REA is making the world smarter."

ACKNOWLEDGMENTS

In addition to our author, we would like to thank Larry B. Kling, Vice President, Editorial, for his overall guidance; Pam Weston, Vice President, Publishing, for setting the quality standards for production integrity and managing the publication to completion; Diane Goldschmidt, Senior Editor, for coordinating this edition and editorial quality assurance; Christine Saul, Senior Graphic Artist, for designing our cover; and Jeff LoBalbo, Senior Graphic Artist, for post-production file mapping.

We also extend our thanks to Kathy Caratozzolo of Caragraphics for typesetting this edition and Amazing Voice for recording our audio CDs.

Chapter 1

Excelling on the AP Italian Language and Culture Exam

Chapter 1

Excelling on the AP Italian Language and Culture Exam

About This Book

This book provides an accurate and complete representation of the Advanced Placement Examination in Italian Language and Culture. Our practice tests are based on the format of the most recently administered Advanced Placement Italian Language and Culture exam. Each model exam lasts three hours and includes every type of question that you can expect to encounter on the real test. Following each of our practice exams is an answer key, complete with detailed explanations designed to clarify the material for you. By using the subject review, completing the practice tests, and studying the explanations that follow, you will pinpoint your strengths and weaknesses and, above all, put yourself in the best possible position to do well on the actual test.

About the Advanced Placement Program

The AP Italian Language and Culture examination is offered each May at participating schools and multi-school centers throughout the world.

The Advanced Placement Program is designed to allow high school students to pursue college-level studies while attending high school. The participating colleges, in turn, grant credit and/or advanced placement to students who do well on the examinations.

The Advanced Placement Italian Language and Culture course is designed to be the equivalent of a college introductory Italian language class.

For registration bulletins or more detailed information about the AP Italian Language and Culture exam, contact:

AP Services
Educational Testing Service
P.O. Box 6671
Princeton, NJ 08541-6671
Phone: (609) 771-7300 or (888) 225-5427
E-mail: apexams@ets.org
Website: *www.collegeboard.com*

Format and Content of the
AP Italian Language and Culture Exam

The AP Italian Language and Culture exam is approximately three hours long. It tests your ability to understand both written and spoken Italian. It also tests the ease and fluency with which you can respond in speaking and writing.

The exam is divided into two sections:

Section I: The multiple-choice section of the exam assesses the test-taker's listening and reading comprehension.

> Part A requires the student to listen to dialogues or short narratives and answer multiple-choice questions based on what the student heard. Students are given time to read the printed questions before listening to the recorded segment. This section contains 30 to 34 questions and 35 minutes is allowed for completion.

> Part B, the reading portion, requires the student to read passages and answer multiple-choice questions based on the passages. This 55-minute section can contain up to 48 questions.

Section II: This free-response section assesses the test-taker's writing and speaking abilities and contains three parts:

> Part A assesses the student's writing ability by requiring the student to complete two fill-in exercises and write a composition. The first fill-in exercise tests verb forms and the second exercise tests other grammar points. The essay portion, which is 30 minutes long, requires the student to write a 150-word essay in Italian on a general topic.

> Part B assesses the student's cultural knowledge by requiring the student to write a 150-word essay on a cultural topic normally covered in an AP Italian Language and Culture course. Students are allowed 30 minutes to complete their composition.

Part C of the exam assesses the student's speaking skills. Students are required to narrate a story suggested by a series of pictures and also to respond to a series of questions based on a general topic.

Each of the five parts of the exam has the same value for scoring purposes and each part contributes 20 percent to the student's final AP grade.

About the Multiple-Choice Sections

Listening and reading skills are tested with multiple-choice questions. You will be expected to choose the correct answer from four possibilities for each question. You mark your answer choice (A, B, C or D) on an answer grid that is provided in your test booklet.

In the listening portion of the exam, you will generally hear a series of dialogues between two speakers, or a short narrative. Each dialogue or narration is heard only once. You then answer five multiple-choice questions for each recorded segment. You will be able to read the questions but you will not see the spoken dialogues. You have about 25 minutes to complete this listening portion of the exam.

You will then have approximately 55 minutes to complete the reading segment of the test. The passages vary in length and subject matter. They usually come from Italian media, newspaper or magazine articles, or virtually any non-technical text or literary excerpt. Each passage is followed by a series of questions with four answer choices. Again, mark your answer choice by blackening the corresponding letter on the answer grid in your text booklet.

About the Writing Sections

There are four writing exercises in the AP Italian Language and Culture exam—two fill-in exercises and two essays.

The first fill-in exercise is related to supplying verbs. The blank will indicate the infinitive form of the verb you are to use. You must provide the correct tense. The verb could also be a command form, or you may have to determine whether to use the indicative or the subjunctive. The verb you supply must match its subject. If the verb is reflexive, you will need to include the reflexive pronoun that matches it. If the verb is in a compound tense you will need the correct auxiliary verb, the correct past participle, and possibly agreement.

The second fill-in exercise requires you to write in single words that are missing in the passage provided. The missing words are represented by numbered blanks. You are expected to write out the missing word in a column of blanks to the right of the text. None of the answers in this second fill-in segment will be verbs.

The final writing segment requires you to write two compositions in Italian. There is no choice of topic for the essay questions given. You are expected to write a coherent and well-organized essay in response to the given question. Your answer should showcase your mastery of verbs and grammatical structures. Your vocabulary must be varied, well-chosen, and as idiomatic as possible. That means you should not think in English and then try to translate into Italian. Being idiomatic means thinking like an Italian, or at least asking yourself how an Italian would express what you mean. Plan to write a minimum of three paragraphs and at least 150 words per essay. You will have one hour and twenty minutes to complete the writing section of the test. Always read over what you have written, check your spelling, accent marks, and agreement.

Don't be nervous about the essays. The general question essay topic is always very open-ended and usually requires your thoughtful opinion rather than specific facts. You will definitely be able to think of an answer. Your challenge will be how to express it as best you can. The cultural essay gives you an opportunity to showcase what you know about Italian culture. The range of topics is very broad. You could be asked to discuss an Italian custom of your choice, an industry, a facet of art, architecture, music, literature, film, politics, food, geography, or a well-known tourist destination. Again, there is the same open quality in these questions that will allow you to answer comfortably.

About the Speaking Sections

You will be recording your own voice during the two speaking segments of the exam. These sections are entirely free-response, that is, you may say whatever you think best answers the question. You will have approximately 15 minutes for these segments of the exam.

The first speaking section asks you to comment on a series of six simple sketches. The sketches invariably depict a typical life experience and, in that respect, are not difficult at all. You must tell what takes place in the sequence of drawings. You may also add your own personal commentary as you narrate your story. Observe carefully as you look over the sketches. You will have two minutes to look at and think about the drawings. Jot down details and ideas if you like. You will then have two minutes to record your actual narration.

The second part of the speaking segment is a simulated conversation in Italian. You will hear a series of questions that relate to a single topic. Each question is heard twice. *You do not have to answer the first question!* It is given as a practice question. It cues you into the coming topic and gives you a chance to compose yourself and to get ready to answer the next five questions on the same topic. The remaining questions will also be spoken twice. After each question you will hear a *tone*. Once you hear the tone, you have exactly 20 seconds to record your response. Begin speaking as soon as you hear the tone. It will sound again 20 seconds later to signal the end of the time allowed. Be sure to use all of the time allotted. If you make an error that you can correct, do it and move on. Keep talking! If the end tone sounds before you have finished, stop talking or you will miss the next question. It is not a cause for concern if you don't finish what you were saying. Remain focused and continue on.

It is important that you make an effort to familiarize yourself with the recording equipment you will be using. Ask about this well in advance. If your testing location is your school, ask to see the equipment. Get permission to practice using the device well before the exam. This will help you so much! If you are experienced using the equipment, you will be calm during the exam. You will be able to concentrate on what you are going to say, rather than worrying about whether or not the volume is adequate or if you're close enough to the microphone. Work out all of those details before the exam, and practice until using the equipment is a cinch for you. Some schools allow students to use their own recording device. This is ideal. If you're expected to use your own recording device, purchase it well ahead of time and get comfortable using it.

Tools to Help You Prepare for the Exam

Read and study this book thoroughly and do all of the drills provided. Keep a notebook in which you can compile all your written answers. Keep track of what you have completed and what you have yet to cover. Make notes on things you've mastered. Identify your weaknesses and devote extra effort to those areas. *Take your time.* Work no more than two or three hours at a sitting. Come back to it later when you are fresh. You will have the best possible result from a steady series of two-hour sessions spread over a long period of time. Schedule time to work with this book on a regular basis, just as you might schedule a regular fitness workout. When you have completed the drills, try your hand at the pre-exam exercises. Then move on to the three practice tests. Explanations are provided for every answer! Read them carefully.

No dictionaries or reference materials can be used during the exam. For studying, however, you should invest in the best and most complete Italian-English dictionary you can afford. There are many good dictionaries to choose from. *Zanichelli* and *Oxford-Paravia* are both excellent choices. You might also consider the very fine *Ragazzini English and Italian Dictionary* on CD-ROM that is very convenient to use.

It might also be useful to have access to an all-Italian dictionary such as the inimitable *Garzanti*. This would be a wise investment, especially if you will be continuing your study of Italian in college. Looking up a word in an all-Italian dictionary allows you to study the *way* the word is explained, as well as its meaning. It exposes you to authentic expression. You glimpse the actual choreography of the words in use. The more you delve into this all-Italian medium, the easier it is to come away with a truly Italic turn of phrase.

You should acquire a recording device with which to record your voice. You can also use your telephone answering machine to practice speaking Italian. Call yourself up and leave a message in Italian! Do it every day. The more you do it, the easier it becomes. Recording your voice allows you to hear how you actually sound. You can then evaluate what you hear. Is your accent authentic? Are your vowels pure? Are you trilling your *r*'s ? Is your stress on the correct syllable? Once you have your recording device, record yourself reading a passage aloud, reciting a poem or singing a song in Italian. This is the best kind of activity for working on your accent and correct pronunciation. Ad-lib into the microphone; describe your room or your current state of mind. Mute the television and do your own voice-over in Italian.

Studying for the Exam

Ideally, you should begin your preparation six months ahead of your testing date. This deluxe approach produces the best possible result. Look at your calendar, map out your plan. Set aside time to work regularly with this book. Schedule time to watch Italian films, to read Italian novels and periodicals, to listen to Italian singers. Allow some time each week to explore Italian chat rooms and various Italian language sites on the Internet. Team up with other friends who are also preparing for the test. Vow to speak to one another in Italian on a regular basis. Send each other instant messages and e-mails in Italian.

Starting four months ahead of your test date will still give you enough time to do an adequate job of preparing. This is would be a "good" plan for success, provided that you remain faithful to a regular regimen of review, study, reading, writing, speaking, and listening.

Planning a calendar, no matter which plan you adopt, gives you an excellent over-view of just how much time you have at your disposal. You can schedule what you'd like to have accomplished by a certain date. It's also a good idea to record how much time you've actually spent working. Time will slip by quickly. Suddenly you may notice that it's been two weeks since you last studied. Not good!

The bare-bones approach gives you only two months to prepare for this behemoth of an exam. That is really not much time at all. Yet, with unswerving dedication, you could probably finish this book, possibly catch a few films and do some reading, writing, and speaking.

What to Read

Try to read at least two short Italian novels a month. That comes out to a dozen books in six months, eight books in four months, or four books on the bare-bones two-month plan. You will find some excellent titles to choose from on the list provided in this chapter. The books were selected for their ease in reading, their relative short length, and the pleasure that you will undoubtedly experience while reading them.

How do you get your hands on these books? They are all available in paperback. One of the best sources of these *libri tascabili* is your own Italian teacher. Happily for you, most teachers have a considerable personal library of paperbacks, which they are willing to lend to responsible students.

You can also scrounge for Italian paperbacks wherever good used books congregate. If you live near a college or university, the student bookstore may have different titles at different times of the year, depending on the courses offered. Once you've found a good title, share it with a friend.

In addition to the novels listed in this chapter, make an effort to read as many Italian newspapers and magazine articles as possible. All Italian publications have websites where you can read articles daily. Simply use your search engine and type in *Corriere della Sera, La Stampa, La Gazzetta dello Sport, Oggi, Gente, l'Espresso* or *Panorama*. There is a huge variety of specialty magazines as well. *Donna Moderna* and *Abitare* are just two examples. Read about whatever interests you. There are Italian magazines about cycling, skiing, cars, soccer, tennis, and fashion. There are also gossipy movie star magazines, if that's what you like. Friends and family who fly often should also be pressed into service. Italian language magazines may be available during a flight and in airport lounges, usually without cost. Make an effort and you'll be amazed at the possibilities you will find.

Once you have begun your preparation for the AP exam you should be reading in Italian *daily*.

Below is a list of some very enjoyable Italian paperbacks. None of them are very long or very hard to read. This is by no means a complete list, but rather a starting point.

The list is arranged alphabetically by author.

Author	Title
Baricco, Alessandro	Barnum
Baricco, Alessandro	Oceano mare
Baricco, Alessandro	Seta
Benni, Stefano	Saltatempo
Calvino, Italo	Lezioni americane
Calvino, Italo	Se una notte d'inverno un viaggiatore…
Calvino, Italo	Il visconte dimezzato
Cardella, Lara	Volevo i pantaloni
Deledda, Grazia	Canne al vento
Di Lampadusa	Il Gattopardo
Eco, Umberto	Il nome della rosa*
Fallaci, Oriana	Un uomo*
Fallaci, Oriana	Se il sole muore
Faletti, Giorgio	Fuori da un evidente destino
Faletti, Giorgio	Niente di vero tranne gli occhi
Ginzburg, Natalia	Caro Michele
Ginzburg, Natalia	Lessico famigliare
Levi, Carlo	Cristo si è fermato ad Eboli
Levi, Primo	La tregua
Mazzantini, Margaret	Non ti muovere
Morante, Elsa	L'isola di Arturo
Moravia, Alberto	Gli Indifferenti
Passolini, Pierpaolo	Angelo
Pirandello, Luigi	Uno, nessuno e centomila
Pratolini, Vasco	Cronache di poveri amanti
Sciascia, Leonardo	Il giorno della civetta
Sereni, Clara	Casalinghitudine
Svevo, Italo	La Cosienza di Zeno
Tabucchi, Antonio	Noturno Indiano
Tamaro, Susanna	Va' dove ti porta il cuore
Tozzi, Federigo	Con gli occhi chiusi

* These two books are longer and perhaps somewhat harder to read than the other titles, but they are worth the time and effort.

Just a few pointers on how to approach this kind of reading:

1. Remember that you are not writing essays or book reports on these novels. Try to read them the way you would read any book for pleasure. The secret lies in finding one that you will enjoy. Try a few pages, and if it's not going to hold your attention, stop. With a little luck, you should be able to find one that you will enjoy.

2. It is not a crime if you don't understand every single word on a page. Dive in, if you've read the whole page and have a pretty good idea about what's going on, that's good enough. As you read further, things will become clearer and you will discover that you can learn new words just by context. Sometimes you will have a hunch about what a word means. Don't run right to the dictionary. Be patient. You may find that you were right all along. Once you get the hang of this kind of reading, your comfort level will increase and your vocabulary will quadruple.

3. Don't allow yourself to go to the dictionary more than once per page. Trust me. If you have only one ticket (for a trip to the dictionary) per page, you will slowly begin to analyze which word you should spend it on. Which word is most crucial to your understanding of the passage? The more conscientious the student, the harder this is to learn. Go with the flow, and guess if you can. The point is not to get bogged down with too many stops and starts. Just try it. The dictionary is a great tool, but here you should try to wean yourself from it long enough to develop confidence in your ability to figure out what's going on.

What to Watch

While preparing for this exam, watch as many movies in Italian as you can. Short of visiting Italy, this is the absolute best way to prepare yourself for the listening portion of your test. Films provide an ideal opportunity to hear spoken Italian, and that is what you need! Try to work in a film at least once a week. If you're not in the mood to study your book one evening, pop in a video or DVD. Italian films are probably available at your local video store. If not, again, try the Internet! Take full advantage of this excellent resource at your fingertips!

Below is a list of wonderful Italian films for you to enjoy. They are listed alphabetically by director.

Director	Title
Antonioni, Michelangelo	Professione: reporter
Begnini, Roberto	Pinocchio
Begnini, Roberto	Johnny Stecchino
Begnini, Roberto	La Tigre e la neve
Begnini, Roberto	La Vita è bella
Bertolucci, Bernardo	Novecento
Crialese, Emanuele	Nuovomondo
de Sica, Vittorio	Il giardino dei Finzi Contini
de Sica, Vittorio	Ladri di biciclette
de Sica, Vittorio	Miracolo a Milano
de Sica, Vittorio	L'oro di Napoli
Fellini, Federico	Amarcord
Fellini, Federico	Otto e mezzo
Fellini, Federico	Lo Sceicco bianco
Fellini, Federico	La Strada
Garrone, Matteo	L'Imbalsamatore
Germi, Pietro	Divorzio all'italiana
Giordana, Marco Tullio	I Cento passi
Martone, Mario	Morte di un matematico napoletano
Mazzacurati, Carlo	Il Toro
Monicelli, Mario	I Soliti ignoti
Olmi, Ermanno	L'Albero degli zoccoli
Radford, Michael	Il Postino
Risi, Dino	Il Sorpasso
Rossellini, Roberto	Bellissima
Rossellini, Roberto	Mamma Roma
Rossellini, Roberto	Roma, città aperta
Pasolini, Pierpaolo	Uccellacci uccellini
Salvatores, Gabriele	Mediterraneo
Steno	Un Americano a Roma
Tornatore, Giuseppe	Io non ho paura
Tornatore, Giuseppe	Malèna
Tornatore, Giuseppe	Nuovo cinema Paradiso
Verdone, Carlo	Bianco rosso e verdone
Visconti, Luchino	Il Gattopardo
Visconti, Luchino	Morte a Venezia
Wertmüller, Lina	Ciao, Professore!

Don't forget that American DVDs sometimes feature foreign sound tracks or subtitles as options. If your family has a DVD collection, be sure to look through your titles to see if you can listen to any of them in Italian. Being familiar with the story enhances your ability to understand what you hear. You may already have an Italian sound track that you weren't aware of somewhere in your collection of films at home.

A word of caution: DVDs purchased in Italy (region 2) will not work on standard American DVD players (region 1).

What to Listen To

Try to obtain some CDs with Italian lyrics. Whenever you're doing a chore at home, or just relaxing, Italian can be on in the background. When you drive a long distance, listen to Italian. Read Italian magazines designed for young people, such a *Groove,* to find out who is currently popular. There are Italian rappers and hip-hop artists. The artist doesn't really have to be hip and new for you to benefit from listening. Old smoothies like Domenico Modugno, Patty Pravo, Mina or Zucchero will do just as well.

Record your own voice and listen to it. You don't have to sing, just read aloud. There are wonderful audio programs you can subscribe to as well. *Acquarello* sends a monthly CD or audiocassette with an interesting and authentic radio broadcast format. All the speakers are native and a magazine that allows you to follow the script verbatim is also available. Notations for study are included.

You may be able to get an Italian radio program if you live near a metropolitan area. Check your television schedule for Italian films or Italian programming. Don't dismiss listening to Italian songs as unnecessary fluff. Your goal should be to increase your exposure to spoken Italian as much as possible. Listening to songs is a legitimate and effective way to do this. The musical format is also an ideal conduit for learning and remembering. It's a painless way to stay in contact with Italian. Another unexpected bonus is that the music and words don't have to be your primary focus for you to benefit from them. Do your nails, clean out a drawer, or wash the car while you listen. Let the words seep into your consciousness on a secondary level, just as the words of any other song would. It's this very relaxing and indirect route that allows music to leave its impression on us so effortlessly.

What to Write

If your Italian teacher does not already require you to write on a regular basis, you need to begin doing so now. The simplest and easiest thing to do is to keep a diary or *diario*. Place a notebook and pencil by your bed. Write a few paragraphs each night as you settle in. Try to capture a few thoughts, maybe what you did today, or what you hope to accomplish tomorrow. Students often enjoy this routine and relish the privacy afforded them by writing in Italian instead of English. They are able to collect themselves and reflect a bit. Many find themselves writing at length. Of course you can always try your hand at writing poetry or writing a story to which you add a chapter each evening. Make your hero suffer the consequences if you've had a bad day. The more you write the easier it becomes. As you step up your reading and listening exposure to Italian, your writing skills will improve in tandem.

Where to Go

If you should have the good fortune to travel to Italy on a school trip, or with your family, you must make every effort to use your language skills. Don't make the mistake so many students do—staying together en masse and maintaining their English idiom just as though they were back in the United States. If you've traveled that far, be brave enough to wean yourself from the group long enough to make a purchase by yourself, to exchange pleasantries with the gentleman at the front desk of your hotel, or to strike up a conversation with the person riding down in the elevator with you. Each little success begets another.

For those who aren't traveling to Italy, the Internet is the next best thing. There are Italian chat rooms, forums on film, politics, and cheese. You can make a virtual visit to the Uffizi, to the Colosseum, or to any region you so desire. For the AP Italian student the Internet provides a dizzying array of current and interesting articles to read, as well as the opportunity to interact with other Italian speakers.

There are audio dictionaries that pronounce words for you. You can listen to speeches by Berlusconi. You can hear interviews with famous authors, actors, artists and directors about their work. Avail yourself of these wonderful resources. They will help you keep your commitment to your goal of preparing fully and well for the AP Italian Language and Culture exam.

Thinking in Italian!

If you immerse yourself in Italian for an extended period of time you may very well discover yourself thinking in the language. It is very exciting the first time you realize that this has happened to you. The immersion must be extended, let's say a full day, and you must have been actively using the language, speaking or writing at length. Suddenly it will dawn on you that you are thinking in Italian.

It is a very gratifying moment. Many people remember when it first happened to them. Of course, the more often you use the language exclusively, the more frequently it will happen, and, over time, just becomes routine. When you begin to think spontaneously in Italian your mind is comfortable and at ease in its new medium.

It is possible to experiment with thinking in Italian before it comes to you spontaneously. Try making a deliberate effort to think in Italian and see how you fare. It is best to try this when you are alone so that no one interrupts your thoughts. Do whatever you would normally do but make a conscious effort to think about each step in Italian. It's fun to try. You don't need a pencil or any equipment to do it, and it's excellent training. You are giving yourself a chance to think in Italian when there is no pressure to perform, and therein lies the beauty of it. When you've used Italian all day long and drift off to sleep after having written in your journal or having read your novel for a while, who's to say that you won't dream in Italian too?

Course Review

AP Italian Language and Culture

Chapter 2

AP Italian Review

Alphabet and Pronunciation

The Italian Alphabet

Letter	Italian Name	Sample Word	English Approximation	Observations
a	a (ah)	ala	Mama	
b	bi	babbo	boy	
c	ci	ciao, cento	chin, chest[1]	[1] The sound [tʃ] occurs whenever **c** appears in front of the vowels **i** or **e**.
		caro, culla	car	The hard [**k**] (as in car) occurs if **c** appears in front of any other letter.
d	di	dado	day	
e	e (ay)	sera, bene	bay, bet	
f	effe	farfalla	fee	
g	gi	Gino, gentile gatto, gomma	jeep, gentle go[2]	[2] Similarly, **g** is soft (**G**ino) in front of **i, e,** and hard (**g**o) in front of any other letter.
h	acca	silent		
i	i (ee)	ieri	bee	
l	elle	latte	low	

Letter	Italian Name	Sample Word	English Approximation	Observations
m	emme	mamma	**m**y	
n	enne	nonna	**n**o	
o	o (oh)	po', poco	h**o** ho!, h**u**t	
p	pi	pepe	**p**eep[3]	[3] The Italian **p** does not produce the little puff of air which escapes when **p** is pronounced in English. The same is true for the sound of **t**.
q	cu	qui	**qu**ip	
r	erre	raro	**r**ear, butter	
s	esse	sasso	**s**ea	
t	ti	tetto	**t**ea	
u	u	uva	sch**oo**l	
v	vu	vino	**v**eal	
z	zeta	zero, pizza	**z**oo	

Italian uses only twenty-one letters in its alphabet. It does have names for the 5 letters it considers foreign. They are needed for the spelling of foreign words adopted directly into Italian, such as **jazz, whiskey,** or **yogurt**. They also combine in many hybrid words such as **raggi X** for X-ray, or for foreign words used in Italian with new meanings, such as **water** for flush toilet. The letter **j** persists in some ancient names, **Jacopo, Jacopone, Juventus**.

Foreign Letters Used in Italian

Letter	Italian Name	Sample Word
j	i lunga	**j**azz, **J**acopo, **J**uventus
k	kappa	**k**arate, **k**eniano
w	vu doppio	**w**ater, **w**hiskey
x	ics	**r**aggi X
y	ipsilon	**y**acht, **y**ogurt

The International Phonetic Alphabet Symbols Used in Italian
A Useful Guide to Correct Italian Pronunciation

Symbol	Sound	Sample Words to SAY ALOUD *Pronuncia queste parole ad alta voce:*
consonants		
p	**p**a**p**à	paio pepe piano popolo pupa primo oppure sopra zoppo zuppa
b	**b**ene	babbo barba bello bianco bocca buco abbaio bubbola cribbio
m	**m**ale	mai mano mela mio moto mura come mamma memento mimo
t	**t**an**t**o	tatto tetto tipo titolo totale toto tutto contento ottanta patata
d	**d**a**d**o	dai dama dedalo denaro dito dodici domani dubbio addio ladro
n	**n**oi	nano nero nido ninnananna nonna notte numero inganno renna
ɲ	**gn**occo	gnomo gnorri assegno bagno campagna montagna spagnolo
k	**c**arta	cane come cura chi che classe crudo questo ricotta scacchi
g	**g**atto	gancio gamba gara gomma guaio ghetto ghiaccio sgabello
ts	pi**zz**a	zazzera zampa zeppo zio zia zoo zucca zuppa negozio piazza
dz	**z**ero	zanzara zebra zigolo zolletta zona zonzo zotico zuavo zumata
tʃ	**c**ento	c'è cera cesta ciao cielo cinque doccia goccio piccino uccello
ʤ	**Gi**no	già Giotto Giulia giusto gelo gentile gesto raggio regina rigido
f	**f**a	fai farfalla fede fiaba foglio fumetto flauto frutta gufo ufficio
v	**v**oi	vai vela vita volta vulcano avanti avverbio avvocato evviva

Symbol	Sound	Sample Words to SAY ALOUD *Pronuncia queste parole ad alta voce:*
s	sera	sasso sega sito sosta sussurro scala scherzo schiena sfumatura spento squalo stato
z	casa	chiuso preso rosa sbaffo sdegno sdentato sgabello sgherro slitta smalto snello sregolato sveglia
ʃ	**sci**	scelta scena scienza scimmia asciugare asciutto ascensore
r	**raro**	rado regio ritmo rotto ruota rumore barra errore sera serra
l	**lilla**	lamella latte letto limetta lotta luce lupo allegro alto Liliana
ʎ	**gli**	maglia meglio famiglia foglio luglio gagliardo glieli Guglielmo
semi-vowels		
j	p**ie**de	ieri miele piatto pieno pietra più rialto siede siete tiepido vietato
w	t**uo**i	buon cuore fuori guaio guerra guido nuovo quando questo suoi
vowels		*Pronuncia ad alta voce:*
a	mamma	acca afa ala alba alta audio aiuto palla pazza rato sala tazza
e	sera	deciso dei età mela messo metà pera rete sega seta tela
ɛ	bene	è esempio era erba etto bello fede gelo segno sette tetto
i	vino	cibo cin cin dimmi ditalini giro ittico lieto mito piccino rito sito vita
o	sole	oca bocca dopo duomo gioco foto sopra sotto topo Toto voto
ɔ	modo	brodo con donna poco tonno osso otto rosa sorta volo volta
u	uva	burro cura Euro futuro giù giusto più muro su sussurro TV vu

Learn how to distinguish an open syllable (it ends in a vowel sound) from a closed syllable (it ends in a consonant sound). The word **po'** [po] is an open syllable. In the word **poco** the first syllable is closed by the consonant sound [k].

The vowels **e** and **o** appear exclusively in OPEN syllables, while **ɛ** and **ɔ** generally appear in CLOSED syllables.

Accent Marks Used in Italian

There are two accent marks in Italian. An accent mark may signal stress on the syllable it appears in, or it may be applied to distinguish one short word from another.

1. The acute accent appears on the letter e (**é**). It usually signals stress, as in **éta**, or **perché**.

2. The grave accent may appear on any vowel, signaling stress for the syllable it appears in.

    a (città)

    e (caffè)

    i (lunedì)

    o (farò)

    u (virtù)

3. The grave accent can be used to avoid confusion in short, similar words. Compare:

    è (is) versus **e** (and)

    dà (he gives) versus **da** (from)

    lì (there) versus **li** (them).

    papà (daddy) versus **papa** (pope)

Drill 1: Italian Pronunciation

Complete the statement by writing a letter or IPA symbol in the blank:

1. The consonant *c* produces a soft sound in front of the vowels _____ _____ or _____. The transcription for this soft sound is *tʃ*. In front of any other letter *c* is hard (k) as in "car."

2. The consonant *g* also produces a soft sound in front of the vowels _____ or _____. The transcription for this soft sound is ʤ. In front of any other letter *g* is hard (g) as in "go."

3. This letter has no sound attribution. It is used principally to prevent *c* and *g* from touching the vowels *i* and *e*. In this manner it preserves the hard sound of the consonant. It also appears in some forms of the verb *avere*: _____ _____.

4. The combination of these two consonants _____ + _____ _____ makes a "shhh" sound (as in "sheet") in front of the vowels *i* or *e*. In front of any other letters the sound is hard (as in the English words "sky" or "scout").

5. When the letter combination *gn* appears in an Italian word, the resulting sound will always be transcribed as _____. The sound can be heard in the English words "onion" and "canyon."

6. The combination of these two consonants _____ + _____ produces a *liquid* sound as in the English names "William" or "Lillian." The phonetic symbol for this sound is ʎ.

7. The consonant _____ makes a *hissing* sound when it is doubled. It usually makes a *buzzing* sound when it appears in between two vowels (ca*s*a). The resulting phonetic sound is _____.

8. The consonant _____ is always followed by the vowel *u*. Its pronunciation in Italian and English is the same. In both languages the resulting phonetic combination is k + the semivowel _____.

9. The consonant _____ is always *trilled* in Italian. The closest corresponding sound in American English is the casual pronunciation of the "tt" sound in "better butter."

10. When an *e* shares its syllable with a following consonantal sound, as in *etto*, it is pronounced _____.

11. This type of syllable (which ends in a consonant) is called a closed syllable. If *e* appears in an open syllable as in *sera* (ending in the vowel sound) it is pronounced _____.

12. When the letter *o* appears in a closed syllable, as in the first syllable of *otto*, it is pronounced _____.

13. When the letter *o* appears in an open syllable, as in the second syllable of *otto*, it is pronounced _____.

14. The combination of *c+h* is always pronounced _____.

15. The combination of *g+h* is always pronounced _____.

16. The consonant _____ will hiss in front of unvoiced consonants such as *p* or *t*. It is buzzed in front of voiced consonants like *b*, *n* or *v*.

17. The consonants _____ + _____ emit a little puff of escaping air when pronounced in English. This is called aspiration. In Italian these consonants are never aspirated.

18. When the consonants _____ + _____ are pronounced in Italian, the tongue is farther forward in the mouth than it is in English.

19. The consonant _____ *may* be pronounced like a *v*.

20. When the vowel *i* ends the syllable, and the next syllable begins with another vowel (as in *ieri*, or *piatto*) the syllable containing the *i* will produce the semi-vowel _____.

21. The letter *c*, in front of an *i,e* produces the sound _____.

22. The letter **g**, in front of an **i,e** produces the sound _____.

23. The vowel _____ is always pronounced like the double **ee** in in the English word "bee."

24. The vowel _____ is pronounced "**ay**" (remember Fonzie!) when it's the last sound in the syllable. It is pronounced "**eh**" if a consonant sound closes its syllable.

25. The semi-vowel _____ is produced whenever the sound **u** shares its syllable with another vowel sound.

Answers and Explanations to Drill 1

1. *c* is soft (*tʃ*) *only* when it appears in front of the vowels *i* or *e*.

2. Exactly like *c*, the consonant *g* is soft (*dʒ*) *only* in front of the vowels *i* or *e*.

3. The letter *h* is always silent. It appears after *c* and *g* if needed to keep those consonant sounds hard, that is, in front of *i* or *e*. It also appears in 4 forms of the verb avere: *h*o, *h*ai, *h*a, *h*anno. In each case it is present only to prevent confusion with other words: *o* (or) *ai* (to the) *a* (to, at) *anno* (year)

4. The combination *s* + *c* produces the soft sound ʃ in front of *i* or *e*. In front or any other letters *s* + *c* produce the hard sound sk as in the English words "sky" or "scout." English speakers commonly mispronounce this combination when it appears in front of *h*. Compare: sc*i* versus sc*h*iena, sc*e*lto versus sc*h*eletro. American supermarkets now sell *bruschetta* nationwide. It is almost always mispronounced! The correct pronunciation is *bruskɛtta*.

5. When the letter combination *gn* appears in an Italian word, the resulting sound will always be ɲ. This is always true. Here are more sample words: dise*gn*o, *gn*occho, ma*gn*o, pu*gn*o, Spa*gn*a.

6. The combination *g* + *l* produces the *liquid* sound ʎ and is always followed by the vowel *i*. More sample words: mo*gl*ie, gi*gl*io, Gu*gl*ielmo, pa*gl*ia.

7. A double *s* hisses: ca*ss*a, lu*ss*o, pi*ss*i pi*ss*i, sa*ss*o. A single *s* between two vowels (ca*s*a) usually results in the buzzing sound *z*. Worth remembering! More examples: ingle*s*e, chiu*s*o, ri*s*o, spe*s*o, u*s*o.

8. The letter *q* is always followed by the vowel *u*. In both Italian and English the phonetic sounds produced are *k+w*: quaderno, quel, questo, quindici, quotidiano.

9. The consonant *r* is always *trilled* in Italian.

10. When *e* is followed by a consonantal sound in the same syllable it is pronounced ɛ.

11. When *e* is the last sound heard in the syllable, it is pronounced **e** "*ay*" phonetically.

12. When the letter *o* shares its syllable with a following consonant, as in *otto*, it is pronounced ɔ.

13. When the letter *o* is the last sound heard in the syllable, as in *otto*, it is pronounced o.

14. The combination of *c+h* is always pronounced *k*!

15. The combination of *g+h* always creates the hard phonetic sound *g*.

16. *S* will hiss in front of unvoiced consonants: s*f*era, s*c*opa, s*p*ort, s*q*uama, s*t*udente. *S* will buzz in front of voiced consonants: s*b*aglio, s*d*entato, s*g*arbo, s*l*ancio, s*m*eraldo, s*n*odo, s*r*otolato, s*v*olta.

17. The consonants *p + t* do not produce escaping air in Italian. With two hands, hold *just the corner of a piece of paper* close to your mouth. Your fingers should be about two inches from the corner. Now pronounce the rhyming English words "pair" and "tear." The paper tip will move slightly as a puff of air escapes. Now, holding the paper in the same way, pronounce the Italian words *pera* and *terra* so that the paper tip does NOT move. Tricky, but that's the difference.

18. When the consonants *d + l* are produced in Italian, the tongue actually touches the gum behind the front teeth.

19. The foreign consonant *w* can be pronounced **v**, as in *water*, [vater]. Otherwise give its English value as in *whiskey* [wiski].

20. The semi-vowel **j** is produced whenever the sound *i* ends its own syllable *and* another vowel sound begins the next syllable.

21. The letter *c*, in front of an *i, e* always makes the soft sound *t∫*.

22. The letter *g*, in front of an *i* or an *e* always makes the soft sound ʤ.

23. The vowel *i* is always pronounced like the double *ee* in "bee."

24. The vowel *e* is pronounced "*ay*" when it's the last sound in the syllable. (Remember Fonzie!) It is pronounced ɛ if a consonant sound closes its syllable.

25. When *u* combines with another vowel in the same syllable, as in ***cuore***, it always create the semi-vowel *w* (kwɔre). We have already observed that this same semi-vowel appears consistently after the letter *q*.

Cardinal and Ordinal Numbers

Cardinal Numbers (one, two, three) are as follows:

1 uno	21 ventuno	50 cinquanta
2 due	22 ventidue	60 sessanta
3 tre	23 ventitré	70 settanta
4 quattro	24 ventiquattro	80 ottanta
5 cinque	25 venticinque	90 novanta
6 sei	26 ventisei	100 cento
7 sette	27 ventisette	1.000 mille
8 otto	28 ventotto	2.000 duemila
9 nove	29 ventinove	3.000 tremila
10 dieci	30 trenta	4.000 quattromila
11 undici	31 trentuno	5.000 cinquemila
12 dodici	32 trentadue	10.000 diecimila
13 tredici	33 trentatré	1.000.000 un milione
14 quattordici	34 trentaquattro	2.000.000 due milioni
15 quindici	35 trentacinque	1.000.000.000 un miliardo, (i)
16 sedici	36 trentasei	1.000.000.000.000 un bilione, (i)
17 diciassette	37 trentasette	
18 diciotto	38 trentotto	
19 diciannove	39 trentanove	
20 venti	40 quaranta	

Rules governing cardinal numbers:

1. Only the numbers **uno** and **zero** can change. All others are invariable.
   Uno has four forms (*un, uno, un'* and *una*) (See: Indefinite Article)
   Zero has a plural form, *zeri.*

2. When spelling cardinal numbers, all the parts are strung together to make one word, no matter how long. This true up to a million (un miliardo).

3. *Never* put the word **un** in front of *cento* or *mille*.

4. Italian uses a comma where we would use a decimal: $(7,^{50}$ versus $7.50)$

5. Italian uses a decimal where we would use a comma: $(2.000 = 2,000)$

6. Use an accent on **tre**, *only* if it appears after another number: cinquantatré

Ordinal Numbers (first, second, third) are as follows:

1st	primo / last ultimo	26th	ventiseiesimo
2nd	secondo	27th	ventisettesimo
3rd	terzo	28th	ventottesimo
4th	quarto	29th	ventinovesimo
5th	quinto	10th	decimo
6th	sesto	30th	trentesimo
7th	settimo	31st	trentunesimo
8th	ottavo	32nd	trentaduesimo
9th	nono	33rd	trentatréesimo
10th	decimo	34th	trentaquattresimo
11th	undicesimo	35th	trentacinquesimo
12th	dodicesimo	36th	trentaseiesimo
13th	tredicesimo	37th	trentasettesimo
14th	quattordicesimo	38th	trentottesimo
15th	quindicesimo	39th	trentanovesimo
16th	sedicesimo	40th	quarantesimo
17th	diciassettesimo	50th	cinquantesimo
18th	diciottesimo	60th	sessantesimo
19th	diciannovesimo	70th	settantesimo
20th	ventesimo	80th	ottantesimo
21st	ventunesimo	90th	novantesimo
22nd	ventiduesimo	100th	centesimo
23rd	ventitréesimo	1.000th	millesimo
24th	ventiquattresimo	1.000.000th	milionesimo
25th	venticinquesimo		

Rules governing ordinal numbers:

1. The ordinal numbers from *first* to *tenth* must be learned by heart. All are irregular.

2. For all other numbers, starting with *eleventh*, simply remove the last vowel of the cardinal number and add *–esimo*.

3. Cardinal numbers are preceding *adjectives,* and as such, show agreement with the nouns they modify. Each one exists in four forms: *terzo, terza, terzi, terze.*

Drill 2: Cardinal and Ordinal Numbers

Supply the number indicated by the English cue. Remember that ordinals *agree* with the noun. Spell each number correctly.

1. la loro _____ figlia (first)

2. Benedetto _____ (sixteenth)

3. il papa Giovanni _____ (twenty-third)

4. _____ più _____ fa venti. $(5 + 15 = 20)$

5. _____ meno due fa _____. $(19 - 2 = 17)$

6. _____ per due fa _____. $(8 \times 2 = 16)$

7. la _____ volta (sixth)

8. il _____ nano (seventh)

9. _____ giorni (three hundred sixty-five)

10. il _____ esercizio (fourth)

11. il _____ figlio (second)

12. due _____ (thirds)

13. due _____ (fifths)

14. la _____ posizione (fourth)

15. _____ mese (eighth)

16. il _____ circolo (ninth)

17. il _____ presidente (twentieth)

18. le _____ luci (last)

19. la _____ tempesta (fourteenth)

20. il _____ compleanno (ninetieth)

Answers and Explanations to Drill 2

1. la loro **prima** figlia (first)
   Notice how the number agrees with its noun, just like any other adjective.

2. Benedetto **sedicesimo** (sixteenth)
   Titles of popes and kings don't use a definite article as they do in English.
   In English we'd say Benedict *the* Sixteenth.

3. il papa Giovanni **ventitréesimo** (twenty-third)
   Pope John *the* Twenty-third

4. **Cinque** più **quindici** fa venti. (5 + 15 = 20)
   Students often confuse these two numbers, along with *cinquanta*, 50.

5. **Diciannove** meno due fa **diciassette**. (19 – 2 = 17)
   These are two of the most commonly misspelled numbers in Italian!
   Diciannove has two **n**'s, *diciassette* has the **double s**.

6. **Otto** per due fa **sedici**. (8 × 2 = 16)
   Sedici has only two **i**'s. Don't spell it with three!

7. la **sesta** volta (sixth)
   Make your ordinal number agree with its noun.

8. il **settimo** nano (seventh)
   Learn the forms for 1st through 10th by heart, each is irregular.

9. **trecentosessantacinque** giorni (three hundred sixty-five)
   When spelling a long number, link all parts together, no matter how many.

10. il **quarto** esercizio (fourth)
    Another irregular form to remember.

11. il **secondo** figlio (second)
    Also irregular but so like English it's not hard to remember.

12. due **terzi** (thirds)
    Every ordinal adjective has two plural forms.

13. due **quinti** (fifths)
    Every ordinal adjective has two plural forms.

14. la **terza** posizione (third)
    Here we need the feminine singular.

15. l'**ottavo** mese (eighth)
    Note the special article before the vowel.

16. il **nono** circolo (nineth)
    One of the ten irregular forms to learn by heart.

17. il **ventesimo** presidente (twentieth)
    An easy one, remove the last vowel from the cardinal form and add –esimo.

18. le **ultime** luci (last)
    Le luci is a feminine plural noun. The adjective form matches exactly.

19. la **quattordicesima** tempesta (fourteenth)
    Regular formation. Remove last vowel, add –esimo.

20. il **novantesimo** compleanno (ninetieth)
    Another regular formation. Simply remove the last vowel, and add –esimo.

The Indefinite Article

The singular indefinite article exists in four forms in Italian. There are two masculine forms: **un** and **uno**, and two feminine forms: **una** and **un'**. They are the equivalent of *a* or *an* in English.

Use and Omission of the Indefinte Article

1. The singular indefinite article is used after **c'è**.

> C'è **un** pacco per te sulla tavola.
> *There's a package for you on the table.*

> C'è anche **una** lettera.
> *There's also a letter.*

2. When a **pronoun**, **noun** or **name** precedes **essere**, the indefinite article is possible but **not necessary** with the noun that follows. The article can drop out because the noun takes on the role of an adjective:

> Carla è studentessa.
> *Carla is a student.*

This construction is frequently encountered when expressing one's occupation or profession. Study the following examples:

> È avvocato.
> *He's a lawyer.*

> Mio padre è contabile.
> *My father is an accountant.*

> Filomena è insegnante.
> *Filomena is a teacher.*

The indefinite article will reappear if the profession is modified:

> È una brava professoressa.
> *She's a great teacher.*

> Mio padre è un contabile esperto.
> *My father is an experienced accountant.*

> Mario è un automobilista eccezionale.
> *Mario is an exceptionally fine driver.*

3. The indefinite article is never used in exclamations with **che**:

    Che peccato!
    What a shame!

    Che sorpresa!
    What a surprise!

4. The indefinite article drops out in **apposition**, after **senza**, and after **con** (if the noun is abstract) just like the definite article.

    Ho visto Fabio Cannavaro, capitano azzurro, alla TV ieri sera.
    I saw Fabio Cannavaro, the national team captain, on TV last night.

    È uscito senza cappello.
    He went out without a hat.

    Ti aiuterò con piacere.
    I'll gladly help you. (with pleasure = abstract noun)

    Taglio la torta con un coltello.
    I cut the cake with a knife. (knife = concrete noun)

Drill 3: The Indefinite Article

Suppy the correct form of the indefinite article if it is necessary. If there is no article required, place an **X** on the blank.

1. Mio fratello è _____ idraulico.

2. È _____ buon chirurgo.

3. C'è _____ uccello sull'albero.

4. Che _____ bella ragazza!

5. È _____ falegname.

6. È cascato come _____ pera cotta.

7. Il Papa Alessandro VI ha condannato Savonarola, _____ frate domenicano.

8. È riuscito senza _____ problema.

9. "Meglio _____ uovo oggi che _____ gallina domani."

10. La nonna cammina con _____ difficoltà.

Explanations and Answers to Drill 3

1. Mio fratello è **X** idraulico. *My brother is a plumber.*
   Italian omits the definite article with profession and trades.

2. È **un** buon chirurgo. *He's a good surgeon.*
   The indefinite article is required if the profession is modified.

3. C'è **un** uccello sull'albero. *There's a bird in the tree.*
   The indefinite article is required after c'è.

4. Che **X** bella ragazza! *What a pretty girl!*
   The indefinite article is never used after che.

5. È **X** falegname. *He's a carpenter.*
   Italian omits the definite article with profession and trades.

6. È cascato come **una** pera cotta. This old idiom *(he dropped like a cooked pear),* the rough equivalent of "he fell head over heels in love," illustrates the basic use of the indefinite article as it is used in both Italian and English.

7. Il Papa Alessandro VI ha condannato Savonarola, **X** frate domenicano. Pope Alexander VI condemned (to death) Savonarola, a Dominican friar. The article is omitted when the noun is placed in apposition.

8. È riuscito senza **X** problema.
   He succeeded without a problem.
   The article is routinely omitted after senza.

9. "Meglio **un** uovo oggi che una gallina domani."
   "Better an egg today than a chicken tomorrow."
   The Italian version of " A bird in the hand is worth two in the bush."
   Another illustration of the basic use of the indefinite article.

10. La nonna cammina con **X** difficoltà.
    Grandmother walks with difficulty.
    This is an example of omission of the article after con with an abstract noun.

The Definite Article

The English definite article *the*, has seven possible forms in Italian. Each is based on the gender, number, or sound of the noun which follows.

1. **LO** is used in front of masculine singular nouns whose initial sound is made of **two strong consonant sounds**, such as in **lo ps**icologo.

    This doubly strong initial sound is most common in the combination of **s** plus **another consonant**:

    > **lo s**conto **lo s**gabello **lo s**lancio **lo sm**acco **lo sp**untino **lo st**udente

    in the voiced consonant **z**, which is pronounced [**dz**]:

    > **lo z**enzero **lo z**ero **lo z**ingaro **lo z**io **lo z**occolo **lo z**oo **lo z**ucchero

    in the double consonant **gn**:

    > **lo gn**occo **lo gn**omo **lo gn**orri

    and in the voiced foreign consonant **y**:

    > **lo y**acht **lo y**eti **lo y**ogurt

    By substituting **lo** for the standard **il** (which will be presented shortly) Italian prevents the juxtaposition of a third consonantal sound to the beginning of of these words. What may seem like a tediously exacting of rules does allow Italian to maintain its beautiful, melodic pronunciation.

    If the two initial consonants do not result in a strong pair, we don't need to use **lo**, as in *il treno*.

2. **L'** is required before all singular nouns beginning with a vowel, regardless of gender:

    > **l'**amico **l'**amica **l'**estate **l'**esagono **l'**inverno **l'**isola
    > **l'**ora **l'**otto **l'**uomo **l'**università

3. **IL** is used in front of all remaining masculine singular nouns which do not require **LO** or **L'**:

    > **il** libro **il** quaderno **il** ragazzo **il** teatro

4. **LA** is used in front of all singular feminine nouns beginning in a consonant:

   la ragazza   **la** sedia   **la** scimmia   **la** zia   **la** zingara

5. **I** is used for all masculine plural nouns which required *il* in the singular:

   i libri   **i** quaderni   **i** ragazzi   **i** teatri

6. **GLI** is the masculine plural form of **LO**. It also serves as the masculine plural form of **L'** as follows:

   lo spaghetto = **gli** spaghetti

   lo zio = **gli** zii

   lo gnocco = **gli** gnocchi

   lo yacht = **gli** yacht

   l'amico = **gli** amici

   l'uomo = **gli** uomini

7. **LE** is the plural form for **ALL** feminine nouns:

   la ragazza = **le** ragazze

   la sedia = **le** sedie

   l'amica = **le** amiche

   l'isola = **le** isole

Special Uses of the Definite Article Peculiar to Italian

1. Unlike English, Italian requires the definite article when the noun is used in **general**. Study these examples:

   Le sigarette sono cattive per la salute.
   Cigarettes are bad for your health.

   Il grasso è cattivo per **il** cuore.
   Fat is bad for the heart.

   This use extends to **liking** or **disliking** something:

   Vi piace **il** vino rosso?
   Do you like red wine?

No, preferisco **il** vino bianco.
No, I prefer white wine.

Odio **il** latte.
I hate milk.

Vado pazzo per **il** cioccolato.
I'm crazy about chocolate.

2. The definite article is required in front of **geographical names**—of continents, countries, regions, mountains, and rivers:

l'Europa, **la** Francia, **l'**Umbria, **il** Veneto
le Alpi, **gli** Appennini, **il** Tevere, **l'**Adige

3. The definite article is used with the names of the **seasons**:

l'estate, **l'**autunno, **l'**inverno, **la** primavera

but is **omitted** after **prepositions**:

in estate, d'autunno, d'inverno, in primavera

4. The definite article is used in expressing **the date, without the day**:

Oggi è **il** 3 settembre.
Today is September 3rd.   ***but***

Oggi è martedì, 3 settembre.
Today is Tuesday, September 3rd.

If the definite article is used with the name of a weekday, it indicates a **repetition** of that day of the week.

Non mi piace lavorare **il** sabato.
I don't like to work on Saturdays.

5. Italian uses the definite article with **body parts**:

Ho **gli** occhi castani.
My eyes are brown.

Ha **i** capelli lunghi.
Her hair is long.

Hai **il** naso rosso.
Your nose is red.

6. The definite article is used with **quantities**, **prices** and **letters**:

    Queste uova vengono 1 Euro **la** dozzina.
    These eggs cost 1 Euro per dozen.

    Le banane si vendono a 2⁵⁰ **al** chilo.
    Bananas sell at 2⁵⁰ per Kilo.

    C'è una scelta dall'A alla Z.
    There's a selection from A to Z.

7. The definite article is used with **the names of languages** and with **subjects of study**:

    Lo spagnolo e l'italiano si somigliano molto.
    Spanish and Italian are very similar.

    La chimica è interessante.
    Chemistry is interesting.

    Chi insegna **la** matematica quest'anno?
    Who's teaching Math this year?

    Mi piace **l'**iformatica.
    I like Computer Science.

Omission of the Definite Article

1. The definite article is omitted when the name of a language follows the verb **parlare**. Compare:

    Mi piace **l'**italiano.   with   Parlo italiano.
    I like Italian.   *I speak Italian.*

    If parlare is modified, the article is retained:

    Parlo bene **l'**italiano.
    I speak Italian well.

2. Omit the article if the language is preceded by the preposition **in**:

    Gli ho scritto in italiano.
    I wrote to him in Italian.

3. Omission of the definite article is also common after the verb **studiare**:

    Studio fisica.
    I study Physics.

The same omission occurs with feminine countries and feminine provinces preceded by **in**:

> Andiamo in Francia.
> *We're going to France.*

> Era ceramista in Umbria.
> *He was a potter in Umbria.*

But:

> Andiamo negli Stati Uniti.
> *We're going to the USA.*

> Viaggiano nel Senegal.
> *They traveling in Senegal.*

4. The article is **retained** after **di** with geographical names:

> Sono venuti dall'Inghilterra.
> *They came from England.*

> Viene dalla Val d'Aosta.
> *He comes from Val d'Aosta.*

5. The definite article is often omitted after **di** when one noun modifies another. Here are some examples:

> Mi piace il pan di Spagna.
> *I like sponge cake.*

> Vorrei una coperta di lana.
> *I'd like a woolen blanket.*

> Giasone cercava il Toson d'oro.
> *Jason went in search of the Golden Fleece.*

> Preparava una crostata di mele.
> *She was making an apple pie.*

> Vittorio Emanuele, re d'Italia
> *Victor Emmanuel, king of Italy*

But:

> il leone, re degli animali
> *the lion, king of beasts*

Note also that the article is retained after **presidente**:

il Presidente della Comunità Europea
the President of the European Community

il Presidente degli Stati Uniti
the President of the United States

5-1. The definite article is omitted after **di** when the noun which follows is used adverbially:

Piango **di gioia**.
I'm crying for joy. (it tells *how* I'm crying)

Muoio **di fame**.
I'm dying of hunger.

La stanza era **piena di gente**.
The room was full of people.

5-2. The definite article is omitted after expressions which require **di**:

Sembrava una principessa, **vestita di** seta.
She looked like a princess dressed in silk.

Sono **sovraccarico di** lavoro.
I'm overloaded with work.

Mi piace vedere gli alberi **coperti di** neve.
I like to see the trees covered with snow.

Gli occhi dei bimbi **scintillavano di** gioia.
The children's eyes sparkled with joy.

6. The definite article is also omitted after **da,** and **in** when one noun modifies another:

uno spazzolino **da denti**
a tooth brush

una borsa **in pelle**
una borsa **in cuoio**
a leather bag

7. The definite article is omitted after the preposition **senza** if the noun which follows is unmodified:

    È riuscito senza aiuto.
    He succeeded without help.

    L'abbiamo trovato senza problema.
    We found it without a problem.

But:

    Ho cominciato senza la minima idea di quello che facevo.
    I began without the slightest idea of what I was doing.

8. The definite article may be omitted after the preposition **con**, especially if the noun which follows is more abstract than concrete. Compare:

    Lo farò con piacere.
    I'll do it with pleasure.

    Lo farò con i soldi che mi hai dato.
    I'll do it with the money you gave me.

9. The definite article is omitted after **in** and **a** in many set expressions. Here are some common examples:

in aereo	a cavallo
in automobile	a fondo
in biblioteca	a piedi
in chiesa	a scuola
in cima	a tavola
in città	a volontà
in cucina	
in ginocchio	
in macchina	
in piedi	
in spiaggia	
in testa	
in treno	

10. The definite article is omitted in **all idiomatic expressions** based on the verb **avere**. Here are some examples:

>   avere caldo
>   avere bisogno
>   avere fame
>   avere freddo
>   avere fretta
>   avere paura
>   avere pazienza
>   avere ragione
>   avere sete
>   avere sonno
>   avere torto
>   avere vergogna
>   avere voglia

11. The definite article is omitted if the descriptive noun is used in apposition to the first noun. Apposition means that the second noun has the same value or status as the first noun. Here's an example:

>   Boccaccio, poeta inimitabile, scrisse Il Decamerone.
>   *Boccaccio, the inimitable poet, wrote the Decameron.*

But:

>   Dante, il Sommo Poeta, scrisse la Divina Commedia.
>   *Dante, the Supreme Poet, wrote the Divine Comedy.*

12. In enumeration the definite article may be retained or omitted:

>   Ho preso **la** maglietta rossa, **i** pantaloni blu, e **i** calzini in saldo.
>   *I got the red sweater, the blue slacks, and the socks on sale.*

>   Vorrei spaghetti alle vongole, manzo ai ferri e insalata.
>   *I'd like the spaghetti with clams, grilled beef and a salad.*

13. The definite article is usually omitted after **né**:

>   Non ha né fratelli né sorelle.
>   *He has neither brother nor sister.*

It is retained with **l'uno e l'altro**:

>   Né l'uno né l'altro non ha risposto.
>   *Neither one nor the other answered.*

Drill 4: The Definite Article

Supply the correct form of the definite article if it is necessary. If there is no article required, place an **X** on the blank.

1. Le piace leggere _____ fumetti.

2. Vogliono vedere _____ Appennini.

3. Un suo amico parla _____ spagnolo.

4. _____ azzurro ti sta bene.

5. Passiamo _____ estate in spiaggia.

6. Hai _____ guance abbronzate.

7. Ha imprecato senza _____ vergogna.

8. Ho _____ fretta di andarmene.

9. Studia _____ biologia.

10. Caterina de Medici, _____ moglie di Enrico II, ha introdotto la forchetta in Francia.

Answers and Explanations to Drill 4

1. Le piace leggere **i** fumetti.
   She likes to read the comics.
   The article accompanies the noun in Italian, and is required when expressing general likes and dislikes.

2. Vogliono vedere **gli** Appennini.
   They want to see the Appenines.
   The article is required with geographical expressions such as the Appenines.

3. Un suo amico parla **X** spagnolo.
   A friend of hers speaks Spanish.
   The article is omitted when the name of a language appears after the verb **parlare**.

4. **L'** azzurro ti sta bene.
   Blue suits you, looks good on you.
   The article always accompanies a noun used in the general sense.

5. Passiamo **l'**estate in spiaggia.
   We spend the summer at the beach.
   The article is required with *summer,* the name of a season.

6. Hai **le** guance abbronzate.
   Your cheeks are suntanned.
   Italian generally uses the definite article with body parts, avoiding the possessive adjectives used in English.

7. Ha imprecato senza **X** vergogna.
   She swore without shame.
   The definite article is routinely omitted after the preposition **senza**.

8. Ho **X** fretta di andarmene.
   I'm in a hurry to get going.
   The article is omitted with all idioms based on the verb **avere**.

9. Studia biologia.
   She's studying Biology.
   The definite article is usually omitted after the verb **studiare**.

10. Caterina de Medici, **X** moglie di Enrico II, ha introdotto la forchetta in Francia.
    Catherine di Medici, the wife of Henri II, introduced the fork to France.
    The article is omitted here as *the wife of Henri II*, has been placed in apposition by the commas.

The Partitive Article

Partitive articles are made by combining the **definite article** with the preposition **di** as follows:

di + il = **del**	di + i = **dei**
di + lo = **dello**	di + gli = **degli**
di + l' = **dell'**	**degli** masculine *OR* **delle** feminine
di + la = **della**	di + le = **delle**

The partitive is used in front of the noun to express **a part** or **a portion** of that noun. The partitive articles stand for **some** in the affirmative and **some** or **any** in the interrogative. The use of the partitive in English and Italian is similar. Here are some examples:

Ci vorrebbe del burro.
This could use some butter.

Lei beve caffè, io tè.
She drinks coffee, I drink tea.

Vorrei della panna sulla mia granita di caffè.
I'd like some cream on my coffee ice.

Lei prende del pollo.
She's having chicken.

Omission of the Partitive in Italian

Italian often leaves out the partitive, even when we would not.

1. The partitive is omitted when negated:

Non compro burro.
I'm not buying (any) butter.

Lei non beve caffè.
She doesn't drink coffee.

Non voglio panna.
I don't want any cream.

2. It *can* be omitted in the interrogative:

> Ci sono fragole?
> *Are there any strawberries?*

> Hai fratelli?
> *Do you have any brothers?*

3. The partitive article is reduced to **di** after **nouns of quantity**:

> una **goccia di** vino
> *a drop of wine*

> un **mazzo di** fiori
> *a bunch of flowers*

> una **bottiglia di** acqua minerale
> *a bottle of mineral water*

> una **fetta di** prosciutto
> *a slice of ham*

> una **cucchiaiata di** zucchero
> *a spoonful of sugar*

> una **dozzina di** uova
> *a dozen eggs*

> uno **spruzzo di** grappa
> *a splash of acquavite*

> un **chilo di** carne
> *a kilo of meat*

> un **litro di** latte
> *a litre or milk*

> un **pezzo di** gesso
> *a piece of chalk*

> un **pacchetto di** sigarette
> *a pack of cigarettes*

> un **cestino di** mele
> *a basket of apples*

> un **pizzico di** sale
> *a pinch of salt*

una **manciata di** basilico
a fistful of basil

un **sacco di** caramelle
a bag of candies

una **tazza di** tè
a cup of tea

un **bicchiere di** spremuta
a glass of juice

Ho **bisogno di** soldi.
I need money.

4. The entire partitive is eliminated after most **adjectives and adverbs of quantity**:

Hai **abbastanza** soldi.
You have enough money.

Mamma ha **molte** ricette.
Mom has many recipies.

Quante volte?
How many times?

Ha **molto poca** pazienza.
She has very little patience.

Hai messo **troppo** sale.
You put in too much salt.

Exceptions to this rule include:

Ho **meno di** 20 cugini.
I have fewer than 20 cousins.

Ho **più di** 20 cugini.
I have more than 20 cousins.

Hai **un po' di** nastro adesivo?
Do you have a little scotch tape?

Mi è piaciuta **la maggior parte del** film.
I liked most of the film.

5. You can express the partitive with the indefinite adjective **QUALCHE** + *SINGULAR* **NOUN**:

> L'ho visto **qualche anno** fa.
> *I saw him a few years ago.*

> Avresti **qualche minuto**?
> *Would you have a few minutes?*

> Vorrei scegliere **qualche formaggio**.
> *I'd like to choose some cheeses.*

Drill 5: The Partitive Article

Complete the sentence according to the English cue, leave blank when necessary:

1. Non mangia _____ (any) carne.

2. Ho fregato un pezzo _____ (of) cioccolato.

3. Abbiamo _____ (too much) compiti.

4. Ci sono _____ (some) mele rimaste.

5. Vuoi _____ (some, any) fragole?

6. Vorrebbe _____ (some) latte per il suo caffè.

7. La maggior parte _____ (of) donne sposate hanno votato di sì.

8. Ho visto quel film _____ (many) volte.

9. Non ho _____ (any) soldi.

10. Ho _____ fortuna. (a lot of).

11. Ci sono _____ stelle stanotte. (so many)

12. Ho chiesto un caffè corretto con uno spruzzo _____ sambuca (of).

13. Prendi _____ pane? (any)

14. Lei ha _____ amici. (so many)

15. Ho fatto un mazzo con _____ fiore. (some, a few)

Answers and Explanations to Drill 5

1. Non mangia carne.
   She doesn't eat any meat.
   The partitive is routinely omitted in the negative.

2. Ha fregato **un pezzo di** cioccolato.
   He swiped (snitched) a piece of chocolate.
   The definite article is always omitted from the partitive construction after a noun of quantity.

3. Abbiamo **troppi compiti**.
   We have too much homework.
   After adjectives of quantity the partitive is omitted much as it is in English.

4. Ci sono **delle** mele rimaste.
   There are some apples left.
   This is the basic use of the complete partitive to express a part or portion.

5. Vuoi **delle** fragole?
   Do you want (some, any) strawberries?
   This is another example of the basic use of the complete partitive before the noun to express a part or portion of that noun. It is also possible to leave out the partitive in a question like this.

6. Vorrebbe **del** latte per il suo caffè.
   He'd like some milk for his coffee.
   He'd like **some** milk, not all the milk in the world, just enough (a portion) for his cup. Basic use of the complete partitive.

7. La maggior parte **delle** donne sposate hanno votato sì.
   Most married women voted yes.
   This expression retains *di*. Combine *di* + *le* to make *delle*. *Più di* and *meno di* follow the same pattern.

8. Ho visto quel film **molte** volte.
   I've seen that film many times.
   Like English, Italian does not use the partitive with most adjectives and adverbs of quantity.

9. Non ho soldi.
   I don't have any money.
   The partitive is omitted when the noun is negated.

10. Ho **molta** fortuna.
    I have lots of luck.
    Similar to examples 8 and 11. The partitive nature of adjectives of quantity is built in. No additional partitive words are required.

11. Ci sono **tante** stelle stanotte.
    There are so many stars tonight.
    Omit the partitive with adjectives of quantity.

12. Ho chiesto un caffè corretto con uno spruzzo **di** sambuca.
    I asked for a coffee laced with a splash of anise-flavored liqueur.
    Uno spruzzo is a noun of quantity, all of which are followed by *di*. Caffè *corretto* always has some brandy, cognac or other liquor added to it. Sambuca is a popular licorice-flavored addition.

13. Prendi **del** pane?
    Do you want any bread?
    Basic use of the complete partitive to express a part or portion of the whole. Remember that you may also leave it out entirely in a question.

14. Lei ha **tanti** amici.
    She has so many friends.
    We omit the partitive after adverbs of quantity.

15. Ho fatto un mazzo con **qualche** fiore.
    I made a bouquet with a few flowers.
    Only *qualche* can give a singular noun a plural meaning.

Drill 6: The Partitive versus the Definite Article

Explain the presence or the absence of the partitive, or part of it, in the following sentences by assigning to each sentence one of these five reasons:

A – omission of the definite article from the partitive after an adjective or adverb of quantity

B – omission of the definite article from the partitive formula after a noun of quantity

C – use of the complete partitive to express SOME or ANY

D – omission of the complete partitive when expressing a NEGATED SOME or ANY

E – use of the definite article to express general preference or dislike

1. Ha preso una bottiglia di vino rosso. _____

2. Vorresti un bicchierino di vin santo? _____

3. Non le piace il vino. _____

4. Non beve vino. _____

5. Compro del vino stasera. _____

6. Rimane un po' di vino. _____

7. Ha bevuto troppo vino. _____

8. Lei odia il vino. _____

9. Le piace molto il vino. _____

10. Prenderei volentieri una goccia di vino. _____

Answers and Explanations to Drill 6

1. Ha preso una bottiglia di vino rosso.   **B**
   He ordered a bottle of red wine.
   Bottiglia is a noun of quantity, therefore we omit the definite article portion of the partitive.

2. Vorresti un bicchierino di vin santo?   **B**
   Would you like a little glass of sweet white wine?
   Another noun of quantity. Omit the article. Vinsanto is a dessert wine frequently offered with *panettone* or little hard cookies like *cantucci*.

3. Non le piace il vino.   **E**
   She doesn't like wine.
   We retain the definite article to express general preference.

4. Non beve vino.   **D**
   She doesn't drink (any) wine
   The definite article is routinely omitted from the partitive to express a negated quantity.

5. Compro del vino stasera.   **C**
   I'll get some wine tonight.
   Here the complete partitive expresses *some wine*.

6. Rimane un po' di vino.   **B**
   Un po' works as a noun of quantity, it requires *di* before the noun.

7. Ha bevuto troppo vino.   **A**
   He drank too much wine.
   Troppo is an adjective of quantity here. Drop the definite article.

8. Lei odia il vino.   **E**
   She hates wine.
   Use the definite article to express general like or dislike.

9. Le piace molto il vino.   **E**
   She likes wine a lot. She really likes wine.
   Tricky one. Here *molto* simply tells us how much she likes wine. This is an expression of preference. Retain the definite article.

10. Prenderei volentieri una goccia di vino.   **B**
    I'd love to have a drop of wine.
    Goccia, like *bottiglia*, is a noun expressing quantity, the definite article drops.

The Gender of Nouns

All Italian nouns are either masculine or feminine. Knowing the gender of nouns is essential in Italian! The gender of the noun determines the formation of the adjective, as well as how the article assigned to the noun will contract.

Here are a few tips worth remembering:

1. Nouns ending in **-o** are generally **masculine**. Exceptions to this basic rule are **l'auto, la foto, la mano, la moto** and **la radio**. Many of these exceptions occur because longer feminine nouns were abbreviated to make them: **la foto**grafia, **la moto**cicletta, **la radio**fonia.

2. Nouns ending in a consonant are generally **masculine**.

   l'alcol, **il** bar, **il** box, **il** gol, **il** film, **lo** sport

3. Nouns ending in **-a** are generally **feminine**. An exception to this rule is **il cinema**, which has been shortened from the longer masculine word, **il cinematografo.** Also: **il poeta**

   Another exception to this rule are those nouns of Greek origin ending in **-ma**. There are many, such as **il clima, il programma, il tema**

4. Nouns ending in **-ame, -ale, -ere, -iere, -one** and **-ore** are **masculine**.

   il falegn**ame**, **il** mai**ale**, **l'**ingegn**ere**, **il** camer**iere**, **il** minestr**one**, **il** profess**ore**

5. **Domenica** is the only day of the week which is feminine, all the others are **masculine**. All the **months** of the year are **masculine**.

6. All **colors** used as nouns are **masculine**.

7. All **languages** are **masculine**.

8. The names of all **metals** and all **elements** are **masculine**.

   l'argento *massiccio,* **il** rame, **il** ferro, **l'**oro *pur*o, **il** cobalto, **lo** zolfo

9. **Adjectives**, **verbs**, and **adverbs** used as nouns are always **masculine**:

    il bello, **il** reale

    il sapere, **il** dovere, **il** potere

    il bene, **il** male

10. Nouns ending in **-ione are** always **feminine**:

    la lezione, **la** nazione, **la** regione, **la** stazione

11. Nouns ending in **-tà** or **-tù** are always **feminine**:

    la città, **la** facoltà, **la** gioventù, **la** virtù

12. Nouns ending in **-trice** are always **feminine**:

    la calcolatrice, **la** protettrice, **la** scrittrice, **la** vincitrice

13. The names of most **sciences** and **subjects of study** are **feminine**.

    la botanica, **la** chimica, **la** fisica, **la** biologia, **l'**informatica, **la** storia

14. Most **abstract** or figurative nouns are **feminine**:

    l'amicizia, **la** bontà, **la** gentilezza, **la** paura

15. The names of many **fruits** are **feminine** while the names of most **trees** are **masculine**. Compare:

la mela	**il** melo
la pera	**il** pero
la ciliegia	**il** ciliegio

    Exceptions: some masculine fruits, such as:

    il limone, il pompelmo, il melone

16. The distinction between feminine fruits and the masculine trees they come from exists for **nuts** as well. Compare:

la noce	il noce
la castagna	il castagno
la mandorla	il mandorlo

17. Some nouns can be either masculine or feminine without changing in form:

      un nipote, **una** nipote   a nephew, a niece

      un collega, **una** collega   a male colleague, a female colleague

      un musicista, **una** musicista a male or female musician

18. Some nouns change meaning through gender. Compare:

      il porto (port) ↔ **la** porta (door)

Drill 7: The Gender of Nouns

Decide if the word is masculine or feminine.

Mark **M** or **F** in the box and then check your answers:

1. ☐ verde

2. ☐ mattone

3. ☐ colazione

4. ☐ fiore

5. ☐ contessa

6. ☐ gennaio

7. ☐ calcolatrice

8. ☐ università

9. ☐ blu

10. ☐ principe

11. ☐ re

12. ☐ diploma

13. ☐ attore

14. ☐ carabiniere

15. ☐ platino

16. ☐ idrogeno

17. ☐ carota

18. ☐ zucchero

19. ☐ rosa

20. ☐ temporale

21. ☐ sabato

22. ☐ ottone

23. ☐ tedesco

24. ☐ scrittore

25. ☐ pilota

Answers and Explanations to Drill 7

1. **M** verde is a **color**, all of which are masculine when used as nouns.

2. **M** mattone, like all nouns ending in **-one**, is masculine.

3. **F** colazione is feminine, as are all nouns ending in **-ione**.

4. **M** fiore and all nouns ending in **-ore** are masculine.

5. **F** contessa ends in a common feminine suffix, **-essa**.

6. **M** gennaio is a **month** of the year, all are masculine.

7. **F** calcolatrice ends in a common feminine suffix, **-trice.**

8. **F** università is feminine, as are all nouns ending in **-à**.

9. **M** blu is a **color** used as a noun, all of which are masculine.

10. **M** principe is a masculine noun. Its feminine version is principessa; like studente and studentessa.

11. **M** re is a masculine noun. Its feminine form is regina.

12. **M** diploma is masculine, as are all nouns of Greek origin ending in **-ma**.

13. **M** attore, like fiore in problem 4, is masculine.

14. **M** carabiniere has a characteristic masculine ending: **-iere**.

15. **M** platino is a metal, all **metals** are masculine.

16. **M** idrogeno is **chemical element**, all of which are masculine.

17. **F** carota is a typical feminine noun ending in **-a**.

18. **M** zucchero is a typical masculine noun ending in **-o**.

19. **M** a tricky one, rosa is a **color** used as a noun, therefore masculine.

20. **M** temporale has a characteristic masculine ending: **-ale**.

21. **M** sabato is a **day of the week**. All, except domenica, are masculine.

22. **M** ottone means *brass*. All **metals** are masculine.

23. **M** tedesco is the name of a **language**, all of which are masculine.

24. **F** pittrice is feminine, as are all nouns ending in **-trice**.

25. **M** or **F** pilota, like collega, can be masculine or feminine.

The Plural of Nouns

An Italian noun usually makes its plural by **changing its last vowel** according to one of these three rules:

1. **o to i**: il libro → i libri

   il numero → i numeri

   il fungo → i fun**h**i*

2. **a to e**: la gomma → le gomme

   l'amica → le ami**h**e*

   la penna → le penne

   a few exceptions: l'ala = le ali

   l'arma = le armi

   * The addition of the letter **h** preserves the hard sound of the consonants **c** and **g** in front of **i** and e. Exceptions to this rule like **amico** to **amici**, **Greco** to **Greci**, and **porco** to **porci**, change in sound from [k] to [tʃ].

3. **e to i**: il paese → i paesi

   la madre → le madri

Exceptions to the above rules include the same abbreviated words we've already encountered. They remain invariable in the plural:

   l'auto → le auto

   la foto → le foto

   la moto → le moto

   la radio → le radio

   il cinema → i cinema

Similarly, la bici (from la **bici**cletta) le bici

   Note: la mano, while it may look funny, makes its plural regularly:

   la mano → le mani

4. Nouns ending in a consonant are invariable:

> la e-mail → le e-mail
>
> il bar → i bar
>
> il film → i film
>
> lo sport → gli sport

5. Nouns ending in an accented vowel are also invariable:

> il caffè → i caffè
>
> la città → le città
>
> la virtù → le virtù

6. Other invariable nouns include:

> il re → i re
>
> lo sci → gli sci

7. Nouns ending in unstressed **-io** become **-i** in the plural:

> il calendario → i calendari
>
> il dizionario → i dizionari
>
> l'orologio → gli orologi

If the letter **-i** is stressed in pronunciation, it will double in the plural:

> lo zio → gli zii

8. Nouns ending in **-cia** and **-gia** generally drop their **-i** in the plural:

> la boccia → le bocce
>
> la coscia → le cosce
>
> la faccia → le facce
>
> la guancia → le guance
>
> la spiaggia → le spiagge

unless a vowel directly precedes the ending:

> la camicia → le camicie
>
> la ciliegia → le ciliegie
>
> la valigia → le valigie

9. Masculine nouns ending in **-a** make their plural in **-i**. This is also true for the masculine plural of dual gender nouns ending in **-a**.

> il tema → i temi
>
> il problema → i problemi
>
> il/la collega → i colleghi/ le colleghe

10. A few masculine singular nouns become feminine in the plural. This odd phenomenon triggers the use of an atypical plural ending, **-a**. Thus branded, they are pretty easy to distinguish from the normal feminine plural. The unusual **-a plural** reminds us that they're derived from the masculine singular. These oddball, gender-bending nouns should be learned by heart as they are all quite common:

> il dito → le dita
>
> il braccio → le braccia
>
> il ginocchio → le ginocchia
>
> il labbro → le labbra
>
> il lenzuolo → le lenzuola
>
> il miglio → le miglia
>
> il paio → le paia
>
> l'uovo → le uova

11. Nouns with TWO plural forms include:

> braccio: braccia (human) / bracci (thing)
>
> ciglio: ciglia (human) / cigli (street curbs)
>
> dito: dita (all together) / diti (individually)
>
> labbro: labbra (of the mouth) / labbri (of a wound)
>
> lenzuolo: lenzuola (a set, all together) / lenzuoli (individually)
>
> membro: membra (of the human body) / membri (of a club)
>
> muro: mura (surrounding a town or city / muri (of a house)
>
> osso: ossa (human) / ossi (other)

12. Some nouns have completely irregular plurals:

>   il bue → i buoi
>
>   il dio → *gli* dei
>
>   l'uomo → gli uomini

13. Family names are invariable and masculine in Italian. Make their plurals accordingly:

    I Cavallini, I LoBianco, Gli Smith, I Tomba

Drill 8: The Plural of Nouns

Change these singular nouns to plural:

1. il quaderno = _____

2. l'amica = _____

3. il lago = _____

4. il formaggio = _____

5. lo spago = _____

6. la matita = _____

7. la zia = _____

8. l'amico = _____

9. la lezione = _____

10. il gol = _____

11. il lemma = _____

12. il chiodo = _____

13. il tè = _____

14. il fermaglio = _____

15. la buccia = _____

Answers and Explanations to Drill 8

1. **i quaderni**
   A masculine noun ending in **o**, il quaderno makes its plural using the basic rule of **o to i**.

2. **le amiche**
   L'amica makes its plural using the basic rule of **a to e**. It requires the addition of the letter **h** to preserve the hard **c** sound in front of the **e**.

3. **i laghi**
   Il lago makes its plural using the basic rule of **o to i**. We must add the **h** to preserve the hard **g** sound in front of the **i**.

4. **i formaggi**
   Simply drop the **o** to make formaggi.

5. **gli spaghi**
   Lo spago follows the **o to i** rule and requires the **h** to keep the **g** hard in front of **i**.

6. **le matite**
   Like most feminine nouns ending in **-a,** matita follows the **a to e** rule to make its plural.

7. **le zie**
   La zia follows the **a to e** rule to make its plural.

8. **gli amici**
   L'amico loses the hard **c** sound in its plural. It does not take an **h**. Porco becomes **porci**, and medico **medici**, in the same way.

9. **le lezioni**
   La lezione uses the basic rule of **e to i** to make its plural.

10. **i gol**
    Il gol ends in a consonant, therefore it does not change in the plural.

11. **i lemmi**
    Nouns of Greek origin, like lemma, make their plural in **-i.**

12. **i chiodi**

    Like most masculine nouns ending in **o**, chiodo follows the basic **o to i** rule to make its plural.

13. **i tè**

    Il tè ends in an **accented vowel**, so it's invariable.

14. **i fermagli**

    Il fermaglio drops its **o** to make fermagli.

15. **le bucce**

    La buccia follows the **a to e** rule and drops its **i**, like boccia.

The Plural of Compound Nouns

There are a variety of compound nouns in Italian. Rules for making these compounds plural vary based on which parts of speech are combined to make the noun. This is actually easier than it sounds.

Remember that only **nouns** and **adjectives** change their last vowels to become plural. **Verbs, adverbs** and **prepositions** NEVER change their form. They **always** remain **invariable** in the compound noun.

1. NOUN with NOUN → if **both** words are **nouns**, usually only one of them, becomes **plural**. It is generally the second noun:

    l'arcobaleno = gli arcobaleni

    il capolavoro = i capolavori

    la ferrovia = le ferrovie

    il manometro = i manometri

    il pescecane = i pescecani

    However, when **capo** is the head of the noun group which follows it, *it* will be the only part to change:

    il capocaccia = i capicaccia   *Masters of the hounds*

    il capofamiglia = i capifamiglia   *Heads of the family*

    il caposquadra = i capisquadra   *Team captains*

    Exceptions: il capobandito = i capibanditi

                   il capobrigante = i capibriganti

2. NOUN followed by ADJECTIVE → Both noun and adjective become plural:

    la cassaforte = le casseforti

    la primadonna = le primedonne

    il pellerossa = i pellirosse

    la terracotta = le terrecotte

    but, some common exceptions: il palcoscenico = i palcoscenici

                                       il manoscritto = i manoscritti

ADJECTIVE followed by NOUN → Change the noun on the end:

il francobollo = i francobolli

l'altoparlante = gli altoparlanti

3.   ADJECTIVE with ADJECTIVE → only the end changes

il pianoforte = i pianoforti

il chiaroscuro = i chiaroscuri

il neonato = i neonati

il sordomuto = i sordomuti

4.   VERB with NOUN → **only** the **noun** becomes **plural**, the verb remains unchanged.

l'asciugamano = gli asciugamani

il cacciavite = i cacciaviti

il grattacielo = i grattacieli

il passaporto = i passaporti

lo spezzacuore = gli spezzacuori

5.   PREPOSITION and NOUN → **only** the **noun** becomes **plural**, the preposition stays the same:

l'avamposto = gli avamposti

il soprannome = i soprannomi

6.   TWO SINGULAR NOUNS separated by a PREPOSITION → generally only the **first noun** is made **plural**:

il foglio di carta = i fogli di carta

il pezzo di gesso = i pezzi di gesso

la luna di miele = le lune di miele

7.   INVARIABLE COMPOUNDS → Here are some frequently used compound nouns which **NEVER** change in the plural:

il/i guastafeste, il/i lasciapassare, il/i mangiatutto, il/i pesapersone,

il/i portavoce, il/i posacenere, il/i rompicollo, il/i rompicapo,

il/i rompighiaccio, il/i senza tetto, il/i lecca lecca

Drill 9: The Plural of Compound Nouns

Which part (or parts) of the compound noun change in the plural?

    A both parts?   **C** just the second word?

    B just the first word?   **D** neither word?

1. ☐ la chiave del successo

2. ☐ il cacciachiodo

3. ☐ il manoscritto

4. ☐ il mal di testa

5. ☐ il retrogusto

6. ☐ il portacenere

7. ☐ l'acquaforte

8. ☐ il capoluogo

9. ☐ il capobarca

10. ☐ il mezzocerchio

11. ☐ il capomastro

12. ☐ la cava di marmo

13. ☐ il portafoglio

14. ☐ il sottobicchiere

15. ☐ l'avambraccio

Answers and Explanations to Drill 9

1. **B** le chiavi del successo: When two nouns are separated by a preposition, only the first noun is made plural.

2. **C** i cacciachiodi: *Caccia*, a verb, is invariable, only the noun *chiodo* can change to plural.

3. **C** i manoscritti: Only the end changes for *manuscripts*. Like palcoscenico.

4. **B** i mali di testa: Two nouns separated by a preposition. Only the first noun becomes plural in *headaches*.

5. **C** i retrogusti: Adjective before noun. Make the noun plural. *Aftertaste* works like francobollo.

6. **D** i/le portabandiera: Like portavoce and posacenere, the *standard-bearer* is invariable.

7. **A** le acqueforti: Noun before adjective. Both become plural in *etchings*.

8. **C** i capoluoghi: Noun plus noun. We make only the second noun plural for this compound meaning (regional or provincial) *capitals*.

9. **A** i capibarca: The *cockswain* leads the crew, therefore **capo** becomes plural.

10. **C** i mezzocerchi: Adjective before noun. Only the noun changes in *semicircles*.

11. **D** i capomastri: Noun plus noun. We make only the second noun plural for this compound meaning *master builder, master mason*.

12. **A** le cave di marmo: Two nouns separated by a preposition. Only the first noun becomes plural in *marble quarries*.

13. **C** i portafogli: Verb plus noun. Only the noun can change in *wallets*.

14. **C** i sottobicchieri: Preposition and noun combination. Only the noun becomes plural in *coasters*.

15. **C** gli avambracci: Preposition and noun combination. Only the noun becomes plural to make *forearms*.

Adjective Formation— Making Feminine Forms

Adjectives must match the gender and number of the nouns or pronouns they describe. Here are the rules for making an adjective feminine:

1. Masculine adjectives ending in **-o** in the singular change to **-a**:

   chiaro = chiara

   piccolo = piccola

2. If the masculine singular adjective ends in **-e,** it is also used for the feminine singular form. There is no change. Compare:

   il ragazzo frances**e**   la ragazza frances**e**

3. If the masculine singular adjective ends in any letter other than **-o** or **-e,** it will not change in the feminine form. Compare:

   il gesso blu   la gomma blu

   il ragazzo belga   la ragazza belga

4. The masculine adjective ending in **-tore** becomes **-trice** in the feminine. Adjectives ending in **-tore**, **-trice** can also function as nouns.

   il gol vincitore   la squadra vincitrice

   uno strato protettore   una vernice protettrice

Drill 10: Making Adjectives Feminine

Make the following adjectives feminine:

1. creatore _____

2. bugiardo _____

3. orgoglioso _____

4. canoro _____

5. rosa _____

6. verde _____

7. viola _____

8. migliore _____

9. netto _____

10. canadese _____

Answers and Explanations to Drill 10

1. creatore = **creatrice** Typical change of the suffix **-tore** to **-trice**.

2. bugiardo = **bugiarda** Standard change from **-o** to **-a**. There are literally thousands of adjectives that work this way.

3. orgoglioso = **orgogliosa** Standard change from **-o** to **-a**.

4. canoro = **canora** Another typical formation of the feminine singular adjective.

5. rosa = **rosa** There is no change from masculine to feminine. Remember that any ending other than **-o** or **-e** on a masculine singular adjective is **invariable**.

6. verde = **verde** There is no change from masculine to feminine. Remember that adjectives ending in **-e** in the masculine singular are the same in the feminine singular.

7. viola = **viola** Like **rosa,** there is no change. The **-a** ending is invariable.

8. migliore = **migliore** There is no change from masculine to feminine. Use **-e** for both.

9. netto = **netta** The most common type of feminine adjective formation, **-o** to **-a**.

10. canadese = **canadese** No change from masculine to feminine. Use **-e** for both.

The Plural of Adjectives

A singular adjective usually makes its plural by **changing its last vowel** according to one of these basic rules, just as we saw with nouns:

1. **o to i**:

    alto → alti

    piccolo → piccoli

    a to e:

    alta → alte

    piccola → piccole

2. Singular adjectives ending in **-e: e to i**
   Remember that this type of adjective can be masculine or feminine.

    gentile → gentili

    cinese → cinesi

3. Masculine singular in **-a: i**

    un uomo egoista → uomini egoisti

    una donna egoista → donne egoiste

4. Adjectives ending in **-io:** Just as we saw with the plural of nouns like **calendario** to *calendari*, the masculine plural has only one **-i** if it is unstressed:

    serio, seri, seria, serie

    If the **-i** is stressed in pronunciation, it will work like the noun **zio** to *zii*:

    natio, natii, natia, natie

5. Adjectives ending in **-co,-ca:** Just as we learned in the plural of nouns like **banco** to *banchi*, or **amica** to *amiche* (which are stressed on the next to last syllable), we add the letter **h** to preserve the hard **c** in pronunciation [k]:

    poco, pochi. poca, poche

    bianco, bianchi, bianca, bianche

    pazzesco, pazzeschi, pazzesca, pazzesche

6. Adjectives ending in **-ico, -ica**: When the stress falls *before* the next to the last syllable, no **h** is added to the masculine plural:

    nemico, nemici, nemica, nemiche

    domestico, domestici, domestica, domestiche

    pubblico, pubblici, pubblica, pubbliche

    simpatico, simpatici, simpatica, simpatiche

    Exception: carico, carichi, carica, cariche

7. Adjectives ending in **-go, -ga:** We made the plural of nouns like **lago** to *laghi*, by adding the letter **h** to preserve the hard **g** in pronunciation. We'll treat adjectives the same way:

    lungo, lunghi, lunga, lunghe

8. Adjectives ending in **-cio, gio:** Some adjectives with these endings will drop their **-i** in the feminine plural, just as we did with **coscia** to *cosce*, **guancia** to *guance*, and **spiaggia** to *spiagge*:

    liscio, lisci, liscia, lisce

    grigio, grigi, grigia, grige (grigie is also accepted)

9. If the masculine singular adjective ends in any letter other than **-o**, **-e**, or **-a**, it is invariable and will not change:

    Otto è un numero **pari**.

    Mettiti i calzini **blu**.

10. Invariable plural of some colors: If the adjective of color is derived from the name of a **fruit**, a **flower**, a **nut**, a **food**, or a **gem stone**, it usually remains invariable as an adjective. Here are some examples:

    rosa: le gomme rosa

    viola: il naso viola dal freddo

    nocciola: gli occhi nocciola

    oliva: pantaloni verde oliva

    latte: la pelle bianco latte

    rubino: le labbra color rubino

    fucsia: un cappello fucsia

Exception: castano: (exists in all forms) i capelli castani Some 40 year-old textbooks and dictionaries I still have include the colors *arancione* and *marrone* as invariable. Reliable current sources, such as Oxford *Paravia* 2007, and Zanichelli 2007 list them as regular **-e** to **-i** adjectives. All other colors follow the general agreement rules: **o to i, e to i, a, u invariable.**

11. All **numbers** are also **invariable** as adjectives:

     cinque fratelli

     i **sette** nani

     tremila soldati

12. When one adjective refers back to more than one noun, that adjective will be **masculine plural** in form, unless **ALL** of the nouns are feminine:

     compare: Il cinghiale e la volpe sono selvatici.

     Sua madre e suo padre sono americani.

     Sua madre e sua nonna sono basse.

13. All Italian adjectives can be placed into one of three groups to help you predict which ending rules they'll follow. This is an easy, useful tool to master. You must always consider what the adjective looks like in the **masculine singular** form to identify it.

     Class I
     Adjectives ending in **o** in the masculine singular exist in four forms: **o, i, a, e**. The majority of Italian adjectives work this way.

     Class II
     Adjectives ending in **e** in the masculine singular have only two possible forms: **e** and **i**.

     Class III
     Masculine singular adjectives ending in any letter other than **o, a,** or **e** are **invariable.**

The three groups can be visualized in a inverted triangle. The class on the top represents the largest group of adjectives and has the most forms (4). Class II is a much smaller group, and has only 2 forms. The bottom tip of the triangle represents the group with the fewest adherents, the invariables, which have only one form.

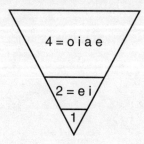

Drill 11: Making Adjectives Plural

Change these singular adjectives to plural:

1. un lago azzurro = laghi _____

2. un vecchio amico = _____ amici

3. un ragazzo francese = ragazzi _____

4. un formaggio stagionato = formaggi _____

5. un guanto nero = guanti _____

6. un fiore bianco = fiori _____

7. uno scritto pio = scritti _____

8. un'amica cortese = amiche _____

9. una parola saggia = parole _____

10. un voto comunista = voti _____

11. una sciarpa avana = sciarpe _____

12. un gesto automatico = gesti _____

13. una famiglia tedesca = famiglie _____

14. una matita gialla = matite _____

15. una scimmia selvatica = scimmie _____

Answers and Explanations to Drill 11

1. laghi **azzurri**
   A masculine adjective ending in **o**, *azzurro* makes its plural using the basic rule of **o to i**, and in the feminine, **a to e**.

2. **vecchi amici**
   Vecchio simply drops its **o** to make the masculine plural. Like the nouns *orologio, formaggio*, and the adjectives *serio, saggio*.

3. ragazzi **francesi**
   Francese uses the basic rule of **e to i** to make its plural.

4. i formaggi **stagionati**
   Stagionato, like *azzurro*, makes its plural using the basic rules, **o to i, a to e**.

5. guanti **neri**
   Nero also follows the basic rules **o to i, a to e**.

6. fiori **bianchi**
   If stressed on the next to last syllable, adjectives ending in **-co** and **-ca** require the addition of the letter **h** in front of **i** and **e**. Thus: bianco, bianchi, bianca, bianche.

7. scritti **pii**
   Pio is pronounced with stress on the letter **i**, so it makes its plural like the noun *zio to zii*.

8. amiche **cortesi**
   Whether masculine or feminine, *cortese* follows the **e to i** rule.

9. parole **sagge**
   From the adjective group ending in **-gio -gia**, *saggia* drops the **i** in the feminine plural, like the noun *spiaggia to spiagge*. The masculine form, *saggi*, drops the **o** like *calendario to calendari*.

10. voti **comunisti**
    Comunista, like *egoista*, makes a standard masculine plural with **i**.

11. sciarpe **avana**

    The tawny, light brown color **avana** comes from the color of the Havana cigar. It is invariable, along with the names of flowers, fruits, nuts, foods and gem stones used as colors.

12. gesti **automatici**

    Adjectives ending in **-ico, -ica** do not take an **h** in the masculine plural if they are stressed *before* the next to the last syllable. Therefore: automatico, automatici, automatica, automatiche.

13. famiglie **tedesche**

    Adjectives ending in **-co** and **-ca** that are stressed on the next to last syllable require the addition of the letter **h** in front of **i** and **e**. Thus: tedesco, tedeschi, tedesca, tedesche.

14. matite **gialle**

    Feminine singular adjectives ending in **-a** make regular plurals in **-e**. Regular in all forms: giallo, gialli, gialla, gialle.

15. scimmie **selvatiche**

    Adjectives ending in **-ico, -ica** are regular in all forms except the masculine plural: selvatico, selvatici, selvatica, selvatiche.

The Position of Adjectives Relative to the Noun

Most Italian adjectives **FOLLOW** the noun they modify. There is a small group of common adjectives which precede the noun and there are adjectives which change in meaning depending on their placement.

English speakers generally learn the preceding adjectives with ease as this is the position they are familiar with in their native language. Not remembering to **place the majority of Italian adjectives after the noun** is the most common student error.

Adjectives which **PRECEDE** the noun in Italian include:

All interrogative, demonstrative and possessive adjectives:

↓   ↓   ↓

Quali libri?   Questi libri.   I miei libri.

All cardinal and ordinal numbers:

↓   ↓

tre libri   il mio primo libro

The following BANGS adjectives:

(B = Beauty)	**bello, brutto**
(A = Age)	**giovane**, **vecchio** (but not anziano!) and **nuovo**
(N = Number)	**alcuno, altro, ciascuno, certo*, molto, parecchio, qualche, stesso, tale, tutto** *when certo appears after the noun its meaning is "assured" **differente**, **diverso** and **nuovo** appear in both with positions with slight changes in meaning
(G = Goodness)	**bravo, buono** and **cattivo**
(S = Size) *only*	**piccolo**, and **grande.** Other adjectives of size follow!!

Adjectives which **FOLLOW** the noun in Italian include:

All adjectives of COLOR

All adjectives expressing NATIONALITY, ORIGIN, or RELIGION

All adjectives denoting SHAPE or TEXTURE

Adjectives denoting POSITION or OFFICE

Most adjectives DESCRIPTIVE of PHYSICAL or MENTAL STATE

Study these examples. Observe the position of the adjectives and then try the drill:

Era una **piccola** ragazza **sottile**.

È un **giovane** pastore **tedesco**.

Ho scelto una **grande** cornice **dorata**.

Cercavo una stoffa **vellutata**.

Mi sono messo i sandali **bianchi**.

La mia **migliore** amica ha comprato una **nuova** macchina **giapponese**.

Piangeva lacrime **amare**.

Era una ragazza **svampita**.

Drill 12: Position of Adjectives

Choose the correct position for the adjective, **in front of** or **after** the noun:

1. un __?__ ragazzo __?__ (cattivo)

2. un __?__ ragazzo __?__ (americano)

3. un __?__ ragazzo __?__ (divertente)

4. un __?__ ragazzo __?__ (alto)

5. un __?__ ragazzo __?__ (noioso)

6. una __?__ donna __?__ (vecchia)

7. una __?__ donna __?__ (bionda)

8. una __?__ donna __?__ (norvegese)

9. una __?__ sorella __?__ (gemella)

10. una __?__ sorella __?__ (minore)

11. una __?__ minestra __?__ (buona)

12. una __?__ minestra __?__ (calda)

13. una __?__ minestra __?__ (gustosa)

14. __?__ scarpe __?__ (blu scuro)

15. __?__ piedi __?__ (stanchi)

Answers and Explanations to Drill 12

1. un **cattivo** ragazzo   *Buono* and *cattivo*, two degrees of goodness, precede.

2. un ragazzo **americano**   Adjectives of nationality always follow.

3. un ragazzo **divertente**   Like the majority of Italian adjectives, *divertente* follows.

4. un ragazzo **alto**   *Piccolo* and *grande* are the only adjectives of size which precede. All others, like *alto*, follow.

5. un ragazzo **noioso**   Normal adjective placement following the noun.

6. una **vecchia** donna   *Giovane* and *vecchio* are BANGS adjectives which precede. *Anziana* would have followed as an ordinary adjective descriptive of state.

7. una donna **bionda**   Typical adjective placement for *bionda*.

8. una donna **norvegese**   All nationalities follow.

9. una sorella **gemella**   Like most Italian adjectives, *gemella* follows the noun.

10. una sorella **minore**   *Minore* follows the noun.

11. una **buona** minestra   Like *cattivo*, *buona* precedes the noun (BANGS).

12. una minestra **calda**   Common adjective descriptive of state, *calda* follows.

13. una minestra **gustosa**   Usual placement of the adjective after the noun.

14. scarpe **blu scuro.**   Colors always follow. Note the absence of agreement!

15. piedi **stanchi**   Another example of an adjective in its usual post-noun position.

The Irregular Forms of *Bello*, *Buono*, and *Grande*

When these three BANGS adjectives precede the noun they take on the special forms we are about to see. When they appear elsewhere they behave normally. Let's look at their normal usage first:

Tuo figlio è **bello**.

Tua figlia è **bella**.

Questi fiori sono **belli**.

Le tue scarpe sono **belle**.

We see that, in this position, BELLO behaves just like any other Class I adjective, with four possible forms. We can say the same of BUONO:

Questo vino è **buono**.

Questa torta è **buona**.

Questi pompelmi sono **buoni**.

Queste fragole sono **buone**.

GRANDE behaves like a regular Class II adjective, with two forms:

La nostra famiglia è **grande**.

Questi quadri sono **grandi**.

These adjectives transform when they are placed directly in front of the noun so as to accommodate the initial sound of the noun in question. **BELLO** changes much the same way as the definite article would:

Andrea è un **bel** ragazzo. (**il** ragazzo)

Mi è piaciuto quel **bello** stadio. (**lo** stadio)

È una **bell'**aula. (**l'**aula)

Emilia è una **bella** ragazza. (**la** ragazza)

Sono **bei** ragazzi. (**i** ragazzi)

Sono **begli** studenti. (**gli** studenti)

Emilia e Sara sono **belle** ragazze. (**le** ragazze)

You will learn this exact same pattern with the forms of **quello** (that, those):

> quel, quello, quell', quella, quei, quegli and quelle

as well as with the contractions made from **di + article**:

> **del, dello, dell', della, dei, degli and delle**

Let's take a look at **BUONO** which, in its singular forms, follows the same pattern as the indefinite article:

> Tu sei un **buon** ragazzo. (**un** ragazzo)
>
> Lui è un **buono** studente. (**uno** studente)
>
> È un **buon** orologio. (**un** orologio)
>
> È una **buon'**automobile. (**un'**automobile)
>
> Sei una **buona** ragazza. (**una** buona)
>
> Sono **buoni** ragazzi, spaghetti, orologi.
>
> Sono **buone** ragazze.

GRANDE may be shortened to **gran** in front of consonants as long as they are not strong (ie, not to be shortened in front of **z, s+consonant, gn, ps, or y**).

GRANDE may be shortened to **grand'** in front of a vowel, without regard to gender. The plural form is always **grandi.**

Here are some examples:

> Sei un **gran** ragazzo adesso.
>
> Garibaldi era un **grand'**uomo.
>
> Giovanna d'Arca era una **grand'**eroina francese.
>
> Che **grande** zaino!
>
> Mi piacerebbe una **gran** casa.
>
> I bambini devono ubbidire alle persone **grandi**.

Italians use the shorter forms to a lesser extent today, substituting **grande** whenever a singular form is needed. Perhaps in time, these "picky" rules and their usage will fade away.

Drill 13: Bello, Buono, and Grande

1. Non trovi questi guanti _____? (beautiful))

2. Che _____ denti! (beautiful)

3. Che _____ lavoro! (good)

4. L'elefante ha _____ zampe. (big)

5. Che _____ libro. (big)

6. Ha una _____ villa sul lago di Como. (big)

7. Che _____ stadio! (big)

8. È una _____ aula. (big)

9. Il Daniele è un _____ albergo. (great)

10. Che _____ uomo! (handsome)

11. È una _____ minestra. (good)

12. Sono arrivati due _____ Spagnoli. (handsome)

13. Dammi un _____ etto di prosciutto. (good)

14. Questo voto è molto _____. (good)

15. È una _____ idea. (good)

Answers and Explanations to Drill 13

1. Non trovi questi guanti **belli**?
   Don't you think these gloves are beautiful?
   Since the adjective isn't in front of the noun we use the regular masculine plural form to match *guanti*.

2. Che **bei** denti!
   What beautiful teeth!
   This preceding adjective is designated for masculine plural nouns using the definite article *i*. Like *dei* and *quei*.

3. Che **buon** lavoro!
   What good work!
   Just like *un*, the indefinite article which matches *lavoro*, **buon** ends in the letter *n*.

4. L'elefante ha **grandi** zampe.
   The elephant has big feet.
   This is the only plural form for *grande*.

5. Che **gran** libro!
   What a big book!
   Grande reduces to **gran** when the singular noun which follows it begins with a weak consonant, regardless of gender.

6. Ha una **gran** villa sul lago di Como.
   He has a big villa on Lake Como.
   Just like the preceding problem, use **gran** in front of *villa*.

7. Che **grande** stadio!
   What a big stadium!
   We must use the complete form in front of a strong consonant combination such as *s + t*.

8. È una **grand'**aula.
   It's a big classroom.
   The *e* drops and is replaced by the apostrophe in front of the singular noun beginning in a vowel, regardless of gender.

9. Il Daniele è un **grand'**albergo.
   The Daniele is a great hotel.
   This problem is exactly like the previous one.

10. Che **bell'**uomo!
    What a handsome man.
    This preceding adjective is designated for singular nouns which use the article *l'*, that is, those beginning with a vowel.

11. È una **buona** minestra.
    It's a good soup.
    Just like *una*, the indefinite article which matches *minestra*, **buona** ends in *a*.

12. Sono arrivati due **begli** Spagnoli.
    Two handsome Spaniards arrived.
    This preceding adjective is designated for masculine plural nouns using the definite article *gli*.

13. Dammi un **buon** etto di prosciutto.
    Give me a good 100 grams of ham. (one etto equals 100 grams)
    Like *un*, the indefinite article which matches *etto*, **buon** ends in *n*.
    Do <u>not</u> use the apostrophe with masculine nouns.

14. Questo voto è molto **buono**.
    This grade is very good.
    This adjective does not precede the noun and is therefore regular.

15. È una **buon'** idea.
    It's a good idea.
    Like *un'*, the indefinite article which matches *idea*, **buon'** ends with the apostrophe. The apostrophe is only needed for feminine singular nouns with this adjective. **Grand'** use the apostrophe regardless of gender. Why are they different? The apostrophe on **buon'** replaces an **a** (from buona) and so can only be applied to a feminine word. The apostrophe on **grand'** replaces an **e** (from grande) which is used in front of both masculine and feminine nouns.

Adjectives That Change in Meaning According to Placement

This is a very interesting feature of Italian adjectives. Adjectives tend to be FIGURATIVE in meaning when placed in front of the noun. When they follow the noun the meaning is usually more LITERAL or concrete. Here are some examples worth remembering:

une **cara** amica *a dear friend*	versus	un vesito **caro** *an expensive dress*
il mio **povero** bambino! *my poor, unfortunate child!*		la gente **povera** *poor people, destitute, without money*
con le **proprie** mani *with my own hands*		il linguaggio **proprio** *proper, correct language*
lo **stesso** giorno *the same day*		il giorno **stesso** *the very day*
Gentile Signora Dear Madame (in a letter)		una signora **gentile** a nice lady
diversi problemi *several, various problems*		un problema **diverso** *a different problem*
una **magra** scusa *a weak, lame excuse*		un cane **magro** *a lean, thin dog*
un **certo** tempo *an unspecified amount of time*		la morte **certa** *certain death*

The speaker can inject subjectivity with the placement he chooses:

tristi notizie *subjective, he feels sad about the news*	notizie tristi *more objective, factual*
un lungo discorso *a long and probably boring speech*	capelli lunghi *long hair*

Drill 14: Adjectives That Change Meaning

Place the adjective in the proper blank to convey the meaning desired:

1. una __?__ ragazza __?__ (place **magra** to mean very thin, skinny)

2. una __?__ ricompensa __?__ (place **magra** to mean meager, paltry)

3. i miei __?__ nonni __?__ (place **cari** to mean dear)

4. un __?__ nome __?__ (place **proprio** to mean proper)

5. un __?__ regalo __?__ (place **caro** to mean pricey, expensive)

6. la mia __?__ casa __?__ (place **propria** to mean my own)

7. un __?__ paese __?__ (place **povero** to mean financially poor)

8. il/lo __?__ cappello __?__ (place **stesso** to mean same, identical)

9. una __?__ cosa __?__ (place **certa** to mean sure, definite)

10. una __?__ cosa __?__ (place **certa** to mean some, indefinite thing)

Answers and Explanations to Drill 14

1. una ragazza **magra**

   The literal meaning *thin* is conveyed by placing *magra* after the noun.

2. una **magra** ricompensa

   Positioned in front of the noun, *magra* is no longer concrete. Here it suggests a *meager, paltry* reward.

3. i miei **cari** nonni

   In front of the noun, *cari* is figurative. Translate it as *dear, loveable, sweet* or *kind*.

4. un nome **proprio**

   After the noun, *proprio* translates literally as *proper.*

5. un regalo **caro**

   After the noun, *caro* has the literal meaning *expensive.*

6. la mia **propria** casa

   Preceding the noun, *propria* means *own.*

7. un paese **povero**

   The literal meaning of *poor, without money*, is expressed when *povero* follows the noun.

8. lo **stesso** cappello

   In front of the noun *stesso* means *same.*

9. una cosa **certa**

   After the noun *certa* is concrete. Here it means *sure, definite.*

10. una **certa** cosa

    In front of the noun *certa* becomes imprecise. Here it conveys something *indefinable.*

Indefinite Adjectives

Indefinite adjectives may determine nouns in place of an article. Like any other adjectives, some agree in gender and number with the nouns they modify, and some are invariable. As adjectives of number, they generally precede. We will see that many of these adjectives also function as indefinite pronouns.

Ogni

Use the invariable **ogni** to convey **each** when you wish to stress the singularity of the thing. Use a form of **tutto + article** when you want to stress the purality of the thing. Compare:

> Lei sceglie ogni ciliegia con cura.
> *She picks each, every cherry carefully.*

> Corro ogni mattina.
> *I run each morning.*

but also:

> Corro tutte le mattine.
> *I run every morning.*

Ciascuno

Ciascuno also means **each, every**. Unlike the invariable **ogni**, however, it matches each noun it modifies:

> ciascun uomo, ciascuno zero, ciascuna donna, ciascun'aula

Qualunque and Qualsiasi

Qualunque and **qualsiasi** are synonyms meaning *any one at all*. Both are invariable and may appear in front of or after the noun:

> Me ne frego! Mettiti una cravatta qualsiasi!
> *I don't care (which one you choose)! Put on just any tie.*

> Sa cucinare qualunque piatto.
> *She knows how to cook any dish.*

> Puoi telefonarmi a qualsiasi ora.
> *You can call me at any hour.*

Both can also take on the meaning of *ordinary* or *run of the mill*.

> Non è un uomo qualsiasi!
> *He's no ordinary man!*

> Non sono piatti qualunque, sono di porcellana!
> *They're not just any plates, they're porcelain.*

Nessun

Nessun(o) means *not one, not any, no*. It can also be translated as *not a single, not one single*. **Nessuna** and **nessun'** are the feminine forms. Nessun is frequently used as a negation in combination with **non**:

> Non ho nessun'idea.
> *I have no idea.*

It can also appear without **non**:

> **Nessuno** di questi pesci è abbastanza fresco.
> *Not one of these fish is fresh enough.*

> **Nessun** riposo per la mamma.
> *No rest for Mom.*

> **Nessun** uccello è arrivato.
> *Not a single bird came.*

Qualche

Qualche suggests *an indefinite amount, some, a few*. Note that the noun it modifies always remains singular, despite the English translations in the plural. Study these examples:

> Avresti qualche minuto?
> *Would you have a few minutes?*

> È rimasto qualche gnocco?
> *Are there any gnocchi left?*

> C'è qualche valigia da caricare.
> *There are a few suitcases to bring up.*

Alcuno

Alcuno and its forms can also be translated as **some, a few, any**.

> Alcuni miei amici mi hanno aiutato.
> *Some, a few of my friends helped me.*

> Ci sono alcune ragazze in squadra.
> *There are a few girls on the team.*

Altro, Altri

Study the slight differences in these translations of **altro, altri**:

> Vuoi un **altro** caffè?
> *Do you want **another** coffee? (a second one)*

> Potrebbe mostrarmi un **altro** colore?
> *Could you show me **another** color? (a different one)*

> Chi **altro** può essere?
> *Who **else** can it be?*

> Non c'e **altri** che lui.
> *There's **nobody** but him.*

Certo

> Certi studenti portano il loro cellulare in classe.
> **Some** *students bring their cell phones to class.*

> Un certo bimbo farà meglio a lavarsi le mani!
> *A **certain** child had better wash his hands!*

Note that **certo** loses its indefinite quality when it appears after the noun; there it means **certain** in the sense of **sure**:

> Quel film sarà un fiasco certo.
> *That film will be a flop, for **sure**.*

Diverso and Vario

Diverso can mean *different, unlike, or dissimilar*. Like **vario**, it also takes on the indefinite meaning of *several, quite few, various,* or *sundry*:

> Abbiamo diverse idee.
> *We have different ideas. (We disagree.)*

C'è una scelta diversa.
There's a variety of choice, there are many choices.

… in vari modi.
…in several, different, various ways.

Parecchio

Parecchio means *quite a lot of*. It always precedes the noun it modifies. Its use is very common:

C'è parecchia nebbia stamattina.
It's quite foggy this morning.

Ci sono parecchi ristoranti cinesi qui vicino.
There are quite a few Chinese restaurants near here.

Molto and Poco

Molto conveys *a lot, a good or great deal of, plenty of, much*:

Una madre deve avere molta pazienza.
A mother must have a lot of patience.

In the plural it can be translated as *lots of, plenty of, many:*

… dopo molti anni.
after many years.

Poco means *little* or *not much* in the singular, *few* or *not many* in the plural:

C'è rimasto poco vino.
There isn't much wine left.

Il nonno era un uomo di poche parole.
Grandfather was a man of few words.

Tale

Tale can precede a noun with no other determiner to mean *like or such:*

Tale padre, tale figlio.
Like father, like son.

When preceded by *un, una,* or *di* it still means *such, like* or *similar:*

Non ho mai visto una tale bellezza.
I never saw such beauty.

Tale + quale are used to mean *exactly like, just like:*

> Ne vorrebbe uno tale e quale il mio.
> *He would like one just like mine.*

Tutto

Tutto may appear in front of a noun with no other determiner. This usage translates as *complete* or *absolute*:

> Vorrei parlare con tutta franchezza.
> *I would like to speak quite frankly.*

> È partito in **tutta** fretta.
> *He left very hurriedly.*

Tutto may be followed by a variety of other determiners to express *all*, or *the whole*:

> **tutta la** notte – followed by a definite article
> *all night long*

> **tutta una** serie – followed by an indefinite article
> *a whole series*

> **tutti questi** libri – followed by a demonstrative adjective
> *all of these books*

> **tutti questi** – followed by a demonstrative pronoun
> *all of these*

> **tutti i miei amici** – followed by a possessive adjective
> *all my friends*

> **tutti i tuoi** – followed by a possessive pronoun
> *all of yours*

> **tutti e tre** – followed by *and + number*
> *all three of them*

> **tutte e due** le mani
> *both hands*

> **tutti e quattro** i fratelli
> *all four brothers*

> **tutte quante** le opere di Dante – followed by an adjective
> *all the works of Dante.*

Tutto can also refer to a noun or pronoun *via a verb:*

> Veniamo **tutti**.
> *We're all coming.*

> Vi invito **tutte**.
> *I'm inviting all of you (girls).*

Tutto often functions as an adverb meaning *completely, entirely:*

> È rincasato **tutto** bagnato.
> *He came home completely soaked.*

Oddly enough this adverb *may agree* with a feminine adjective:

> Hai le mani **tutte** sporche.
> *Your hands are totally filthy.*

> La bimba è venuta **tutta** sola.
> *The little girl came all alone.*

Drill 15: Indefinite Adjectives

Supply the Italian equivalent for the English cue. Use an indefinite adjective as part of each answer.

1. Prendi cioccolato, vaniglia o fragola? _____ gusto andrà bene.
   (any at all)

2. _____ casa le piaceva.
   (not one, not any)

3. Rimangono _____ gnocchi.
   (very few)

4. Ho colto questi fiori stamattina e li ho messi _____ in un vaso.
   (all)

5. Dove sono _____ ragazzi?
   (all the)

6. Ci vediamo _____ giorno.
   (every)

7. Sceglie _____ bicchiere con cura.
   (each)

8. Mi piacciono le tue scarpe. Le voglio comprare _____.
   (exactly like them)

9. Mi sono impegnata per _____ giorno.
   (the whole, the entire)

10. I bambini sono arrivati _____ sudati.
    (completely, totally)

11. Te li do, _____!
    (all three of them)

12. C'è _____ afa!
    (such a)

13. Scenderà fra _____ minuto.
     (a few)

14. Ha indossato _____ vestiti prima di sceglierne uno.
     (quite a few)

15. Abbiamo questo modello in tutte le misure e in _____ colori.
     (various, different)

Answers and Explanations to Drill 15

1. Prendi cioccolato, vaniglia o fragola? **Qualsiasi/qualunque** gusto andrà bene.
   Will you have chocolate, vanilla or strawberry? Any flavor will be fine with me.
   Either answer is possible.

2. **Nessuna** casa le piaceva.
   She didn't like any of the houses.
   This is a typical use of *nessuno* to mean **not one**, **not any**. Notice that it's *feminine* to match *casa*.

3. Rimangono **pochi** gnocchi.
   They are very few gnocchi left.
   Notice the addition of the letter *h* to preserve the original *hard c* sound of *poco*. Did you answer with **alcuni** gnocchi? That would mean there are some left, or a few left, but without the subjective judgment *very few* implies. *Pochi* is the best answer.

4. Ho colto questi fiori stamattina e li ho messi **tutti** in un vaso.
   I picked these flowers this morning and I put them all in a vase.
   Here *tutti* refers to *them*, *the flowers*, via the verb mettere. Like the participle, it reflects the plural nature of the flowers.

5. Dove sono **tutti i** ragazzi?
   Where are all the boys?
   This is an example of *tutto + definite article* to mean **all the**.

6. Ci vediamo **tutti i** giorni.
   We see each other every day.
   Tutti i giorni is the best way to express **every day**. It stresses the *multiple* or *plural* nature of these get togethers.

7. Sceglie **ogni/ciascun** bicchiere con cura.
   She chooses each glass with care.
   Using *ogni* or *ciascun* puts emphasis on **each** *single* glass.

8. Mi piacciono le tue scarpe! Le voglio comprare **tali e quali**.
   I like your shoes. I want to buy the exact same ones.
   Use *tale* + *quale* to mean **exactly**, **just like** them.

9. Mi sono impegnata per **tutto il** giorno.
   I'm tied up all day.
   Use *tutto* + *definite article* to express **the whole**, **the entire** day.

10. I bambini sono arrivati **tutti** sudati.
    The children arrived all sweaty.
    Tutti is treated as part of the adjective here, therefore it agrees.

11. Te li do, **tutti e tre**!
    You can have all three of them! (I give all three of them to you!)
    Tutto combines with **e plus number** here. Taking our cue from *li*, we make the masculine plural. Had the sentence been *Te le do*, we would answered with *tutte e tre*.

12. C'è **una tale** afa!
    It's sooo hot!
    Literally **such a** heat!

13. Scenderà fra **qualche** minuto.
    She'll be down in a few minutes.
    Use *qualche* to express the indefinite amount **a few**. Note the singular noun.

14. Ha indossato **parecchi** vestiti prima di sceglierne uno.
    She tried on quite a few dresses before choosing one of them.
    Parecchi is placed in front of the noun to mean **quite a few**. **Molti** would also work, but with the translation of **a lot of**, **many**.

15. Abbiamo questo modello in tutte le misure e in **diversi/vari** colori.
    We have this style in every size and a variety of colors.
    Either answer works.

Indefinite Pronouns

Many of the indefinite adjectives we discussed earlier also exist as pronouns. They stand on their own, in place of nouns. Here are some of the most useful indefinite pronouns:

alcuno	*some, a few*
altro	*other, another*
certo	*some, some people, some of them*
ciascuno	*each, each one, everyone*
nessuno	*nobody, none, not one*
ognuno	*each, each one, everyone*
parecchio	*several, a lot, quite a few, many*
qualcosa	*something*
qualcuno	*someone*
tale	*someone, a man, a woman*
tutto	*all, everybody, everyone*

Here are examples of each:

Vorrei leggere **alcuni** di questi libri.
I would like to read some, a few of these books.

Ho rovinato questo foglio Signora, potrei averne un **altro**?
I messed up this paper Ma'am, may I have another one?

Certi sono molto audaci.
Some of them are very daring.

Mi è piaciuto **ciascuno** dei suoi film.
I liked each one of his films.

Non ha letto **nessuno** dei suoi libri.
She has read none of his books.

Ognuno si sbaglia.
Everyone makes mistakes.

Scegli una caramella. Ce ne sono **parecchie**.
Choose a candy. There are many.

Vuoi **qualcosa** da bere?
Do you want something to drink?

C'è **qualcuno** alla porta.
There's someone at the door.

C'è **un tale** che ti cerca.
There's a man looking for you.

Tutto è pronto adesso.
Everything is ready now.

Drill 16: Indefinite Pronouns

Supply the Italian equivalent for the English cue. Use an indefinite pronoun for each answer.

1. Mamma, chiedono _____ da mangiare!
   (something)

2. Hai visto le foto? _____ sono veramente buone.
   (some of them)

3. Ha dato una moneta ad _____ di noi.
   (each one, every one)

4. Hai letto _____ delle mie lettere!
   (each one)

5. Sono partiti _____.
   (all)

6. Hai trovato un bel vestito per la serata? No, _____!
   (not one)

7. Qual'è andato in California, Arturo o Andrea?
   Ci sono andati _____.
   (both of them, i.e., all)

8. Perché non ci è andato anche Antonio?
   Aveva _____ cose da fare.
   (other)

9. C'è _____ all'apparecchio per Carlo. Credo che sia Daniela.
   (someone)

10. Quanti lecca lecca ci rimangono? Ce ne sono _____.
    (several)

Answers and Explanations to Drill 16

1. Mamma, chiedono **qualcosa** da mangiare!
   Mom, they're asking for something to eat.
   Qualcosa literally means **something**.

2. Hai visto le foto? **Certe** sono veramente buone.
   Have you seen the photos? Some of them are really good.
   The indefinite pronoun standing in for *le foto* must be feminine and plural, hence *certe*.

3. Ha dato una moneta ad **ognuno** di noi.
   He gave a coin to each one of us.
   While you may have considered *ciascuno, ad* tells us that the next word begins with a vowel.

4. Hai letto **ciascuna** delle mie lettere!
   You read each one of my letters!
   The indefinite pronoun stands for a feminine noun, thus *ciascuna*.

5. Sono partiti **tutti**.
   They've all left.
   Tutto agrees with the subject of the verb.

6. Hai trovato un bel vestito per la serata? No, **alcuno/nessuno**!
   Did you find a nice dress for the party? No, not one!
   The indefinite pronoun reflects that the noun it stands for is masculine.

7. Qual' è andato in California, Arturo o Andrea?
   Ci sono andati **tutti e due**.
   Which one went to California, Arthur or Andy?
   They both went.
   Tutti e + number is the same as *tutti i + noun*. It means **all of them**, in this case, **both**, as there are only two.

8. Perché non ci è andato anche Antonio?
   Aveva **altre** cose da fare.
   Why didn't Tony go too?
   He had other things to do.
   The indefinite pronoun is plural here, to match *cose*.

9. C'è **qualcuno** all'apparecchio per Carlo. Credo che sia Daniele.
   There's someone on the phone for Carlos. I think it's Danielle.
   Use the indefinite pronoun *qualcuno* for an **unknown person**.

10. Quanti lecca lecca ci rimangono? Ce ne sono **parecchi**.
    How many lollipops do we have left? There are several left.
    The indefinite pronoun *parecchio* means **several** or **many**.

Adverbs

Adverbs modify verbs, adjectives, and other adverbs. All adverbs are invariable. The following are groups of common adverbs which you should know.

Adverbs of Time (rispondono alla domanda QUANDO?)

adesso	now	**poi**	then
allora	then	**presto**	early, soon
ancora	again, still, yet	**prima**	before, previously
appena	barely, only just, as soon as	**qualche volta**	sometimes
domani	tomorrow	**di rado**	seldom, infrequently
dopo	after	**raramente**	rarely
già	already	**sempre**	always
ieri	yesterday	**spesso**	often
finalmente	at last, finally	**di solito**	usually
fra poco	soon	**subito**	immediately, right away
nel **frattempo**	meanwhile	**tardi**	late
oggi	today	**una volta**	once, formerly
a lungo	a long time		

Adverbs of Place (rispondono alla domanda DOVE?)

altrove	elsewhere	**là, lì**	there
dappertutto	everywhere	**lontano**	far
davanti	in front	**qui, qua**	here
dentro	inside	**sopra**	above, up, on top
dietro	behind	**sotto**	under, underneath
fuori	outside	**vicino**	near

Adverbs of Manner (rispondono alla domanda COME?)

apposta	deliberately, on purpose	**male**	badly
bene	well, very	**presto**	quickly
insieme	together	**volentieri**	willingly

Adverbs of Quantity (rispondono alla domanda QUANTO?)

abbastanza	enough, quite	**poco**	little
molto	a lot	**più**	more
meno	less	**troppo**	too

Adverbs of Relative Degree (chiarificano i gradi del senso)

anche	also, too, even	**pressappoco**	approximately, about
almeno	at least	**piuttosto**	rather
come	like, as	**quasi**	almost
così	so	**soltanto**	only
molto	very	**sopratutto**	especially

Adverb Formation

RULE 1.   Adverbs are generally made from **feminine singular adjectives** by adding **-mente**, the Italian equivalent of **-ly**, like this:

> solo → sola = sol**amente**
>
> raro → rara = rar**amente**
>
> rapido → rapida = rapid**amente**
>
> veloce → veloce = veloc**emente**
>
> vero → vera = ver**amente**

RULE 2.   If the feminine singular adjective ends in **-le** or **-re**, DROP the **e** before adding -mente, like this:

> genti**le** = gentilmente
>
> ugua**le** = ugualmente
>
> regola**re** = regolarmente

RULE 3.   Some Special Irregularities in Adverb Formation.

These irregular forms are quite common and should be learned by heart:

> **buono** good → **bene** well
>
> **cattivo** bad → **male** badly
>
> **migliore** better → **meglio** better

RULE 4.   Adjectives with No Adverbial Form.

There are many adjectives which have no adverbial form. In this case we use a prepositional phrase which retains the adjective. Here are some examples:

> assiduo → Lavora **in modo assiduo**.
>
> incantevole → Ci ha accolti **in modo incantevole**.
>
> interessante → Ha spiegato la lezione **in modo interessante**.
>
> ripugnante → Mangia **in maniera ripugnante**.

Drill 17: Adverb Formation

Make adverbs from the following adjectives:

1. attento _____

2. assoluto _____

3. verticale _____

4. normale _____

5. breve _____

6. strano _____

7. lungo _____

8. paziente _____

9. perpendicolare _____

10. chiaro _____

Answers and Explanations to Drill 17

1. attento = attentamente
   Replace **attento** with its feminine form, then add **-mente**. (Rule 1)

2. assoluto = assolutamente
   Assoluto must be made feminine before it can accept **-mente**. (Rule 1)

3. verticale = verticalmente
   Adjectives ending in **-le** drop the **e** before accepting **-mente**. (Rule 2)

4. normale = normalmente
   Another adjective ending in **-le.** Drop the **e** before adding **-mente**. (Rule 2)

5. breve = brevemente
   Basic adjective formation, like **veloce** in Rule 1.

6. strano = stranamente
   We use the feminine form **strana** as a base for **-mente**. (Rule 1)

7. lungo = lungamente
   Lungo is replaced by its feminine form **lunga** before accepting **-mente**. This is the most common type of adverb formation. (Rule 1)

8. paziente = pazientemente
   Basic adjective formation, like **veloce** in Rule 1.

9. perpendicolare = perpendicolarmente
   When the adjective form ends in **-re** we drop the **e** before adding **-mente**. (Rule 2)

10. chiaro = chiaramente
    Basic adverb formation here, add **-mente** to the feminine form of the adjective.

Adverb Position

Italian adverbs come as close to the words they modify as possible.

RULE 1.   The adverb must come directly in front of the adjective or adverb it modifies:

> Cerco una tavola **meno** alta. La nebbia è **tanto** spessa.
>
> Qui si sta **troppo** stretti.   Parla **molto** forte.

RULE 2.   The adverb must come directly **after** the simple verb it modifies: (a simple verb has just one part)

> Lo vedo **di rado**.   Esce **tardi** il sabato sera.

Notice that this common adverb position in English is to be avoided in Italian:

> He **often** drinks wine. =   Beve **spesso** vino.
>
> He **always** orders fish. =   Prende **sempre** il pesce.
>
> He **never** orders meat. =   Non prende **mai** la carne.
>
> He **already** knows. =   Lo sa **già**.
>
> I **hardly ever** see him. =   Non lo vedo **quasi mai**.

RULE 3.   In compound tenses **single syllable adverbs** are placed **in between** the auxiliary verb and the past participle. Other short adverbs may also appear in this position.

> È **ben** riuscito.
>
> Abbiamo **già** pranzato.
>
> Non ha **mai** capito.
>
> È **sempre** riuscito.

RULE 4.   In compound tenses longer adverbs and those ending in **-mente** are placed **after** the past participle.

> Mi ha salutato **cordialmente**.
>
> Ci siamo scritti **fedelmente**.

Exceptions: **certamente**, **completamente**, and **probabilmente** are placed in between the auxiliary and the participle:

> Ho **completamente** dimenticato.

RULE 5.   In compound tenses adverbs of **TIME** and **PLACE** are also positioned after the past participle, (even the short ones).

> L'ho visto **ieri**.   Mi sono alzato **presto**.   Li ho lasciati **fuori**.

Drill 18: Position of Adverbs

Place the adverb correctly. Use one of the two blanks provided.

1. _____ chiede _____ vin santo. (sempre)

2. Lo _____ vedo _____. (spesso)

3. Ho _____ visto _____ quel film. (già)

4. Avete _____ mangiato _____? (bene)

5. Mi ha _____ convinto _____. (poco a poco)

6. Hanno _____ finito _____. (velocemente)

7. Hai _____ mangiato _____? (troppo)

8. Sono _____ partiti _____ stamattina. (presto)

9. Ho _____ cercato _____. (ovunque)

10. Non è _____ venuto _____. (mai)

Answers and Explanations to Drill 18

1. Chiede **sempre** vin santo.
   Never place an Italian adverb in front of the simple verb it modified. (2)

2. Lo vedo **spesso**.
   Never place an Italian adverb in front of the simple verb it modified. (2)

3. Ho **già** visto quel film.
   Single syllable adverbs come **between** the auxiliary and the participle. (3)

4. Avete mangiato **bene**?
   With two syllables, **bene** follows.

5. Mi ha convinto **poco a poco**.
   Long adverbs come after the participle. (4)

6. Hanno finito **velocemente**.
   Adverbs ending in **-mente** come after the participle. (4)

7. Hai mangiato **troppo**?
   Troppo, like most Italian adverbs of two or more syllables, follows the participle. (3)

8. Sono partiti **presto** stamattina.
   Adverbs of **time** come after the participle. (5)

9. Ho cercato **ovunque**.
   Adverbs of **place** come after the participle. (5)

10. Non è **mai** venuto.
    Single syllable adverbs come **between** the auxiliary and the participle. (3)

Adjectives Used as Adverbs

There are quite a few adjectives which are used as adverbs in some fixed expressions. The **adjective** always **remains masculine and singular** to indicate its adverbial role. Here are some common examples:

Siamo arrivati giusto in tempo.
We arrived just in time.

Saranno state giusto le cinque.
It must have been around 5 o'clock.

Volevo **tagliar corto** la storia.
I wanted to get to the point.

Lei **parla pian piano**.
She speaks very softly.

Lei deve **parlare** più **forte**.
She should speak louder.

È arrabbiata la mamma? Sì, **vede tutto rosso**!
Is Mom angry? Yes, she's seeing red!

Pinocchio **se l'è vista brutta**.
Pinocchio thought he was done for.

Le ragazze **studiano sodo**.
The girls study hard.

Elena, **guarda diritto** davanti a te!
Elena, look straight ahead!

Gli **dirò chiaro** e **tondo** quello che penso.
I will tell him clearly what I think.

Vorrei **parlarti chiaro**.
I'd like to speak to you frankly.

Non ci **vedo chiaro**!
Something's wrong here!

Drill 19: Adjectives Used as Adverbs

Complete the little sentences in Italian. Each one contains an adjective in an adverbial role:

1. Lavorate _____ per riuscire.
   (hard)

2. Possiamo parlarci _____.
   (plainly, frankly)

3. Le ragazze hanno corso _____.
   (slowly)

4. Mamma è arrivata _____ in tempo.
   (just)

5. Vorrei vederci _____!
   (to get to the bottom)

6. Ce la siamo vista _____!
   (we barely made it)

7. Ti sento appena. Parla più _____!
   (loudly, louder)

8. Vai _____ davanti a te!
   (straight)

9. Sei tanto pessimista! Vedi sempre tutto _____!
   (the dark side)

10. Mi ha sussurrato _____.
    (very softly)

Answers and Explanations to Drill 19

1. Lavorate **sodo** per riuscire.
   Work hard to succeed.
   Like all adjectives used in this manner, *sodo* is invariable.

2. Possiamo parlarci **chiaro**.
   We can speak frankly, plainly.
   Chiaro remains invariable. Its use is adverbial, telling *how* we *can speak.*

3. Le ragazze hanno corso **piano**.
   The girls ran slowly.
   Piano tell *how* the girls *ran*. Adverbs remain invariable.

4. Mamma è arrivata **giusto** in tempo.
   Mom arrived just in time.
   Giusto remains invariable. It clearly modifies the verb, telling *when* she *arrived.*

5. Vorrei vederci **chiaro**!
   I want to get to the bottom of this!
   Vederci chiaro is a fixed idiom meaning *to straighten out, clear up a problem.*

6. Ce la siamo vista **brutta**!
   We had a narrow escape.
   Vedersela brutta is a fixed idom meaning to have a difficult time, to make a narrow escape. *Brutta* remains feminine singular, no matter what.

7. Ti sento appena. Parla più **forte**!
   I can hardly hear you. Speak up! Speak louder!
   Use *forte* for **louder**.

8. Vai **diritto** davanti a te!
   Go straight ahead!
   Diritto means **straight**. It's invariable here but does agree in other adverbial expressions:
   Elena, sit up straight = Elena, *siediti diritta!*

9. Sei tanto pessimista! Vedi sempre tutto **nero**.
   You're such a pessimist. You always see the dark side.
   Like *vedere rosso, vedere nero* always remains invariable.

10. Mi ha sussurrato **pian piano**.
   He whispered to me very quietly, very softly.
   The repetition of *piano* is common in this adverbial use to mean *very softly*.

The Comparative of Adjectives

Italian cannot alter the spelling of an adjective for comparison the way we do by adding *-er* or *-est* in English. Italian relies on the placement of an **adverb** in front of the adjective to be compared.

Here are the *comparative adverbs*:

più *more, -er*	Sei più grande di me.
meno *less, fewer*	Sei meno alto di papà.
tanto … quanto *as*	Sei tanto grande quanto Luca.
come *as*	Sei grande come Luca.
così … come *as*	Non sei così alto come me.

When the remainder of the comparative is introduced by **di,** it's translated as *than* or *as*:

Questa gonna è **meno** cara **di** quella.
*This skirt is **less** expensive **than** that one.*

A gennaio fa tanto freddo **quanto** a febbraio.
*It's **as** cold in January **as** (it is) in February.*

Ho **meno di** cinque pagine da finire.
*I have **fewer than** five pages to finish.*

Ce ne rimangono **più di** una dozzina.
We have more than a dozen (of them) left.
Use più **di** (also meno di) with a countable noun.

The Superlative of Adjectives

To make the superlative of adjectives (except for those which are irregular in comparison) we place a form of **il più** or **il meno** directly in front of the adjective in question:

> Il nonno è **il più** vecchio membro **della** nostra famiglia.
> *Grand-Pop is the oldest member of our family.*

> Grazia è **la** ragazza **più** sportiva **che** conosca.
> Grace *is the most athletic girl I know.*

> *Il* Signor Clayton è **il mio** professore **più** interessante.
> *Mr. Clayton is my most interesting teacher.*

> Quel pasto è stato **il meno** caro **del** nostro viaggio.
> *That meal was the least expensive of our trip.*

> Quei libri sono **i meno** interessanti **che** abbia mai letto.
> *Those are the least interesting books that I ever read.*

> Sei **il più** bel ragazzo **del** mondo.
> *You are the most handsome boy **in the** world.*

Looking over the examples, we can make the following observations about the superlative construction:

1. The position of the adjective relative to the noun is the same as usual; most follow, *BANGS* adjectives precede.

2. The article **agrees** with the noun it refers to.

3. The superlative may use a **possessive adjective** instead of an article.

4. The English word **in** is expressed by **di** or a contraction of **di + article**.

5. Verbs following the superlative are subjunctive, unless an actual fact is being related. Verbs are introduced by **che**.

Irregular Comparatives and Superlatives

A few adjectives have irregular forms of comparison. It is interesting to note that they are also irregular in English:

| buono | migliore | il migliore |
| *good* | *better* | *the best* |

| cattivo | peggiore | il peggiore |
| *bad* | *worse* | *the worst* |

| piccolo | più piccolo | il più piccolo (for size) |
| *small* | *smaller* | *the smallest* |

but also:

| | minore | il minimo (for importance) |
| | *lesser, slighter* | *the least, the slightest* |

Here are some examples of irregular comparatives and superlatives in use:

Non ho **la minima** idea **di** quello che farò.
I haven't the slightest idea what I'm going to do.

Sei **la mia migliore** amica.
You are my best friend.

È **il peggior** voto **della** mia vita!
It's the worst grade of my life!

Vogliamo **i migliori** che ci siano!
We want the best ones there are!

È **la peggior** torta **della** mia carriera; è tanto piatta che sembra una crespella!
It's the worst cake of my career; it's so flat it looks like a pancake!

Drill 20: Comparative and Superlative of Adjectives

Write these sentences in Italian. Observe the rules of placement and agreement. Know when to use an irregular form. Use the subjunctive where needed. Know when to use *di* versus *che*. Translate *in* correctly.

1. He's the smartest boy in the class.

   _____

2. It's the least I can do for you.

   _____

3. She is younger than I.

   _____

4. This box is less heavy than yours.

   _____

5. You ate less than half of your dessert.

   _____

6. Your mother is the most patient woman I know.

   _____

7. These are the warmest socks.

   _____

8. Marco is the best electrician there is.

   _____

9. It's the best film of the year.

   _____

10. He is taller than your brother.

    _____

Answers and Explanations to Drill 20

1. **È il ragazzo più intelligente della classe.**
   This a regular superlative formation. The adjective *intelligent* follows the noun. *In the class* is translated by the prepositional phrase **della classe**.

2. **È il minimo che io possa fare per te.**
   This is an irregular superlative based on *piccolo*; the *smallest* in the sense of the *least* or the *slightest*. Note the subjunctive.

3. **È più giovane di me.**
   This is a regular comparative using *più ...di*. Note the disjunctive pronoun after *di*.

4. **Questa scatola è meno pesante della tua/vostra.**
   This is a regular comparative using *meno di*.

5. **Hai mangiato meno della metà del tuo dolce.**
   Avete mangiato meno della metà del vostro dolce.
   Another regular comparative *less than*.

6. **Tua madre è la donna più paziente che conosca.**
   This regular superlative is followed by the subjunctive to reflect the opinion of the speaker.

7. **Questi sono i calzini più caldi.**
   This is a regular superlative using *più* + *adjective*. Notice how the article matches the noun to which it refers.

8. **Marco è l'elettricista più bravo che ci sia.**
   A regular superlative. Note the subjunctive following it.

9. **È il miglior film dell'anno.**
   The best, an irregular superlative in both English and Italian.

10. **È più alto di tuo fratello.**
    This sentence uses a possessive adjective as part of the comparison.

The Comparison of Adverbs

To make the comparative of adverbs we rely on the same combinations we learned for the comparative of adjectives:

più *more, -er*	Quelle scarpe costano più di queste.
meno *less*	Queste scarpe costano meno di quelle.
così…come *as*	Sei così grande come Papà.
tanto…quanto *as*	Sei tanto grande quanto Papà.

The Superlative of Adverbs

To make the superlative of adverbs (except for those which are irregular in comparison) we place a form of **il più** or **il meno** directly in front of the adverb in question. Since adverbs always remain invariable, the masculine singular article is the only one used:

Maria, torna **il più velocemente** possibile.
Maria, come back as quickly as possible.

È il più debole della figliata ed è **il meno** che è cresciuto.
He's the runt of the litter and he grew the least.

Irregular Comparatives and Superlatives

A few adverbs have irregular forms of comparison:

molto	più	il più
a lot, much	*more*	*the most*
bene	meglio	il meglio
well	*better*	*the best*
male	peggio	il peggio
badly	*worse*	*the worst*
poco	meno	il meno
little	*less*	*the least*

Students often confuse adjective and adverb forms. Never try to modify a noun form with *meglio* for example. This is a common mistake as both the **adjective** *migliore* and the **adverb** *meglio* have the same English translation—*better*. In English we can use *better* in either case without giving it a thought. In Italian, we must distinguish between the need for an adjective (to modify a noun) and the need for adverb (to modify a verb or an adjective). Students often report that they understand English grammar better through their study of Italian.

Study these examples:

È una canzone migliore e tu la canti meglio di me.
  It's a better song and you sing it better than I do.

Questo coltello è migliore e tu lo adoperi meglio di me.
  This knife is better and you handle it better than I do.

Drill 21: The Comparative and Superlative of Adverbs

Supply the needed adverb:

1. Canto _____. (badly)

2. Lei canta _____. (well)

3. Mangi _____ _____ di me. (faster)

4. Corro _____ _____ di te. (less fast)

5. Voi lavorate _____ _____ quanto noi. (as well)

6. Papà balla _____ di Mamma. (better)

7. Lei mangia molto _____. (little)

8. Li vedo _____ _____ adesso. (more often)

9. Tu mangi _____ di me. (less)

10. Lei pronuncia _____ _____ di tutti. (the best)

Answers and Explanations to Drill 21

1. Canto **male**.
   I sing badly.
   Male is the adverb meaning *badly*. Its other comparative forms are
   irregular: *peggio and il peggio*.

2. Lei canta **bene**.
   She sings well.
   Bene means *well*. Its other comparative forms are irregular: *meglio* and
   il meglio.

3. Mangi **più velocemente** di me.
   You eat faster than I.
   This is a standard comparative using **pìu + adverb** to mean *more*.

4. Corro **meno velocemente** di te.
   I run less quickly, less fast than you.
   This is a standard comparative using **meno + adverb** to mean *less*.

5. Voi lavorate **tanto bene** quanto noi.
   You work as well as we do.
   Another basic comparative; this one uses **tanto + adverb + quanto** to
   mean *as*.

6. Papà balla **meglio** di mamma.
   Dad dances better than Mom.
   This is the irregular comparative of *bene*.

7. Lei mangia molto **poco**.
   She eats very little.
   Poco means *little*. Its other comparative forms are irregular: *meno* and
   il meno.

8. Li vedo **più spesso** adesso.
   I see them more often now.
   A standard comparative using **più + adverb** to mean *more*.

9. Mangi **meno** di me.
   You eat less than I.
   A standard comparative using **meno** to mean *less*.

10. Lei parla italiano **meglio** di tutti.
    She speaks Italian the best of all.
    Notice the absence of the article in this irregular superlative of *bene*.
    We use *il più* and *il meno* in regular superlatives. There is no *il* in an irregular superlative.

Demonstrative Adjectives

Like their English counterparts, demonstrative adjectives refer to nouns which are at hand, are in full view, or are being discussed. They always precede the nouns they modify and match them in gender and number. Since there are twelve different forms to master in Italian, this is somewhat more complicated than English, or French, which have only four forms to field. Not to worry, however, if you have a good grasp of how to apply the definite article to a noun, demonstrative adjectives are easy. Here they are:

This and These

questo *this* for a singular masculine noun beginning with a consonant

questa *this* for a singular feminine noun beginning with a consonant

quest' *this* for all singular nouns beginning with a vowel

questi *these* for all masculine plural nouns

queste *these* for all feminine plural nouns

That and Those

quel *that* for a singular masculine noun which does **not** begin with a **vowel**, a **z**, a **y**, **gn**, or the combination of **s+consonant**

quello *that* for a singular masculine noun beginning with **s+consonant**, **z**, **gn**, or **y**

quell' *that* for all singular nouns beginning with a vowel

quella *that* for a singular feminine noun beginning with a consonant

quei *those* for all masculine plural nouns **except** those beginning in a **vowel**, a **z**, a **y**, **gn**, or the combination of **s+consonant**

quegli *those* for masculine plural nouns beginning in a **vowel**, a **z**, a **y**, **gn**, or the combination of **s+consonant**

quelle *those* for all feminine plural nouns

Here's a simple little rhyme to help you distinguish *this* and *these* from *that* and *those*: **THIS AND THESE HAVE Ts!**

Study these examples:

Ti piace **questo** vino?
Do you like this wine?

Questi libri sono pesanti.
These books are heavy.

Mi piace **quest'** orologio da polso.
I like this watch.

Questa camicia è troppo cara.
This shirt is too expensive.

Mi hanno regalato **queste** ciabatte .
I got these slippers as a gift.

Quel cappello ti sta bene.
That hat looks good on you.

Quello zaino è pieno zeppo.
That back pack is stuffed full.

Quell'aula è la nostra.
That classroom is ours.

Quella focaccia* era squisita.
That bread was delicious.
Focaccia* is a round, lumpy flat bread, drizzled with olive oil, salt, and a variety of possible toppings such as olives, tomatoes, or cheese.

Potresti raccogliere **quei** libri?
Could you pick up those books?

Mi metterò **quegli** stivali.
I'll wear those boots.

Quelle scarpe da tennis puzzano.
Those sneakers are smelly.

Demonstrative Pronouns

A demonstrative pronoun takes the place of a demonstrative adjective plus noun. They agree in gender and number with the nouns they replace and provide the equivalent of **this one, these** or **that one, the one, the ones,** and **those** in English.

questo	**quello**	masculine singular	*this one, that one, the one*
questa	**quella**	feminine singular	*this one, that one, the one*
questi	**quelli**	masculine plural	*these, those, the ones*
queste	**quelle**	feminine plural	*these, those, the ones*

Questa penna sbava, vado a cercare **quella** nel mio cassetto.
This pen leaks, I'm going to get the one in my drawer.

Quel vestito è troppo lungo, mettiti **quello** di venerdì sera.
That dress is too long, put on the one (you wore) Friday night.

Ecco i tuoi compiti, **quelli** che ripassavi per l'esame.
Here are your assignments, the ones you were reviewing for the test.

Hai visto i miei occhiali, **quelli** con gli strass?
Have you seen my glasses, the ones with the rhinestones?

Ho trovato un anello fantastico, **quello** dei miei sogni.
I found a great ring, the one I've always dreamed of.

Mi piace questo paio, puoi prendere **quello**.
I like this pair, you can have that one.

If you look back over all of the examples we have used for demonstrative pronouns, you will notice that they never stand alone, but are generally supported by a **preposition**, or a **relative pronoun.**

Drill 22: Demonstrative Adjectives and Pronouns

Supply the demonstrative adjective or pronoun suggested by the English cue:

1. Ammiro _____ bravi in matematica.

(those)

2. Chi è _____ uomo mascherato?

(that)

3. Dammi _____ sci, per favore.

(those)

4. Dove hai preso _____ libri?

(those)

5. _____ è troppo spessa, prendi _____, è più sottile.

(That one)   (this one)

6. Ci piacciono _____ gnocchi.

(those)

7. Ho fatto _____ esercizi, ma non _____.

(these)   (those)

8. _____ yogurt viene dalla Grecia.

(That)

9. Qual'è la Signorina Caporello? _____ con gli occhiali.

(The one)

10. Posso sedermi su _____ sedia?

(this)

11. Questa maglia mi sta bene, _____ è troppo attillata.

(that one)

12. Spiegami _____.
    (this)

13. Ho scelto quel paio, puoi prendere _____.
    (this one)

14. Dove hai trovato _____ vino frizzante?
    (that)

15. I quesiti erano facili oggi, ma _____ dell'altro ieri erano molto
    più difficili.   (the ones)

16. Cosa fai _____ fine settimana?
    (this)

17. _____ fotografie sono datate 1946.
    (Those)

18. _____ non sono miei.
    (These)

19. Non credo a _____ pettegolezzi.
    (that)

20. _____ paese è bellissimo.
    (This)

21. Non si dicono _____ parolacce!
    (those)

22. Consola _____ che sono tristi, e aiuta _____ poveri.
    (those)   (those)

23. _____ giocattoli si trovano in tutti i grandi magazzini.
    (These)

24. Il mio cellulare è nella mia borsa, _____ è il tuo?
    (this one)

25. Potresti lasciare _____ pacchi all'uffico postale?
    (these)

Answers and Explanations to Drill 22

1. Ammiro **quelli** bravi in matematica.
   I admire those who are good in math.
   With no noun present, use the demonstrative pronoun *quelli* to convey "those." The supporting *relative pronoun and verb*, (che sono) are understood. Unless clearly designated as feminine, use the masculine form in cases where both are possible.

2. Chi è **quell'**uomo mascherato?
   Who is that masked man?
   Quell' is the adjective form needed in front of this singular noun beginning with a vowel.

3. Dammi **quegli** sci, per favore.
   Give me those skis, please.
   This plural masculine noun beginning in the strong consonant combination of *s+ c* requires the special demonstrative pronoun form *quegli.*

4. Dove hai preso **quei** libri?
   Where did you get those books?
   Quei is needed here; the plural form of the demonstrative adjective *quel.*

5. **Quella** è troppo spessa, prendi **questa**, è più sottile.
   That one is too thick; take this one, it's thinner.
   The adjective *spessa* is a clue that a distinction is being made between two unnamed nouns that are both feminine and singular.

6. Ci piacciono **quegli** gnocchi*.
   We like those little potato dumplings.
   Like number 3, this is a plural masculine noun beginning in a strong consonant combination, **gn**. It also requires the special demonstrative pronoun form *quegli*. Gnocchi* are tiny dumplings served like pasta, but are made with potatoes, rather than semolina.

7. Ho fatto **questi** esercizi, ma non **quelli**.
   I did these exercises but not those.
   You can distinguish between two identical nouns, one named, and one unnamed, in this manner.

8. **Quello** yogurt viene dalla Grecia.
   That yogurt comes from Greece.
   A masculine noun beginning in the foreign letter *y* requires the definite article *lo*, and, therefore, the special demonstrative adjective form *quello*.

9. Qual'è la Signorina Caporello? **Quella** con gli occhiali.
   Which one is Miss Caporello? The one with the glasses.
   The feminine singular demonstrative adjective *quella* refers to the woman in question.

10. Posso sedermi su **questa** sedia?
    May I sit on this chair?
    The noun *sedia* requires a feminine singular demonstrative adjective to modify it.

11. Questa maglia mi sta bene, **quella** è troppo attillata.
    This sweater fits me well; that one is too tight.
    We distinguish between two similar nouns, one named, and one unnamed.

12. Spiegami **questo**.
    Explain this to me.
    Choose the masculine form when no gender has been specified.

13. Ho scelto quel paio, puoi prendere **questo**.
    I chose that pair, you can have this one.
    We know that the pronoun stands for *pair,* so we chose the masculine form for *this one*.

14. Dove hai trovato **quel** vino frizzante?
    Where did you find that sparkling wine?
    Quel is the masculine singular adjective form needed to modify *vino*.

15. I quesiti erano facili oggi, ma **quelli** dell'altro ieri erano molto più difficili.
    The questions were easy today, but the ones the other day were much harder.
    We know the pronoun refers to *questiti*, so we choose the masculine plural form of the pronoun to stand for them.

16. Cosa fai **questo** fine settimana?
    What are you doing this week-end?
    Fine settimana is tricky. It isn't feminine! It's invariable and requires the
    masculine form of the adjective, *questo*.

17. **Quelle** fotografie sono datate 1946.
    Those photos are dated 1946.
    Choose the feminine plural form of the demonstrative adjective to match
    fotografie.

18. **Questi** non sono miei.
    These are not mine.
    We take our cue from the masculine plural *miei* and supply the same
    form of the demonstrative adjective to stand for the unnamed noun.

19. Non credo a **quei** pettegolezzi.
    I don't believe that gossip.
    Choose a masculine plural adjective form to match *pettegolezzi*.

20. **Questo** paese è bellissimo.
    This is a very beautiful country.
    Can't remember if *paese* is masculine or feminine? Look for other clues.
    The masculine adjective *bellissimo* is a tip-off.

21. Non si dicono **quelle** parolacce.
    We don't (one doesn't) say those bad words.
    Match the feminine form of *those* with *parolacce*.

22. Consola **quelli** che sono tristi, e aiuta **quelli** poveri.
    Comfort those who are sad and help (those who are) poor.
    We choose a plural form of the pronoun to convey *those*, and when no
    gender is specified, we always choose the masculine, thus *quelli*. The
    absence of any noun reminds us that we need a pronoun.

23. **Questi** giocattoli si trovano in tutti i grandi magazzini.
    These toys can be found in all the big department stores.
    Use the masculine form of *these*.

24. Il mio cellulare è nella borsa, **questo** è il tuo?
    My cell phone is in my purse; is this one yours?
    We are distinguishing between two identical masculine singular nouns. One has been named, and the other is being shown. The pronoun, therefore, must also be masculine and singular.

25. Potresti lasciare **questi** pacchi all'ufficio postale?
    Could you drop off these packages at the post office?
    Questi is required here as the standard form of the demonstrative adjective for masculine plural nouns beginning in ordinary consonants.

Interrogative Adjectives and Pronouns

The adjective **quale** means *which* or *what*. It exists in one singular and one plural form:

for masculine singular:	Quale gelato hai scelto?
and feminine singular:	Di quale città si tratta?
for masculine plural:	Quali libri vuoi prendere in prestito?
and feminine plural:	Quali scarpe dovrei mettere?

The adjective asks a direct question in the examples above, but may also be used in indirect questions, like this:

Non so quale può essere il problema.
I don't know what the problem can be.

Vorrei sapere quale piatto preferisci.
I'd like to know which dish you prefer.

Non hai detto quali libri vuoi prendere in prestito.
You didn't say which books you want to borrow.

Mi chiedo quali scarpe scegliere.
I wonder what shoes to pick.

Interrogative Pronouns: CHI, CHE, CHE COSA

Chi ami?	*Whom do you love?*
Chi canta?	*Who's singing?*
Che succede?	*What's happening?*
Che cosa mangi?	*What are you eating?*
Cosa bevi?	*What are you drinking?*

When the interrogative pronoun CHI is the *subject* of the verb, use the 3rd person singular form of that verb. If the verb in question is *essere*, any one of its forms may appear:

Chi parla?
Who is speaking?

Chi siete?
Who are you?

Chi may appear as the object of a preposition, in which case it means *whom*. Study these examples:

Con chi esci?	*With whom are you going out?*
Per chi lavori?	*For whom do you work?*
A chi parli?	*To whom are you speaking? OR* (more casually) *Who are you talking to?*

Che and **che cosa** can also be the object of a preposition if the object is a *thing*. They translate as *what*:

Con che cosa scrive?	*What are you writing with?*
Di che cosa hai bisogno?	*What do you need?*
A che stai pensando?	*What are you thinking about?*

(Che) cosa + avere can express that something is wrong:

Cosa hai?
What's the matter? What's wrong (with you)?

Che cos' ha questo televisore?
What's the matter with this TV set?

Che is frequently used in exclamations. Note the absence of the article in the Italian construction:

Che bella casa!	*What **a** beautiful house.*
Che bel figlio!	*What **a** handsome son!*
Che fortuna!	*What luck!*
Che bei bimbi!	*What beautiful children!*
Che afa!	*What (**a**) suffocating heat!*

If you have not heard something clearly, it is considered bad manners to use *Che?* for *What?* It is preferable to ask instead, *Come?* You will, however, hear both in modern usage.

Drill 23: Interrogative Adjectives and Pronouns

Complete the question or exclamation, incorporating the English cue:

1. _____ _____ vuoi?   (what)

2. _____ vuoi?   (what)

3. _____ viene?   (who)

4. _____ succede?   (what)

5. _____ accadrà?   (what)

6. _____ vuoi dire?   (what)

7. _____ _____ ti piace?   (what)

8. _____ ragazzo inviti?   (which)

9. _____ sorpresa!   (what a)

10. _____ gemelli carini!   (what)

11. _____ ragazzi inviti?   (which)

12. Sai _____ bibita servire?   (which)

13. Di _____ hai bisogno?   (whom)

14. Di _____ _____ hai paura?   (what)

15. Dimmi _____ volo prenderai.   (which)

Answers and Explanations to Drill 23

1. **Che cosa** vuoi?
   What *do you want?*
   Here we used the complete two-part version of *what*. Literally, *what thing?*

2. **Che** vuoi? *OR* **Cosa** vuoi?
   What *do you want?*
   You may use either interrogative, or the two combined, as in the preceding question.

3. **Chi** viene?
   Who*'s coming?*
   Chi provides a human subject for the verb.

4. **Che** succede?
   What *will happen?*
   Supply an inanimate subject.

5. **Cosa** accadrà?
   What*'s coming?*
   Another inanimate subject.

6. **Che / cosa** vuoi dire?
   What do you mean?
   Any of the three variants is acceptable here.

7. **Che cosa** ti piace?
   What *do you like?*
   Here *che cosa* is the subject of *piacere*. It can also be the object of the verb, as in the first problem.

8. Quale ragazzo inviti?
   Which *boy are you inviting?*
   We've used an interrogative *adjective* for the noun *ragazzo*.

9. **Che** sorpresa!
   ***What** a surprise!*
   This is a common exclamation.

10. **Che** gemelli carini!
    ***What** cute twins!*
    Another exclamation with *che*.

11. **Quali** ragazzi inviti?
    ***Which** boys are you inviting?*
    The same problem as number 8, but plural.

12. Sai **quale** bibita servire?
    *Do you know **which** drink to serve?*
    Use *quale* in front of the noun again, this time in an indirect question.

13. Di **chi** hai bisogno?
    ***Whom** do you need?*
    Chi is the human object of the preposition *di*.

14. Di **che cosa** hai paura?
    ***What** are you afraid of?*
    Che cosa is the inanimate object of the preposition *di*.

15. Dimmi **quale** volo prenderai.
    *Tell me **which** flight you'll be on.*
    Use the singular *quale* to match *volo* in this indirect question.

Possessive Adjectives

Italian possessive adjectives are generally preceded by a corresponding definite article. They match the nouns they modify in gender and number. There are rules governing the omission of the definite article which must also be learned, and which will be explained.

Here are the various *complete* forms of the possessive adjectives:

il mio	**i miei**	**la mia**	**le mie**	my
il tuo	**i tuoi**	**la tua**	**le tue**	familiar your
il suo	**i suoi**	**la sua**	**le sue**	his, her, its, one's, polite your
il nostro	**i nostri**	**la nostra**	**le nostre**	our
il vostro	**i vostri**	**la vostra**	**le vostre**	plural your
il loro	**i loro**	**la loro**	**le loro**	their

Use of the Possessive Adjectives

1. Avoid the common error of trying to match the gender of the owner instead of the gender of the thing owned. This is a difficult concept for English speakers to grasp. We are so used to giving the gender of the owner with **his** and **her** in English, that we can lose sight of the basic tenet of possession in ITALIAN, that is, we **ALWAYS identify the gender of the thing possessed**, and NEVER the gender of the owner. Thus, **il suo**, **la sua**, **i suoi,** and **le sue** translate as *either* **his** or **her** as follows:

his father = **suo** padre	her father = **suo** padre
his mother = **sua** madre	her mother = **sua** madre
his book = **il suo** libro	her book = **il suo** libro
his pencil = **la sua** matita	her pencil = **la sua** matita
his brothers = **i suoi** fratelli	her brothers = **i suoi** fratelli
his sisters= **le sue** sorelle	her sisters = **le sue** sorelle

If you are left wondering how Italian distinguishes between his and her, the answer is simple. It doesn't! Remember that the English possessors **my, your, our** and **their** don't reveal the gender of the owner either, and it never mattered to you. In Italian the same is true with **his** and **her**.

2. Be careful to respect which form of **you** the sentence requires before selecting **il tuo, il Suo** or **il vostro**:

> Signora, **ha** lasciato **il Suo** pacco!
> *You left your package Ma'am.*

> Tonio, **hai** lasciato **il tuo** pacco!
> *Tony, you left your package!*

> Ragazzi, **avete** lasciato **il vostro** pacco.
> *Boys, you left your package!*

3. Always choose from the **il suo** forms to match indefinite subjects such as **chi**, **nessuno**, or **ognuno**. This makes good sense as those subjects also use the third person form of the verb:

> Chi ha dimenticato il suo biglietto?
> *Who forgot his ticket?*

> Nessuno vuole perdere il suo biglietto.
> *No one wants to lose his ticket.*

> Ognuno si mette il pigiama prima di dormire.
> *Everyone puts on his or her pajamas before sleeping.*

4. The possessive adjective must be repeated in Italian for each noun included in the possession. This is not necessary in English:

> Mio fratello e mia sorella sono gemelli.
> *My brother and sister are twins.*

> Mia zia e mio zio non sono ancora arrivati.
> *My aunt and uncle have not yet arrived.*

5. **Ciascuno** can also use **il suo** as its possessor:

> Ciascuno ha il suo biglietto.
> *Each one has his ticket.*

If **ciascuno** relates back to another pronoun, however, use the possessor which matches that pronoun:

> (**Noi**) abbiamo **ciascuno** il nostro biglietto.
> *We each have our ticket.*

> **Voi** avete **ciascuno** il vostro biglietto?
> *Do you each have your ticket?*

If **ciascuno** refers back to the 3rd person plural (loro or a plural noun), it is common to see **il suo** forms, as well **il loro** forms:

> Si sono sedute, ciascuna accanto a sua propria madre.
> *They sat down, each one next to her own mother.*

> Si sono addormentate, ciascuna nella loro camera.
> *They went to sleep, each in their rooms.*

6. Choose from the **il suo** group to match an inanimate object, just as you would in English:

> la nuvola e le sue lacrime...
> *the cloud and its tears ...*

> l'inverno, nel suo abbraccio gelido
> *winter in its icy embrace...*

7. Remember that Italian generally avoids the use of the possessive adjective with parts of the body.

> Hai gli occhi azzurri.   *His eyes are blue.*

> Mi fanno male i piedi.   *My feet hurt.*

The possessive adjective is also avoided with clothing.

> I bimbi si tolsero il cappello e il cappotto.
> *The children took off their hats and coats.*

Note that when each member of a group possesses one thing in English, we generally use a plural noun and a corresponding plural possessor. This is not the case in Italian, which emphasizes that each single member of the group has *one*. Compare the use of the plural noun in English versus the singular noun in Italian. Note, as well, the absence of the possessive adjective in the Italian sentence above. Here's another example:

> Gli uccelli fanno il nido nei rami alti.
> *Birds make their nests in the upper branches.*

Omission of the Definite Article with Family Members

1. All possessive adjectives → EXCEPT **LORO** ← drop **il** and **la** in front of **UNMODIFIED** SINGULAR FAMILY MEMBERS. Compare:

    la mia famiglia   **mia** sorella

    il mio cane   **mio** fratello

2. The dropped article only applies to SINGULAR FAMILY MEMBERS! We **DO** use **i** and **le** if the family member is plural:

    i miei fratelli

    le mie sorelle

3. The family member must be UNMODIFIED as well as SINGULAR to drop the definite article. Notice that we **DO** use **il** and **la** if the family member is modified in any way:

    la mia bella sorella

    il mio zio **calabrese**

    il tuo fratell**accio**

4. Because Mamma, Babbo and Papà are considered terms of endearment, they are not supposed to drop **il** and **la**. An older rule retained **il** and **la** with *nonno* and *nonna* as well. Many Italians disregard these rules today.

    The tendency in everyday speech is to simplify. Picky distinctions are being ignored and will eventually be eliminated entirely. *Loro* and its special placement as an indirect object, for example, is on the way out.

5. Since the word **loro** never changes its form, it always keeps the definite article when it acts as a possessive adjective. It has no other way of matching the noun it modifies:

    il loro fratello   **la loro** sorella

Drill 24: Possessive Adjectives

Supply the possessive adjective which matches the **subject of the verb**. Omit the definite article where necessary.

1. Cercate _____ libro.

2. Hai _____ libro?

3. Domenico è venuto con _____ cugina.

4. Credo che _____ padre e _____ madre verrano anche loro.

5. Chi rompe paga e i cocci sono _____.

6. Silvio vuole raccogliere _____ lettere.

7. Martino fa scendere _____ madre dal medico

8. I bimbi che guardavano sfilare la parata hanno agitato _____ piccola bandiera.

9. Preferiamo ciascuno _____ guanciale.

10. Vorrei che _____ figlio riesca.

11. Volevano invitare _____ zio.

12. Abbiamo visitato _____ nipotina.

13. La mia casetta e _____ vecchie pareti spesse mi tengono caldo.

14. Ognuno ha _____ biglietto.

15. Qual è _____ indirizzo, Signora?

Answers and Explanations to Drill 24

1. Cercate **il vostro** libro.
   Get your book.
   The verb form ending in **-ate** narrows the choice to a **voi** form possessor.

2. Hai **il tuo** libro?
   Do you have your book?
   A **tu** form is required to match the second person verb.

3. Domenico è venuto con **sua** cugina.
   Domenico came with his cousin.
   The possessor must be feminine because his cousin is female. The definite article is omitted with this singular, unmodified family member.

4. Credo che **mio** padre e **mia** madre verrano.
   I think my father and mother will come too.
   Italian repeats the possessor in its appropriate form for each member included in the possession.

5. Chi rompe paga e i cocci sono **suoi**.
   Whoever breaks it pays for it, and the shards are his.
   An impersonal subject uses a third person possessor here. *Suoi* is actually a pronoun in this sentence, thus no *i* after *essere*. This is a very old and commonly used saying. Look for it posted in a gift shop.

6. Silvio vuole raccogliere **le sue** lettere.
   Sylvio wants to pick up his mail.
   The feminine plural possessor is required to match the feminine plural noun *le lettere*.

7. Martino fa scendere **sua** madre dal medico.
   Martino drops his mother at the doctor's.
   Madre, a feminine singular noun, requires a feminine singular possessor.

8. I bimbi che guardavano sfilare la parata hanno agitato **la loro** piccola bandiera.
   The children who were watching the parade pass waved their little flags.
   Each child in the group possesses one flag, consequently Italian uses the singular noun and possessor, while English uses the plural.

9. Preferiamo ciascuno **il nostro** guanciale.
   We each prefer our own pillow.
   Since *ciascuno* refers back to *noi*, the possessor matches *noi*.

10. Vorrei che **mio** figlio riesca.
    I would like my son to succeed.

11. Volevano invitare **il loro** zio.
    They wanted to invite their uncle.
    Loro always retains the definite article with its possessor, even with singular unmodified family members.

12. Abbiamo visitato **la nostra** nipotina.
    We visited our little granddaughter (niece).
    Since *nipote* is modified with a suffix here, we retain the definite article.

13. La mia casetta e **le sue** vecchie pareti spesse mi tengono caldo.
    My little house and its old, thick walls keep me warm.
    Match a third person possessor to an inanimate object, just as in English.

14. Ognuno ha **il suo** biglietto.
    Everyone has his ticket.
    Use a third person possessor to match the indefinite pronoun *ognuno*.

15. Qual è **il suo** indirizzo, Signora?
    What is your address, Ma'am?
    This is polite address, use the third person possessor.

Possessive Pronouns

Possessive pronouns replace the combination of a possessive adjective plus noun. They match the noun they replace in gender and number, and, as with possessive adjectives, show the gender of the thing possessed, rather than the gender of the possessor.

Here is a list of the possessive pronouns:

il mio	la mia	i miei	le mie	mine
il tuo	la tua	i tuoi	le tue	yours (familiar singular)
il suo	la sua	i suoi	le sue	his, hers, its, one's, yours (polite singular)
il nostro	la nostra	i nostri	le nostre	ours
il vostro	la vostra	i vostri	le vostre	yours (plural)
le loro	la loro	i loro	le loro	theirs, yours (polite plural)

Special Uses and Omission of the Possessive Pronoun

1. The masculine plural of the possessive pronoun may be used to convey the meaning of one's closest friends, relatives, followers or supporters:

   Buon Natale a te e ai tuoi.
   Merry Christmas to you and yours.

   Ha voluto vivere fra i suoi.
   He wanted to live among his own (kind).

   Sei dei nostri?
   Are you one of us?

2. To express ownership with the verb **essere**, we drop the definite article portion of the possessor, like this:

   These books are *mine*.   *Questi libri sono **miei**.*

   Those books are *yours*.   *Quei libri sono **tuoi**.*

3. The definite article portion of the possessive pronoun will contract with a preposition, just as it would if it were free standing. Compare:

   Scrivo **al** professore.
   I write to the teacher.

Scrivo **al** mio.
I write to mine.

Scrivi **a** tuo padre.
You write to your father.

Scrivo **al** mio.
I write to mine.

Parlo **dei** professori.
I'm talking about the teachers.

Parlo **dei** miei.
I'm talking about mine.

Drill 25: Possessive Pronouns

Supply the possessive pronoun which best translates the English cue.

1. La tua sedia è più comoda di + _____.
   (mine)

2. La vostra casa è grande quanto _____.
   (ours)

3. La nostra macchina è vecchia, ma _____ è nuova di zecca!
   (theirs)

4. Non trovo i miei guanti. Puoi prestarmi _____?
   (yours)

5. Se il tuo cellulare è guasto, chiedigli se _____ è disponibile.
   (his)

6. Il nostro professore di matematica è romano, _____ è milanese.
   (theirs)

7. Il mio giardino non è ancora fiorito ma _____ è in piena fioritura.
   (yours, voi form)

8. Di chi sono questi fogli? Sono _____.
   (mine)

9. Auguri a te e a + _____.
   (to yours)

10. Non ha una matita, puoi prestargliene una di + _____?
    (of yours)

Answers and Explanations to Drill 25

1. La tua sedia è più comoda **della mia**.
   Your chair is more comfortable than mine.
   Select the feminine singular pronoun to represent the unnamed *chair*.
   Contract di + la.

2. La vostra casa è grande quanto **la nostra.**
   Your house is as big as ours.
   Here the feminine singular pronoun represents the unnamed *house*.

3. La nostra macchina è vecchia, ma **la loro** è nuova di zecca.
   Our car is old, but theirs is brand new!
   The feminine singular pronoun is needed to represent the *neighbors' car*.

4. Non trovo i miei guanti. Puoi prestarmi **i tuoi**?
   I can't find my gloves, may I borrow yours?
   Here the masculine plural pronoun stands for the needed *gloves*. Note that Italian doesn't have a comfortable way to ask *to borrow*. Flip the question like the Italians do, and ask the other person *to lend*.

5. Se il tuo cellulare è guasto, chiedigli se **il suo** è disponibile.
   If your cell is dead, ask him if his is available.
   The masculine singular pronoun represents *cell phone*.

6. Il nostro professore di matematica è romano, **il loro** è milanese.
   Our math teacher is from Rome, theirs is from Milan.
   Their teacher is represented by the masculine singular pronoun.

7. Il mio giardino non è ancora fiorito ma **il vostro** è in piena fioritura.
   My garden hasn't blossomed yet, but yours is in full bloom.
   Here the masculine singular pronoun stands for *your garden*.

8. Di chi sono questi fogli? Sono **miei**.
   Whose papers are these? They're mine.
   Remember to omit the definite article from the possessive pronoun after a form of the verb **essere**.

9. Auguri a te e **ai tuoi**.
   Best wishes to you and to yours.
   Here the masculine plural pronoun combines with the preposition **a** and means *to your closest family and friends.*

10. Non ha una matita, puoi prestargliene una **delle tue**?
    He doesn't have a pencil, can you lend him one of yours?
    Now the masculine plural pronoun combines with the preposition **di** to mean *one of your pencils.*

Subject Pronouns

io—I	noi—we
tu—you familiar, singular v	oi—you, plural
lui—he	loro—they
lei—she	Loro—you, formal plural
Lei—you polite, singular	

The following pronouns are no longer used in modern speech. You will only encounter them in formal documents and in literature written in the past.

egli → (only in reference to a human being) (lui)

ella → (only in reference to a human being) (lei)

Ella → (only in reference to a human being) (Lei)

esso → (for inanimate thing or animal) (it)

essa → (for inanimate thing, animal OR *rare:* human)

(it, *rare*: she, her)

essi → (for inanimate, animal OR human) (loro)

esse → (for inanimate, animal OR human) (loro)

All of the pronouns beginning in the letter **e** are obsolete. You are not expected to use them in speech or writing. They are included here so that you will recognize and understand them when you see them in an older text, perhaps like this:

A questo punto, **egli** balzò in piedi.

C'è la possibilità che **egli** venga.

Ella vestiva di rosso.

Vuole **Ella** farci il piacere di venire cenare?

Cercai di prendere l'uccellino, ma **esso** volò via.

Alzai la lettera, e sotto di **essa**, trovai la chiave.

Omission of Subject Pronouns

Since most verb forms have a distinctly different ending in Italian, it is very easy to discern the subject of the verb without a pronoun to identify it. That is why subject pronouns are optional in Italian and are frequently omitted. They are retained for emphasis, or for clarity when necessary. If you need to specify *she* as subject, for instance, include *lei*. Sometimes a pronoun is needed to clarify the subject of a subjunctive verb (*io* possa?, *tu* possa?, or *lui* possa?). Otherwise you can omit them just as the Italians do.

You

Italian has four forms for YOU. Only three of them are used in everyday speech. **Tu** is familiar. It is used with intimate friends, relatives, small children and animals. Students commonly use the **tu** form when speaking to their classmates.

Lei is the polite or formal counterpart to **tu**. It is always used with strangers, superiors, or anyone to whom you wish to show respect. **Loro** is the corresponding polite plural form of address. It is extremely formal, however, and is generally replaced by **voi** today.

Object Pronouns

Object pronouns replace **direct** and **indirect** objects. **Ci** and **ne** replace inanimate nouns introduced by prepositions. If you need to replace a person introduced by a preposition, see **disjunctive pronouns**.

Here are *all* of the object pronouns.

mi *(me, to me)*	**lo** *(him, it)*	**gli** *(to him)*	**ne** *(some)* *(for him)*
ti *(you, to you)*	**la** *(her, it)*	**le** *(to her, to you)* *(for her, for you)*	
ci *(us, to us) (there)*	**li, le** *(them)*		
vi *(you, to you)*			
si *(himself, herself, yourself, to himself, to herself, to yourself)* *for reflexive verbs*			

Use and Position of Object Pronouns

With the exception of LORO, an object pronoun is usually positioned directly in front of the verb which governs it in a declarative sentence:

> **Lo** vedo.   **Gli** parlo.   **Vi** manda la lettera.
>
> **La** vedo.   **Le** parlo.   Manda **loro** la lettera.

If the verb is in a compound tense such as the *passato prossimo*, all object pronouns (except for LORO) appear directly in front of the auxiliary verb. **Lo** and **la** become **l'** in this position. **Li** and **le** never take the apostrophe! The past participle always agrees with the direct object pronoun when it appears in front of the auxiliary verb, like this:

> Ho visto Maria ieri = **L'**ho vist**a** ieri.
>
> Ho visto i gemelli ieri. = **Li** ho vist**i** ieri.

Note that indirect object pronouns in this same position NEVER agree with their participles. Compare:

> Ho scritto a Raffaele ieri. = Gli ho scritto ieri.
>
> Ho scritto a Maria ieri. = Le ho scritto ieri.

Study these examples of position:

> La vedo.
> *I see her.*

L'ho vista.
  I saw her.

Le parlo.
  I speak to her.

Le ho parlato.
  I spoke to her.

Mi stai parlando?
  Are you speaking to me?

Special attention should be given to distinguishing between the third person direct object forms (**lo, la** and **li, le**) and the third person indirect object forms (**gli, le** and **loro**). The **mi, ti, ci** and **vi** forms are fairly user friendly as their direct and indirect objects forms are identical. This is NOT the case with third person object pronouns, so we must select them with great care. You should always ask yourself if the Italian verb requires a direct object or an indirect object before choosing your answer. This is complicated by the fact that a verb which requires a direct object in English may require an indirect object in Italian. The reverse is also true! Furthermore it is very common to place the indirect object in an English sentence in such a way that it seems like a direct object. Study these examples.

Gli ho dato la mia matita.
  I gave him my pencil.   (I gave my pencil to him!)

Gli ho venduto la mia bici.
  I sold him my bike.   (I sold my bike to him!)

Abbiamo inviato loro i regali.
  We sent them the gifts.   (We sent the gifts to them!)

Le rispondi.
  You answer her.   rispondere a

Gli telefoni.
  You call him.   telefonare a

Chiedigli.
  Ask him.   chiedere a

Ascoltala!
  Listen to her!   ascoltare does not use a preposition in Italian!

Aspettala!
  Wait for her!   aspettare does not use a preposition in Italian!

The Pronoun *Ci*

When a pronoun is needed for *a place* or *a thing introduced by a preposition*, use **ci**. (If the partitive is involved, we use **ne**, which is explained next.) Study these examples of **ci** replacing inanimate nouns introduced by **a** or **di**:

Tua sorella gioca **a tennis**?
Does your sister play tennis?

Sì, **Ci** gioca bene.
Yes, she plays it well.

Penso **ai miei compiti**.
I'm thinking about my homework.

Non pensar**ci**!
Don't think about it!

Sei mai stato **a Filadefia**?
Have you ever been to Philadelphia?

Sì, **Ci** sono stato molte volte.
Yes, I've been there many times.

Mi abituo **alla dieta**.
I'm getting used to the diet.

Mi **ci** abituo.
I'm getting used to it.

Ci can also replace inanimate nouns introduced by other prepositions. Here are examples with **in** and **su**:

Vado **in Italia** il mese prossimo.
I'm going to Italy next month.

Ci vado il mese prossimo
I'm going there next month.

Ha messo le sue chiavi **nella borsa**.
She put her keys in her bag.

Ci ha messo le sue chiavi.
She put her keys in it.

Ci is commonly used with the verb **andare** (to go) when the destination is not specified:

Ci vai?
Are you going there?

Ci is frequently added to verb **avere** *plus pronoun object*, to flesh out very short utterances. When used this way, it doesn't translate into English:

Ce l'hai?
Do you have it?

Sì **Ce** l'ho?
Yes, I've got it.

The Pronoun *Ne*

Ne is generally translated as *some* or *any,* but it also replaces an inanimate noun introduced by the preposition **di**. Like **ci**, it has many possible translations when used this way. Here are some examples:

Quanti francobolli hai?
How many stamps do you have?

Ne ho tre.
I have three of them.

Ce **ne** sono abbastanza?
Are there enough? (of them)

Sì, ce **ne** sono tre
Yes, there are three. (of them)

Vuoi **del gelato**?
Do you want some ice cream?

Certo, **ne** voglio!
Of course, I want some.

Ha paura **del babau**?
Is she afraid of the bogeyman?

No, non **ne** ha paura.
No. She's not afraid of him.

Sei felice **del tuo regalo?**
Are you happy with your gift?

Sì, **ne** sono molto contenta.
Yes, I'm very happy with it.

Non ho bisogna **di quella pala**.
I don't need that shovel.

Non **ne** hai bisogno?
Don't you need it?

Parla **dei suoi problemi**?
Does she talk about her problems?

Sì, **ne** parla.
Yes, she does. Yes, she talks about them.

Non abbiamo **piu vino**.
We don't have any more wine.

Ne comprerò qualche bottiglia domani.
I'll buy a few bottles (of it) tomorrow.

Object Pronouns with Two Verbs

It is quite common for two verbs to appear in the same phrase. The first verb is conjugated and the second one appears in the infinitive. For more about this construction, see **modal verbs.**

There are two ways to place the OBJECT PRONOUN in this type of sentence:

<u>I want to see</u> her.

Compare: **La** voglio vedere.   **OR**   Voglio veder**la**.

You may place the pronoun in front of the conjugated verb *OR* you may *attach* it to the end of the infinitive, having first removed the final *e*.

Here are more examples:

Lo vuole leggere.   *OR*   Vuole leggerlo.
  He wants to read it.

Ne vuoi assaggiare?   *OR*   Vuoi assaggiarne?
  Do you want to taste some?

Non la posso sentire.   *OR*   Non posso sentirla.
  I can't hear her.

Li dobbiamo imparare.   *OR*   Dobbiamo impararli.
  We have to learn them.

Object Pronouns in Commands

In the *familiar affirmative* command, the pronoun object will *follow* the verb and will *attach* to that verb (except for loro). Study these examples of position:

Spiega**mi** perché sei in ritardo.
  Explain to me why you are late.

Scriv**ici** una lettera!
  Write us a letter!

Sveglia**ti**!
  Wake up!

The same position is used for *noi* and *voi* affirmative commands:

Proviamo**lo**.
  Let's try it.

Tagliamo**la** mentre è calda.
  Let's cut it while it's hot.

Degustate**li**.
  Try them, taste them.

In negative commands, all three forms place the pronoun in front of the verb, like this:

Non **mi** dire una bugia.

Non **lo** dimentichiamo.

Non **li** prendete.

In polite commands, both the affirmative and the negative take the pronoun object in front of the verb, like this:

> **Si** accomodi.
> Non **si** preoccupi.
>
> **Si** accomodino.
> Non **si** preoccupino.
>
> **La** prenda.
> Non **la** prenda.
>
> **La** prendano.
> Non **la** prendano.

When the *familiar affirmative* command is only one syllable long, as in **dai** or **da'**, **di'**, **fai** or **fa'**, **stai** or **sta'**, **vai** or **va'**, attaching pronouns (except for **gli**) will double their initial consonant like this:

> Dai questa lettera <u>a Silvia</u>.   =   Dal**le** questa lettera.
> *Give this letter to Sylvia.*   *Give her this letter.*
>
> Dai questi soldi <u>a papà</u>.   =   Da**gli** questi soldi.
> *Give this money to Dad.*   *Give him this money.*
>
> Sta' vicino a me!   Sta**mmi** vicino!
> *Stay close to me. same:*   *Stay close to me.*
>
> Fai' una pizza per per noi!   Fa**cci** una pizza!
> *Make a pizza for us!*   *Make us a pizza!*

Drill 26: Single Object Pronoun Placement

Rewrite the sentence by replacing the underlined words with an appropriate pronoun.

1. Scrivo <u>ai genitori</u>. _____

2. Parlo <u>al professore</u>. _____

3. Vediamo spesso <u>la nonna</u>. _____

4. Ho comprato <u>quei regali</u>. _____

5. Vanno <u>in Umbria</u> quest'estate. _____

6. Abbiamo spedito il pacco <u>a Maria</u>. _____

7. Dove hai visto <u>la macchina</u>? _____

8. Non trovo <u>le tazze</u>. _____

9. Metto le caramelle <u>in questo sacchetto</u>. _____

10. Va <u>al mercato</u> il sabato. _____

11. Di' la verità <u>a me</u>. _____

12. Vorrei conoscere <u>Maria</u>. _____

13. Compriamo <u>la macchina rossa</u>! (command!) _____

14. Puoi fare un favore <u>a me</u>? _____

15. Non prendere <u>il mio gelato</u>! _____

Answers and Explanations to Drill 26

1. Scrivo <u>ai genitori</u>.
   I write to my parents.
   Scrivo **loro**. Also: **Gli** scrivo.
   I write to them.

2. Parlo <u>al professore.</u>
   I speak to the teacher.
   Gli parlo.
   I speak to him.

3. Vediamo spesso <u>la nonna</u>.
   We see Grandmother often.
   La vediamo spesso.
   We see her often.

4. Ho comprato <u>quei regali</u>.
   I bought those gifts.
   Li ho comprati.
   I bought them.

5. Vanno <u>in Umbria</u> quest'estate.
   They're going to Umbria this summer.
   Ci vanno quest'estate.
   They're going there this summer.

6. Abbiamo spedito il pacco <u>a Maria</u>.
   We sent the package to Maria.
   Le abbiamo spedito il pacco.
   We sent her the package.

7. Dove hai visto <u>la macchina</u>?
   Where did you see the car?
   Dove **l'**hai vist**a**?
   Where did you see it?

8. Non trovo <u>le tazze</u>.
   I can't find the cups*.
   Non **le** trovo.
   I can't find them*. While *Non posso trovare le tazze* is a more literal translation, it is very idiomatic, and quite common, to leave out the counterpart to "can".

9. Metto le caramelle <u>in questo sachetto</u>.
   I put the candies in this bag.
   Ci metto le caramelle.
   I put the candies in there.

10. Va <u>al mercato</u> il sabato mattina.
    She goes to market on Saturday mornings.
    Ci va il sabato.
    She goes there Saturday mornings.

11. Di' la verità <u>a me</u>.
    Tell the truth to me.
    Dimmi la verità.
    Tell me the truth.

12. Vorrei conoscere <u>Maria</u>.
    I'd like to meet Maria.
    La vorrei conoscere. *OR* Vorrei conoscer**la**.
    I'd like to meet her.

13. Compriamo <u>la macchina rossa</u>!
    Let's buy the red car!
    Compriamo**la**!
    Let's buy it!

14. Puoi fare un favore <u>a me</u>?
    Can you do a favor for me?
    Mi puoi fare un favore? *OR* Puoi far**mi** un favore?
    Can you do me a favor?

15. Non prendere <u>il mio gelato</u>!
    Don't take my ice cream!
    Non **lo** prendere!
    Don't take it!

Double Object Pronouns

It is common for one verb to have two objects (one direct and one indirect) in both Italian and English. If you must place two objects with a single verb, that **pair** of objects will be positioned exactly as we learned to place them separately. The difficulty lies in knowing which one to place first.

Here are five rules to guide you in placing two objects in the right order. They apply to all types of sentences, including the commands:

1. **Ne** is the caboose. No matter what other object you combine with it, **ne** will always be last.

2. Always place **ci** first, no matter how it is translated, no matter what combines with it.

3. Both **gli** and **le** change to **glie** and attach to the next pronoun.

4. **Mi**, **ti**, **ci**, **vi** and **si** become **me**, **te**, **ce**, **ve** and **se** when they appear in combination with other pronouns. They do not attach to each other in front of the verb. If they follow the verb, all pronouns except loro, attach to the verb and to each other.

5. Always place the INDIRECT OBJECT PRONOUN in front of the DIRECT OBJECT PRONOUN.

Here are some examples, observe how the pronouns combine according to the rules:

> **Ve ne** ha dato un po'.
> *He gave you some, a little.*

> **Ce li** ho messi.
> *I put them there.*

> Non **ce n'**è più.
> *There isn't any more (there).*

> **Te li** do.
> *I'm giving them to you.*

> **Me la** spiega.
> *He explains it to me.*

Ve le mostro.
I show them to you.

Glielo restituisci.
You give it back to her/him.

Ho mandato **loro** una lettera.
I sent them a letter.

When placing a *pair* of pronouns in the **tu**, **noi** or **voi** affirmative command, attach them to the rear of the verb, *and to each other*, except for loro. Remember that with all other command forms, the pronoun pair is placed in front of the verb and remains free standing.

Let's review the basic rules we learned for combining all pronoun objects except loro. Here is a condensed version:

1. **ne** is *always* last, **ci** is *always* first.

2. Place the *indirect object* **in front of** *the direct object*

3. Make spelling changes needed: **Ci** to **ce**, **mi** to **me**, etc. Also change **gli** and **le** to **glie**.

Observe how the pronouns combine according to these simplified rules:

Manda**melo**!
Send it to me!

Spieghiamo**lo loro**!
Let's explain it to them!

Date**cene** un po'!
Give us some!

Drill 27: Combining Object Pronouns
(first drill of two)

Each sentence already contains one pronoun object. Replace the underlined words with *another object pronoun* and combine it with the one that is already present.

Example: Vi do <u>la mia parola</u>.   **Ve la** do.
I give you my word.   I give it to you.

1. M'invia <u>dei soldi</u>. _____

2. Ti mostriamo <u>la nostra casa nuova</u>. _____

3. Mettili <u>sulla sedia</u>. _____

4. Dammi <u>i fogli</u>. _____

5. Raccontami <u>la storia</u>. _____

6. Dacci <u>le chiavi</u>. _____

7. Non gli dire <u>il segreto</u>. _____

8. Ci racconta <u>le sue avventure</u>. _____

9. Le prometto <u>la più bella fetta di torta</u>. _____

10. Mamma ci prepara tre <u>bibite</u>. _____

Answers and Explanations to Drill 27

1. M'invia <u>dei soldi</u>.
   He sends me money.
   Me ne invia. (**ne** is always last in combination, change **mi** to **me**)
   He sends me some.

2. Ti mostriamo <u>la nostra casa nuova</u>.
   We show you our new house.
   Te la mostriamo. (indirect before direct, change **ti** to **te**)
   We show it to you.

3. Mettili <u>sulla sedia.</u>
   Put them on the chair.
   Metti**celi**. (**ci** is always first and changes to **ce** in combination)
   Put them there.

4. Dammi <u>i fogli</u>.
   Give me the papers.
   Dam**meli**. (place indirect before direct, change **mi** to **me**)
   Give them to me.

5. Raccontami <u>la storia</u>.
   Tell me the story.
   Racconta**mela**. (place indirect before direct, change **mi** to **me**)
   Tell it to me.

6. Dacci <u>le chiavi</u>.
   Give us the keys.
   Dac**cele**. (**ci** is always first and changes to **ce** in combination)
   Give them to us.

7. Non gli dire <u>il segreto</u>.
   Don't tell him the secret.
   Non **glielo** dire. (indirect before direct. **Gli** becomes **glie** and attaches to the next pronoun)
   Don't tell it to him.

8. Ci racconta <u>le sue avventure.</u>
   He tells us his adventures.
   Ce le racconta. (**ci** is first and remains freestanding in front of the verb)
   He tells them to us.

9. Le prometto <u>la più bella fetta di torta</u>.
   I promise her (you) the best slice.
   Gliela prometto. (indirect before direct. **Le** becomes **glie** and attaches to the next pronoun)
   I promise it to her, you.

10. Mamma ci prepara tre <u>bibite</u>.
    Mom prepares three soft drinks for us.
    Mamma **ce ne** prepara **tre**. (**ne** is always last, here it conveys *of them*)
    Mom prepares three of them for us.

Drill 28: Combining Object Pronouns
(second drill of two)

Rewrite the sentence, replacing the underlined words with two object pronouns.

Example: Spiego <u>la lezione agli alunni</u>.   **La** spiego **loro**.
                I explain the lesson to the pupils.   *I explain it to them.*

1. Leggo <u>la storia a mio figlio</u>. _____

2. <u>Maria</u>, ti do <u>i soldi</u>. _____

3. Spediamo <u>il regalo alla nonna</u>. _____

4. Do <u>il lecca lecca al bimbo</u>. _____

5. Scegli <u>i fiori per la mamma</u>. *command* _____

6. Tu versi <u>dell'acqua nei bicchieri</u>. _____

7. Mostrate <u>le foto a Valentina</u>. _____

8. Consiglia <u>il sangiovese a te e a Mario</u>. _____

9. Di' <u>la verità ai genitori</u>. _____

10. Ho inviato un pacco <u>di biscotti ad Andrea</u>. _____

11. <u>Maria</u>, ecco <u>il tuo limoncello</u>. _____

12. Lasci <u>la sua giacca sulla sedia</u>. _____

13. Non mettere <u>i gomiti sulla tavola</u>. _____

14. Lui presta <u>i soldi a suo fratello</u>. _____

15. Colgono <u>fiori per la loro mamma</u>. _____

Answers and Explanations to Drill 28

1. Leggo la storia a mio figlio.
   I read the story to my son.
   Gliela leggo. Indirect before direct, gli becomes glie and attaches.
   I read it to him.

2. <u>Maria</u> (ti) do <u>i soldi</u>.
   Maria, I give you the money.
   Te li do. Place the indirect object before the direct object.
   I give it to you.

3. Spediamo <u>il regalo alla nonna</u>.
   We send the gift to Grandmother.
   Glielo spediamo. Indirect before direct, le becomes glie and attaches.
   We send it to her.

4. Do <u>il lecca lecca al bimbo</u>.
   I give the lollipop to the little boy.
   Glielo do. Indirect before direct, gli becomes glie and attaches.
   I give it to him.

5. Scegli <u>i fiori per la mamma</u>.
   Choose the flowers for mom.
   Scegli**glieli**.
   Choose them for her. That's a mouthful to pronounce! Attach the pronouns onto the end of this familiar affirmative command.

6. Tu versi un po' d'<u>acqua nei bicchieri</u>.
   You pour a little water in the glasses.
   Tu **ce ne** versi un po'. (**ne** is always last)
   You pour a little in.

7. Mostrate <u>le foto a Valentina</u>.
   You show the photos to Valentina.
   Gliele mostrate.
   You show them to her.

8. Consiglia <u>il sangiovese a te e a Mario</u>.
   He recommends the sangiovese to you and Mario.
   Ve lo consiglia.
   He recommends it to you (both).
   Sangiovese is a red grape, the #1 varietal in Italy.

9. Di' <u>la verità ai genitori</u>.
   Tell your parents the truth.
   Dilla loro. Only **la** can attach to the verb. **Loro** must follow.
   Tell it to them. Note the doubled consonant.
   Today many Italians replace loro, and its obstinant positioning, with *gli*.
   Following this modern substitution, you could use di**gliela** here.

10. Ho inviato un pacco <u>di biscotti ad Andrea</u>.
    I sent a package of cookies to Andrew.
    Gliene ho inviati un pacco. (**ne** is always last, gli becomes glie and attaches.)
    I sent him a package of them.

11. <u>Maria</u>, ecco <u>il tuo limoncello</u>.
    Maria, here is your lemon liqueur.
    Ecco**telo**. Ecco accepts attached pronoun objects. Indirect before direct.
    Here you are, here it is for you.

12. Lasci <u>la sua giacca sulla sedia</u>.
    Leave your jacket on the chair.
    Ce la lasci. This a polite command. Pronoun objects precede the verb.
    Ci is first and does not attach in this position.
    Leave it there.

13. Non mettere <u>i gomiti sulla tavola</u>.
    Don't put your elbows on the table.
    Non **ce li** mettere. Ci is first and does not attach in front of the verb.
    Don't put them there.

14. Lui presta <u>i soldi a suo fratello</u>.
    He lends the money to his brother.
    Glieli presta.
    He lends it to him.

15. Colgono <u>fiori per la loro mamma</u>.
    They pick some flowers for their mother.
    Gliene colgono. Either rule applies: Indirect before direct, or ne is last.
    They pick some for her.

Relative Pronouns

Che, Cui, Il Quale, Il Cui

Relative pronouns allow us to link a descriptive clause to a person or a thing in the main clause. The relative pronoun *relates back* to that noun in the main clause. Since that noun in the main clause always comes first, it is often called the **antecedent.**

Che refers back to a noun used as either the subject or the object of the verb. It may be a *person*, or a *thing*. When it refers to a person, **che** is translated as **who, whom** or **that**. When it refers to a *thing*, it's translated as **which** or **that**. Here are some examples:

> Come si chiama la donna **che** parla al prete?
> *What's the name of the woman who's talking to the priest?*

> Ecco il pacco **che** è arrivato ieri.
> *Here is the parcel which arrived yesterday.*

> È una donna **che** non conosco.
> *It's (she's) a woman whom I don't know.*

> È il pacco **che** aspettavo.
> *It's the package I was waiting for.*

In English the relative pronoun is often left out of the sentence entirely. In Italian the relative pronoun may NEVER be omitted. Compare:

> Ecco il libro **che** volevi.
> *Here's the book you wanted.*

> Guarda a sinistra la ragazza **che** sbadiglia!
> *Look at the girl yawning on the left!*

Cui replaces **che** when that person or thing is the object of a simple (one word) preposition. Its translation is **that, which,** or **whom.**

> Era una ragazzina **con cui** giocavo spesso.
> *She was a little girl I used to play with often.*

> Ecco il cane **di cui** ho paura.
> *There's the dog I'm afraid of.*

> Tecnocasa è l'agenzia immobilare **per cui** lavora.
> *Tecnocasa is the real estate agency he/she works for.*

Dove *(where)* and **quando** *(when)* can be used to replace the combination of **in cui** like this:

> È la casa in cui sono nato.
> *It's the house in which I was born.*

> È la casa dove sono nato.
> *It's the house where I was born.*

> Era un periodo in cui sono cresciuta molto.
> *It was a time in which I grew a lot.*

If the preposition is a compound (made of two or more words) use **il quale (or one of its forms: i quali, la quale, le quali)** instead of *cui*, like this:

> I bimbi giocano nel parco **davanti al quale** abitiamo.
> *The children play in the park in front of which we live.*
> Note the normal contraction of the article.

Since its forms are gender and number specific, **il quale** is useful for clarification: Compare:

> Ho inviato una cartolina al padre di mia nuora che sta all'ospedale.
> *I sent a card to my daughter-in-law's father, who's in the hospital.*
> (Who's in the hospital? *Che* could refer back to either one)

> Ho inviato una cartolina al padre di mia nuora, il quale sta all'ospedale.
> *Same translation, but much clearer as to who's in the hospital.*

The combination of **definite article + cui + noun** is the equivalent of **whose, of whom, of which** in English. Here are some examples:

> Come si chiamava quella donna **i cui** gemelli hanno traslocato a Milano?
> *What was the name of that woman whose twins moved to Milan?*

> Ho visto alla TV quella scrittrice inglese **il cui** nome ora mi sfugge. Ha scritto la serie Harry Potter.
> *I saw that English best-selling author whose name escapes me at the moment. She wrote the Harry Potter series.*

È la professoressa **ai cui** studenti abbiamo scritto.
She's the teacher whose students we wrote to.

Non è il vetraio **di cui** ho il numero di telefono.
He's not the glass-cutter whose phone number I have.

Quello Che, Ciò Che, and Il Che

All three forms mean **what** or **that which**. These pronouns never refer to people, only to *things*. They may also refer to a *whole phrase* or *idea*. They are only suitable when no noun object is present. Compare:

La pizza **che** mangi sembra deliziosa.
The pizza you're eating looks delicious.

Quello che mangi sembra delizioso.
What you're eating looks delicious.

Il dolce **che** arriva sarà indimenticabile.
The dessert which is coming will be unforgettable.

Ciò che arriva sarà indimenticabile.
What's coming will be unforgettable.

Non vuole lavorare per riuscire, **il che** è peccato.
He doesn't want to work to succeed, which is a shame.

Ciò a Cui, Ciò Di Cui

Like the preceding group, these two pronoun combinations can only apply to things, never people. They are only used instead of QUELLO CHE or CIÒ CHE when the object is introduced by the preposition **a** or **di**, compare:

Hai sentito **ciò che** ho detto?
Di you hear what I said?

Hai capito **ciò a cui** mi riferivo?
Did you understand what I was referring to? (riferirsi **a**)

Ho letto **quello che** hai scritto.
I read what you wrote.

Ho dimenticato **ciò di cui** ti lamentavi. (lamentarsi **di**)
I've forgotten what you were complaining about.

Italians simplify wherever possible:
*Ho dimenticato **perché** ti lamentavi.*

Drill 29: Che, Cui, il Cui, il Quale

Supply the needed pronoun.

1. Ecco il martello di _____ abbiamo bisogno

2. È la giovane coppia _____ figli conosci.

3. La ragazza _____ piange è molto triste.

4. Cè un piccolo alborello accanto (a +) _____ ti aspetterò.

5. Non mi piace la cravatta _____ hai messo.

6. Conosco gemelli fra _____ non riesco a distinguere.

7. Sono i vicini _____ cane abbaia tutta la notte.

8. Liliana sceglie un libro _____ le sembra interessante.

9. Ho la vecchia camicia strappato _____ di hai perso i bottoni.

10. Ha cancellato il voto di _____ aveva vergogna.

Answer and Explanations to Drill 29

1. Ecco il martello di **cui** abbiamo bisogno.
   Here's the hammer we need.
   Il martello is the object of the verbal expression avere bisogno *di*.
   Cui is the best choice with which to follow a single word preposition.

2. È la giovane coppia **i cui** figli conosci già.
   It's the young couple whose children you already know.
   Use the combination of *article + cui + noun* to create **whose**.

3. La ragazza **che** piange è molto triste.
   The girl who's crying is very unhappy.
   We need a basic relative pronoun to refer back to the girl. Use *che*.

4. Cè un piccolo alberello accanto **al quale** ti aspetterò.
   There's a little tree next to which I'll wait for you.
   Since *accanto a* is a two word preposition, it requires *il quale* instead of *cui*. Note the contraction of *il + a* to make *al*.

5. Non mi piace la cravatta **che** hai messo.
   I don't like the tie you put on.
   Che refers back to the tie, the object of the verb *mettere*.

6. Conosco gemelli fra **cui** non riesco a distinguere.
   I know twins between whom I cannot distinguish.
   Remember to use *cui* after a simple (one word) preposition.

7. Sono i vicini **il cui** cane abbaia tutta la notte.
   They're the neighbors whose dog barks all night.
   Here we use *article + cui + noun* to create **whose**.

8. Liliana sceglie un libro **che** le sembra interessante.
   Lillian chooses a book which seems interesting to her.
   Here *che* refers back to an inanimate antecedent, the book.

9. Ho strappato la vecchia camicia di **cui** hai perso i bottoni.
   I cut up for rags the old shirt whose buttons you lost.
   Notice how the article matches the noun in this combination meaning
   whose.

10. Ha cancellato il voto di **cui** aveva vergogna.
    She crossed out the grade she was ashamed of.
    Il voto is the object of the verb phrase *avere vergogna di*. Remember we
    cannot use *che* for the object of a preposition. Choose *cui* for this simple
    preposition.

Drill 30: il Quale, Dove, Quando

Supply the needed pronoun.

1. Benedetto è un collega con _____ ho un buon rapporto.

2. Ecco la ricetta con _____ preparo la mia focaccia.

3. È il dizionario (di +) _____ mi fido.

4. È il dizionario (di +) _____ mi servo il più spesso.

5. Sono ricordi (a +) _____ penso di quando in quando.

6. Ecco il piccolo paese _____ abitavamo.

7. Hai visto Giacomo, il figlio della Signora Lupo _____ abita vicino a me? (who = la Signora)

8. Hai visto Giacomo, il figlio della Signora Lupo _____ abita vicino a me? (who = Giacomo)

9. Erano le anni sessanta _____ ci siamo sposati.

10. Ecco la fontana di Trevi _____ lanciamo monete.

Answers and Explanations to Drill 30

1. Benedetto è un collega con **il quale** ho un buon rapporto.
   Benedict is a co-worker with whom I have a good relationship.

2. Ecco la ricetta con **la quale** preparo la mia focaccia.
   Here's the recipe with which I make my focaccia. (a round flat bread with a bumpy surface and seasonings on the top)
   Use the feminine singular form of **il quale** for the inanimate object of the preposition *con*.

3. È il dizionario **del quale** mi fido.
   It's the dictionary I trust.
   Here the preposition from the verb *fidarsi di* contracts with **il quale**.

4. È il dizionario **del quale** mi servo il più spesso.
   It's the dictionary I use most often.
   The verb *servirsi* uses *di* in front of its object, thus *del quale (of which)*

5. Sono ricordi **ai quali** penso di quando in quando.
   They're memories I think of from time to time. (about which I think)
   The preposition from *pensare a* contracts with *i quali*.

6. Ecco il piccolo paese **dove** abitavamo.
   Here's the little village where (in which) we used to live.
   Dove provides a handy replacement for *in cui*.

7. Hai visto Giacomo, il figlio della Signora Lupo **la quale** abita vicino a me?
   Have you seen Jack, Mrs. Wolf's son, who lives near me? (She does)

8. Hai visto Giacomo, il figlio della Signora Lupo **il quale** abita vicino a me?
   Have you seen Jack, Mrs. Wolf's son, who lives near me? (He does)

9. Erano gli anni sessanta **quando** ci siamo sposati.
   It was the sixties when (in which, during which) we got married.
   Quando conveniently replaces *in cui*.

10. Ecco la fontana di Trevi **dove** lanciamo monete.
    Here's the Trevi Fountain where (in which) we throw coins (for luck).

Drill 31: Quello Che, Ciò Che, Il Che, Ciò a Cui, Ciò Di Cui

Supply the needed pronoun.

1. _____ vuoi non è possibile!

2. Dimmi _____ ti piace.

3. Non aiuta mai con i lavori domestici, _____ mi dà fastidio.

4. È _____ riesco.

5. Mostrami _____ hai in mano.

6. Raccontami _____ succede.

7. Dite loro tutto _____ volete.

8. Dite loro _____ avete voglia.

9. Capisco _____ vuoi dire.

10. Vorrei sapere _____ ti secca.

Answers and Explanations to Drill 31

1. **Ciò che** vuoi non è possible!
   What you want isn't possible.
   The unnamed OBJECT of the verb *volere* is represented by either CIÒ CHE or QUELLO CHE.

2. Dimmi **ciò che** ti piace.
   Tell me what you like. Tell me what pleases you.
   The unnamed SUBJECT of the verb *piacere* requires CIÒ CHE or QUELLO CHE.

3. Non aiuta mai con i lavori domestici, **il che** mi dà fastidio.
   He never helps with the chores, which bothers me.
   IL CHE refers back to the entire phrase that he doesn't help at home.

4. È **ciò in cui** riesco.
   It's what I'm good at.
   We need CIÒ IN CUI to express the unnamed OBJECT of the verb riuscire **in**.

5. Mostrami **quello che** hai in mano.
   Show me what you have in your hand.
   We use QUELLO CHE to stand for the unnamed OBJECT of the verb *avere*.

6. Raccontami **ciò che** succede.
   Tell me what's happening.
   CIÒ CHE stands for the unnamed SUBJECT of the verb *seccarsi*.

7. Dite loro tutto **quello che** volete.
   Tell them everything you want.
   QUELLO CHE represents the unnamed OBJECT of *volere*.

8. Dite loro **ciò di cui** avete voglia.
   Tell them what you want.
   CIÒ DI CUI is required to convey the unnamed OBJECT of the verb phrase *avere voglia* **di**.

9. Capisco **quello che** vuoi dire.
   I see what you mean.
   The unnamed OBJECT of the verb phrase *volere dire* is represented by
   QUELLO CHE.

10. Vorrei sapere **quello che** ti secca.
    I'd like to know what's bothering you.
    The verb *seccarsi* is governed here by an unnamed SUBJECT.

Disjunctive Pronouns

me—me	noi—us
te—you	voi—you
lui—him	loro—them
lei—her	
sé – oneself, himself, herself	

Disjunctive or *stressed* pronouns can only refer to people. They replace object pronouns in the following circumstances:

1. After prepositions—a disjunctive pronoun is required if the object of the preposition is human, as in these examples:

    Ecco una lettera **per te**.
    Here's a letter for you.

    Andiamo a cena **da lui** stasera.
    We're going have dinner at his house this evening.

    Guarda davanti **a te**!
    Look in front of you!

    Abito vicino **a loro**.
    I live near them.

2. For emphasis:

    Parla **con te**!
    He's speaking to you!

3. In exclamations:

    Beato **te**!
    Lucky you!

    Povero **te**!
    You poor thing!

4. In a comparison:

> Sono alto come **lei**.
> *I'm as tall as she is.*

> Sei più alto di **me**.
> *You are taller than I am.*

5. As the second pronoun in multiple subjects or objects:

> Io e te, ci siamo intesi.
> *You and I hit it off.* (got along from the start)

> Vi vedo, tu e lei.
> *I see both you and her.*

The pronoun **sé** can be translated as oneself, himself, herself, itself, themselves **or** one, him, her, it, them. Always use it with an indefinite subject:

> Il bimbo si è vestito da **sé**.
> *The little boy dressed himself.*

> Le piace parlare di **sé**.
> *She likes to talk about herself.*

> Si dovrebbe essere sicuri di **sé** stessi.
> *One should be self confident.*

> Va da **sé**.
> *It goes without saying.*

Drill 32: Disjunctive Pronouns

Supply the necessary pronoun to convey the English meaning:

1. Questo regalo è per _____?
   This gift is for me?

2. Contento _____!
   Suit yourself! (tu form)

3. Ama il prossimo tuo come _____ stesso.
   Love thy neighbor as thyself.

4. Ognuno per _____!
   Each man for himself!

5. Tocca a _____!
   It's my turn!

6. Sei più fortunato di _____.
   You are luckier than he is.

7. Vuoi venire con _____?
   Do you want to come with me?

8. Guardami! Parlo con _____!
   Look at me! I'm speaking to you!

9. Ecco un mazzo di mimose per _____.
   Here is a bunch of mimosa for you. (tu form)

10. Mi sono seduto accanto a _____.
    I sat down next to them.

Answers and Explanations to Drill 32

1. Questo regalo è per **me**?
   The human object of a preposition must be disjunctive.

2. Contento **te**!
   Disjunctive pronouns regularly appear in exclamations.

3. Ama il prossimo tuo come **te** stesso.
   The human object of a preposition is disjunctive.

4. Ognuno per **sé**!
   Himself refers back to the indefinite subjet *ognuno*.

5. Tocca a **me**.
   The human object of a preposition is always disjunctive.

6. Sei più fortunato di **lui**.
   Disjunctives are always used in comparisons.

7. Vuoi venire con **me**?
   Use a disjunctive pronoun for the human object of a preposition.

8. Guardami! Parlo con **te**!
   The disjunctive pronoun is used emphatically here.

9. Ecco un mazzo di mimose per **te**.
   The human object of a preposition is always disjunctive.
   Sprigs of mimosa are traditionally given on March 8th, la festa della donna.

10. Mi sono seduto accanto a **loro**.
    Another human object of a preposition.

Prepositions

A preposition may be a single word or an expression of two or three words in Italian. Italian prepositions can be followed by nouns, pronouns, or infinitives. Choosing the right preposition will be crucial in your writing sample. Since each one may have several meanings, learning to master prepositions can feel like walking through a minefield. One needs to go slowly and pay attention!

What follows is a study of the most useful common prepositions. They are presented in small groups that juxtapose similar prepositions which are frequently confused. With some earnest study, you will be able to avoid the errors which commonly plague student writing.

Per, Durante, Da

Avoid the error of using the preposition **per** (for) with the verbs *aspettare*, *cercare*, *chiedere*, and *pagare*. The preposition is already built into the verb. Thus we say:

> Aspetto i miei amici.
> *I wait for my friends.*

> Cerco i miei occhiali.
> *I'm looking for my glasses.*

> Chiedo le chiavi della macchina.
> *I ask for the car keys.*

> Pago la pizza.
> *I pay for the pizza.*

Use **per** to convey *intent* or *destination*.

> Per fare una frittata, occorrono le uova.
> *To make an omelette, you need eggs.*

> Uso quelle forbici per tagliare la stoffa.
> *I use those scissors to cut fabric.*

> È partito per l'Italia.
> *He left for Italy.*

Use **per** with the verbs like *andare*, *venire*, *viaggiare*, *partire* and *uscire* to indicate a period of time:

> La mia amica italiana è venuta per Natale.
> *My Italian girl friend came for Christmas.*

> Quest'estate spero di andare in Francia per un mese.
> *This summer I hope to go to France for a month.*

Durante means *during* or *all through*. See how it changes the meaning slightly in the sentence about the girl coming for Christmas.

> La mia amica italiana è stata con noi durante le feste natalizie.
> *My Italian girl friend was with us for the Christmas holidays.*

> Non mette scarpe durante l'estate.
> *She doesn't wear shoes during the summer.*

Da is needed to express *for* if the period of time began in the past and continues into the present.

> Studio l'italiano da cinque anni.
> *I have been studying Italian for five years.*

Notice the use of the *present tense* in the Italian construction, much simpler than the clumsy "I have been studying" in the English sentence. If the action began in the past and continued to a point also in the past, you use the *imperfect tense* with **da:**

> Studiavo l'italiano da cinque anni quando ho ricevuto la borsa di studio.
> *I had been studying Italian for five years when I got the scholarship.*

Thus we have two very simple constructions:

> present tense verb + da + time element
> (*have been*)

> imperfect verb + da + time element
> (*had been*)

The preposition **da** can also mean *since* when referring to a point in time. If you want to express *since* meaning *because*, you must use an expression like *dato che* or *visto che*. Compare:

> Non ho mangiato da stamattina. Ho fame.
> *I haven't eaten since this morning. I'm hungry.*

Dovrai andare solo visto che non posso venire.
You'll have to go alone since I can't come.

Da is also used to mean *at the home of or place of business*. It has no real equivalent in English. Here is how to use it:

Si mangia bene da Maria.
They eat well at Maria's house.

Vado dal dentista dopo scuola.
I'm going to the dentist's office after school.

Dentro, In, Su, Sopra, Sotto

Use **dentro** when *in* means *inside, within, indoors.*

È tanto raccolto qui dentro!
It's so cozy in here!

Che cosa c'è dentro?
What's inside?

Dentro tremavo di paura.
I was trembling inside.

Ho messo la lettera dentro la busta.
I put the letter in the envelope.

In is used rather than **su** when referring to a street location.

Abita in via Maleretta.
She lives on via Maleretta.

Benetton si trova in Piazza del Popolo.
Benetton is on the Piazza del Popolo.

In conveys how much time is or was spent doing something.

Ho letto il romanzo in tre ore.
I read the novel in three hours.

Ha fatto i suoi compiti in meno di dieci minuti.
He did his homework in less than 10 minutes.

In is NOT used to refer to a period of time that has not yet taken place. Italian uses **tra** instead:

Partiranno tra un'ora.
They're going to leave in an hour.

La nuova succursale aprirà tra un mese.
The new branch will open in a month.

In expresses *in* or *to* in front of all feminine countries and regions.

L'ho conosciuta in Germania.
I met her in Germany.

Ho passato due settimane in Umbria.
I spent two weeks in Umbria.

Compare:

Ho passato due settimane negli Abruzzi.
I spent two weeks in Abruzzi.
Gli Abruzzi are masculine, plural.

In can also mean *in* as in *made of.*

Cerco una borsa in cuoio.
I'm looking for a leather purse.

In can be translated as *by* with a means of transportation:

Mi piace viaggiare in aereo.
I like to travel by plane.

The use of **su** to mean **on** is limited to being physically on the surface of something. **Su** does not translate the many idiomatic uses of **on** in English. There are so many that you should make an effort to memorize those that you encounter. Here are some examples:

On foot: a piedi

On the right: a destra

On the floor: per terra

On purpose: di proposito

On fire: in fiamme

Sotto is translated as *under*. It can be physical as well as historical.

Non si può respirare sott'acqua.
One cannot breath under water.

Le arti sono fiorite sotto Lorenzo il Magnifico.
The arts flourished under Lorenzo the Magnificent.

È scomparso sotto gli occhi.
He disappeared in plain sight.

Italian uses **sotto** to express the idea of *in the rain*.

> Ti piace camminare sotto la pioggia?
> *Do you like to walk in the rain?*

Prima di, Dopo, Davanti, Dietro a

Prima di and **davanti** both mean *before*. **Prima di** is used exclusively for *time*, and **davanti** is for *physical placement* (in front of). **Prima che** is followed by the subjunctive.

> Cenerentola doveva tornare a casa prima di mezzanotte.
> *Cinderella was supposed to come home before midnight.*

> Prima di addormentarmi, tiro fuori ciò che indosserò l'indomani.
> *Before going to bed, I lay out what I'm going to wear the next day.*

> Studiate prima che sia troppo tardi!
> *Study before it's too late!*

> Ho visto la tua borsa davanti alla porta.
> *I saw your bag in front of the door.*

Dietro a (behind), like **davanti** is only for physical placement.

> La fanciulla si è nascosta dietro alla quercia.
> *The little girl hid behind the oak tree.*

Dietro is NOT suitable for time expressions.

> Sono lenta a scrivere le mie lettere.
> *I'm behind in my letter writing.*

> L'aereo è in ritardo.
> *The plane is behind schedule.*

> Lascio questa valigia. La riprenderò più tardi.
> *I'm going to leave this suitcase behind. I'll pick it up later.*

Dopo (after) is the opposite of **prima di** (before).

> Partiremo dopo cena.
> *We're going to leave after dinner.*

To create the equivalent of the English *after + present participle* construction, Italian requires **dopo + infinitive + past participle**:

> Dopo aver sistemato la mia camera, sono uscito.
> *After straightening my room, I went out.*

Dopo aver vinto al totocalcio, hanno costruito una casa nuova.
After winning the lottery they built a new house.

Dopo essersi truccata, ha messo il vestito.
After putting on her make-up, she put on her dress.

À causa di, Perché

A causa di (because of) is always followed by a noun group or a pronoun. **Perché** (because) is needed in front a whole clause with a subject, a verb and possibly an object. Compare:

Abbiamo perso il volo a causa tua!
We missed the flight because of you!

Abbiamo perso il volo perchè eri in ritardo.
We missed the plane because you were late.

Malgrado, nonostante

Malgrado and *nonostante* translate as *in spite of*, or *despite*.

È stato bocciato malgrado gli sforzi fatti all'ultimo minuto.
He failed in spite of his last minute effort.

Sono uscita nonostante la pioggia battente.
I went out despite the driving rain.

Eccetto, Salvo, Tranne

All three prepositions are translated as *except* or *but*. They may be used interchangeably.

Ho fatto tutti gli esercizi eccetto il numero 17.
Ho fatto tutti gli esercizi salvo il numero 17.
Ho fatto tutti gli eserczi tranne il numero17.
I did all of the exercises except for number 17.

Fra, Tra

Fra (tra) means *between* and is used much as it is in English.

Il bimbo si è seduto fra noi.
The child sat down between us

C'è una scelta fra carne e pesce.
There's a choice between meat and fish.

C'è una grande differenza tra volere e potere.
There's a big difference between wanting to and being able to.

In the expressions **nel frattempo** it conveys *meanwhile*, or *in the meantime*.

Ti aspetterò qui, nel frattempo leggerò.
I'll wait for you here, I'll read in the meantime.

Fra (tra) also means *among* or *amongst*.

Sceglieranno fra noi.
They're going to choose amongst us.

Attenzione! C'è un ladro fra voi.
Be careful! There's a thief in your midst.

Verso, Circa

Verso means *toward* or *towards*:

Il girasole si volta verso il sole.
The sunflower turns towards the sun.

I corsi riprenderanno verso aprile.
Courses start again around (towards) April.

Il bimbo muove un passettino verso di me.
The baby takes a little step towards me.

Both verso and circa can be translated as *around, roughly*:

Ci vedremo verso le tre.
We'll see each other around three o'clock.

Sono circa le tre.
It's about three o'clock.

Con, Senza

Con and **senza** are discussed under Omission of the Definite Article for use with nouns. **Senza** may also be followed by the infinitive:

Ho risposto senza pensare.
I answered without thinking.

Secondo

Secondo means according to, or in the opinion of.

Come sarà la moda di questo inverno, secondo te?
What, in your opinion, according to you, will be in fashion this winter?

Per quanto mi riguarda metterò gli stessi vestiti dell'anno
scorso.
As for me, I'll wear the same outfits I wore last year.

A

The preposition **a** has a myriad of different meanings. It is often translated as *to*, *at*, *in*, *on*, *by* or *with*. It is featured in a variety of idioms which
gives rise to many other translations as well. As you study the following
examples, observe the different nuances in the English translations, all of
which use **a** in Italian:

Vanno al cinema.
They're going TO the movies.

L'ho comprato al supermercato.
I bought it AT the supermarket.

Lei è a sinistra.
She's ON the left.

Noi verremo a piedi.
We'll come ON foot.

A proposito, come sta tua mamma?
BY the way, how's your Mom?

Noi abitiamo a cinque chilometri da Roma.
We live five kilometers AWAY from Rome.

Sometimes the preposition is entirely lost in the English translation as
follows:

Alla prossima volta!
(See you) next time!

Oggi facciamo una passeggiata a cavallo.
Today we're going horseback riding.

Ieri sera hanno preso a noleggio un film.
They rented a film last night.

A can also express *possession*, or *style*:

Questo bicchiere appartiene a me.
This glass belongs to me.

È un sugo alla bolognese.
It's a Bolognese style sauce.

A can be followed by a pronoun or an infinitive:

> Tocca a te.
> *It's your turn.*

> Mi abbasso a raccogliere la penna.
> *I bend down to pick up the pen.*

You will also find that many verbs require **a** before the infinitive, while others take **di**. They are discussed under **VERBS (a o di)**.

Di

Di also has multiple uses. It can be translated as *from, of, to, with, in,* or *than*:

> Lei è di Filadelfia.
> *She is from Philadephia.*

> Prenderei volontieri una tazza di caffè.
> *I'd love to have a cup of coffee.*

> Sono lieta di fare la Sua conocenza.
> *I'm delighted to meet you.*

> Non entrare! Le tue scarpe sono coperte di fango!
> *Don't come in! Your shoes are covered WITH / IN mud.*

This is a common construction, that is, a past participle used as an adjective + di + noun.

> Ho bevuto più di due tazze.
> *I drank more THAN two cups.*

Di has other translations as in these expressions:

> Non perdere di vista i bambini.
> *Don't let the children OUT OF your sight.*

> Sono morta di fatica.
> *I'm dead tired.*

Di can express possession too:

> Ho messo la sciarpa di mia sorella.
> *I wore my sister's scarf.*

Drill 33: Prepositions

Supply the preposition suggested by the English cue:

1. Cosa c'è d'importante nella vita, _____ te?
   (according to, in your opinion)

2. Ho dovuto pulire il bagno _____ (+la) tua prigrizia.
   (because of)

3. Ho letto quel libro _____ tu me l'hai consigliato.
   (because)

4. Ha ereditato l'annello _____ sua nonna.
   (belonging to)

5. Ha trovato il suo vecchio orsetto _____ i giocattoli in soffitta.
   (among)

6. _____ quale regione venite?
   (From)

7. _____ la tua indifferenza io continuo a volerti bene.
   (Despite)

8. _____ il mese di agosto siamo stati in Basilicata.
   (During, for)

9. Andremo in Basilicata _____ un mese.
   (for)

10. Siamo in Basilicata _____ un mese.
    (for)

11. Aspettami _____ al cinema.
    (in front of)

12. Mi faresti scendere _____ centro commerciale?
    (at the)

13. Cosa c'è _____ frigo?
    (in the)

14. Ama la figlia _____ le lentiggini.
    (with)

15. Si sono conosciuti _____ aereo.
    (on the)

16. Telefonagli _____ (+le)17.
    (before)

17. Telefonagli _____ le 17.
    (towards)

18. È partito _____ salutarci.
    (without)

19. Ci invita _____ lui.
    (to his home)

20. _____ me, vado a letto.
    (As for)

Answers and Explanations to Drill 33

1. Cosa c'è d'importante nella vita, **secondo** te?
   What's important in life, according to you?
   Secondo te conveys *in your opinion*.

2. Ho dovuto pulire il bagno **a causa della** tua pigrizia.
   I had to clean the bathroom because of your laziness.
   Since we follow with a noun group, *la tua pigrizia*, we must use *a causa di* to express *because*.

3. Ho letto quel libro **perché** tu me l'hai consigliato.
   I read that book because you recommended it to me.
   This time we have a clause (subject and verb) following *because*. In this case we must use *perché*.

4. Ha ereditato l'anello **di** sua nonna.
   She inherited her grandmother's ring.
   Here *di* means *belonging to*.

5. Ha trovato il suo vecchio orsetto **fra** i giocattoli in soffitta.
   He found his old teddy among / amongst the toys in the attic.
   Some people say *tra* instead of *fra*. Either is fine.

6. **Da** quale regione venite?
   What region do you come from?
   A basic example of *da* meaning *from*.

7. **Malgrado** la tua indifferenza io continuo a volerti bene.
   I still love you, inspite of your indifference.
   Nonostante is also correct.

8. **Durante** il mese di agosto siamo stati in Basilicata.
   We spent the month of August in Basilicata.
   Because the month was spent *in the past*, choose *durante* to translate *for*.

9. Andremo in Basilicata **per** un mese.
   We're going to Basilicata for a month.
   Because the month has *not yet taken place*, choose *per* to translate *for*.

10. Siamo in Basilicata **da** un mese.
    We've been in Basilicata for a month.
    Because the month *began in the past* and is still *continuing into the present*, use *da* to translate *for*.

11. Aspettami **davanti** al cinema.
    Wait for me in front of the movie theatre.
    Here we want *IN FRONT OF* (position), so we use *davanti* instead of *prima di* (time).

12. Mi faresti scendere **al** centro commerciale?
    Could you drop me off at the mall?
    A combines with *il* to produce *AT THE*.

13. Cosa c'è **nel** frigo?
    What's in the fridge?
    Here we contract *in + il* to make *IN THE*.

14. Ama la ragazza **con** le lentiggini.
    He loves the girl with the freckles.
    An easy one, *con* is the only choice for *with*.

15. Si sono conosciuti **in** aereo.
    They met on the plane.
    Always use *IN* for a vehicle of transportation.

16. Telefonagli **prima** delle 17.
    Call him (or them) before 5 pm.
    To express *before* in the sense of time, we choose *prima di*.

17. Telefonagli **verso** le 17.
    Call him (or them) around 5 pm.
    To express *towards* in the sense of time, we need *verso*.

18. È partito **senza** salutarci.
    He left without saying good-bye.
    Senza is the only choice for *without*.

19. Ci invita **da** lui.
    He's inviting us to his place.
    Da expresses *at his home* succinctly and neatly.

20. **Quanto a** me, vado a letto.
    As for me, I'm going to bed.
    Quanto a means *as for*.

Prepositional Contractions

The definite article contracts with many common prepositions to allow for fluidity in pronunciation. Study the following chart and you will see that the formation rules are easy to discern:

le preposizioni articolate

di	del	dello	dell'	della	dei	degli	delle
a	al	allo	all'	alla	ai	agli	alle
da	dal	dallo	dall'	dalla	dai	dagli	dalle
in	nel	nello	nell'	nella	nei	negli	nelle
su	sul	sullo	sull'	sulla	sui	sugli	sulle
	il	**lo**	**l'**	**la**	**i**	**gli**	**le**

The preposition **con** no longer contracts in modern Italian, but you will still see an occasional **col** and sometimes **coi**. **Per**, **tra** and **fra** do not contract at all.

Drill 34: Prepositional Contractions

Supply the correct form of the necessary CONTRACTION.

1. Il professore spiega la lezione _____ studenti. (a)

2. Ci sono due semestri _____ anno accademico. (in)

3. Mi piace mettere il limone _____ tè freddo. (in)

4. Non metto zucchero _____ caffè. (in)

5. In autunno le foglie colorate cadono _____ alberi. (da)

6. In primavera ci sono molti bei fiori _____ giardini. (in)

7. Gli zii arrivano _____ otto domani mattina. (a)

8. Oggi pranziamo _____ una. (a)

9. Parliamo _____ amici italiani. (di)

10. Spedisco una lettera _____ nonni. (a)

11. Ho bisogno _____ penna rossa per correggere. (di)

12. Ho messo i tovaglioli accanto _____ piatti. (a)

13. Io lavoro _____ ristorante (in) vicino _____ banca. (a)

14. Pago in contanti _____ cassa. (a)

15. Ci sediamo _____ sedie. (su)

16. Metto un po' di formaggio _____ gnocchi. (su)

17. Tengo il quaderno _____ zaino. (in)

18. Ecco la casa _____ nonni. (di)

19. Ecco il foglio _____ studente. (di)

20. Vuoi un po' di sugo _____ spaghetti? (su)

Explanations and Answers to Drill 34

1. Il professore spiega la lezione **agli** studenti.
   *The teacher explains the lesson **to the** students. **a + gli = agli***

2. Ci sono due semestri **nell'** anno accademico.
   *There are two semesters **in the** academic year. **in + l' = nell'***

3. Mi piace mettere il limone **nel** tè freddo.
   *I like to put lemon in ice tea. **in + il = nel***
   Note the presence of the definite article in front of both generalized nouns.

4. Non metto zucchero **nel** caffè.
   *I don't put sugar in my coffee. **in + il = nel***
   Note that the possessive adjective is omitted. The coffee is presumed to be mine.

5. In autunno le foglie colorate cadono **dagli** alberi.
   *Colorful leaves fall from the trees in autumn. **da + gli = dagli***

6. In primavera ci sono molti bei fiori **nei** giardini.
   *In spring, there are many beautiful flowers **in the** gardens. **in + i = nei***

7. Gli zii arrivano **alle** otto domani mattina.
   *My aunt and uncle arrive tomorrow morning at 8 o'clock. **a + le = alle***
   Remember we say *sono le otto* when telling time.

8. Oggi pranziamo **all'** una.
   *We're having lunch at 1:00 today. **a + l' = all'***
   An Italian *pranzo* is hearty fare, usually the largest meal of the day.

9. Parliamo **degli** amici italiani.
   *We're talking about our Italian friends. **di + gli = degli***

10. Spedisco una lettera **ai** nonni.
    *I send a letter to my grandparents. **a + i' = ai***

11. Ho bisogno **della** penna rossa per correggere.
    *I need the red pen to correct (the papers). bisogna **di + la = della***

12. Ho messo i tovaglioli accanto **ai** piatti. *accanto **a** + **i** = **ai***
    I put the napkins next to the plates.

13. Io lavoro **nel** ristorante vicino **alla** banca.
    *I work in the restaurant near the bank. **in** + **il** = **nel**, vicino **a** + **la** = **alla***

14. Pago in contanti **alla** cassa.
    *I pay cash at the register. **a** + **la** = **alla***

15. Ci sediamo **sulle** sedie.
    *We sit on the chairs. **su** + **le** = **sulle***

16. Metto un po' di formaggio **sugli** gnocchi.
    *I put a little cheese on the potato dumplings. **su** + **gli** = **sugli***

17. Tengo il quaderno **nello** zaino.
    *I keep my notebook in my bookbag. **in** + **lo** = **nello***
    Italian consistently leaves out the possessive adjective wherever owner-
    ship is obvious.

18. Ecco la casa **dei** nonni.
    Here's my grandparent's house. la casa ***di** + **i** = **dei** (possession with di)*

19. Ecco il foglio **dello** studente.
    Here's the student's paper. il foglio ***di** + **lo** = **dello** (possession with di)*
    Here the contraction acts a possessor.

20. Vuoi un po'di sugo **sugli** spaghetti?
    *Do you want a little sauce on the spaghetti? **su** + **gli** = **sugli***

Conjunctions

There are two types of conjunctions. *Coordinating* conjuctions simply **link** two words or phrases. *Subordinating* conjunctions connect a **dependent clause** to a **main clause**.

Coordinating Conjunctions

Many coordinating conjunctions express *sequence*, such as **prima** and **anzitutto** *(first)*, **infine** *(finally)*, **poi** and **dopo** *(then)*. Others, like **e** *(and)*, **inoltre**, or **d'altronde** *(besides)* and **ancora** *(in addition)*, simply *add* or *enhance*. Still others, such as **o** *(or)*, **ma** *(but)*, **purtroppo** *(yet)*, **comunque**, **però**, **tuttavia** (all variants of *however)* and **nondimeno** *(nevertheless)*, provide *opposition* or *contrast*.

There is also a group of coordinating conjunctions which conveys *consequence*. Examples include: **quindi**, **perciò** *(therefore)*, and **di conseguenza** *(consequently)*. **Allora** can fit into either category as it may mean *then* sequentially, as well as *then* or *so*, consequentially.

A few conjunctions have two parts, like this:

> O resti o te ne vai.
> *Either you stay or you go.*

> Metterò **sia** gli zoccoletti **sia** i tacchi alti.
> *I'm going to wear either my clogs or my heels.*

> Non aveva **né** il carattere **né** la pazienza per essere madre.
> *She had neither the temperament nor the patience to be a mother.*

> Vuoi prendere *sia* la tua valigia *che* la mia?
> *Would you take both your suitcase and mine?*

Study the following examples and you will see that Italian coordinating conjunctions work much like their English counterparts.

> Ho messo **e** sale **e** pepe.
> *I added both salt **and** pepper.*

> Vorresti qualcosa da mangiare **o** da bere?
> *Would you like something to eat **or** to drink?*

> Le piacerebbe andare **ma** non può.
> *She would like to go but she can't.*

Ti lascerò questa porcellana **perchè** ti piace tantissimo.
I'll leave you this china because you like it so much.

Faceva tanto freddo ieri sera, **allora** non sono uscita.
*It was cold last night **so** I didn't go out.*

Non ho studiato affatto, **quindi** sono stato bocciato.
*I didn't study at all, **so** (therefore) I flunked.*

Finalmente gli ha concesso il permesso.
*He **finally** gave his permission.*

Non ho molta fame. **Inoltre**, sono a dieta.
*I'm not very hungry. **Besides**, I'm on a diet.*

Suo marito è morto giovane, **perciò** ha dovuto provvedere ai suoi figli da sola.
Her husband died young, so she had to support her children all by herself.

Anzitutto, devi stendere la tovaglia.
***First**, you must spread the tablecloth.*

Dopo, tu apparecchi la tavola.
***Next** (then, after) you set the table.*

Poi, disponi i fiori.
Then *you arrange the flowers.*

È un buon voto, **comunque** non è un 10.
*It's a good grade, **however**, it's not a 10 (100).*

È vegetariana, **tuttavia**, mangia un po' di pesce di quando in quando.
*She's a vegetarian, **yet**, she'll have a little fish once in a while.*

Questo film ti piacerà. **D'altronde** ha vinto un David di Donatello.
*You will like the film. **Besides**, it won a David.* (Italian film award)

Il povero ometto **non** ha **né** tetto, **né** amici.
*The poor fellow has **neither** home nor friends.*

Subordinating Conjunctions

It's essential to know which subordinating conjunctions are followed by the *indicative*, and which require the *subjunctive*. The asterisk (*) signals expressions requiring the subjunctive. Note them with care. Subordinating conjunctions can be categorized just like the coordinating conjunctions. Temporal conjunctions and conjunctions of *sequence* include: **quando** (*when*), **appena**, *(as soon as)*, **dopo che** and **prima che*** (*before and after*), **mentre,** and **tanto che**, (variations of *while*), and **finché** (*as long as*).

Conjunctions which convey *consequence* or *cause* include: **poiché, giacché** and **siccome**, *(since)*, **perchè** *(because)*, **come**, and **come che*** *(as, just as, anyway)*. Other conjunctions of *consequence* are **perciò, affinché*, cosicché***, and **di / in maniera che***, all of which are variants of *so, so that,* or *in order that.*

The subordinating conjunctions which *oppose* include **benché*, sebbene*, quantunque*** and **malgrado*** *(even though, although, in spite of)*.

There are also subordinates which *qualify* by *restricting* or *limiting*. They include: **a meno che non***(*unless*), **finché non** *(until)*, **purché*, a patto che*** *(provided that)*, and **per paura che*** *(for fear that)*.

Study the following examples carefully:

> Vorrei essere un suo studente **prima che** *vada* in pensione.
> *I'd like to be in his class before he retires.*

> Ti farò segno **appena** il volo atterrerà.
> *I'll let you know as soon as my flight lands.*

> Verrà, **a meno che non** *abbia* una partita di calcio.
> *He'll come unless he has a soccer game.*

> Vi manderò in vacanza **a patto che** vi comportiate bene.
> *I'll send you on vacation provided that you behave.*

> Mia sorella gioca a tennis con nostro fratello, **mentre** leggo.
> *My sister plays tennis with our brother while (during which time) I read.*

> Aspetta **finché non** l'avrai visto.
> *Wait until you've seen it.*

Drill 35: Coordinating and Subordinating Conjunctions

First select the conjunction needed to convey the English cue. Then provide the required verb form, deciding carefully between the *indicative* and the *subjunctive*.

1. Mi metto a dieta _____ _____ qualche chilo.
    until   I lose

2. Papà taglia la carne a pezzettini _____ il bambino _____
    so that   can
    prenderli con le dita.

3. Andremo in Italia _____ noi _____ il tempo e i soldi
    as soon as   have
    necessari.

4. _____ _____, porto sempre il mio vecchio apparecchio
    When I   travel
    _____ qualcuno me _____.
    for fear that   will steal

5. Sceglieranno _____ una casa di campagna _____ una villa
    either   or
    vicino alla spiaggia.

6. Questo abito dell'anno scorso non ti va più, _____ _____
    since   you grew
    di 30 centimetri!

7. _____, _____ darlo al tuo fratellino.
    Therefore   you can

8. Non ci hanno invitati, _____ per me _____ uguale.
    yet   is

9. Vogliono partire presto domani mattina, _____ mi dà molto
    however
    fastidio.

10. Spiacente, ma sono sommersa di lavoro e _____, non mi sento
    besides
    tanto bene.

Answers and Explanations to Drill 35

1. Mi metto a dieta **finché non perdo** qualche chilo.
   I'm going on a diet until I lose a few pounds. (1 chilo = 2.2 lbs.)

2. Papà taglia la carne a pezzettini **affinché** il bambino **possa** prenderli con le dita.
   Dad cuts the meat into little pieces so the baby can pick it up with his fingers.
   Other correct answers include: **cosicché**, **in modo che** and **in maniera che**. All require the subjunctive.

3. Andremo in Italia **appena avremo** il tempo e i soldi necessari.
   We'll go to Italy as soon as we have the time and the money.
   Did you remember to use the future tense here? (see rules on implied future)

4. **Quando viaggio**, porto sempre il mio vecchio apparecchio **per paura che** qualcuno me lo **rubi**.
   When I travel I always bring my old camera for fear that someone will steal it.
   An expression of fear is followed by the subjunctive.

5. Sceglieranno **o** una casa di campagna **o** una villa vicino alla spiaggia.
   They'll choose either a country house or a villa near the beach.
   You can also use **sia**, repeated.

6. Questo abito dell'anno scorso non ti va più, **siccome sei cresciuto** di 30 centimetri!
   Last year's suit doesn't fit you any more since you've grown almost a foot taller!
   You could also use **poiché**. (1 foot = 30.48 centimeters)

7. **Quindi / perciò, puoi** darlo al tuo fratellino.
   So (therefore) you can give it to your little brother.
   Either conjunction works here.

8. Non ci hanno invitati, **tuttavia / comunque / però** per me è uguale.
   They didn't invite us but that's fine with me.
   We use the coordinating conjunction *tuttavia* to convey *yet*.
   But or *however* would work as well.

9. Vogliono partire presto domani mattina, **tuttavia** mi dà molto fastidio.
   They want to leave early tomorrow morning but that's a big hassle for me.
   You could also use **però**.

10. Spiacente, ma sono sommersa di lavoro e **d'altronde**, non mi sento tanto bene.
    I'm so sorry but I'm up to my neck in work and besides, I don't feel well.
    You could also use **inoltre** here to mean *besides*.

Negations

Besides the basic **non**, all other Italian negations have at least two parts which surround the verb entirely. They consist of **non**, which precedes the verb, and a **second word** which follows the verb directly. Here are the negations which you should know:

non	not	Non capisce.
non...affatto	not at all	Non capisce affatto
non...mai	never, not ever	Non capisce mai.
non...né...né...	neither, nor	Non capisce né te né me.
non...neanche nemmeno neppure	not even	Non ama neanche sua madre. Non ama nemmeno sua madre. Non ama neppure sua madre.
non...nessuno	no one, nobody	Non ama nessuno.
non...niente	nothing, not anything	Non capisce niente.
non ...nulla	nothing, not anything	Non capisce nulla.
non...più	no longer, no more	Non mi ama più.
non...nessun	no, not one, not any	Non capisce nessuna domanda.
...alcun		Non è fiorito alcun bulbo.

Nessuno, nessun + noun, and niente can also act as subjects. In this case, they drop **non**:

> Nessuno mi capisce.
> *Nobody, no one understands me.*

> Nessun giardino è fiorito.
> *Not one garden bloomed.*

> Non succede niente.
> *Nothing's happening.*

If a negation appears without a verb, there is no need for **non**.

> Chi è? Nessuno.
> *Who's there? No one.*

> Che cosa fai? Niente.
> *What are you doing? Nothing.*

> Non gli piace il pesce. Neanche a me.
> *He doesn't like fish. Neither do I. (Me neither.)*

Positioning Negations

If there is a pronoun in front of the verb, the **non** will move back to accommodate it, so that the negation encircles the pronoun and verb combination.

> **Non** si alza **mai**.
> *He never gets up.*

> **Non** la vcdo **affatto**.
> *I don't see her at all.*

In compound tenses **mai** and **più** follow the auxiliary verb. Most other negations, and those that combine with nouns, follow the participle. Compare:

> **Non** l'ho **mai** visto.
> *I never saw him.*

> **Non** ha detto **niente**.
> *He said nothing. He didn't say anything.*

> **Non** sono **più** venuti.
> *They no longer came. They didn't come anymore.*

> **Non** ha visto **nessuno**.
> *He didn't see anyone. He saw no one.*

> **Non** hai mangiato **né** verdure, **né** carne.
> *You ate neither vegetables nor meat.*

> **Non** ho inviato **nessuna/alcuna** cartolina.
> *I didn't send one card.*

It is possible to combine negative expressions just as we would in English. Place **mai** or **più** first in the series of multiple negations. If they are both in the series, use the order **mai più**.

> **Non** ho **più niente**.
> *I have nothing more.*

> **Non** vedo **più nessuno**.
> *I don't see anyone anymore.*

> **Non** capisce **mai niente**.
> *He never understands anything.*

Non vedrò **mai nessuno!**
I won't ever see anyone!

Non vedrò **più nessuno!**
I won't see anyone anymore!

Non vedrò **mai più nessuno!**
I won't ever see anyone anymore!

Drill 36: Negations

Make a sentence with the opposite meaning by using a negation:

1. Ho un fratello.

   _____

2. Fa sempre i suoi compiti.

   _____

3. È giovane e bello.

   _____

4. Ama il suo cane. (Say that he doesn't even love his dog.)

   _____

5. Sono venuti tutti.

   _____

6. C'è ancora un po' di gelato nel congelatore.

   _____

7. Capiamo completamente.

   _____

8. Ho tutto.

   _____

9. Le è piaciuto il film. Anche a noi.

   _____

10. Gli piace tutto.

   _____

11. Vedo sempre tutti.

_____

12. Ha sempre fatto i suoi compiti

_____

13. È già pronta.

_____

14. Condivide tutto.

_____

15. Vuoi qualcosa?

_____

16. Tutte le ragazze sono andate via. (verb must change to singular!)

_____

17. Tutti i ragazzi sono rimasti. (verb must change to singular!)

_____

18. Hai detto qualcosa.

_____

19. È stata bocciata in matematica. Anch'io.

_____

20. Ho ricevuto molte cartoline.

_____

Answers and Explanations to Drill 36

1. Ho un fratello.
   Non ho fratelli.
   Note the loss of *un* and the switch to the plural!
   (The *indefinite article* is omitted in a *partititve* negation.)

2. Fa sempre i suoi compiti.
   Non fa **mai** i suoi compiti.
   NON... MAI is the negative opposite of SEMPRE.

3. È giovane e bello.
   Non è **né** giovane **né** bello.
   NON NÉ... NÉ... is needed to negate TWO adjective traits at the same time.

4. Ama il suo cane.
   Non ama **neanche** il suo cane.
   You could also use **nemmeno** or **neppure**.

5. Sono venuti tutti.
   Nessuno è venuto.
   NESSUNO provides the negative opposite of TUTTI. Observe the switch from plural to singular in the verb form as *nessuno* is inherently singular.

6. C'è ancora un po' di gelato nel congelatore.
   Non c'è **più** gelato nel congelatore.
   Note the absence of an article in front of *gelato* in the *partitive* negation.

7. Capiamo completamente.
   Non capiamo **affatto**.
   We create the opposite of *completely* with NON...AFFATTO (not at all).

8. Ho tutto.
   Non ho **niente**.
   NON... NIENTE is the negative opposite of TUTTO.

9. Le è piaciuto molto il film. Anche a noi.
   Non le è piaciuto il film. **Neanche** a noi.
   Non le è piaciuto **affatto** il film. **Neanche** a noi. (also possible)
   As there is no exact *negative* opposite for *molto*, more than one response
   is possible. The exact opposite, *poco*, is not a negation.

10. Gli piace tutto.
    Non gli piace **niente**.
    Non … NIENTE is the opposite of TUTTO.

11. Vedo sempre tutti.
    Non vedo **mai nessuno**.
    NESSUNO is the opposite of TUTTI, and MAI is the opposite of
    SEMPRE. *Mai* precedes all other negatives.

12. Ha sempre fatto i suoi compiti
    Non ha **mai** fatto i suoi compiti
    Notice the position of the single syllable *mai* in the compound past,
    directly after the auxiliary verb.

13. È già pronta.
    Non è **ancora** pronta.
    NON …ANCORA, *not yet* opposes GIÀ, *already*.

14. Condivide tutto.
    Non condivide **niente**.
    As in problem number 8, NON… NIENTE, *nothing*, opposes TUTTO,
    everything.

15. Vuoi qualcosa?
    Non vuoi **niente**.
    NON… NIENTE is also the opposite of QUALCOSA, *something*.

16. Tutte le ragazze sono andate via.
    Nessuna ragazza è andata via.
    Not one girl went away, as opposed to *All the girls went away*, hence the
    verb change to singular. *Non* is absent when the negation is the subject
    of the verb.

17. Tutti i ragazzi sono rimasti.
    Nessun ragazzo è rimasto.
    The verb must now be singular to match. *Not one boy remained.*

18. Hai detto qualcosa.
    Non hai detto **niente**.
    Use NON... NIENTE, *nothing*, to oppose QUALCOSA, *something*.

19. È stata bocciata in matematica. Anch'io
    Non è state bocciata in matematica. **Neanch**'io.
    Me neither, provides the opposite of *me too,* ANCH'IO.

20. Ho ricevuto molte cartoline.
    Non ho ricevuto cartoline.
    Non ho ricevuto **nessuna** cartolina.
    Non ho ricevuto **alcuna** cartolina.

The Infinitive

Every possible manifestation of a given verb is represented by the infinitive; hence its name. We differentiate the three basic verb groups by the last three letters of this primary verb form. Thus we speak of **-are** verbs, **-ere** verbs, and **-ire** verbs. When you look up the meaning of a verb in the dictionary, its definition will be listed under the infinitive form. English requires two words to make its version of the infinitive. Thus *avere* means *to have*.

Italian generally uses the infinitive where English would use a present participle or gerund:

> L'ho sentita piangere.
> *I heard her crying.*

> Li ho visti uscire.
> *I saw them going out.*

> Amo ballare.
> *I love dancing. I love to dance.*

> Ho voglia di dormire.
> *I feel like sleeping. I want to sleep.*

> È partito senza salutarci.
> *He left without saying good-bye.*

> Lavati le mani prima di mangiare.
> *Wash your hands before eating.*

> Invece di aspettare il giorno dopo, apriamo i nostri regali la Viglilia di Natale.
> *Instead of waiting for the next day, we open our gifts on Christmas Eve.*

The Italian infinitive replaces the English gerund used as a noun:

> Aspettare è noioso.
> *Waiting is a bore.*

> Il mio sogno sarebbe di andare in Italia.
> *Going to Italy would be my dream.*

Here it replaces a past participle:

> Vietato introdurre cani.
> *No dogs allowed.*

Infinitives also appear after other verbs in certain set expressions:

> Vuoi andare a prenderci una pizza?
> *Do you want to go get us a pizza?*
> andare a prendere: to go and get

> Mi sono fatta consegnare una pizza a domicilio.
> *I had a pizza delivered.*
> fare portare, fare consegnare: to have delivered, brought

> Ho sentito dire che era tornata.
> *I heard that she had returned.*
> sentire dire: to hear that

> Il bimbo ha lasciato cadere la sua tettarella.
> *The baby dropped his pacifier.*
> lasciare cadere: to drop

> Vieni a prendere i tuoi spiccioli.
> *Come and get your change.*
> venire a cercare: to come and get

> Che vuole dire?
> *What does it mean?*
> volere dire: to mean

The infinitive may replace a command form in directions and instructions. This is quite common in recipes:

> Aggiungere il formaggio fuso e mescolare bene.
> *Add the melted cheese and mix well.*

The PAST INFINITIVE is made with the infinitive of the auxiliary verb (avere or essere) and the past participle:

> Dopo aver finito il mio compito, sono tornato a casa.
> *After finishing my homework, I went home.*

> Gli dispiaceva di esser arrivato in ritardo.
> *He was sorry for arriving late. (for having arrived late)*

Drill 37: The Infinitive

Complete the sentence using an infinitive expression:

1. Ho passato tutta la notte _____.
   $\quad\quad\quad\quad\quad\quad\quad\quad\quad\quad$ without sleeping

2. Vorrei parlarti _____.
   $\quad\quad\quad\quad\quad\quad\quad$ before leaving

3. _____ due uova e _____ i bianchi dai tuorli
   $\quad$ Break $\quad\quad\quad\quad\quad\quad\quad\quad\quad$ separate

4. Ti ho visto _____ la Befana!
   $\quad\quad\quad\quad\quad\quad\quad$ kissing

5. Va pazza _____.
   $\quad\quad\quad\quad\quad$ cooking

6. Vietato _____.
   $\quad\quad\quad\quad$ smoking

7. _____ per _____.
   $\quad$ Seeing $\quad\quad\quad\quad$ believing

8. Che cosa _____ _____?
   $\quad\quad\quad\quad$ mean $\quad\quad\quad$ - tu

9. Tu _____ _____ _____ gli occhiali.
   $\quad\quad\quad\quad\quad\quad\quad$ dropped

10. Non mi ricordo di _____ _____ quella lettera.
    $\quad\quad\quad\quad\quad\quad\quad\quad$ having $\quad\quad\quad$ written

Answers and Explanations to Drill 37

1. Ho passato tutta la notte **senza dormire**.
   I spent the whole night without sleeping.
   Here the English gerund is expressed with an infinitive preceded by a preposition.

2. Vorrei parlarti **prima di partire.**
   I'd like to speak to you before leaving.
   Here is another preposition plus infinitive combination to replace an English gerund.

3. **Rompere** due uova e **separare** i bianchi dei tuorli.
   Break two eggs and separate the whites from the yolks.
   The infinitive is commonly used to replace an imperative in instructions.

4. Ti ho visto **baciare** la Befana!
   I saw you kissing Befana!
   Note how the English present participle converts to the infinitive here.

5. Va pazza per **cucinare**.
   Cooking is her passion.
   When a verb is used as a noun, put it in the infinitive form.

6. Vietato **fumare.**
   No smoking.
   Use the infinitive whenever the verb is used as noun.

7. **Vedere** per **credere**.
   Seeing is believing.
   As in the two preceding problems, these infinitives are used as nouns.

8. Che cosa **vuoi dire**?
   What do you mean?
   Volere dire is one of several fixed expressions constructed with infinitives.

9. Tu **hai lasciato cadere** gli occhiali.
   You dropped your glasses.
   Lasciare cadere is a fixed infinitive expression meaning *to drop*.

10. Non mi ricordo di **aver scritto** quella lettera.
    I don't remember having written that letter.
    This is an example of the perfect or past infinitive.

A or *Di*?

Test questions are sometimes based on which preposition belongs to a given verbal locution. Train yourself to establish the needed preposition (if there is one) whenever you learn a new verb. Here are some common combinations:

abituarsi **a**	*to get used to*
abusare **di**	*to abuse, overindulge in*
accontentarsi **di**	*to be content with*
addossarsi **a**	*to lean on or against*
agganciare qualcosa **a**	*to hook or attach to*
aiutare qualcuno **a** fare qualcosa	*to help someone do something*
appartenere **a**	*to belong to*
arrivare **a**	*to reach, to achieve a result, to find a solution*
cercare **di**	*to try to*
chiedere **a** qualcuno **di** fare qualcosa	*to ask someone to do something*
cominciare **a**	*to begin to*
condannare qualcuno **a**	*to condemn someone to*
consigliare **a** qualcuno **di** fare qualcosa	*to advise someone to do something*
continuare **a**	*to continue to*
costringere qualcuno **a**	*to force someone to*
credere **di, in**	*to believe in* as in: *Crede di no.* *Crede in Dio.*
decidere **di**	*to decide to*
dimenticare **di**	*to forget to*
dire **a** qualcuno **di** fare qualcosa	*to tell someone to do something*
imparare **a** fare qualcosa	*to learn to do something*
insegnare **a** qualcuno **a** fare qualcosa	*to teach someone to do something*
fingere **di**	*to pretend*
finire **di**	*to finish*
giocare **a**	*to play a game, to play at something*

mettersi **a**	*to start to, to begin*
mostrare **a**	*to show*
parlare **a** qualcuno **di** qualcosa	*to speak to someone about something*
pregare qualcuno **di** fare qualcosa	*to beg someone to do something*
proporre **di**	*to suggest, to propose*
provare **a** fare qualcosa	*to try to do something*
ricordarsi **di**	*to remember*
ringraziare qualcuno **di** aver fatto qualcosa	*to thank someone for doing something,* **per** *for something*
risalire **a**	*to go back in time, to trace back*
riuscire **a**	*to succeed in*
scappare **di**	*to escape from*
scrivere **a**	*to write to someone*
smettere **di**	*to stop, to cease an activity as in: Ha smesso di fumare.*
sognare **di**	*to dream of, about*
spedire **a**	*to send to*
sperare **di**	*to hope to*
telefonare **a** qualcuno	*to call someone on the phone*
temere **di**	*to fear*
tentare **di**	*to try*
trattarsi **di**	*to be about, to be a question of – impersonal*
ubbidire **a**	*to obey*
venire **a**	*to come to*

Idioms based on **avere** also use a preposition:

avere bisogno **di**	*to need*
avere voglia **di**	*to feel like, to want*
avere vergogna **di**	*to be ashamed of*
avere paura **di**	*to be afraid of*

Expressions based on **essere** use a preposition as well:

essere contento **di**	*to be happy with*
essere fiero **di**	*to be proud of*
essere geloso **di**	*to be jealous of*
essere pronto **a**	*to be ready to*

Many other prepositions are encountered as integral parts of verbal expressions. Here are just a few examples:

Ho molto **da** fare.
I've got a lot to do.

Ho votato **contro** la mozione.
I voted against the motion.

Scoppiò **in** lacrime.
She burst into tears.

Drill 38: Using the Correct Preposition After the Verb

Supply the appropriate preposition, make a contraction with the article if necessary:

1. Ho tentato _____ scappare _____ casa quando ero piccolo.

2. Dovrei scrivere _____ (+i) nonni.

3. Credo _____ poter venire.

4. Ho chiesto _____ papà _____ aspettarci qui.

5. Hai ringraziato il tuo professore _____ averti aiutato?

6. Gioca bene _____ calcio.

7. Speriamo _____ tornare in Italia.

8. Il cane ubbidisce _____ (+la) sua proprietaria.

9. Mannaggia! Si mette _____ piovere!

10. Sei fiero _____ (+il) tuo voto?

11. Ho bisogno _____ studiare stasera.

12. Mostra le foto _____ sua sorella.

13. _____ che cosa si tratta?

14. Ho spedito un regalino _____ Mario.

15. Non dimenticare _____ scriverci!

16. Siamo pronti _____ andare.

17. Ha imparato _____ pattinare.

18. Hai finito _____ gridare?

19. Mi sono fatto male _____ (+il) collo!

20. Il bimbo cercava _____ farsi capire.

21. Chi ti ha insegnato _____ sciare così?

22. Cavolo! Non ho più voglia _____ sgobbare!

23. Sono riuscita _____ superare l'esame.

24. Smetti _____ fare lo scemo!

25. Dite _____ (+i) bimbi _____ entrare. È ora di mangiare.

Answers and Explanations to Drill 38

1. Ho tentato **di** scappare **di** casa quando ero piccolo.
   I tried to run away from home when I was little.
   Both *tentare* and *scappare* use *di*.

2. Dovrei scrivere **ai** nonni.
   I should write to my grandparents.
   Scrivere always uses **a** in front of its **human** object.

3. Credo di poter venire.
   I think I can come.
   Credere uses **di** in front of the infinitive, and also before *sì* and *no*.

4. Ho chiesto **a** papà **di** aspettarci qui.
   I asked Dad to wait for us here.
   Chiedere uses **a** for its human object, and **di** in front of an infinitive.

5. Hai ringraziato il tuo professore **di** averti aiutato?
   Did you thank your teacher for helping you?
   Ringraziare uses **di** to thank someone *for doing something* and **per** when thanking someone for *a thing*.

6. Gioca bene **a** calcio.
   He/she plays soccer well.
   Giocare always uses **a** with games.

7. Speriamo **di** tornare in Italia.
   We hope to return to Italy.
   Suppy **di** in front of the infinitive when using *sperare*.

8. Il cane ubbidisce **alla** sua proprietaria.
   The dog obeys its owner.
   Combine *a* + *la* to make *alla*.

9. Mannaggia! Si mette **a** piovere!
   Darn! It's starting to rain.
   Mettersi uses *a* in front of an infinitive.

10. Sei fiero **del** tuo voto?
    Are you proud of your grade?
    This is a combination of *essere* plus adjective. **Di** often follows.

11. Ho bisogno **di** studiare stasera.
    I need to study tonight.
    Avere expressions use **di.**

12. Mostra le foto **a** sua sorella.
    She shows the photos to her sister.
    Mostrare uses **a** in front of its human (indirect) object.

13. **Di** che cosa si tratta?
    What's it about?
    Trattarsi is a useful verb to master. It always takes **di.**

14. Ho spedito un regalino **a** Mario.
    I sent a little gift to Mario.
    Spedire needs **a** in front of its human (indirect) object.

15. Non dimenticare **di** scriverci.
    Don't forget to write to us.
    Dimenticare and *ricordarsi* both require **di** in front of an infinitive.

16. Siamo pronti **ad** andare.
    We're ready to go.
    Essere pronto uses **a** before an infinitive. The letter "*d*" is added to the little preposition **a** when the following word also begins with a vowel. This is done to make pronunciation easier and prevents the vowel sound from being lost. The same "*d*" is added to the conjunction **e** (and) if a vowel follows. Thus we say *"Gianni ed io"*. This is similar to the English use of *an* instead of *a* in front of a noun like *effort*.

17. Ha imparato **a** pattinare.
    He learned to skate.
    Use **a** with *imparare*.

18. Hai finito **di** gridare?
    Have you finished yelling?
    Finire uses **di**. Note how the infinitive is used to convey the English gerund.

19. Mi sono fatto male **al** collo!
    I hurt my neck!
    Compare this construction to *Mi fa male il collo. (My neck hurts.)*

20. Il bimbo cercava **di** farsi capire.
    The baby tried to make himself understood.
    Cercare needs **di** *before an infinitive.*

21. Chi ti ha insegnato **a** sciare così?
    Who taught you to ski like that?
    Insegnare uses **a** in front of an infinitive *as well as* in front of its human object, making **ti** an *indirect* object pronoun.

22. Cavolo! Non ho più voglia **di** sgobbare!
    Hey! I don't feel like cramming anymore!
    The expression *avere voglia* takes **di** in front of an infinitive *or* an object. (Ho voglia di un gelato.)

23. Sono riuscita **a** superare l'esame.
    I was able to pass the exam.
    Use **a** with *riuscire.*

24. Smetti **di** fare lo scemo!
    Stop clowning around!
    Smettere uses **di** before an infinitive.

25. Dite **ai** bambini **di** entrare. È ora di mangiare.
    Tell the children to come in, it's time to eat.
    Dire needs **a** for its **human** object and **di** in front of an infinitive.

The Present Participle

To make the present participle we add **-ante** to the infinitive stem of -ARE verbs, and **-ente** to the infinitive stem of -ERE and -IRE verbs. This creates the equivalent of *-ing* in English.

Uses of the Present Participle

1. The present participle is often used as an adjective. Since it ends in **e**, it behaves just like any other class II adjective, with one singular form for both masculine and feminine nouns, and one plural form for both, like this:

   una vittoria schiacciante
   a crushing victory

   un vino spumeggiante
   a sparkling wine

   un film divertente
   an entertaining film

   occhi raggianti
   bright, shining eyes

   granite rinfrescanti
   refreshing flavored ices

2. The Italian present participle may be used just like its English counterpart, *however*, its use is much less common in Italian than it is in English. It can appear as a noun, like this:

   l'insegnante, *teacher*, from insegnare
   il conoscente, *aquaintance*, from conoscere

   It can also replace a relative clause, like this:

   I limoni provenienti da Sorrento sono i migliori.
   *Lemons **that come** from Sorrento are the best.*

Drill 39: The Present Participle

Supply the correct form of the present participle in the following sentences:

1. C'era una pioggia _____. (hard, driving)

2. Il mio zaino è molto _____. (heavy)

3. In Italia ci sono molti _____ popolari. (singers)

4. Il sole era _____. (shining)

5. Il volo _____ da Filadefia arriva con 15 minuti d'anticipio. (coming from)

Answers and Explanations to Drill 39

1. C'era una pioggia **battente**.
   There was a driving rain.
   This is a present participle used as an adjective.

2. Il mio zaino è molto **pesante.**
   My book bag is very heavy.
   Used as an adjective, this present participle comes from the verb *pesare*,
   to weigh.

3. In Italia ci sono molti **cantanti** popolari.
   There are many popular singers in Italy.
   This present participle is used as a noun. It comes from *cantare*.

4. Il sole era **splendente**.
   The sun was shining.
   Here we use the present participle of the verb *splendere*.

5. Il volo **proveniente** da Filadelfia arriva con quindici minuti d'anticipio.
   The flight coming from Philadelphia is 15 minutes ahead of schedule.
   The present participle replaces the clause *che proviene*.

The Gerund

To make the Italian gerund we add **-ando** to the infinitive stem of -ARE verbs, and **-endo** to the infinitive stem of -ERE and -IRE verbs. There are only a few irregulars, as follows:

bere: *bevendo*

condurre: *conducendo*

dire: *dicendo*

fare: *facendo*

porre: *ponendo*

trarre: *traendo*

The Italian gerund is invariable; it doesn't *agree* like a past or present participle.

Uses of the Gerund

1. The gerund can simply express *how* the main action is achieved:

   Mi ha risposto, sorridendo.
   She answered me smiling.

2. The **gerund** is the best construction to translate an English *verb of motion plus preposition*, such as *to run up to*, or *to skip across:*

   Il bambino si è precipitato verso suo padre correndo.
   The child ran up to his father.

   Abbiamo attraversato il ponte saltando.
   We skipped across the bridge.

3. Use the **gerund** of **AVERE** or **ESSERE** with **a past participle** to create a compound for an activity that took place before the action of the main verb, like this:

   Avendo lavorato ben bene, mi sono addormentata soddisfatta.
   Having worked hard, I fell asleep pleased with myself.

   Essendo già caduta una volta, scendeva le scale con attenzione.
   Having already fallen once, she came down the stairs carefully.

4. Combine the gerund with the present tense of *stare* to create *the present progressive*, a special present tense used to emphasize the continuing present activity. A mother who is constantly interrupted by her child might turn to him and state firmly *Sto parlando!* This easy construction stresses the on-going nature of her activity. Combining the gerund with the imperfect of *stare* creates the past tense version.

> Stavo parlando con la nonna e tu mi interrompevi sempre!
> *I was talking to Grandma and you kept interrupting me.*

Drill 40: The Gerund

Supply the correct form of the gerund in the following sentences:

1. Si torceva una ciocca di capelli mentre stava _____ (talking) al suo ragazzo.

2. Camminavo in punta di piedi, _____ (knowing) che il bambino dormiva.

3. Ci ha salutati _____ (on his way out).

4. Il bimbo mi ha baciato _____. (jumped up to)

5. _____ (having passed) gli esami, gli alunni sono partiti.

6. _____ (having forgotten) la mia chiave, sono tornato a cercarla.

7. _____ (having arrived) troppo tardi, siamo rincasati.

8. _____ (cooking), mi sono bruciata il dito.

9. Camminavano _____ (laughing).

10. È tornata a casa _____ (dancing).

Answers and Explanations to Drill 40

1. Si torceva una ciocca di capelli mentre stava **parlando** al suo ragazzo.
   She twirled a lock of hair while talking to her boyfriend.
   The gerund conveys that two actions by the same person were taking place simultaneously.

2. Camminavo in punta di piedi, **sapendo** che il bimbo dormiva.
   I was tip-toeing, knowing that the baby was sleeping.

3. Ci ha salutati **uscendo.**
   He waved to us on his way out.
   The gerund is the best way to render an English expression of motion + preposition.

4. Il bambino mi ha baciato **saltando.**
   The child jumped up to kiss me.
   This problem is similar to the previous one. Use the gerund to recreate an English expression of motion + preposition.

5. **Avendo superato** gli esami, gli alunni sono partiti.
   Having passed their exams, the pupils left.
   A compound is created with the gerund of the auxiliary verb and the past participle of the main verb.

6. **Avendo dimenticato** la mia chiave, sono tornato a cercarla.
   Having forgotten my key, I came back to get it.
   Another example of the past compound.

7. **Essendo arrivati** troppo tardi, siamo rincasati.
   Having arrived too late, we went home.
   This past compound uses *essere* as the auxiliary verb. Note the anticipatory agreement of the participle *arrivati.*

8. **Cucinando,** mi sono bruciata il dito.
   I burned my finger cooking.
   The gerund explains how it happened.

9. Camminavano **ridendo.**
   They were walking and laughing. (at the same time)
   Two simultaneous actions; one subject.

10. È tornata a casa **ballando.**
    She came home dancing.
    Here the gerund tells how the main action (coming home) was achieved.

The Imperative

The command form of a verb is used to tell someone *what to do*, or *what not to do*. Therefore we say a command is either *affirmative* or *negative*.

A command always involves direct address as you must be speaking to someone in order to use it. Therefore it only exists in the ***you*** forms: **tu**, **Lei**, **Loro**, **voi**, and in the **noi** form which is used if you make a suggestion that includes yourself.

Commands are given in both Italian and English **without** a subject pronoun. We use the verb alone, or the verb with its object.

The Affirmative Command

Let's examine the **tu**, **noi**, and **voi** commands first. They are exactly like the present indicative forms, *with the exception of one change* which takes place in the **tu** form of the -**ARE** verb. The final letter becomes **a**, instead of *i*. There are no other changes in regular commands, just this one. Let's look at some examples of the affirmative command:

Guarda!	*Look!* (note the **a**)
Guardate!	*Look!*
Guardiamo!	*Let's look!*
Dormi bene!	*Sleep well!*
Dormite bene!	*Sleep well!*
Dormiamo bene!	*Let's sleep well!*
Finisci!	*Finish!*
Finite!	*Finish!*
Finiamo!	*Let's finish!*
Rispondi in italiano!	*Answer in Italian!*
Rispondete in italiano!	*Answer in Italian!*
Rispondiamo in italiano!	*Let's answer in Italian!*

Irregular Commands

The verbs AVERE, ESSERE, and SAPERE have irregular command forms as follows:

Abbi pazienza!	Sii gentile!	Sappi la verità!
Abbiate pazienza!	Siate gentili!	Sappiate la verità!
Abbiamo pazienza!	Siamo gentili!	Sappiamo la verità!

Some irregular verbs have two possible forms for the affirmative familiar (tu form):

Andare:	vai or va'
Dare:	dai or da'
Fare:	fai or fa'
Stare:	stai or sta'

Also irregular in the tu form: Dire: di'

Now let's take a look at the **Lei** and **Loro** command forms which are based on the present subjunctive, as follows:

Signore, parli più forte!
Signori, parlino più forte!

Dorma bene, Signore!
Dormano bene, Signori!

Metta la sua giacca qui.
Mettano la loro giacca qui.

Stia attento!
Stiano attenti!

Capisca bene quello che dico!
Capiscano bene quello che dico!

Signora, venga pure!
Signore, vengano pure!

Signora, dica pure!
Signore, dicano pure!

The Negative Command

The negative commands are easy. For **tu** we use *non* and the *entire infinitive*, like this:

Non insistere!

Non esitare!

Non piangere più!

Non dimenticare!

Non andartene!

Non dire una bugia!

Non prendere la mia fetta!

Non finire tutto il gelato!

For **noi** and **voi**, **Lei** and **Loro** we simply add *non* if front of the same verb form we used for the affirmative command:

Non mangiate quella fetta!

Non facciamo più niente!

Non aspetti!

Non aspettino!

You will find all of the rules regarding of the use of pronoun objects in command forms under **Object Pronouns in Commands**.

Drill 41: The Imperative

Change the negative command into an affirmative one:

1. Non venire alle 5! _____

2. Non stare zitto! _____

3. Non essere così! _____

4. Non andiamo stasera! _____

5. Non andare via! _____

Change the affirmative command into a negative one:

6. Abbi paura! _____

7. Spieghino perché. _____

8. Dimentichiamo. _____

9. Finisci quella bibita! _____

10. Finisca quella bibita! _____

Answers and Explanations to Drill 41

1. **Vieni alle 5!**
   Come at 5 o'clock!
   This command form is exactly like the present indicative.

2. **Stai / Sta' zitto!**
   Be quiet!
   Both forms are acceptable.

3. **Sii così!**
   Be like that!
   This is an irregular but common command form of *essere*.

4. **Andiamo stasera!**
   Let's go tonight!
   Simply remove the *non*!

5. **Vai / Va' via!**
   Go away!
   Either form is acceptable.

6. **Non avere paura!**
   Don't be afraid!
   Use *non +infinitive* for the negative **tu** form command.

7. **Non spieghino perché!**
   Don't explain why!
   Just add *non*.

8. **Non dimentichiamo!**
   Let's not forget!
   Just add *non*.

9. **Non finire quella bibita!**
   Don't finish that drink!
   Remember to use *non* plus the entire infinitive for the negative **tu** command.

10. **Non finisca quella bibita!**
    Don't finish that drink!
    Just add *non*.

Reflexive Verbs

A reflexive verb is one whose subject is also its object, as in the sentence *I cut myself*. I am the subject of *to cut* as well as the object of *to cut*. Most verbs can be both transitive and reflexive. Compare:

Ho lavato il cane.   versus   Mi sono lavato.
I washed the dog.   *I got washed.*

Here are the reflexive pronouns. Their position relative to the verb is just like any other pronoun object:

(Io) **mi** alzo.   (Io) **mi** siedo.

(Tu) **ti** alzi.   (Tu)**ti** siedi.

(Lui) **si** alza.   (Lui) **si** siede.

(Noi) **ci** alziamo   (Noi) **ci** sediamo.

(Voi) **vi** alzate.   (Voi) **vi** sedete.

(Loro) **si** alzano.   (Loro) **si** siedono.

Reciprocal Meaning in Plural Forms

The **noi, voi** and **loro** forms of reflexive verbs often express **reciprocity**. The plural subjects perform the action and receive the action:

Si baciano.   *They kiss each other.*

Reflexives in the Compound Tenses

Reflexive verbs must be conjugated with ESSERE in the compound tenses. Agreement is always made between the past participle and the subject.

Si sono addormentati a mezzanotte.
They went to sleep at midnight.

Mi sono seduta.
I sat down. (female)

Drill 42: Reflexive Verbs

Practice making the necessary agreement:

1. Elena si è addormentat_____ tardi.

2. Maria e Francesca si sono abbracciat _____ strette.

3. I ragazzi si sono fatt_____ male.

4. Tiziana, ti sei sbagliat_____!

5. Stefania si è tagliat_____ i capelli.

6. Luca si è fermat_____ al semaforo rosso.

7. Le due attrici si sono sempre odiat_____.

8. Gli studenti si sono dett_____ "arrivederci".

9. Rosario e Fabiola, quando vi siete sposat_____?

10. Francesca si è mess_____ a lavorare.

Answers and Explanations to Drill 42

1. Elena si è addormentata tardi.
   Elena fell asleep late. Elena put *herself* to sleep late.
   Note how the pronoun functions as a direct object.

2. Maria e Francesca si sono abbracciate strette.
   Maria and Francesca hugged each other tightly.

3. I ragazzi si sono fatti male.
   The boys got hurt.
   Literally: They did harm *to* themselves.

4. Tiziana, ti sei sbagliata!
   Tiziana, you were mistaken.
   Always remember to show subject agreement with reflexive verbs in any compound past.

5. Stefania si è tagliata i capelli.
   Stephanie cut her hair.
   Note how the reflexive pronoun functions as a possessive marker here.

6. Luca si è fermato al semaforo rosso.
   Luke stopped at the red light.
   A man's name can end in **a**! Make masculine singular agreement.
   Andrea (Andrew) is another example.

7. Le due attrici si sono sempre odiate.
   The two actresses always hated each other.
   This is an example of a reciprocal verb.

8. Gli studenti si sono detti "arrivederci".
   The students said goodbye to *each other.*
   Another reciprocal verb.

9. Rosario e Fabiola, quando vi siete sposati?
   Rosario and Fabiola, when did you get married?
   Reciprocal verb, when did you marry *each other*?

10. Francesca si è messa a lavorare.
    Francesca began to work.
    Literally: She put *herself* to work.

Modal Verbs

The modal verbs are DOVERE, POTERE and VOLERE. They enable, or give modality to, the infinitives that follow them. Mastery of modal verbs will expand and enhance your speaking and writing abilities immeasurably. The impersonal verbs OCCORRERE and BISOGNARE work exactly the same way.

The verb DOVERE expresses obligation, probability, or expectation.

> Mi devi 5 Euro.
> *You owe me 5 Euros.*

> Devo prendere i bambini alle tre.
> *I have to pick up the children at three.*

> Dev'essere tardi.
> *It must be late.*
> *It's probably late.*

> L'aereo dovrebbe decollare fra poco.
> *The plane should take off in a moment.*

When giving advice, use the **present conditional** of DOVERE to suggest what should or shouldn't be done, and the **past conditional** to suggest what should have or should not have been done, like this:

> Dovresti stare più attento.
> *You should be more careful.*

> Non dovreste essere insolenti.
> *You shouldn't be insolent.*

> Avrei dovuto aspettare i saldi.
> *I should have waited for the clearance sales.*

> Non avremmo dovuto mangiare tanto.
> *We shouldn't have eaten so much.*

The passato prossimo of DOVERE + infinitive creates *had to:*

> Ho dovuto fare la fila.
> *I had to wait in line.*

The imperfect of DOVERE + infinitive expresses what *was supposed to* take place as well as the *hypothetical must have*.

> Dovevano arrivare ieri.
> *They were supposed to arrive yesterday.*

> Doveva avere 5 o 6 anni.
> *She must have been about 5 or 6.*

POTERE expresses possibility. It is used to seek permission as well:

> Non può nascere oggi perché si è slogato la caviglia.
> *He can't swim today because he sprained his ankle.*

> Posso sedermi qui?
> *May I sit here?*

> Non poteva aiutarci.
> *He couldn't help us.*

> Avrei potuto aiutare.
> *I could have helped.*

The present conditional of POTERE suggests what could be done:

> Potresti dire grazie.
> *You could (might) say thank you.*

VOLERE relates desire (real or wishful) as well as intention:

> Vuole cenare prima delle otto.
> *He wants to have dinner before eight.*

> Lei vorrebbe essere famosa.
> *She would like to be famous.*

SAPERE + infinitive express capacity or ability (to know how):

> Sa cucinare bene.
> *She really knows how to cook.*

OCCORRERE and BISOGNARE always express necessity. They appear in the third person singular and plural only:

> Bisogna aspettare per sapere il risultato.
> *We have to wait to get the results.*

> Non occorre disturbarlo adesso.
> *It's not necessary to bother him now.*

Occorrono tre uova per fare quella torta.
Three eggs are needed to make that cake.

The modals may also be used without a following infinitive:

Devi!
You have to!

Lo so!
I know it!

Si può?
May I…may one?

Non posso!
I can't!

Non occorre!
It's not necessary!

Drill 43: Modal Verbs

Supply the modal verb in the appropriate tense to create the Italian equivalent of the English cue:

1. _____ (tu) aiutarci più tardi?
        (can)

2. (Tu) _____ vergognartene!
        (should)

3. (Noi) _____ finire.
        (must)

4. (Tu)_____ giocare a scacchi?
    (do you know how)

5. _____ aspettare qui.
    (it is necessary)

6. (Voi) _____ mangiare prima di partire.
      (should have)

7. (Tu)_____ scusarti!
      (could)

8. (Tu) _____ scusarti!
      (should)

9. (Lui) _____ imparare a pilotare un aereo.
    (would like)

10. _____ aiutarLa?
    (may I)

Answers and Explanations to Drill 43

1. **Puoi** aiutarci più tardi?
   Can you help us later?

   Potrai aiutarci più tardi?
   Will you be able to help us later?

   Potresti aiutarci più tardi?
   Would you be able to help us later?

   Each tense lends a slightly different meaning.

2. **Dovresti** vergognartene!
   You should be ashamed!
   Use the *conditional* of **dovere** to suggest what *should* be done.

3. **Dobbiamo** finire.
   We have to, we must finish.
   Use the *present* of **dovere** to tell what *must* be done.

4. **Sai** giocare a scacchi?
   Do you know how to play chess?
   Always use **sapere + infinitive** to express *knowing how.*

5. **Bisogna** aspettare qui. **Occorre** aspettare qui.
   It is necessary to wait here.
   Either impersonal verb works here.

6. **Avreste dovuto** mangiare prima di partire.
   You should have eaten before leaving.
   The *past conditional* of **dovere** is used to express what *should have been done.*

7. **Potresti** scusarti!
   You could excuse yourself.
   The *conditional* of **potere** creates the suggestion of what *could be* done.

8. Tu **dovresti** scusarti!

   You should excuse yourself.

   Use the *conditional* of **dovere** to suggest what *should be* done.

9. **Vorebbe** imparare a pilotare un aereo.

   He would like to learn to be a pilot.

   The conditional of **volere** can be used to express a desired goal or intention, what one *would like*.

10. **Posso** aiutarLa?

    May I help you?

    Use the present tense here. Save the conditional for an affirmation rather than a question: Potrei aiutarLa domani. *I could help you tomorrow.*

Modal Verbs in the Compound Past Tenses

In the compound past, deciding on *avere* or *essere* as auxiliary depends on the nature of the infinitive which follows the modal. This is an interesting grammatical point peculiar to Italian. The modal verb assumes the auxiliary verb appropriate for the coming infinitive, like this:

Noi abbiamo voluto parlare loro.
We wanted to talk to them.

Noi siamo voluti andare con loro.
We wanted to go with them.

Liliana ha dovuto aspettare a casa.
Lillian had to wait at home.

Liliana è dovuta rimanere a casa.
Lillian had to stay (remain) at home.

Drill 44: Modal Verbs in the Compound Past Tenses

Supply the modal verb in the appropriate compound tense to create the equivalent of the English cue:

1. (Tu) _____ _____ partire in anticipio.
   (had to)

2. (Tu) _____ _____ svolgere un tema.
   (had to)

3. (Voi) non _____ _____ finire.
   (weren't able)

4. Gina _____ _____ venire con noi.
   (should have)

5. Gina _____ _____ venire con noi.
   (wanted)

6. (Loro) _____ _____ entrare alle nove.
   (were able)

7. Le ragazze non _____ _____ venire.
   (couldn't)

8. Io non _____ _____ partire ieri.
   (wasn't able)

9. Papà _____ _____ come fare.
   (would have known)

10. Io non _____ _____ seguirli.
    (wasn't able)

Answers and Explanations to Drill 44

1. **Sei dovuto** partire in anticipio.
   You had to leave early.
   We use *essere* as auxiliary for *dovere,* in anticipation of the intransitive verb which comes next, *partire.*

2. **Hai dovuto** svolgere un tema.
   You had to write an essay.
   Here we need *avere* as auxiliary verb for *dovere,* to match the transitive *svolgere un tema* which follows.

3. Non **avete potuto** finire.
   You weren't able to finish.
   We use *avere* to match the transitive verb *finire.*

4. Gina **sarebbe dovuta** venire con noi.
   Gina should have come with us.
   Here we make the *past conditional* with *essere,* to match the coming intransitive verb, *venire.* Note the agreement!

5. Gina **è voluta** venire con noi.
   Gina wanted to come with us.
   Volere assumes the intransitive nature of *venire,* and uses *essere* as a helping verb.

6. **Sono potuti** entrare alle nove.
   They were able to get in at 9:00.
   Potere assumes the intransitive nature of *entrare,* and uses *essere* as a helping verb.

7. Le ragazze non **sono potute** venire.
   The girls weren't able to come. The girls couldn't come.
   Here *potere* assumes the intransitive nature of *venire,* and uses *essere* as a helping verb.

8. Non **sono potuto/a** partire ieri.

   I wasn't able to leave yesterday.

   You should be catching on by now. Did you choose *essere* as your auxiliary verb, to match the intransitive *partire?*

9. Papà **avrebbe saputo** come fare.

   Daddy would have known what to do.

   Here *sapere* is conjugated with *avere* as a helping verb, to match *fare.*

10. Non ho **potuto** seguirli.

    I wasn't able to follow them.

    Seguire, with its direct object attached to it, is obviously transitive. We use *avere* as auxiliary for *potere.*

The Causative Construction

The little formula **fare + infinitive + person or thing** allows us to express *making or having someone do something, or having something done.*

If the fare + infinitive construction has only one object, it will be *direct.*

> Fai piangere tua madre.
> *You make your mother cry.*

> **La** fai piangere.
> *You make her cry.*

> Tu **l'**hai fatta piangere.
> *You made her cry.*

> Faccio tagliare l'erba oggi.
> *I'm having the lawn (the grass) cut today.*

> **La** faccio tagliare oggi.
> *I'm having it cut today.*

> **L'**ho fatta tagliare oggi.
> *I had it cut today.*

> Fai fare il vestito?
> *Are you having the dress made?*

> **Lo** fai fare?
> *Are you having it made?*

> **L'**hai fatto fare?
> *Did you have it made?*

If fare *and* the infinitive *each* have an object, the object of fare will be *indirect.* The participle of fare agrees with the direct object but never with the indirect object. Study these sentences with two objects:

> Faccio mangiare le verdure ai bimbi.
> *I make the children eat their vegetables.*

> Glie**le** faccio mangiare.
> I make them eat them.
> *Le* is the direct object of fare mangiare.

Gliele ho fatte mangiare.
I made them eat them.
Gli(e) is the indirect object of fare mangiare.

Faccio tagliare i capelli al bambino.
I have the child's hair cut.

Glieli faccio tagliare.
I have his cut.
Li is the direct object of fare tagliare.

Glieli ho fatti tagliare.
I had his cut.
Gli(e) is the indirect object of fare taglaire.

Le faccio inviare il pacco.
I have the package sent to her.
Le is the indirect object of fare inviare.

Glie**lo** faccio inviare.
I have it sent to her.
Lo is the direct object of fare inviare.

Gliel'ho fatto inviare.
I had it sent to her.
Gli(e) is the indirect object of fare inviare.

When making or having a person do something which involves a reflexive verb, we eliminate the reflexive pronoun, like this:

La faccio sbrigare.
I make her hurry.

Drill 45: Causative Construction

Express these causative sentence in Italian:

1. He makes his mother worry.

   _____

2. I will have the children get up early.

   _____

3. I'm having the house repainted.

   _____

4. She has the students write.

   _____

5. She makes the students speak Italian.

   _____

6. We make him understand.

   _____

7. We make him understand Italian.

   _____

8. I have them sing.

   _____

9. I have the children drink their milk.

   _____

10. I had the boy tell the story.

    _____

Answers and Explanations to Drill 45

1. **Fa preoccupare sua madre.**
   The reflexive pronoun is omitted in the causative construction.

2. **Farò alzare i bambini presto.**
   Use the future tense of fare, eliminate the reflexive pronoun.

3. **Faccio riverniciare la casa.**
   This is the basic causative construction with one object.
   fare + infinitive + person or thing

4. **Fa scrivere gli studenti.**
   Another basic single object construction.

5. **Fa parlare italiano agli studenti.**
   Two objects are involved. *Italian* is the direct object of *fare parlare*, and the students become the indirect object.

6. **Lo facciamo capire.**
   The single object of *fare capire* is the direct object *him*.

7. **Gli facciamo capire l'italiano.**
   With two objects, *Italian* is the direct object of *fare capire*, and *him* now becomes the indirect object.

8. **Li faccio cantare.**
   Basic single direct object construction.

9. **Faccio bere il latte ai bimbi.**
   Two objects, *their milk* is direct, *the children* become indirect.

10. **Ho fatto raccontare la storia al ragazzo.**
    A past tense construction. You can clarify that the boy told the story by using *dal* instead of *al*. Otherwise it could mean that I had the story read *to* the boy.

Sapere versus *Conoscere*

Italian has two verbs meaning **to know**. This very same type of differentiation also exists in Spanish, French and Portuguese. Of the two verbs, **sapere** has the broadest range of use. **Conoscere** is restricted to a much narrower application as we shall see.

The Uses of Sapere

1. To express KNOWING HOW to do something, always use the verb *sapere* followed by an infinitive.

   > Non **sa nuotare**.
   > *He doesn't know how to swim.*

   Note the absence of the adverb *come* in this construction! It is usually left out with skills.

   Come, while never necessary, can be used to add emphasis:

   > Sa farlo.
   > *He knows how to do it.*

   > Sa come fare, lui.
   > **He** *knows how.*

2. Use *sapere* when *to know* simply suggests GENERAL AWARENESS. This usage includes:

KNOWING WHEN	Voglio **sapere quando** verranno.
	I want to know when they're coming.
KNOWING WHERE	Non so **dove** ho messo la mia penna
	I don't know where I put my pen.
KNOWING WHY	**Sai perché** piange?
	Do you know why she's crying?
KNOWING WHAT	Non **sa che** succede.
	He doesn't know what's happening.
	Non **so cosa** vuole.
	I don't know he wants.
KNOWING WHICH	Non **so quale** film scegliere.
	I don't know which film to choose.

KNOWING WHO	**Sapete chi** ha mangiato le mie polpette? *Do you guys know who ate my meatballs?*
KNOWING IF	Non **sappiamo** ancora **se** veniamo. *We don't know yet if we're coming.*
KNOWING THAT	**Sai che** ti amo. *You know that I love you.*
KNOWING HOW	Non **so com'**è morta. *I don't know how she died.*

3. Use *sapere* for knowing TELEPHONE NUMBERS and ADDRESSES.

> Sai il mio numero?
 Do you know my number?

4. Use *sapere* for knowing something BY HEART, *a memoria*. This usually includes anything that has been memorized or learned by rote, such as the abc's, multiplication tables, verb endings, or the capitals of countries.

> Sai qual'è la capitale italiana?
 Do you know the capital of Italy?

5. Use *sapere* when the verb *to know* is USED ALONE.

> Lo so!
 I know!

> Non so!
 I don't know!

The Uses of Conoscere

1. To express KNOWING A PERSON always use *conoscere*. It is the *only* verb you may use for aquaintance with *people*.

> Conosce la Signora Piscitelli?
 Do you know Mrs. Piscitelli?

2. To express IN DEPTH KNOWLEDGE, gained through FAMILIARITY due to lengthy association, research or personal experience, use *conoscere*.

This usage includes:

KNOWING A PLACE WELL	Non **conosco** troppo **bene** Roma.
KNOWING THE BEST	Conosci **i migliori** ristoranti!
KNOWING ONE'S JOB	Dopo 40 anni, **conosco il mio mestiere.**
KNOWING THE WORK OF AN ARTIST OR AUTHOR	**Conosce Boccaccio,** lui!

Conoscere and Sapere in the Past Tense

Both verbs take on special meanings in the Passato Prossimo. *Sapere* takes on the meaning of **finding out**:

> L'ho saputo da Maria.
> *Maria told me.*

> L'abbiamo saputo appena ieri.
> *We just found out yesterday.*

Conoscere takes on the meaning of **meeting** for the first time, or **making the aquaintance** of another person:

> Si sono conosciuti all'università.
> *They met in college.*

Drill 46: Sapere or Conoscere?

Complete the sentence with the appropriate form of *sapere* or *conoscere*:

1. (Lui) non _____ pattinare sul ghiaccio.

2. (Tu) _____ dove abito?

3. Vuole _____ se pioverà oggi.

4. (Voi) _____ i film di Luchino Visconti?

5. Loro non _____ i miei genitori.

6. (Io) _____ bene questo quartiere.

7. (Lui) _____ che non possiamo venire stasera.

8. _____ (tu) quali scarpe mettere?

9. (Noi) _____ chi vincerà.

10. (Tu) _____, credo che dobbiamo tirare giù la serranda.

Answers and Explanations to Drill 46

1. Non **sa** pattinare sul ghiaccio.
   He doesn't know how to ice skate.
   Always use SAPERE for knowing how to do something.

2. **Sai** dove abito?
   Do you know where I live?
   This is a good example of general awareness, knowing WHERE. Use
   SAPERE.

3. Vuole **sapere** se pioverà oggi.
   He wants to know if it's supposed to rain today.
   General awareness; knowing IF. Use SAPERE.
   Note the need for the infinitive form (*sapere*) after the conjugated modal
   (*vuole*).

4. **Conoscete** i film di Luchino Visconti?
   Do you know (are you familiar with) the films of Luchino Visconti?
   FAMILIARITY with the work of an artist. Use CONOSCERE.

   Visconti (1906-1976) was an Italian film-maker, director and screenwriter.
   His best known work is probably *Il Gattopardo*, starring Burt Lancaster
   in 1963. Visconti's screenplay *La Caduta degli Dei* (The Damned) was
   nominated for an Academy Award in 1969, but didn't win.

5. Non **conosce** i miei genitori.
   He doesn't know my parents.
   Parents are human beings! Always use CONOSCERE with people.

6. **Conosco** bene questo quartiere.
   I know this neighborhood well.
   FAMILIARITY with a place. Use CONOSCERE.

7. **Sanno** che non possiamo venire stasera.
   They know (that) we can't come tonight.
   General awareness; knowing THAT. Use SAPERE.

8. **Sai** quali scarpe mettere?
Do you know which shoes to wear (to put on)?
General awareness; knowing WHICH. Use SAPERE.

9. **Sappiamo** chi vincerà.
We know who's going to win.
General awareness; knowing WHO. Use SAPERE.

10. **Sai**, credo che dobbiamo tirare giù la serranda.
You know, I think we should pull down the shade.
Use SAPERE when *to know* is used alone, as it is here.

Using *Piacere* and *Mancare*

These two verbs present problems for the English speaker because English and Italian approach what they mean from totally opposite directions.

Let's examine PIACERE first. The actual meaning of PIACERE is TO PLEASE. That is the only thing it means. **It does not mean TO LIKE**! When Italians use it, it *always* means TO PLEASE. It is *we* who say we *like* something. *They* say it is *pleasing* to them. Sure, what the Italian **means** is that he likes it, but what he **says** is that it pleases him! If you understand and accept this basic truth, you will save yourself a lot of confusion.

There are some important ramifications to consider. In the English sentence the thing or person being liked is the DIRECT OBJECT of the verb. The person who *likes* is the subject of the verb:

> **He** (subject) **likes** (verb) **beer** (direct object).

The Italian sentence, expressing the same thought, comes out like this:

> **Gli** (indirect object) **piace** (verb) **la birra** (subject).
> *To him beer is pleasing.*

The verb *piacere*, which can only mean *to please*, has for its subject the thing that pleases, *beer*. The person who was the subject in the English sentence becomes the indirect object (to him) in the Italian construction. Here's another example.

> **She** (subject) **likes** (verb) **strawberries** (direct object).

The Italian thinks and says:

> **Le** (indirect object) **piacciono** (verb) **le fragole** (subject).
> *To her strawberries are pleasing.*

Notice how the verb *piacere* matches its subject! Here is one more example:

> **I** (subject) **like** (verb) **you** (direct object).

The same thought, expressed in Italian:

> **Tu** (subject) **mi** (direct object) **piaci** (verb).
> *You are pleasing to me.*

Italian does have the verb **amare** which means *to love* or *to like*. Students tend to stick with it because it's safe and easy. While the Italians have both *piacere* and *amare* at their disposal, more often than not they'll use *piacere*.

When using the verb *mancare* for feeling the absence of someone, we will see a similar pattern unfold. In this usage the verb *mancare* means **TO BE MISSING**. Hold that thought! In English **we** miss someone. In Italian that person **is missing** to us. The same construction that we used with *piacere* now works for *mancare*. Compare:

> **I miss you.** = (tu) Mi manchi.
> (omitted subject), indirect object pronoun, verb
> *You are missing to me.*

> **We miss him.** = (lui) Ci manca.
> (subject—usually omitted), indirect object
>   pronoun, verb
> *He is missing to us.*

> **I miss them.** = (loro) Mi mancano.
> (omitted subject) , indirect object pronoun, verb
> *They are missing to me.*

> **Do you miss me?** = (io)Ti manco?
> (omitted subject), indirect object pronoun, verb
> *Am I missing to you?*

Two chairs are missing. = Mancano due sedie.
                      verb, subject

Both PIACERE and MANCARE require ESSERE as an auxiliary verb in the PASSATO PROSSIMO:

> Non mi sono piaciuti gli asparagi.
> *I didn't like the asparagus.*
> Note the agreement of the past participle with its subject, *gli asparagi.*

> *Ci sei mancata, Maria.*
> *We missed you, Maria.*
> The past participle agrees with its subject, *Maria.*

Drill 47: Using Piacere and Mancare

Match the Italian sentence with its English translation:

_____ 1. Gli mancano i soldi.　　A. You like him.

_____ 2. Gli piaccio.　　B. We like you.

_____ 3. Mi piacciono.　　C. We miss you.

_____ 4. Le manchi.　　D. I like them.

_____ 5. Ti manca.　　E. He doesn't have the money.

_____ 6. Gli piaci.　　F. She misses you.

_____ 7. Ti piace.　　G. They like me.

_____ 8. Ti piacciamo.　　H. You miss him.

_____ 9. Ci mancate.　　I. You like us.

_____ 10. Ci piaci.　　J. He likes you.

Answers and Explanations to Drill 47

E 1. Gli mancano i soldi.
To him the money is missing. = He doesn't have (enough) money.

G 2. Gli piaccio.
To them I am pleasing. = They like me.
Note that modern Italian often substitutes *gli* for *loro*, thus avoiding the post-verb placement *manco loro*.

D 3. Mi piacciono.
To me they are pleasing. = I like them.

F 4. Le manchi.
To her you are missing. = She misses you.

H 5. Ti manca.
To you he is missing. = You miss him.

J 6. Gli piaci.
To him you are pleasing. = He likes you.

A 7. Ti piace.
To you he is pleasing. = You like him.

I 8. Ti piacciamo.
To you we are pleasing. = You like us.

C 9. Ci mancate.
To us you (plural) are missing. = We miss you.

B 10. Ci piaci.
To us you are pleasing. = We like you.

The Present Indicative

	AMARE *to love*	VENDERE *to sell*	APRIRE *to open*	FINIRE *to finish*
io	amo	vendo	apro	finisco
tu	ami	vendi	apri	finisci
lui, lei, Lei	ama	vende	apre	finisce
noi	amiamo	vendiamo	apriamo	finiamo
voi	amate	vendete	aprite	finite
loro, Loro	amano	vendono	aprono	finiscono

Tips on Pronouncing and Spelling -ARE Verbs

Verbs whose roots end in **c**, like cer**c**are, dimenti**c**are, gio**c**are or man**c**are, need the addition of the letter **h** whenever those roots contact an ending beginning in the vowel **i**. This contact occurs in the *tu* and *noi* forms. The inserted **h** preserves the hard sound [**k**] heard in the infinitive.

Verbs with roots ending in g, such as pagare or spiegare also need the **h** under the exact same circumstances, that is, in the *tu* and *noi* forms. Again, the added **h** preserves the hard sound [**g**] heard in the infinitive.

Roots ending in **i**, as in **mangiare** or **studiare** drop that **i** in the *tu* and *noi* forms, as those endings begin in the same letter.

Irregular ARE verbs include:

andare *(to go):*	**vado, vai, va, andiamo, andate, vanno.**
fare *(to do, make):*	**faccio, fai, fa, facciamo, fate, fanno**
dare *(to give):*	**do, dai, dà, diamo, date, danno**
stare *(to be, to sta):*	**sto, stai, sta, stiamo, state, stanno**

Tips on -ERE Verbs

There are a number of irregular ERE verbs which should be learned by heart. Here are some of the most frequently encountered:

avere *(to have)*	**ho, hai, ha, abbiamo, avete, hanno**
bere *(to drink)*	**bevo, bevi, beve, beviamo, bevete, bevono**
cogliere *(to gather, to pick)*	**colgo, cogli, coglie, cogliamo, cogliete, colgono**
raccogliere *(to pick up, to collect)*	**raccolgo, raccogli, raccoglie, raccogliamo, raccogliete, raccolgono**
scegliere *(to choose, to select)*	**scelgo, scegli, sceglie, scegliamo, scegliete, scelgono**
sciogliere *(to melt)*	**sciolgo, sciogli, scioglie, sciogliamo, sciogliete, sciolgono**
togliere *(to remove, take out, off)*	**tolgo, togli, toglie, togliamo, togliete, tolgono**
cuocere *(to cook)*	**cuocio, cuoci, cuoce, c(u)ociamo, c(u)ocete, cuociono**
dolere *(to ache, to hurt)*	**dolgo, duoli, duole, do(g)liamo, dolete, dolgono**
dovere *(to have to, "must")*	**devo, devi, deve, dobbiamo, dovete, devono**
essere *(to be)*	**sono, sei , è, siamo, siete, sono**
piacere *(to please)*	**piaccio, piaci, piace, piacciamo, piacete, piacciono**
potere *(to be able, "can")*	**posso, puoi, può, possiamo, potete, possono**
sapere *(to know)*	**so, sai, sa, sappiamo, sapete, sanno**
sedere, sedersi *(to sit)*	**siedo, siedi, siede, sediamo, sedete, siedono**
rimanere *(to remain)*	**rimango, rimani, rimane, rimaniamo, rimanete, rimangono**
tacere *(to be silent)*	**taccio, taci, tace, tacciamo, tacete, tacciono**
tenere *(to hold, to keep)*	**tengo, tieni, tiene, teniamo, tenete, tengono**
valere *(to be worth, of value)*	**valgo, vali, vale, valiamo, valete, valgono**
volere *(to want)*	**voglio, vuoi, vuole, vogliamo, volete, vogliono**

Tips on -IRE Verbs

There are two types of regular **-ire** verbs. The number of consonants the root ends in determines how to proceed. If the root ends in *two or more consonants*, we apply the ending directly to the root. Verbs which work this way include:

> apr**ire** *(to open)*
>
> dorm**ire** *(to sleep)*
>
> offr**ire** *(to offer)*
>
> part**ire** *(to leave)*
>
> segu**ire*** *(to follow, take a course)*
>
> sent**ire** *(to hear, to feel)*
>
> serv**ire** *(to serve)*
>
> soffr**ire** *(to suffer)*

If the root ends in *a single consonant, we insert the letters **isc*** in four of of the six forms (all except noi and voi), before attaching the endings. Here are some common verbs which work this way:

capire *(to understand)*	**cap*isc*o, cap*isc*i, cap*isc*e, capiamo, capite, cap*isc*ono**
finire *(to finish)*	**fin*isc*o, fin*isc*i, fin*isc*e, finiamo, finite, fin*isc*ono**
preferire *(to prefer)*	**prefer*isc*o, prefer*isc*i, prefer*isc*e, preferiamo, preferite, prefer*isc*ono**
pulire *(to clean)*	**pul*isc*o, pul*isc*i, pul*isc*e, puliamo. pulite, pul*isc*ono**
riferire *(to refer)*	**rifer*isc*o, rifer*isc*i, rifer*isc*e, riferiamo, riferite, rifer*isc*ono**
suggerire *(to suggest)*	**sugger*isc*o, sugger*isc*i, sugger*isc*e, suggeriamo, suggerite, sugger*isc*ono**
ubbidire *(to obey)*	**ubbid*isc*o, ubbid*isc*i, ubbid*isc*e, ubbidiamo, ubbidite, ubbid*isc*ono**

If the root ends in *u*, as in restit<u>u</u>ire or seg<u>u</u>ire, **we evaluate the quality of the preceding consonant.** If the consonant is *voiced* (and therefore strong) no *isc* is required. If the consonant is *unvoiced* (and therefore weak) we add the *isc*.

The following IRE verbs are irregular in the present indicative:

dire *(to say, to tell)*	**dico, dici, dice, diciamo, dite, dicono**
morire *(to die)*	**muoio, muori, muore, moriamo, morite, muoiono**
salire *(to go up, to climb)*	**salgo, sali, sale, saliamo, salite, salgono**
udire *(to hear, but not commonly used)*	**odo, odi, ode, udiamo, udite, odono**
uscire *(to go out, to exit)*	**esco, esci, esce, usciamo, usite, escono**
venire *(to come)*	**vengo, vieni, viene, veniamo, venite, vengono**

Irregular Verbs Ending in Arre, Urre

trarre *(to pull, to drag, to draw)*	**traggo, trai, trae, traiamo, traete, traggono**
attrarre *(to attract, to draw)*	**attraggo, attrai, attrae, attraiamo, attraete, attraggono**
distrarre *(to divert, distract)*	**distraggo, distrai, distrae, distraiamo, distraete, distraggono**
estrarre *(to extract, to pull out)*	**estraggo, estrai, estrae, estraimo, estraete, estraggono**
condurre *(to lead, to conduct)*	**conduco, conduci, conduce, conduciamo, conducete, conducono**
tradurre *(to translate)*	**traduco, traduci, traduce, traduciamo, traducete, traducono**

Drill 48: The Present Indicative

Supply the correct form of the present tense. Make sure your answer agrees with its subject:

1. Quale _____, aranciata o limonata?
   (preferire – tu)

2. Papà _____ tanta gente.
   (conoscere)

3. _____ in ferie oggi.
   (partire – io)

4. A che ora _____?
   (finire – loro)

5. _____ profondamente.
   (dormire – lui)

6. La mia gattina _____ Fiducia.
   (chiamarsi)

7. _____ spesso a Briscola.
   (giocare – noi)

8. La nonna _____ questo programma in TV.
   (seguire)

9. Lo _____ già.
   (sapere – loro)

10. Non _____ mai il mio compleanno.
    (dimenticare – tu)

11. Non _____ ancora pronti?
    (essere – voi)

12. _____ una bibita.
     (scegliere – io)

13. _____ ballare con me?
     (volere – tu)

14. Ti _____ il tuo libro domani.
     (restituire – io)

15. _____ presto negli Stati Uniti.
     (cenare – noi)

16. _____ nel parco.
     (studiare – tu)

17. La professoressa _____ i compiti.
                      (raccogliere)

18. _____ il nostro pasto.
     (pagare – tu)

19. _____ le pantofole sotto il letto?
     (lasciare – tu)

20. Che cosa _____ lassù?
            (vedere – voi)

21. Dove _____ così?
         (andare – tu)

22. _____ lo stesso fotogiornale.
     (ricevere)

23. Quanti anni _____?
                (avere – tu)

24. _____ dall'inglese.
     (tradurre – loro)

25. _____ in italiano.
    (rispondere – tu)

26. Quello che _____ è vero.
    (dire – voi)

27. Che cosa _____?
    (prendere – voi)

28. Che cosa _____?
    (fare – loro)

29. Mamma _____ la cucina.
    (pulire)

30. I nostri parenti _____ a trovarci.
    (venire)

Answers and Explanations to Drill 48

1. Quale **preferisci**, aranciata o limonata?
   Preferire is typical of regular -ire verbs whose roots end in a single consonant. It requires the insertion of the letters *isc* in the first, second, third and last forms of the present indicative. We never add *isc* to noi and voi forms.

2. Papà **conosce** tanta gente.
   Conoscere uses a regulare -ere conjugation.

3. **Parto** in ferie oggi.
   Partire represents regular -ire verbs whose roots end in two or more consonants. No insertion is required. Just apply regular -ire endings directly to the root.

4. A che ora **finiscono**?
   Finire is a regular -ire verb whose root ends in a single consonant. Insert *isc* here before adding the regular -ire ending.

5. **Dorme** profondamente.
   The root of this regular -ire verb ends in two consonants. No insertion necessary here.

6. La mia gattina **si chiama** Fiducia.
   This is a regular -are verb. Since it is also reflexive you must supply the appropriate reflexive pronoun. *(mi, ti, si, ci, vi, si)*

7. **Giochiamo** spesso a Briscola.
   Giocare requires the addition of the letter **h** in the tu and noi forms. This insures the hard sound [K] of the letter **c** by preventing its contact with the letter **i**.

8. La nonna **segue** questo programma in TV.
   If we evaluate the consonant preceding the letter **u**, we see that the **g** is voiced and strong enough to stand alone, without the addition of *isc*.

9. Lo **sanno** già.
   Sapere is very irregular and must be learned by heart. Note the similarity between this form and other irregulars like: hanno, danno, fanno and stanno.

10. Non **dimentichi** mai il mio compleanno.
    Did you remember to add the **h**?

11. Non **siete** ancora pronti?
    Essere is probably one of the first irregular verbs you ever learned. It is essential. Forget taking the AP exam if you don't know this verb inside and out! It would be easier to nail polenta to the ceiling!

12. **Scelgo** una bibita.
    Scegliere is a commonly used irregular verb. You should know this conjugation by heart.

13. **Vuoi** ballare con me?
    Volere is highly irregular and must be learned by heart. Like: *puoi*.

14. Ti **restituisco** il tuo libro domani.
    When the -ire root ends in a **u**, evaluate the strength of the consonant which precedes it. In this case, a single unvoiced consonant (t) requires the addition of *isc*.

15. **Ceniamo** presto negli Stati Uniti.

16. **Studi** nel parco.
    Studiare, like mangiare and viaggiare, drops one **i** in the tu and noi forms of the present tense.

17. La professoressa **raccoglie** i compiti.
    Raccogliere follows the irregular pattern set by cogliere.

18. **Paghi** il nostro pasto.
    You must insert the letter *h* in the *tu* and *noi* forms of the present indicative. This preserves the hard [g] sound of the infinitive, and permits all six forms to have the same initial sound, including the tu and noi forms whose endings begin with *i*.

19. **Lasci** le pantofole sotto il letto?
    When a root ending in **i** meets an ending beginning in **i**, drop one **i**!

20. Cosa **vedete** lassù?
    Vedere uses a regular -ere conjugation.

21. Dove **vai** così?
    Part of the irregular conjugation of *andare*. This form brings to mind similar second person forms such as: *dai, hai, fai, stai*

22. **Ricevo** lo stesso fotogiornale.
    Ricevere uses a regular -ere conjugation, like vedere.

23. Quanti anni **hai**?
    Like *essere*, the verb *avere* is one of the veritable founding blocks on which Italian is based. Attempting the AP exam without learning every little idiosyncracy there is to know about this irregular verb would be foolish.

24. **Traducono** dall'inglese.
    Like all infinitives ending in -urre, tradurre is irregular.

25. **Rispondi** in italiano.
    Rispondere is a regular -ere verb and follows the standard conjugation.

26. Quello che **dite** è vero.
    Dire is irregular and the *voi* form is a teacher favorite to catch the unaware!

27. Che cosa **prendete**?
    Prendere uses a regular -ere conjugation.

28. Che cosa **fanno***?*
    Fare is irregular and must be learned by heart. Here it is just like hanno, danno, stanno and vanno.

29. Mamma **pulisce** la cucina.
    Pulire is a regular -ire verb whose root ends in a single consonant. Use *isc* and then the ending.

30. I nostri parenti **vengono** a trovarci.
    Venire is an important and commonly used irregular verb worth knowing by heart.

The Future

The future tense uses one set of universal endings which are applied to all verbs. The regular root is the entire infinitive *minus the last letter*. What could be easier? There is only one change that occurs in the root of all regular -are verbs: The **-a** changes to **-e** as follows:

> abitare = abit**er**
>
> cantare = cant**er**
>
> parlare = parl**er**
>
> studiare = studi**er**

In infinitives ending in *-care* and *-gare*, this -a to -e change will require the addition of the letter **-h** to preserve the hard sound of **-c** or **-g** in the -are future root as follows:

> cercare = cerc**her**
>
> dimenticare = dimentic**her**
>
> giocare = gioc**her**
>
> litigare = litig**her**
>
> pagare = pag**her**

In infinitives ending in *-iare*, this **-a** to -e change also causes the vowel **i** to drop out after the soft sound of **-c** or **-g** in the -are future root as follows:

> bac**i**are = bac**er**
>
> lasciare = lasc**er**
>
> mang**i**are = mang**er**

Here are samples from each of the three verb groups with the universal future endings attached:

> ARE: parler**ò**, parler**ai**, parler**à**, parler**emo**, parler**ete**, parler**anno**
>
> ERE: vender**ò**, vender**ai**, vender**à**, vender**emo**, vender**ete**, vender**anno**
>
> IRE: finir**ò**, finir**ai**, finir**à**, finir**emo**, finir**ete**, finir**anno**

The irregular future roots are not too troublesome as virtually all of them result in a shorter, condensed version of the root, allowing faster and smoother pronunciation.

The following verbs have condensed or irregular roots in the future:

andare	**andr**	(andrò)	*I will* go
avere	**avr**	(avrò)	*I will* have
bere	**berr**	(berrò)	*I will* drink
cadere	**cadr**	(cadrò)	*I will* fall
dare	**dar**	(darò)	*I will* give
dire	**dir**	(dirò)	*I will* say, tell
dovere	**dovr**	(dovrò)	*I will* have to
essere	**sar**	(sarò)	*I will* be
fare	**far**	(farò)	*I will* do, make
godere	**godr**	(godrò)	*I will* enjoy
parere	**parr**	(parrò)	*I will* seem, appear
potere	**potr**	(potrò)	*I will* be able
rimanere	**rimarr**	(rimarrò)	*I will* remain
sapere	**sapr**	(saprò)	*I will* know
stare	**star**	(starò)	*I will* be
tenere	**terr**	(terrò)	*I will* keep, hold
mantenere	**manterr**	(manterrò)	*I will* maintain
ottenere	**otter**	(otterrò)	*I will* obtain
sostenere	**sosterr**	(sosterrò)	*I will* uphold, support
trattenere	**tratterr**	(tratterrò)	*I will* restrain, entertain
valere	**varr**	(varrò)	*I will* be worth
vedere	**vedr**	(vedrò)	*I will* see
venire	**verr**	(verrò)	*I will* come
vivere	**vivr**	(vivrò)	*I will* live
volere	**vorr**	(vorrò)	*I will* want

You will get to recycle your knowledge of future roots, both regular and irregular, as they are also used in the formation of the conditional.

Use of the Future Tense

The future tense expresses future action in Italian just as it does in English. This use is obvious and easy to grasp. There is a problem, however, for English speakers because Italian often uses the future tense where we would use the present in English. This happens when the future is *implied*. Key words which often trigger this phenomenon are:

> **appena**, *as soon as*
>
> **finchè**, *until, as long as*
>
> **quando**, *when*
>
> **se**, *if, whether*

Study these examples. Note the present tense in English!

> Dove resterai QUANDO **andrai** in Italia?
> *Where will you stay when you go to Italy?*

> Lei verrà a vederci QUANDO **potrà**.
> *She will come see us when she can.*

> Ti telefonerò APPENA **saprò** qualcosa.
> *I will call you as soon as I find out.*

> Andremo a sciare APPENA **torneranno**.
> *We'll go skiing as soon as they get back.*

> Rimarrai FINCHÈ **vorrai**.
> *You'll remain as long as you want.*

> Non so SE li **vedrò**.
> *I don't know whether I'll see them.*

> SE **farà** bello, andrò alla spiaggia.
> *If the weather is good, I'll go to the beach.*

> Ti aspetterò FINCHÈ **arriverai**.
> *I'll wait for you until you arrive.*

> Non potrò bere FINCHÈ **avrò** ventuno anni.
> *I won't be able to drink until I'm twenty-one.*

A word of caution: These same key words can be followed by a variety of other tenses. Remember that we must establish that the future is **implied** to follow with the future tense. Here are some typical examples of other tenses following the same introductory conjunctions:

Ogni giorno QUANDO **torno** a casa, mi fermo per un caffè.
I stop for a coffee every day on my way home.

Sono venuti a prendermi APPENA **sono arrivata**.
They came to pick me up as soon as I arrived.

Expressing Probability, Conjecture, Supposition

In English, when we guess or speculate about what might be, we use the words **probably, could,** or **must.** In Italian, we simply use the **future tense.** If you say *"That'll be for me."* when the phone rings, you are using the future tense just like the Italians do. You are expressing what you suppose will be true.

Here are some examples:

Dove **sarà**?
*Where **could** he be?*

Sarà in ferie.
*He **must be** on vacation.*

Sarà a letto.
*He's **probably** in bed.*

Vorrà qualcosa da bere.
*You'll **probably want** something to drink.*

(after the phone rings):

Sarà per te.
*It's **probably** for you. It **must be** for you.*
*That'**ll be** for you*

Chi **sarà?**
*Who **could** it **be?***

Sarà Mamma, non rispondere!
*It's **probably** Mom, don't answer!*

Be', Cinzia **avrà lavato** i piatti!
Oh, Cynthia must have done the dishes!

(after a knock at the door):

Sarà il postino, aspetto un pacco.
*It's **probably** the mailman, I'm expecting a package.*

Expressing the Immediate Future with the Present Tense

Italians can also express future intent with the present tense exactly as we do in English. This usage is quite common and frequently heard. Here are some examples; note the present tense in both languages:

Domani **tocca** a me.
Tomorrow it's my turn.

Partiamo venerdì.
We leave Friday.

Mamma ci **fa** una pizza stasera.
Mom is making us a pizza tonight.

Vengono la settimana prossima.
They're coming next week.

Drill 49: Future or Present Tense?

Place the indicated verb in either the future OR the present tense. Base your choice on cues in the sentences.

1. Vi scriverò quando _____.
   (I can)

2. Quanti anni _____?
   (I wonder how old she is.)

3. Andremo a sciare appena _____.
   (it snows)

4. Resterò fedele finchè lo _____ lui.
   (he is)

5. Volete andare dal tabaccaio quando _____ in città?
   (you are)

6. _____ per me.
   (It's probably)

7. Avrò finito in un attimo se tu _____ aspettarmi.
   (want)

8. Chiamami quando _____ a casa.
   (you return)   (two answers possible)

9. Tenga la chiave finchè _____.
   (you want)   (two answers possible)

10. I miei genitori non _____ mai la loro vecchia macchina.
    (won't sell)

11. Resteremo in Italia finchè _____.
    (we can)

12. Quando avremo finito tutto il vino rosso, _____ il vino bianco.
    (we'll drink)

13. _____ in ritardo se non ci sbrighiamo.
    (We'll be)

14. Non cominceremo finchè non _____ tutti gli ospiti.
    (arrive)   (can use present, future **or** futuro anteriore!)

15. Ti _____ appena ti vedrò.
    (I'll kiss)

Answers and Explanations to Drill 49

1. Vi scriverò quando **potrò**.
   I will write to you when I can.
   It is best to use the future tense after *when* if a future time is implied, as it is here.

2. Quanti anni **avrà**?
   I wonder how old she is.
   Here the future tense expresses conjecture. Did you remember to use a form of *avere* to express age with *anni*?

3. Andremo a sciare appena **nevicherà**.
   We'll go skiing as soon as it snows.
   Classic use of the future after *appena* with future time implied. Note the addition of the letter **h** to preserve the hard **c** sound.

4. Resterò fedele finchè lo **sarà** lui.
   I'll remain faithful as long as he is.
   Use the future after *as long as* when the future is implied.

5. Volete andare dal tabaccaio quando **sarete/siete** in città?
   Do you want to stop at the tobacco shop when you're in town?
   Italian generally uses the future after *when* if future time is implied. It has become quite common, however, to hear the present tense after QUANDO in every day use.

6. **Sarà** per me.
   (The phone call) is probably for me.
   This is an example of the future used to express supposition or probability.

7. Avrò finito tra un attimo se (tu) **vuoi** aspettarmi.
   I'll be finished in a second if you want to wait for me.
   Use the present tense here, just as you would in English, to express the immediate future.

8. Chiamami quando **torni / tornerai** a casa.
   Call me when you get in.
   After a command you may use the present (immediate future) *or* the usual future after *quando* with future time implied.

9. Tenga la chiave finchè **vuole** / **vorrà**.
   Keep the key as long as you want.
   After a command you may use the present (immediate future) *or* the usual future after *finchè* with future time implied.

10. I miei genitori non **venderanno** mai la loro vecchia macchina.
    My parents won't ever sell their old car.
    Basic use of the future tense, parallel to English here. The presence of the word *mai* reinforces the need for the future tense.

11. Resteremo in Italia finchè **potremo**.
    We'll stay in Italy as long as we can.
    If the future is implied, use the future tense after *as long as*.

12. Quando avremo finito tutto il vino rosso, **berremo** il vino bianco.
    We'll drink the white wine when we've finished all the red.
    Basic use of the future tense to express a future action.

13. **Saremo** in ritardo se non ci sbrighiamo.
    We'll be late if we don't hurry up.
    Another basic use of the future tense to express what will happen.

14. Non cominceremo finchè non **arrivano** / **arriveranno** tutti gli ospiti.
    We won't begin until all the guests arrive.
    You can use the present tense (immediate future) or the future tense. While it is unlikely that you would encounter an exam question with so many correct answers, it would also be possible to say:
    Non cominceremo finchè **saranno arrivati** tutti gli ospiti.
    We won't begin until all the guests have arrived.

15. Ti **bacerò** appena ti vedrò.
    I will kiss you as soon as I see you.
    Classic use of the future tense to express a future action. Note the loss of the letter **i** in the root. In pronunciation, its sound is lost as it blends into the soft **c** sound. Therefore it drops out in spelling as well.

The Imperfect

The imperfect uses one set of universal endings for all verbs. The root is made from the **infinitive minus the last two letters (-re)**. There is only one verb which is completely irregular in the imperfect and should be learned by heart:

ESSERE: **ero, eri, era, eravamo, eravate, erano**

Here are samples from each of the three verb groups with the universal imperfect endings attached:

ARE: parla**vo**, parla**vi**, parla**va**, parla**vamo**, parla**vate**, parla**vano**

ERE: vende**vo**, vende**vi**, vende**va**, vende**vamo**, vende**vate**, vende**vano**

IRE: fini**vo**, fini**vi**, fini**va**, fini**vamo**, fini**vate**, fini**vano**

The following verbs have irregular roots:

BERE: **beve**vo, **beve**vi, **beve**va, **beve**vamo, **beve**vate, **beve**vano

DIRE: **dice**vo, **dice**vi, **dice**va, **dice**vamo, **dice**vate, **dice**vano

FARE: **face**vo, **face**vi, **face**va, **face**vamo, **face**vate, **face**vano

BERE, DIRE and FARE were once *bevere, dicere, and facere*. If you take that into consideration, their roots are not really irregular. They are just based on the original, now defunct, infinitives.

Uses of the Imperfect

1. The imperfect relates CONTINUING action in the past. The action has no discernable beginning or ending within the framework of the sentence. The English translation of the verb invariably uses **was + ing** or **were + ing**. The action may be continuing or on-going in the background while another action takes place.

2. The imperfect is DESCRIPTIVE of a physical or mental state. Verbs which take place in the mind, such as wanting *(volere)*, thinking *(pensare)*, believing *(credere)*, fearing *(temere)*, or knowing *(sapere)*, are generally rendered in the imperfect.

Any verb which is WEATHER-related falls into this category. The verb AVERE in combination with a noun, and the verb ESSERE plus adjective or noun, are also reliable clues to use the descriptive imperfect.

3. The imperfect relates HABITUAL, CUSTOMARY, or REPEATED action in the past. The English translation here is **used to**, or **would**. There are often clue words in the sentence which suggest repetition, such as *sempre, spesso,* or *al, di solito*.

How the *Passato Prossimo* is Different

If the past action is COMPLETED and clear-cut, having either a distinct beginning or ending within the sentence, we use the *passato prossimo*. If it is easy to visualize the action being accomplished within the sentence (He ate the apple: *Ha mangiato la mela*.) we render it in the *passato prossimo*.

In a narrative, it is the *passato prossimo* which propels the action forward, while the use of the imperfect creates a descriptive pause in the forward progression of the story.

Drill 50: Imperfetto or Passato Prossimo?

Supply the most suitable past tense. Study the sentences carefully to determine your choice. Train yourself to pick out hidden cues.

1. _____ quando (noi) _____ stamattina.
   (nevicare)   (partire)

2. (Lei) _____ quando (io) l' _____ .
        (piangere)   (vedere)

3. (Lui) _____ la bottiglia. Poi, (lui) ci _____ il vino.
        (aprire)   (versare)

4. (Noi) _____ quando il telefono _____ .
        (dormire)   (suonare)

5. (Io) _____ uscire ieri sera ma (io) _____ esausto.
       (volere)   (essere)

6. (Loro) _____ quando (noi) _____ .
         (baciarsi)   (entrare)

7. (Io) _____ quando (io) _____ paura.
       (fischiare)   (avere)

8. Noi _____ sempre in chiesa la domenica.
      (andare)

9. _____ il libro che ti _____ ?
   (leggere – tu form)   (prestare)

10. Io _____ un'ape* quando (io) _____ giovane.
       (avere)   (essere)

*ape, a very small three-wheeled truck, named after the drone (bee) for its reliable hard work.

Answers and Explanations to Drill 50

1. **Nevicava** quando **siamo partiti** stamattina.
   It was snowing when we left this morning.
   This is a classic combination; the *imperfect* describes the background weather condition, while the *passato prossimo* conveys the completed action.

2. **Piangeva** quando l'**ho vista**.
   She was crying when I saw her.
   The *imperfect* is used here to express a continuing or on-going action, while the *passato prossimo* plays the only role it can, that of completed action.

3. **Ha aperto** la bottiglia. Poi, ci **ha versato** il vino.
   He opened the bottle. Then he poured us the wine.
   Two successive completed actions. We can visualize their completion as they take place, one after the other. Use the *passato prossimo* for both.

4. **Dormivamo** quando il telefono **è suonato**.
   We were sleeping when the telephone rang.
   The *imperfect* expresses the continuing, on-going background action; the *passato prossimo* provides the completed action.

5. **Volevo** uscire ieri sera ma **ero** esausto.
   I wanted to go out last night but I was exhausted.
   Two *imperfects*. The first one describes a verb which takes place in the mind, we don't *see* it happening. The second one *describes a physical state*. Remember that **essere + adjective** and **essere + noun** are reliable clues for the use of the *imperfect*.

6. **Si baciavano** quando **siamo entrati**.
   They were kissing when we came in.
   The *imperfect* expresses the on-going background action; the *passato prossimo* takes care of the completed action.

7. **Fischiavo** quando **avevo** paura.

   I used to whistle when I was afraid.

   Two *imperfects*. The first one is a repetitive or habitual past action; **used to** or **would** convey the English equivalent. The second one describes a mental activity. We don't *see* it being accomplished. **Avere + noun** is a generally reliable clue for the use of the *imperfect*.

8. **Andavamo** sempre in chiesa la domenica.

   We would always go to church on Sundays.

   This activity took place over and over again. It was habitual. *La domenica* and *sempre* are neon signs for repeated past action. **Used to** or **would** convey the English equivalent. Use the *imperfect*.

9. **Hai letto** il libro che ti **ho prestato**?

   Did you read the book I lent you?

   Two completed past actions. Use the *passato prossimo* for both.

10. **Avevo** un'ape quando **ero** giovane.

    I had (used to have) "a bee" when I was young.

    Two *imperfects*. The first one describes *what used to be*. The second one describes a *physical state*. Both **avere** and **essere** are generally put into the *imperfect*.

The Conditional

The formation of the present conditional is very simple. It uses the identical roots we learned for the future in combination with its own set of universal endings. We simply recombine the *future roots* with the new conditional endings.

If the verb used a regular root in the future, we reuse it in the conditional:

ARE: parler**ei**, parler**esti**, parler**ebbe**, parler**emmo**, parler**este**, parler**ebbero**

ERE: vender**ei**, vender**esti**, vender**ebbe**, vender**emmo**, vender**este**, vender**ebbero**

IRE: finir**ei**, finir**esti**, finir**ebbe**, finir**emmo**, finir**este**, finir**ebbero**

If the verb required an irregular root in the future, we reuse it in the conditional:

andare: *andr**ei**, andr**esti**, andr**ebbe**, andr**emmo**, andr**este**, andr**ebbero***

avere: *avr**ei**, avr**esti**, avr**ebbe**, avr**emmo**, avr**este**, avr**ebbero***

bere: *berr**ei**, berr**esti**, berr**ebbe**, berr**emmo**, berr**este**, berr**ebbero***

essere: *sar**ei**, sar**esti**, sar**ebbe**, sar**emmo**, sar**este**, sar**ebbero***

fare: *far**ei**, far**esti**, far**ebbe**, far**emmo**, far**este**, far**ebbero***

Note how similar the *noi* form endings are in the future and the conditional: parler**emo** versus parler**emmo**. Be sure to pronounce the **m** twice in the conditional ending to distinguish its sound from the future ending.

The Uses of the Conditional

1. The conditional tense is used to be polite and to make requests less demanding. This usage parallels English:

    Vorrei una pizza ai funghi.
    I would like a mushroom pizza.

    Potrebbe aiutarmi a trovare la chiesa?
    Could you help me find the church?

2. The conditional is used to express something one imagines or dreams of:

> La macchina dei miei sogni **dovrebbe** essere su misura.
> *The car of my dreams would have to be custom built.*

3. When a contrary-to-fact condition is set forth with **se** and the **subjunctive**, we follow with the conditional in the result clause, like this:

> Se avessi i miei stivali li **metterei** adesso.
> *If I had my boots, I'd put them on now.*

> Se fossi in te, non **aspetterei** per cominciare.
> *If I were you, I wouldn't wait to get started.*

Drill 51: The Conditional

Place the indicated verb in the conditional tense. Note the cues within the sentence that trigger this tense choice.

1. Il mio marito ideale _____ gentile e tenero.
   (would be)

2. Noi _____ venire con voi.
   (would like)

3. Che cosa _____ (tu) al mio posto?
   (would do)

4. Se avessi la tua età, _____ volentieri con te.
   (would come)

5. A chi _____ un cono gelato?
   (would please)

6. _____ dirmi dov'è la chiesa?
   (Would you be able –Lei)

7. Se ci avessero scelti, ne _____ _____ contenti.
   (would have been)

8. _____ aiutarmi a ripiegare questa carta?
   (Could you, would you be able to – tu form)

9. Chi _____ mai _____ che avrebbe fatto così?
   (would have ever thought)

10. Se non dicessi la verità, i miei genitori lo _____.
    (would know)

Answers and Explanations to Drill 51

1. Il mio marito ideale **sarebbe** gentile e tenero.
   My ideal husband would be kind and loving.
   Here the conditional is used much as it is in English, to express a dreamed of or imagined ideal.

2. Noi **vorremmo** venire con voi.
   We would like to come with you.
   This use parallels English exactly. Expressing what is wanted in the conditional tense makes the request as polite as possible.

3. Che cosa **faresti** al mio posto?
   What would you do in my place?
   The conditional is used here just as it would be in English. *Al mio posto* sets up a situation contrary to fact, the conditional is used for the result.

4. Se avessi la tua età, **verrei** volentieri con te.
   If I were your age, I'd gladly come with you.
   The *subjunctive* in the *if* clause sets up a contrary-to-fact situation; the conditional is used in the subsequent result clause.

5. A chi **piacerebbe** un cono gelato?
   Who would like an ice cream cone?
   The use of the conditional is literal here. The ice cream cone is the subject of *piacere*.

6. **Potrebbe** dirmi dov'è la chiesa?
   Could you (Would you be able to) tell me where the church is?
   This use of the conditional renders the request more polite.

7. Se ci avessero scelti, ne **saremmo stati** contenti.
   If they had chosen us, we would have been happy about it.
   The past subjunctive in the *if* clause sets the stage for the past conditional in the result clause.

8. **Potresti** aiutarmi a ripiegare questa carta?
   Could you, would you be able to, help me fold up this map?
   The conditional allows the speaker to ask for help politely.

9. Chi **avrebbe** mai **pensato** che avrebbe fatto così?
   Who would ever have thought he'd do (like) that?
   The conditional is literal here, a verbatim translation of the English.

10. Se non dicessi la verità, i miei genitori lo **saprebbero**.
    If I weren't telling the truth, my parent would know it.
    A typical construction, the contrary-to-fact *if* clause in the *subjunctive*,
    followed by the conditional in the result clause.

Compound Tenses

In the compound tenses, most Italian verbs use a form of **AVERE** as an auxiliary verb along with the past participle of the verb in question. The **tense** used for the auxiliary varies from one compound past to the next. **Abbiamo studiato,** an example from the *passato prossimo,* is the single equivalent of *we studied, we have studied,* and *we did study* in English.

Regular past participles are based on the infinitive root as follows: **am + ato** for ARE verbs, **fin + ito** for IRE verbs, **vend + uto** for ERE.

There are many irregular past participles in Italian, just as there are in English. Like favorite old sneakers that get misshapen from so much use, it is often the most common verbs that fall into this group. Learn these irregular participles by heart. It takes years to learn the irregulars in English. We hear little children say *I buyed*, or *He gived* and we correct them until they stop.

They are grouped here by similarity:

acceso	*lit*	from accendere
perso	*lost*	from perdere
preso	*took, taken*	from prendere
reso	*gave back*	from rendere
sceso	*came, went down*	from scendere
speso	*spent*	from spendere
steso	*spread*	from stendere
teso	*held out, stretched out*	from tendere
accolto	*welcomed, received*	from accogliere
colto	*gathered, picked*	from cogliere
raccolto	*picked up*	from raccogliere
tolto	*removed, taken out*	from togliere
accorto	*noticed, became aware*	from accorgersi
afflitto	*afflicted*	from affliggere
fitto	*fixed, fastened*	from figgere
fritto	*fried*	from friggere
scritto	*wrote, written*	from scrivere
aggiunto	*added*	from aggiungere
giunto	*arrived*	from giungere
aperto	*opened*	from aprire
coperto	*covered*	from coprire
offerto	*offered*	from offrire
sofferto	*suffered*	from soffrire
apparso	*appeared*	from apparire
assunto	*assumed*	from assumere

chiesto	*asked, asked for*	from chiedere
chiuso	*closed*	from chiudere
concluso	*concluded*	from concludere
deluso	*disappointed*	from deludere
incluso	*included*	from includere
corso	*ran, run*	from correre
discorso	*talked, chatted*	from discorrere
costretto	*forced, compelled*	from costringere
detto	*said*	from dire
diretto	*directed*	from dirigere
letto	*read*	from lire
cotto	*cooked*	from cuocere
condotto	*drove, driven*	from condurre
prodotto	*produced*	from produrre
tradotto	*translated*	from tradurre
dato	*gave, given*	from dare
nato	*born*	from nascere
stato	*was, been*	from essere, from stare
fatto	*did, made*	from fare
deciso	*decided*	from decidere
discusso	*discussed*	from discutere
detto	*said, told*	from dire
benedetto	*blessed*	from benedire
dipinto	*painted*	from dipingere
distinto	*distinguished*	from distingere
finto	*feigned, pretended*	from fingere
espresso	*expressed*	from esprimere
messo	*put, placed*	from mettere
morso	*bit, bitten*	from mordere
morto	*died*	from morire
mosso	*moved, stirred*	from muovere
raso	*shaved, shaven*	from radere
riso	*laughed*	from ridere
rimasto	*remained*	from rimanere
risposto	*answered*	from rispondere
scelto	*chose, chosen*	from scegliere
sciolto	*melted*	from sciogliere
scosso	*shook, shaken*	from scuotere
spento	*extinguished, put out*	from spegnere
valso	*to have been worth*	from valere
venuto	*came*	from venire
vinto	*won*	from vincere
visto	*saw*	from vedere
vissuto	*lived*	from vivere

Verbs Conjugated with *Essere*

There is a small group of intransitive verbs which use **ESSERE** as the auxiliary verb. They are further distinguished from AVERE verbs in that they must show agreement between the past participle and the subject. That means the gender and number of the subject reflect onto the past participle via the final vowel, like this:

> Maria è caduta.
> *Marie fell.*

> Siamo saliti.
> *We went up.*

> Le ragazze sono tornate.
> *The girls came back.*

An unchanged vowel (**o**) means the subject is *masculine* and *singular*. This is agreement too:

> Andrea è tornato a casa.
> *Andrew came home.*

Here are 18 common intransitive verbs which require ESSERE as the auxiliary verb, and which must show agreement between the past participle and the subject. They are listed in a way that allows you to to see the class-room device: **Marc D. + Russ Van Pester**, a mnemonic to help you recall all 18.

> **M**orire
> **A**ndare
> **R**estare
> **C**adere
>
> **D**iventare
>
> +
>
> **R**imanere
> **U**scire
> **S**alire
> **S**cendere
>
> **V**enire
> **A**rrivare
> **N**ascere

Partire
Entrare
Stare
Tornare
Essere
Rincasare

Besides these basic verbs, there are many other intransitives that use essere. Impersonal verbs pertaining to the weather, for example, are also conjugated with essere:

È piovuto ieri sera.
It rained last night.

È nevicato, è grandinato.
It snowed, it hailed.

Observations on Agreement

The following rules of agreement govern ALL compound tenses:

1. Past participle agrees in gender and number with the **subject** of all verbs using *essere* as the auxiliary.

2. Past participle agrees with the **preceding direct object pronoun** of all verbs using *avere* as auxiliary. Direct objects which follow the participle do not affect it.

Compare:

Ho messo le mie scarpe nuove di zecca.
I put on my brand new shoes.
(no agreement, direct object doesn't precede)

Le ho mess**e**.
I put them on.

Quando hai comprato quella gonna?
When did you buy that skirt?

L'ho comprat**a** ieri.
I bought it yesterday.

3. There is **never** agreement with an *indirect* object.

Il Passato Prossimo

This essential past tense is constructed with the present (indicative) of the auxiliary and a past participle:

> Abbiamo capito la lezione.
> *We understood the lesson.*

> Siamo andati al cinema.
> *We went to the movies.*

The Passato Prossimo is the workhorse of the past. It expresses a completed past action in conversation and in informal writing.

Il Trapassato

The Past Perfect is created with the imperfect of the auxiliary verb and a past participle. It is used for an action that had already taken place previous to another point in the past:

> Avevo già restituito il libro quando me l'hai chiesto.
> *I had already returned the book when you asked me for it.*

> Era già partita quando sei arrivato.
> *She had already left when you arrived.*

Il Futuro Anteriore

The Future Perfect is constructed from the future tense of the auxiliary verb and a past participle. It expresses a future action which will have taken place by some other point in time, as follows:

> Sbrighiamoci, avranno già finito di mangiare senza di noi!
> *Let's hurry (or) they will have finished the meal without us.*

> Se arriverai alle 10 loro saranno già partiti.
> *If you get here at 10 they'll have already left.*

Il Condizionale Passato

The Past Conditional uses the conditional of the auxiliary verb and a past participle. It expresses what might have taken place if certain conditions had been met:

> Se avessi avuto il tempo, l'avrei fatto da sola.
> *If I had had the time, I would have done it myself.*

Se avessi avuto il tempo, sarei andato al concerto.
If I had had the time, I would have gone to the concert.

Il Congiuntivo Passato

This compound is made with the present subjunctive of the auxiliary verb and a past participle. It is used in a subordinate clause whose action 1) has taken place prior to that of the main verb or 2) has yet to take place relative to the verb in the main clause:

Dubito che abbiano trovato la strada giusta.
I doubt they took the right road.

Voglio che abbiate finito tutti gli esercizi prima di partire.
I want you to have finished all of the problems before you leave.

Credo che loro siano scesi a Roma.
I think they got off in Rome.

Il Passato Anteriore

This is a **literary** tense based on the passato remoto of the auxiliary verb and a past participle. It has approximately the same meaning as its less formal counterpart, the *trapassato*. It is restricted to literature or formal writing for an action which **had taken place prior** to the action of main verb. Expect to see it used along with the passato remoto like this:

Quando **ebbe finito** il suo caffè, *lavò* la tazza e la *rimise* sul gancio.
When he had finished his coffee, he washed his cup and put it back on its hook.

Drill 52: Formation of the Compound Tenses: The Auxiliary Verb

Select the correct auxiliary verb. Does the verb require **essere** or **avere**?

1. _____ andata a letto verso le undici.
   (è OR ha?)

2. _____ dovuto finire i tuoi compiti.
   (saresti OR avresti?)

3. Se mi fossi sbrigato, _____ finito prima di mezzanotte.
   (avrei OR sarei?)

4. _____ morti in un incidente.
   (Sono OR Hanno?)

5. Ti _____ pettinato i capelli.
   (sei OR hai?)

6. Vi _____ seduti.
   (siete OR avete?)

7. _____ uscite da un'ora.
   (saranno OR avranno?)

8. I tuoi regali mi _____ piaciuti tanto.
   (sono OR hanno?)

9. Qualcuno _____ bevuto la mia birra.
   (serà OR avrà?)

10. Chi _____ preso il mio cellulare?
    (è OR ha?)

Answers and Explanations to Drill 52

1. È andata a letto verso le undici.
   She went to bed around eleven.
   The **a** on the end of the participle is a blinking light that signals agreement with subject, the hallmark of verbs conjugated with *essere*.

2. **Avresti** dovuto finire i tuoi compiti.
   You should have finished your homework.
   Did you remember that *dovere* is conjugated with the auxiliary that matches the coming infinitive? In this case *finire* is a transitive verb, which means it can accept a direct object and, therefore, uses *avere*.

3. Se mi fossi sbrigato, **avrei** finito prima di mezzanotte.
   If I had hurried, I would have finished before midnight.
   Chose *avere* for a transitive verb like *finire*.

4. **Sono** morti in un incidente.
   They died in an accident.
   Agreement with subject is evident in the **i** on the end of the past participle. *Morire* is an *essere* verb.

5. Ti **sei** pettinato i capelli.
   You combed your hair.
   A reflexive verb always uses *essere*!

6. Vi **siete** seduti.
   You (plural) sat down.
   Reflexive again! Choose *essere*!

7. **Saranno** uscite da un'ora.
   They probably went out an hour ago.
   The **e** indicates agreement with a feminine plural subject. *Uscire* is a classic *essere* verb.

8. I tuoi regali mi **sono** piaciuti *tantissimo.*
   I liked your gifts so much.
   In this sentence *piaciuti* agrees with its subject, the gifts. Conjugate with *essere*.

9. Qualcuno **avrà** bevuto la mia birra.

   Someone must have drunk my beer.

   Bere requires *avere* for its auxiliary. Its direct object appears in this sentence *(la mia birra)*, making *bere* easy to nail as a transitive verb.

10. Chi **ha** preso il mio cellulare?

    Who took my cell?

    The cell phone is the direct object of *prendere (to take)*. Use *avere* as the auxiliary for this transitive verb.

Drill 53: Formation of the Compound Tenses: The Past Participle

Provide the correct participle. Show agreement where necessary.

1. I gemelli si sono _____ i capelli.
   (tagliare)

2. Lei si è _____ la doccia.
   (fare)

3. Se avessi letto la storia, avresti _____ la fine.
   (sapere)

4. Hai visto le mie chiavi? Le avevo _____ sulla tavola.
   (mettere)

5. Gli abbiamo _____ la verità.
   (dire)

6. Il bimbo ha _____ sulle candeline.
   (soffiare)

7. Ho _____ tre ore.
   (dormire)

8. Non ha _____.
   (rispondere)

9. Hai _____ le luci?
   (spegnere)

10. A che ora sono _____?
    (partire – loro)

Answers and Explanations to Drill 53

1. I gemelli si sono **tagliati** i capelli.
   The twins cut their hair.
   Tagliarsi is reflexive, show agreement with subject.

2. Lei si è **fatta** la doccia.
   She took a shower.
   Fare uses the irregular participle *fatto*, and here is feminine and singular to match *lei*. Since all reflexive verbs are conjugated with *essere*, they always show subject agreement.

3. Se tu avessi letto la storia, avresti **saputo** la fine.
   If you had read the story, you would have known (found out) the ending.
   The past participle for *sapere* is regular.

4. Hai visto le mie chiavi? Le avevo **messe** sulla tavola.
   Have you seen my keys? I had left them on the table.
   Mettere uses the irregular participle *messo*. The final **e** reflects the *feminine plural direct object* which **precedes the participle.** *(le)* Understanding agreement is very important because it actually changes the sound of the participle.

5. Gli abbiamo **detto** la verità.
   We told him (them) the truth.
   Dire uses the irregular participle *detto*. The preceding object in this sentence *(gli)* is **indirect**. Past participles **never** agree with *indirect* objects; a hard and fast rule worth remembering.

6. Il bimbo ha **soffiato** sulle candeline.
   The child blew out the candles.
   Soffiato is a regular past participle from a typical -are verb.

7. Ho **dormito** tre ore.
   I slept three hours.
   Dormito is a standard past participle from a regular -ire verb.

8. Non ha **risposto**.
   He didn't answer.
   Risposto is a common but irregular past participle.

9. Hai **spento** le luci?
   Did you turn out the lights?
   This is the irregular participle from the verb *spegnere, to extinguish, to turn off*.

10. A che ora sono **partiti**?
    At what time did they leave?
    A regular -ire participle which reflects agreement with its subject, *loro*.

Drill 54: Selection of the Compound Tense

Provide the past compound needed in the following sentences.

1. Se fosse venuta l'_____.
   (vedere – io)

2. Noi _____ quando tornerete.
   (partire + già)

3. Loro _____ le porte quando siamo arrivati.
   (chiudere + già)

4. L'_____ scendere verso le dieci.
   (fare, l' = *her*)

5. Azzurra, dove stavi? Ti _____ dappertutto!
   (cercare)

6. Quando _____ il libro, te lo invierò.
   (leggere – io)

7. _____ la loro villa l'anno scorso.
   (vendere - loro)

8. Se tu gli avessi chiesto, ti _____ volentieri le sue avventure.
   (raccontare)

9. Cecilia _____ il naso, poverina!
   (rompersi)

10. Gli amici _____ ieri.
    (parlarsi)

Answers and Explanations to Drill 54

1. Se fosse venuta, l'**avrei vista.**
   If she had come I would have seen her.
   When the pluperfect subjunctive appears in the *if* clause, as it does here, we must follow with the *past conditional* in the result clause. Note the agreement between the past participle and its *preceding direct object, l' = her.*

2. Noi **saremo già partiti** quando tornerete.
   We will have already left when you get back.
   We need the *futuro anteriore* here for an action that *will have already taken place before* the second action comes to pass. Since the verb *partire* is intransitive, we conjugate it with *essere* as the auxiliary and show subject agreement.

3. **Avevano gìa chiuso** le porte quando siamo arrivati.
   They had already closed the doors when we arrived.
   We use the *trapassato* to express what had happened prior to our arrival.

4. L'**ho fatta** scendere verso le dieci
   I dropped her off around ten o'clock.
   Use the *passato prossimo* to convey a completed past action with a discernable beginning or ending. The past participle shows agreement with its preceding direct object, *l' = her.*

5. Azzurra, dove stavi? Ti **ho cercata** dappertutto!
   Azzurra, where were you? I looked for you everywhere!
   We show agreement with *ti,* in this case feminine, as Azzurra is a girl.

6. Quando **avrò letto** il libro, te lo invierò.
   When I've read the book, I'll send it to you.
   Use the *futuro anteriore* for an action that *needs to take place before* the second action can come to pass. Since the verb is obviously transitive (because of the presence of *il libro,* its direct object) we conjugate with *avere.*

7. **Hanno venduto** la loro villa l'anno scorso.

   They sold their villa last year.

   The *passato prossimo* reports a completed past action here. The verb *vendere* is unmistakably transitive (*villa* = direct object). We use *avere* as auxiliary.

8. Se tu gli avessi chiesto, ti **avrebbe raccontato** volentieri le sue avventure.

   If you had asked him, he would have gladly told you (all about) his adventures.

   This is an example of the *condizionale passato*.

9. Cecilia **si è rotta** il naso, poverina!

   Cecilia broke her nose, poor thing!

   This is a completed past action. We use the *passato prossimo* to report it. *Rompersi* is reflexive, so we conjugate with *essere* as the auxiliary. Did you know the irregular participle?

10. Gli amici **si sono parlati** ieri.

    The friends spoke to each other yesterday.

    This is most likely a completed action. Use *essere* as the auxiliary with this reciprocal verb.

The Literary Past

You must master the Passato Remoto in order to read with understanding. This tense is usually reserved for written narrative in literature. It is not used in everyday speech* and it is not used in informal writing such as a letter or an e-mail. The Passato Remoto replaces the Passato Prossimo in this literary milieu only. The meaning of the two tenses is identical. We often see the Passato Remoto intertwined with the Imperfetto in a literary narrative. Translate the Passato Remoto just as though it were the Passato Prossimo.

The formation of the Passato Remoto employs three sets of endings. Regular roots are taken from the infinitive, minus the three final letters. Irregular verbs generally come from the **-ere** family and are often only irregular in three of the six persons. Here are examples of the three regular formations, followed by the most common irregulars:

ARE: am**ai**, am**asti**, am**ò**, am**ammo**, am**aste**, am**arono**

ERE: vend**ei**, vend**esti**, vend**è**, vend**emmo**, vend**este**, vend**erono**

IRE: fin**ii**, fin**isti**, fin**ì**, fin**immo**, fin**iste**, fin**irono**

Note that the third person of all three regular conjugations is accented.

Irregular verbs:

avere:	**ebbi**, avesti, **ebbe**, avemmo, aveste, **ebbero**
bere:	**bevvi, bev**esti, **bevve, bev**emmo, **beveste, bevvero**
cadere:	**caddi**, cadesti, **cadde**, cademmo, cadeste, **caddero**
condurre:	**condussi, conduc**esti, **condusse, conduc**emmo, **conduc**este, **condussero**
conoscere:	**conobbi**, conoscesti, **conobbe**, conoscemmo, conosceste, **conobbero**
dare:	**diedi, desti, diede, demmo, deste, diedero**
decidere:	**decisi**, decidesti, **decise**, decidemmo, decideste, **decisero**
dire:	**dissi, dic**esti, **disse, dic**emmo, **dic**este, **dissero**
essere:	**fui, fosti, fu, fummo, foste, furono**
fare:	**feci, fac**esti, **fece, fac**emmo, **faceste, fecero**

---

* The Passato Remoto is used in every day speech throughout Sicily, perhaps due to Spanish influence. It can also be heard in parts of Calabria, and in a few areas of Puglia.

leggere:	**lessi,** leggesti, **lesse,** leggemmo, leggeste, **lessero**
mettere:	**misi,** mettesti, **mise,** mettemmo, metteste, **misero**
nascere:	**nacqui,** nascesti, **nacque,** nascemmo, nasceste, **nacquero**
prendere:	**presi,** prendesti, **prese,** prendemmo, prendeste, **presero**
rimanere:	**rimasi,** rimanesti, **rimase,** rimanemmo, rimaneste, **rimasero**
rispondere:	**risposi,** rispondesti, **rispose,** rispondemmo, rispondeste, **risposero**
sapere:	**seppi,** sapesti, **seppe,** sapemmo, sapeste, **seppero**
scegliere:	**scelsi,** scegliesti, **scelse,** scegliemmo, sceglieste, **scelsero**
scendere:	**scesi,** scendesti, **scese,** scendemmo, scendeste, **scesero**
scrivere:	**scrissi,** scrivesti, **scrisse,** scrivemmo, scriveste, **scrissero**
spendere:	**spesi,** spendesti, **spese,** spendemmo, spendeste, **spesero**
stare:	**stetti, stesti, stette, stemmo, steste, stettero**
uccidere:	**uccisi,** uccidesti, **uccise,** uccidemmo, uccideste, **uccisero**
vedere:	**vidi,** vedesti, **vide,** vedemmo, vedeste, **videro**
venire:	**venni,** venisti, **venne,** venimmo, veniste, **vennero**
vivere:	**vissi,** vivesti, **visse,** vivemmo, viveste, **vissero**
volere:	**volli,** volesti, **volle,** volemmo, voleste, **vollero**

Drill 55: Il Passato Remoto

Change the **bold** verbs to the Passato Remoto, adjust the pronoun if necessary:

1. Giovanna **è nata** in un piccolo paese francese. _____

2. Un giorno, mentre guardava le sue pecore **ha sentito** delle voci divine che le dicevano di andare a salvare la Francia e di cacciare gli Inglesi dalla patria. _____

3. **È partita** e **è andata** a trovare il delfino, Carlo VIII, che **è riuscita** a persuadere. _____

4. L'**ha fatto** incoronare re, poi **si è messa** a capo del suo esercito.

   _____

5. Vestita da uomo, **ha vinto** molte battaglie e **ha liberato** la città assediata di Orléans. _____

6. È stata tradita, comunque, e i Bourgignon l'**hanno catturata** e l'**hanno venduta** agli Inglesi. _____

7. Gli Inglesi l'**hanno giudicata** e l'**hanno condannata** a morte.

8. Giovanna **è morta** sul rogo. _____

9. **È diventata** una delle più grandi eroine del mondo.

   _____

10. Per anni dopo la sua morte, la gente credeva di rivederla. La chiesa l'**ha santificata**. Poco dopo il popolo francese l'**ha scelta** come santa patrona. _____

Answers to Drill 55

1. Giovanna **nacque** in un piccolo paese francese.

2. Un giorno, mentre guardava le sue pecore **sentì** delle voci divine che le dicevano di andare a salvare la Francia e di cacciare gli Inglesi dalla patria.

3. **Partì** e **andò** a trovare il delfino, Carlo VIII, che **riuscì** a persuadere.

4. Lo **fece** incoronare re, poi **si mise** a capo del suo esercito.

5. Vestita da uomo, **vinse** molte battaglie e **liberò** la città assediata di Orléans.

6. **Fu** tradita, comunque, e i Bourguigon **la catturarono** e **la venderono/ vendettero** agli Inglesi.

7. Gli Inglesi **la giudicarono** e **la condannarono** a morte.

8. Giovanna **morì** sul rogo.

9. **Diventò** una delle più grandi eroine del mondo.

10. Per anni dopo la sua morte, la gente credeva di rivederla. La chiesa la **santificò**. Poco dopo il popolo francese **la scelse** come santa patrona.

The Passive Voice

The passive voice is generally avoided in Italian. However, it does exist and is made as follows: Conjugate the verb ESSERE in whatever tense is needed and follow with the past participle of the verb in question. You can also make the passive voice in the same way with the verb VENIRE. Both verbs create a sentence in which the subject is *acted upon*. Just remember that Italian prefers, whenever possible, an active verb. Here are samples of the passive voice in Italian:

> Gianni non poteva affrontare la mamma perchè **è stato espulso** dalla scuola.
> *John couldn't face his mother because he was expelled from school.*

> **Sarete accolti** a braccia aperte.
> *You will be welcomed with open arms.*

> Molto vino **viene prodotto** in Italia.
> *A lot of wine is produced in Italy.*

How to Avoid the Passive Voice

1. You can create an active subject by making the verb reflexive:

   > In Italia si beve molto vino.
   > *A lot of wine is drunk in Italy.*

2. The object of the passive sentence can be made into an active subject:

   > La sua accoglienza calorosa mi ha commosso.
   > *I was touched by her warm reception.*

3. If the subject is a person, you may use the **farsi + infinitive** construction to keep your sentence in the active voice:

   > Si è fatto sostituire da un giovane.
   > *He was replaced by a younger worker.*

4. If there is no subject you can supply *qualcuno, nessuno* or *loro*.

   > Qualcuno mi ha fregato le patatine!
   > *Somebody swiped my chips!* (instead of *My chips have been swiped.*)

Drill 56: Avoiding the Passive Voice

Restate the sentence in the active voice, using one of the above methods:

1. È stata chiamata Aurelia.

   _____

2. La mia valigia è stata aperta.

   _____

3. È stato investito da un furgone.

   _____

4. Il vino bianco è servito freddo.

   _____

5. Sono sbalordita dal tuo regalo.

   _____

6. Non siamo stati invitati.

   _____

7. Sei stato dimenticato.

   _____

8. Siete stati rifiutati.

   _____

9. Una nuova torre sarà costruita.

   _____

10. La mia nuova pettinatura non è stata notata.

   _____

Answers and Explanations to Drill 56

1. Si chiamava Aurelia.
   Her name was Aurelia.
   The reflexive construction works well and is widely used.

2. Qualcuno ha aperto la mia valigia.
   We supply *Qualcuno,* an active subject for the unkown individual who opened the suitcase. You could also say *Hanno aperto* to provide a vague but active subject: *they.*

3. Un furgone l'ha investito.
   He was run over (or *hit*) *by a van.*
   We make the *van* the active subject of the verb.

4. Il vino bianco si serve freddo.
   White wine is served cold.
   The reflexive works well here.

5. Il tuo regalo mi ha sbalordito.
   I was astonished by your gift.
   Turn the *gift* into the subject of the sentence.

6. Non ci hanno invitati.
   We weren't invited.
   Supply an active subject with *loro.*

7. Ti hanno dimenticato.
   You were forgotten.
   Supply an active subject with *loro.*

8. Vi hanno rifiutati.
   You were refused.
   Supply an active subject with *loro.*

9. Costruiranno una nuova torre.
   A new tower will be built.
   Supply an active subject with *loro.*

10. Nessuno ha notato la mia nuova pettinatura.
    No one noticed my new hair style.
    Supply the active subject with *Nessuno.*

The Subjunctive

The formation of the present subjunctive is not as daunting as you may have heard. Let's take it one step at a time. The first form of the present subjunctive is used for three persons: io, tu, and lui. The regular root can be made by removing **the last letter** from **the first person** of the present indicative as follows:

> io parlo = parl
>
> io vendo = vend
>
> io dormo = dorm
>
> io finisco = finisc

To these roots we add one of two possible endings, **-i** for -are verbs, and **-a** for all -ere and -ire verbs, thus:

che io parl**i**	che io vend**a**	che io dorm**a**	che io finisc**a**
che tu parl**i**	che tu vend**a**	che tu dorm**a**	che tu finisc**a**
che lui parl**i**	che lui vend**a**	che lui dorm**a**	che lui finisc**a**

Since the verb forms are identical for all three persons, it is quite common, and often necessary, to use the subject pronouns for clarity.

The next form, *noi*, is the same as the present indicative:

> che **parliamo**   che **vendiamo**   che **dormiamo**   che **finiamo**

The *voi* form is easily made by replacing the **-mo** of the *noi* form with **-te**:

> che parlia**te**   che vendia**te**   che dormia**te**   che finia**te**

The *loro* form is made by adding **-no** to whatever we used for the first three persons of the present subjunctive, like this:

> che parli**no**   che venda**no**   che dorma**no**   che finisca**no**

Here, then, are examples of the regular formation of the present subjunctive:

> ARE: parl**i**, parl**i**, parl**i**, parl**iamo**, parl**iate**, parl**ino**
>
> ERE: vend**a**, vend**a**, vend**a**, vend**iamo**, vend**iate**, vend**ano**
>
> IRE: dorm**a**, dorm**a**, dorm**a**, dorm**iamo**, dorm**iate**, dorm**ano**
>
> IRE: finisc**a**, finisc**a**, finisc**a**, fin**iamo**, fin**iate**, finisc**ano**

If the -are root already ends in **-i**, it is not necessary to add another **-i**: io mangio – o = che io mangi

> io cambio – o = che io cambi
>
> io lascio – o = che io lasci
>
> io studio – o = che io studi

Let's recap how to make the present subjunctive. There are 5 steps:

1. Start with the first person present indicative; remove the last letter.

2. Add **-i** to **-are** verbs and **-a** to all other verbs. Use the form you've just created for *io*, *tu* and *lui*.

3. Reuse the present indicative *noi* form for the present subjunctive.

4. Turn the *noi* form into the *voi* form by using **-te** as the last two letters (instead of **-mo**).

5. To make the *loro* form, simply add **-no** to the form which was used for *io*, *tu* and *lui*.

We can apply these same rules to make many common **irregular** verbs. Study these so-called *irregular* present subjunctive verbs and observe that they follow our formation rules exactly:

cogliere *(to gather, to pick)*	**colga, colga, colga, cogliamo, cogliate, colgano**
dire *(to say, to tell)*	**dica, dica, dica, diciamo, diciate, dicano**
esporre *(to expose)*	**esponga, esponga, esponga, esponiamo, esponiate, espongano**
piacere *(to please)*	**piaccia, piaccia, piaccia, piacciamo, piacciate, piacciano**
porre *(to put, to place)*	**ponga, ponga, ponga, poniamo, poniate, pongano**
potere *(to be able)*	**possa, possa, possa, possiamo, possiate, possano**
rimanere *(to remain)*	**rimanga, rimanga, rimanga, rimaniamo, rimaniate, rimangano**
salire *(to go up, to come up)*	**salga, salga, salga, saliamo, saliate, salgano**
scegliere *(to choose)*	**scelga, scelga, scelga, scegliamo, scegliate, scelgano**
sedersi *(to sit)*	**mi sieda, ti sieda, si sieda, ci sediamo, vi sediate, si siedano**

tenere *(to hold, to keep)*	**tenga, tenga, tenga, teniamo, teniate, tengano**
togliere *(to remove)*	**tolga, tolga, tolga, togliamo, togliate, tolgano**
tradurre *(to translate)*	**traduca, traduca, traduca, traduciamo, traduciate, traducano**
uscire *(to go out)*	**esca, esca, esca, usciamo, usciate, escano**
valere *(to be worth)*	**valga, valga, valga, valiamo, valiate, valgano**
venire *(to come)*	**venga, venga, venga, veniamo, veniate, vengano**
volere *(to want)*	**voglia, voglia, voglia, vogliamo, vogliate, vogliano**

The following eight verbs really *are* irregular, do not follow our pattern, and must be learned by heart:

andare *(to go)*	**vada, vada, vada, andiamo, andiate, vadano**
avere *(to have)*	**abbia, abbia, abbia, abbiamo, abbiate, abbiano**
dare *(to give)*	**dia, dia, dia, diamo, diate, diano**
fare *(to do, to make)*	**faccia, faccia, faccia, facciamo, facciate, facciano**
dovere *(to have to, must)*	**debba, debba, debba, dobbiamo, dobbiate, debbano**
essere *(to be)*	**sia, sia, sia, siamo, siate, siano**
sapere *(to know)*	**sappia, sappia, sappia, sappiamo, sappiate, sappiano**
stare *(to be)*	**stia, stia, stia, stiamo, stiate, stiano**

The Subjunctive Mood

The indicative relates actuality or fact. The subjunctive mood allows the speaker to impose his opinion, wish, or emotion onto the verb in the subsequent clause. The construction frequently uses the conjunction **che** to signal that this is taking place. Remember, however, that **che** figures in lots of expressions that do not require the subjunctive. We will address them as well.

Most of the verbs and expressions with which a speaker can project his fears, doubts, or opinions onto the coming verb, can be neatly classified into one of 5 categories. When deciding whether or not to use the subjunctive, ask yourself if the verb or phrase which introduces it fits under one of these broad headings.

Keep in mind that the subjunctive is only needed if the subject of the introductory clause and the subject of the subordinate clause are **different**. One would **never say** *Voglio che io riesca*. The subjunctive would be avoided altogether with the much simpler infinitive construction: Voglio riuscire.

1. **La Volontà**: Will

   Is the speaker expressing a want or desire? Is he giving an order, a requirement, or making a command? Follow with the subjunctive.

   > VUOI **che** ti **faccia** un caffè?
   > *Do you want me to make you a coffee.*

   > Il professore ESIGE **che parliate** italiano.
   > *The teacher requires that you speak Italian.*

   > Papà INSISTE **che siate** responsabili.
   > *Dad insists that you be responsible.*

   Here are some common verbs in this group, all requiring the subjunctive:

comandare *(to order, command)*	**preferire** *(to prefer)*
desiderare *(to wish, desire)*	**proibire** *(to forbid)*
esigere *(to require, demand, exact)*	**suggerire** *(to suggest)*
insistere *(to insist)*	**supplicare** *(to implore, to beseech)*
ordinare *(to order, prescribe)*	**tenere** *(to belive, to maintain)*
pregare *(to beg, to ask, to pray)*	**volere** *(to want)*

2. **Il Dubbio**: Doubt

   Is the speaker expressing doubtfulness? Is he unsure or waivering in his certainty? Follow with the subjunctive.

   > NON CREDO **che possano** venire.
   > *I don't think they can come.*

   > PUÒ DARSI **che vengano** domani.
   > *Maybe they'll come tomorrow.*

   > È POSSIBILE **che** lei non **voglia** venire.
   > *It's possible that she doesn't want to come.*

   > DUBITO **che sia** possibile.
   > *I doubt that it's possible.*

3. **La Necessità**: Necessity

Does the speaker think that what is to follow is necessary or required? Use the subjunctive in the subordinate clause.

BISOGNA **che** io **dimagrisca dopo Natale**!
I need to lose weight after Christmas!

OCCORRE **che ascoltiate** in classe.
You must listen in class.

4. **L'Emozione**: Emotion

Is the speaker expressing a feeling or emotion, such as fear, happiness, hope, or sorrow? Always follow with the subjunctive.

HO PAURA **che piova** il giorno delle loro nozze.
I'm afraid that it will rain on their wedding day.

SONO TANTO FELICE **che** tu **stia** qui!
I'm so glad that you're here.

MI AUGURO **che** Lei **possa** venire.
I hope you can come.

SIAMO SPIACENTI **che** Lei **vada** in ospedale.
We're sorry that you're going into the hospital.

Lei TEME **che** il licantropo la **mangi**.
She's afraid that the werewolf will eat her.

SI TEME **che si siano persi**.
They're feared lost.

Here are some common verbs and expressions from this group:

avere paura *(to fear)*	**essere contento, felice, lieto** *(to be happy)*
arrabbiarsi *(to be angry)*	**essere triste, spiacente** *(to be sad, sorry)*
dispiacersi *(to be sorry, to regret)*	**essere deluso** *(to be disappointed)*
preoccuparsi *(to worry)*	**essere fiero, orgoglioso** *(to be proud)*
rallegrarsi *(to be glad)*	**essere fortunato, sfortunato** *(to be lucky, unlucky)*
sorprendersi *(to be surprised)*	
temere *(to fear)*	

5. **L'Opinione**: Opinion

Is the speaker stating what he thinks or believes? Is he giving his opinion regarding what is to follow? Use the subjunctive carefully here as we shall see that some opinions do not require it.

> CREDO **che**/ PENSO **che sappia** perchè.
> *I believe/I think he knows why.*

> È SECCANTE **che siano** in ritardo.
> *It's irritating that they're late.*

> PENSI **che abbia** la mia chiave?
> *Do you think he has my key?*

> PARE **che** non **voglia** venire.
> *It appears that he doesn't want to come.*

> SEMBRA **che sia** malato.
> *It seems that he's sick.*

> È UN PECCATO **che sia** malato.
> *It's a shame that he's sick.*

There are many IMPERSONAL EXPRESSIONS that belong under the heading of OPINION. They all convey the speaker's *"take"* or opinion on what he is about to say:

> È **bene che** *(it's good that)*

> È **male che** *(it's bad that)*

> È **facile che** *(it's easy that)*

> È **difficile che** *(it's difficult, hard that)*

> È **essenziale che** *(it's essential that)*

> È **importante che** *(it's important that)*

> È **necessario che** *(it's necessary that)*

> È **naturale che** *(it's natural that)*

> È **normale che** *(it's normal that)*

> È **strano che** *(it's strange that)*

> È **giusto che** *(it's right, fair that)*

> È **meglio che** *(it's better that)*

> È **possibile, impossibile che** *(it's possible, impossible that)*

> È **probabile, improbabile che** *(it's probable, improbable that)*

Verbs and Expressions of Certainty

Think of this as a sixth category: LA CERTEZZA. Verbs and expressions in this group DO NOT use the subjunctive UNLESS they are **negated** or **interrogative** (which makes them doubtful).

Here are some expressions of certainty. Remember, NO SUBJUNCTIVE *unless* negated or interrogative:

> **sono certo che** *(I'm certain that)*
>
> **sono sicuro che** *(I'm sure that)*
>
> **è chiaro che** *(it is clear that)*
>
> **è ovvio che** *(it is obvious that)*
>
> **è vero che** *(it is true that)*
>
> **so che** *(I know that)*

The following expression of certainty also uses the indicative:

> **Non dubito che** *(I don't doubt that)*

Subordinating Conjunctions

These common conjunctions must be followed by the subjunctive

> **affinchè** *(so that)*
> a condizione che
>
> **a meno che....non** *(unless)*
> a patto che
>
> **benché** *(although)*
>
> **in modo che*, perché*** *(so that)*
> *When **in modo che** and **perché** are followed by a result already attained, the indicative is used. When the result is desired, but not yet achieved, the subjunctive follows.
>
> **nonostante (che)** *(despite, in spite of)*
>
> **prima che** *(before)*
>
> **purché** *(provided that)*
>
> **sebbene** *(although)*
>
> **senza che** *(without)*

Using the Subjunctive After a Superlative

The subjunctive is used after *solo*, *unico*, *primo*, *ultimo* and *superlative adjectives* if the opinion of the speaker is reflected in the statement. When used to express a fact, they are followed by the indicative:

> Sei IL MIGLIORE amico **che** ci **sia**.
> *You're the best friend there is.*

> È LA macchina PIÙ VELOCE **che ha vinto**.
> *The fastest car won.*

> È IL PIÙ BEL quartiere **che** io **conosca**.
> *It's the nicest neighborhood I know.*

> È L'UNICA gonna **che** mi **piaccia**.
> *It's the only skirt I like.*

> È L'UNICA gonna blu **che ho**.
> *It's the only blue skirt I have.*

The Subjunctive After an Indefinite Antecedent

The subjunctive is used when the desired thing or quality is named but not yet found, like this:

> Cerchiamo una villa **che sia** più vicino al mare.
> *We're looking for a grand house that is closer to the sea.*

> Conoscete qualcuno **che capisca** il cinese?
> *Do you know someone who understands Chinese?*

> Esiste una medicina **che possa guarire** questa malattia?
> *Is there a drug that can cure this disease?*

Note that if the desired object has been found the indicative is used. Compare:

> CERCA un cappello **che** le **stia** bene.
> *She's looking for a hat that suits her.*

> Ha trovato un cappello **che** le **sta** bene.
> *She found a suitable hat.*

The subjunctive is also required after the following indefinite expressions:

> **CHIUNQUE sia,** se ne vada via.
> *Go away, whoever you are.*

> **COMUNQUE** tu **faccia,** riuscirai.
> *However you do (it), you will succeed.*

> Lo seguirò **DOVUNQUE vada**.
> *Wherever he goes, I will follow him.*

> **QUALUNQUE** + adjective or noun
> *(no matter how, no matter what)*
>
> > Qualunque cosa faccia …
> > Qualunque mestiere voglia fare…

> **QUALSIASI COSA dica**, restiamo.
> *We're staying, no matter what he says.*

> **PER QUANTO** ricco **sia**, non è contento.
> *However rich he is, he's not happy.*

> **PER QUANTO** veloce **vada**, arriva sempre in ritardo.
> *No matter how fast he goes, he always arrives late.*

The Subjunctive After a Negative Pronoun

Use the subjunctive after a negative pronoun when expressing an opinion:

> Non c'è **NESSUNO** che **sia** in grado di piacerle.
> *Nobody is able to please her.*

> Non c'è **NIENTE** che **valga.**
> *There is nothing worthwhile.*

How to Avoid the Subjunctive

The subjunctive is always avoided when both verbs in the sentence have the same subject. This is accomplished with a simple infinitve or **di + infinitive**:

> Odio **essere** in ritardo.
> *I hate being late.*

> Sono spiacente **di** non **poter** aiutare.
> *I'm sorry I can't help.*

Most verbs and impersonal expressions can be replaced in a similar manner, even if the subjects of the two verbs are different:

> È bene **tenere** il bimbo per mano.
> *It's (a) good (idea) to hold your child's hand.*

> È meglio **attendere** i nostri bagagli qui.
> *It's better to wait for our bags here.*

A + infinitive replaces the subjunctive in the superlative construction:

> Tu sei **LA SOLA** persona **a** capirmi.
> *You are the only person who understands me.*

Drill 57: The Subjunctive

Supply the correct form of the subjunctive, **or** the indicative, as the case may be. Base your decision on what precedes the **CHE**:

1. Spero che voi _____ felici.
   (essere)

2. Mamma vuole che lui _____ .
   (finire)

3. È certo che tu _____ venire?
   (potere)

4. È ovvio che lui _____ troppo.
   (bere)

5. È chiaro che lei non mi _____ .
   (capire)

6. È seccante che _____ stamattina.
   (piovere)

7. Mi dispiace che tu _____ tanti guai.
   (avere)

8. Dovunque tu _____ , ti troverò.
   (andare)

9. Cerchiamo un regalo che gli _____ .
   (piacere)

10. Esige che loro _____ ad alta voce.
    (leggere)

11. Credo che voi _____ studiare di più.
    (dovere)

12. Vorebbe rincasare prima che suo padre _____.
    (tornare)

13. È urgente che voi _____ subito.
    (andare)

14. Verró a ameno che non _____.
    (nevicare)

15. Posso prestarti il mio vestito a patto che me lo _____.
    (rendere)

16. Mi auguro che questi regali vi _____.
    (piacere)

17. Scrivi affinché io _____ sapere come stai.
    (potere)

18. Occorre che tu _____ una materia di specializzazione.
    (scegliere)

19. Preferisco che voi _____ la verità.
    (dire)

20. Può darsi che noi _____ il treno.
    (prendere)

21. Non c'è nessuno che _____ aspettare.
    (volere)

22. È l'unica casa che loro _____.
    (possedere)

23. Andremo dovunque _____.
    (essere) (it may be)

24. Peccato che non _____ bel tempo.
    (fare)

25. Conoscete una domestica che _____ cucinare?
    (sapere)

Answers and Explanations to Drill 57

1. Spero che voi **siate** felici.
   I hope that you will be happy.
   The speaker projects his wish for happiness onto the subordinate *verb*. *Sperare* is *emotivo* and requires the subjunctive. Note that there is no future form of the subjunctive.

2. Mamma vuole che lui **finisca.**
   Mom wants him to finish.
   Volere, obviously a verb of *volontà*, requires the subjunctive. Mom projects her will onto the verb which follows *what she wants*.

3. È certo che tu **possa** venire?
   Is it certain that you can come?
   Here we have an expression of *certezza* in the interrogative, thus it becomes doubtful and requires the subjunctive.

4. È ovvio che lui **beve** troppo.
   It's obvious that he drinks too much.
   This is a clear expression of *certainty*. The indicative is required.

5. È chiaro che lei non mi **capisce.**
   It's clear that she doesn't understand me.
   Another clear-cut expression of certainty. Use the indicative.

6. È seccante che **piova** stamattina.
   It's irritating that it's raining this morning.
   The speaker's *opinion* that the rain is a nuisance is reflected in the subjunctive form of piovere.

7. Mi dispiace che tu **abbia** tanti guai.
   I'm sorry that you have so many troubles.
   Dispiacere is a verb of *emozione* requiring the subjunctive.

8. Dovunque (tu) **vada**, ti troverò.
   Wherever you go, I will find you.
   You must use the subjunctive after the indefinite *dovunque*.

9. Cerchiamo un regalo che gli **piaccia**.
   We're looking for a gift that will please him.
   The gift being sought has not yet been found; the existence of this antecedent is therefore indefinite. Use the subjunctive here.

10. Esige che loro **leggano** ad alta voce
    He requires that they read aloud.
    He clearly projects his will (*volontà*) onto the subordinate verb. You must use the subjunctive here.

11. Credo che voi **dobbiate** studiare di più.
    I believe you must or *should study more.*
    The verb *credere* is a verb of *belief or opinion.* Use the subjunctive here.

12. Vorebbe rincasare prima che tu suo padre **torni**.
    He would like to be home before his father gets back.
    The subordinating conjunction *prima che* requires the subjunctive.

13. È urgente che voi **andiate** subito.
    It's urgent that you go right away.
    This *opinion* is reflected in the subjunctive which must follow it.

14. Verrò a meno che non **nevichi**.
    I'll come unless it snows.
    A subordinating conjunction, *a meno che...non* requires the subjunctive.

15. Posso prestarti il mio vestito a patto che tu me lo **renda**.
    You can borrow my dress provided that you return it to me.
    Always use the subjunctive after this subordinating conjunction.

16. Mi auguro che questi regali vi **piacciano**.
    I hope that these gifts please or *will please you.*
    Augurarsi expresses the emotive *hope.* Follow with the subjunctive.

17. Scrivi affinché io **possa** sapere come stai.
    Write so that I can know how you are.
    Use the subjunctive after this conjunction as the desired result (clear handwriting) has not yet been attained.

18. Occorre che tu **scelga** una materia di specializzazione.
    You must choose a major.
    Always use the subjunctive after *occorre che*, the quintessential expression of requirement or need (*necessità*). Chances are that you will encounter *occorre che* or *bisogna che* on your exam.

19. Mi sembra che voi **diciate** la verità.
    It seems to me that you're telling the truth.
    The verb *sembrare* is used to express an opinion (*opinione*) and therefore requires the subjunctive.

20. Può darsi che **prendiamo** il treno.
    Maybe we'll take the train.
    A classic example of *dubbio*. Use the subjunctive.

21. Non c'è nessuno che **voglia** apettarti.
    There's nobody who wants to wait for you.
    Here we need the subjunctive to follow the negative pronoun *nessuno*. The person who might wait for you has not been found and the speaker doesn't think he exists.

22. È l'unica casa che **possiedono**.
    It's the only house they own.
    We follow *l'unica* with the indicative here because this is a fact, and not an opinion.

23. Andremo dovunque **sia**.
    We'll go wherever it may be.
    The subjunctive always follows this *indefinite*, and therefore *doubtful* phrase.

24. Peccato che non **faccia** bel tempo.
    It's a shame that the weather's not nice.
    The speaker gives his *opinion* on the weather. Use the subjunctive.

25. Conoscete una domestica che **sappia** cucinare?
    Do you know a maid who knows how to cook?
    This problem is similar to number 9. The existence of the wished-for maid has not yet been confirmed. She is therefore an *indefinite* antecedent. Use the subjunctive here.

The Imperfect Subjunctive

The regular roots come from the infinitive, minus the three final letters. There are three sets of endings, but they differ from each other by just one letter. Each verb type is marked by its characteristic letter, *a, e,* or *i.*

Here are examples of the three regular conjugations:

ARE: parl**assi**, parl**assi**, parl**asse**, parl**assimo**, parl**aste**, parl**asscro**

ERE: vend**essi**, vend**essi**, vend**esse**, vend**essimo**, vend**este**, vend**essero**

IRE: fin**issi**, fin**issi**, fin**isse**, fin**issimo**, fin**iste**, fin**issero**

Here some common irregular verbs:

bere:	**bev**essi, **bev**essi, **bev**esse, **bev**essimo, **bev**este, **bev**essero
dare:	**d**essi, **d**essi, **d**esse, **d**essimo, **d**este, **d**essero
dire:	**dic**essi, **dic**essi, **dic**esse, **dic**essimo, **dic**este, **dic**essero
essere:	**fossi, fossi, fosse, fossimo, foste, fossero**
fare:	**fac**essi, **fac**essi, **fac**esse, **fac**essimo, **fac**este, **fac**essero
stare:	**st**essi, **st**essi, **st**esse, **st**essimo, **st**este, **st**essero
tradurre:	**traduc**essi, **traduc**essi, **traduc**esse, **traduc**essimo, **tra-duc**este, **traduc**essero.

Since the first and second persons are identical, it is common to include the subject pronoun to avoid confusion. Study the following sentences to see how the imperfect subjunctive is used:

Mi dispiaceva che non **mantenesse** la sua promessa.
I was sorry he didn't keep his promise.

Non sapevamo che tu *volessi* venire.
We didn't know that you wanted to come.

Temevo che *vi sbagliaste*.
I feared you were wrong.

Se *avessi* 21 anni, verrei con voi.
If I were 21, I'd come with you.

Se *poteste* venire anche voi, mi piacerebbe.
I would be pleased if you could come too.

Credevo che le lingue straniere **fossero** difficili.
I used to think foreign languages were difficult.

La professoressa insisteva che lo **facessimo** di nuovo.
The teacher insisted that we do it over again.

Speravamo che **nevicasse**.
We were hoping that it would snow.

Che cosa faresti se **piovesse**?
What would you have done if it rained?

The Pluperfect Subjunctive

This compound tense is made with the imperfect subjunctive of the auxiliary verb, either *avere* or *essere*, in combination with a past participle.

Here are some examples of how it is used:

Ignoravo che **fossero tornati**.
I didn't know they had returned.

Se **avessi saputo** che eri ammalato, sarei venuto ad aiutarti.
If I had known that you were sick, I'd have come to help you.

Avevamo paura che **avessero perso** il treno.
We were afraid that they had missed the train.

Avrei preferito che mi **avessi aspettato.**
I would have preferred that you had waited for me.

Sperava che **avessero assaggiato** il suo risotto.
She was hoping that they had tasted her risotto.

General rules governing the use of these two tenses:

1. Use the *imperfect subjunctive* in a contrary-to-fact **if clause**, when the result clause is in the *conditional*.

2. Use the *pluperfect subjunctive* in a contrary-to-fact **if clause**, when the result clause is in the *past conditional*.

3. If the verb in the main clause is expressed in a past tense, put the next verb in the *imperfect subjunctive*, **or**, if the next verb has already taken place, use the *pluperfect*.

Drill 58: The Imperfect and Pluperfect Subjunctive

Supply either the imperfect or the pluperfect subjunctive. Make your choice based on the English cue.

1. Speravo che _____ (they'd leave).

2. Mi aspettavo che _____ (you would understand – voi).

3. Se _____ te, non andrei (were – io).

4. Se _____ te, non sarei andato (had been – io).

5. Non volevo che tu mi _____ (leave – tu).

6. Poteva darsi che _____ ieri. (they had arrived).

7. Benché _____ forte, aveva un cuore debole. (he seemed)

8. Ero felice che _____ all'università. (you were accepted – tu)

9. Non ci aspettavamo che _____ tanto bene. (they would do)

10. Eravamo sbalorditi che _____ tanto bene. (they had done)

Answers and Explanations to Drill 58

1. Speravo che **partissero**.
   I was hoping they'd leave.
   Follow the imperfect of *sperare* with the *imperfect subjunctive* here.

2. Mi aspettavo che **aveste capito.**
   I expected that you would understand.
   The expectation of *aspettarsi* in the imperfect was that the next verb (*capire*) would have already taken place. We need the pluperfect.

3. Se **fossi** in te, non andrei.
   I wouldn't go if I were you.
   The *conditional* in the result clause (*andrei*) tips us off that we need the *imperfect subjunctive* in the contrary-to-fact **if clause**.

4. Se **fossi stato** in te, non sarei andato.
   I wouldn't have gone if I had been you.
   The *past conditional* in the result clause (*sarei andato*) is a clue that we need the *pluperfect subjunctive* in the contrary-to-fact **if clause**.

5. Non volevo che mi **lasciassi**.
   I didn't want you to leave me.
   Follow the imperfect of *volere* with the *imperfect subjunctive* here.

6. Poteva darsi che **fossero arrivati** ieri.
   Maybe it was that (it could have been that) they had arrived yesterday.
   The arrival supposedly took place before this conjecture stated in the imperfect. Use the *pluperfect subjunctive*.

7. Benché **sembrasse** forte, aveva un cuore debole.
   Even though he seemed strong, he had a weak heart.
   As in problems 1 and 5, we combine the *imperfect* with the *imperfect subjunctive*.

8. Ero felice che tu **fossi stata ammessa** all'università.
   I was happy that you were admitted (accepted) to college.
   The reason for my being happy, expressed in the imperfect, was because the next verb (your admission to college) had already taken place. We need the pluperfect.

9. Non ci aspettavamo che **facessero** tanto bene.
   We didn't expect that they would do so well.
   A classic combination of the *imperfect* and *imperfect subjunctive.*

10. Eravamo sbalorditi che **avessero fatto** tanto bene.
    We were astonished (flabbergasted) that they had done so well.
    The doing well has taken place prior to their astonishment. Use the *pluperfect subjunctive.*

Pre-Exam Practice

AP Italian Language and Culture

[*From the Editor:* This Pre-Exam Practice section contains all the sections found on the AP Italian Language and Culture exam. However, in some sections, more material is provided than is on the actual exam, giving you more practice before taking the practice exams that follow.]

Pre-Exam Practice

AP Italian Language and Culture

Answer Sheet

SECTION I: Multiple Choice

Part A: Listening

1. Ⓐ Ⓑ Ⓒ Ⓓ
2. Ⓐ Ⓑ Ⓒ Ⓓ
3. Ⓐ Ⓑ Ⓒ Ⓓ
4. Ⓐ Ⓑ Ⓒ Ⓓ
5. Ⓐ Ⓑ Ⓒ Ⓓ
6. Ⓐ Ⓑ Ⓒ Ⓓ
7. Ⓐ Ⓑ Ⓒ Ⓓ
8. Ⓐ Ⓑ Ⓒ Ⓓ
9. Ⓐ Ⓑ Ⓒ Ⓓ
10. Ⓐ Ⓑ Ⓒ Ⓓ

11. Ⓐ Ⓑ Ⓒ Ⓓ
12. Ⓐ Ⓑ Ⓒ Ⓓ
13. Ⓐ Ⓑ Ⓒ Ⓓ
14. Ⓐ Ⓑ Ⓒ Ⓓ
15. Ⓐ Ⓑ Ⓒ Ⓓ
16. Ⓐ Ⓑ Ⓒ Ⓓ
17. Ⓐ Ⓑ Ⓒ Ⓓ
18. Ⓐ Ⓑ Ⓒ Ⓓ
19. Ⓐ Ⓑ Ⓒ Ⓓ
20. Ⓐ Ⓑ Ⓒ Ⓓ

21. Ⓐ Ⓑ Ⓒ Ⓓ
22. Ⓐ Ⓑ Ⓒ Ⓓ
23. Ⓐ Ⓑ Ⓒ Ⓓ
24. Ⓐ Ⓑ Ⓒ Ⓓ
25. Ⓐ Ⓑ Ⓒ Ⓓ
26. Ⓐ Ⓑ Ⓒ Ⓓ
27. Ⓐ Ⓑ Ⓒ Ⓓ
28. Ⓐ Ⓑ Ⓒ Ⓓ
29. Ⓐ Ⓑ Ⓒ Ⓓ
30. Ⓐ Ⓑ Ⓒ Ⓓ

Part B: Reading

31. Ⓐ Ⓑ Ⓒ Ⓓ
32. Ⓐ Ⓑ Ⓒ Ⓓ
33. Ⓐ Ⓑ Ⓒ Ⓓ
34. Ⓐ Ⓑ Ⓒ Ⓓ
35. Ⓐ Ⓑ Ⓒ Ⓓ
36. Ⓐ Ⓑ Ⓒ Ⓓ
37. Ⓐ Ⓑ Ⓒ Ⓓ

38. Ⓐ Ⓑ Ⓒ Ⓓ
39. Ⓐ Ⓑ Ⓒ Ⓓ
40. Ⓐ Ⓑ Ⓒ Ⓓ
41. Ⓐ Ⓑ Ⓒ Ⓓ
42. Ⓐ Ⓑ Ⓒ Ⓓ
43. Ⓐ Ⓑ Ⓒ Ⓓ
44. Ⓐ Ⓑ Ⓒ Ⓓ

45. Ⓐ Ⓑ Ⓒ Ⓓ
46. Ⓐ Ⓑ Ⓒ Ⓓ
47. Ⓐ Ⓑ Ⓒ Ⓓ
48. Ⓐ Ⓑ Ⓒ Ⓓ
49. Ⓐ Ⓑ Ⓒ Ⓓ
50. Ⓐ Ⓑ Ⓒ Ⓓ

Pre-Exam Practice

AP Italian Language and Culture

SECTION I: Multiple Choice

Part A: Listening

> **DIRECTIONS:** You will now listen to several selections. For each selection you will have time to read over the questions printed in your booklet. Then you will hear the selection. You may take notes in your exam booklet as you listen. Your notes will not be graded. After listening to the selection, you will have time to answer the questions. Blacken the corresponding oval on your answer sheet.

CD 1, Track Number 1

1
La Pelle

1. Sono utili per preparare la pelle per l'estate?

    (A) Sì, preparano bene la pelle.

    (B) Sì, sono obbligatori.

    (C) No, Danneggiano la pelle.

    (D) No, Non hanno nessun' effetto sulla pelle.

2. Cosa fanno i raggi Uva?

    (A) Invecchiano la pelle.

    (B) Aumentano la bellezza della pelle.

    (C) Nutriscano la pelle.

    (D) Purificano la pelle.

3. Cosa sarebbe meglio per abituare la pelle al sole?

   (A) Passare solo una settimana sotto il sole artificiale.

   (B) Espore la pelle gradualmente, pian piano.

   (C) Le docce solari sono utili.

   (D) Portare occhiali di sole.

4. Quali prodotti sono consigliati?

   (A) Asciugamano ampio.

   (B) Filtri solari protettori.

   (C) Sandali.

   (D) Paletta e secchiello.

2
La Pupa

5. Dov'è questa coppia?

   (A) Sono fra i giocattoli.

   (B) Cercano crema solare.

   (C) Sono nel corridoio fardasé.

   (D) Sono fra gli elettrodomestici.

6. A chi credono di offrire questa bambola?

   (A) Non lo sanno ancora.

   (B) A nessuno di particolare.

   (C) A una ragazzina, forse la loro figlia.

   (D) A una loro collega.

7. Cosa c'è di speciale con questa bambola?

   (A) Ha molti accesori.

   (B) Prende la tintarella.

(C) Viene con un cagnolino che abbaia.

(D) Si cambia il colore degli occhi.

8. Sono tutti e due incantati dalla bambola?

(A) Il marito non lo sopporta.

(B) Esitano tutti e due a causa del prezzo.

(C) Ne sono affascinati tutti e due.

(D) Il marito crede che sua moglie spenda troppo.

9. Come si abbronza la bambola?

(A) Si fa scura quando si mette gli occhiali da sole.

(B) Prende colore se rimane sull'asciugamano.

(C) Si fa scura quando si mette i sandalini.

(D) Prende colore sotto l'ombrellone.

10. Gli sembra qualcosa da nuovo?

(A) No, è vecchissima!

(B) Sì, totalmente!

(C) No, tutte le ragazzine ne hanno già una. È comune.

(D) Sì, l'avevano vista alla TV e sono venuti espressamente per comprarla.

3
I Vicini

11. Credi che questa coppia abbia amato essere genitori?

(A) Erano stuffi di essere genitori.

(B) Essere genitori era troppo faticoso.

(C) Si ricordano con tenerezza questo periodo della loro vita.

(D) Non se ne ricordano più.

12. Che cosa sentono oltre all'amichevolezza?

 (A) la nostalgia.

 (B) la curiosità.

 (C) l'invidia.

 (D) l'inquietudine.

13. Chi sono i loro nuovi vicini?

 (A) una coppia anziana.

 (B) uno scapolo e i suoi cani.

 (C) una giovane coppia la cui donna è incinta.

 (D) una grande famiglia calabrese.

14. Qual'è la loro opinione di questi nuovi vicini?

 (A) Non li conoscono affatto.

 (B) Credono che siano gentili, giovani e senza esperienza.

 (C) Credono che siano distacchi e freddi.

 (D) Credono che siano della loro età.

15. Che cosa pensano di fare?

 (A) Lui, verniciare la vecchia culla, lei, fare a ferri scarpette.

 (B) Lui, cavare un pozzo, lei, suggerire un nome femminile.

 (C) Lui, chiamare Martino, lei, invitare i loro genitori.

 (D) Lui, raccontare meravigliosi ricordi, lei, aiutare con la nascita.

4
La Partenza

16. Finisci questa frase: È ovvio che....

    (A) ... questa coppia non s'intende molto bene.

    (B) ... il marito si preoccupa più di sua moglie.

    (C) ... non vogliono perdere il volo.

    (D) ... vanno a Linate e non a Leonardo da Vinci.

17. Perché decidono di partire tanto presto?

    (A) Per fare colazione all'Autogrill.

    (B) Per controllare la carta.

    (C) Per essere sicuri di avere abbastanza tempo prima del volo.

    (D) Vogliono essere i primi arrivati.

18. Si secca di dover partire alle 4:30, il Signore?

    (A) Sì, tantissimo.

    (B) Sì, e non è d'accordo che sia necessario.

    (C) No, la moglie sarà al volante, lui dormirà.

    (D) No, si sentirà assai sollevato di arrivare in anticipio.

19. Che cose prenderanno tempo secondo la moglie?

    (A) Cercare e trovare i passaporti.

    (B) Il traffico, i bagagli e tutti i controlli prima del volo.

    (C) La colazione, le direzioni, la sosta benzina.

    (D) Caricare e scaricare le valigie.

20. Come andranno all'aeroporto?

    (A) In macchina.

    (B) Prenderanno l'autobus.

    (C) Prenoteranno un tassì.

    (D) In treno.

5
Il Livido

21. Secondo te, questa ragazza lo prende in giro spesso?

    (A) No, è sempre seria.

    (B) No, mai.

    (C) Senza volerlo, forse.

    (D) Sì, spesso.

22. Dov'è il livido?

    (A) Sulla fronte, fra gli occhi.

    (B) Sulla tempia.

    (C) Sul naso.

    (D) Sotto l'occhio di sinistra.

23. Perché non vedeva il rastrello per terra?

    (A) Perché non sta mai attento.

    (B) Perché era coperto di foglie.

    (C) Perché il rastrello era vecchio.

    (D) Perché aveva bisogno che qualcuno l'aiutasse.

24. È serio quando chiede se il livido aumenta il blu degli occhi?

    (A) Cercava un complimento.

    (B) È della vanità maschile.

    (C) L'ha detto scherzando.

    (D) Ha gli occhi castagni.

25. Dove lavorava?

    (A) Nello studio suo.

    (B) Nel giardino, sotto gli alberi.

(C)   Sulle scale.

(D)   Nel box.

6
L'Armadio

26.   Il ragazzo riconosce che il suo armadio è un disastro, perché non
       l'avrà sistemato prima?

    (A)   Non ha mai il tempo.

    (B)   Non sa neppure cominiciare.

    (C)   Non è necessario.

    (D)   Gli piace così.

27.   Cosa pensa la donna di sistemare quest'armadio?

    (A)   Crede che sia un lavoraccio odioso.

    (B)   Non sa che cosa fare.

    (C)   Crede che sia facilmente realizzabile.

    (D)   Non le piace affatto questo lavoro.

28.   Che sarà la prima cosa da fare?

    (A)   Sistemare le grucce.

    (B)   Passare l'aspirapolvere.

    (C)   Stroffinare gli scaffali.

    (D)   Vuotarlo interamente.

29.   Come reagisce il ragazzo alle idee della donna?

    (A)   È riconoscente e ottimistà.

    (B)   È dubbioso che siano possibili.

    (C)   È imbarazzato.

    (D)   È maldestro.

30. Perchè l'ultimo mucchio non può superare in altezza gli altri?

    (A) Per non crollare.

    (B) Per essere della stessa altezza.

    (C) Perché vogliono ridurre la quantità di cose conservate.

    (D) Per fare più divertente il lavoro.

Part B: Reading

DIRECTIONS: Read the following passages with care. Each segment is followed by a series of questions or statements to be completed. Choose the best answer, according to what you have read, from the four choices provided. Blacken the corresponding oval on your answer sheet.

1
Chiavi Libreria

A seguito della ripetuta sparizione di molti testi di didattica, con la presente siamo tenuti ad informarvi che gli sportelli della libreria dovranno rimanere tassativamente chiusi a chiave.

Quando gli insegnanti avranno bisogno di consultare i testi dovranno chiedere le chiavi o a Giulia o a Federica e di riconsegnarle appena finito.

Qualora dovesse di nuovo mancare un testo, sarà ritenuto interamente responsabile l'insegnante che non ha riconsegnato le chiavi. Gli studenti che volessero visionare qualsiasi testo sono pregati di rivolgersi agli insegnanti.

31. Perchè gli sportelli devono rimanere chiusi?

    (A) Perchè i libri si rovinano con l'aria.

    (B) Per tenere lontana la polvere.

    (C) Perchè tutti i testi sono tradotti dal greco.

    (D) A causa della scomparsa dei libri.

32. Chi è incaricato di tenere le chiavi?

    (A) Soltanto il direttore.

    (B) Soltanto il bidello.

    (C) L'una o l'altra dipendente della scuola.

    (D) Solo la proprietaria.

33. Cosa succede d'ora in avanti se manca un libro?

    (A) Chi l'ha preso verrà bruciato vivo.

    (B) Chi l'ha preso dovrà pagare una multa salata.

    (C) Chi l'ha preso verrà licenziato.

    (D) Chi non avrà restituito le chiavi verrà considerato responsabile.

34. Come deve fare uno studente che ha bisogno di un libro?

    (A) Deve prendere le chiavi al bar a pianoterra.

    (B) Deve chiedere al suo insegnante.

    (C) Può chiedere una copia del libro al direttore.

    (D) Questi libri non possono essere presi in prestito dagli studenti.

35. È stato sempre così?

    (A) No, prima gli sportelli erano sempre aperti a chiunque.

    (B) Sì, da quando la scuola è aperta.

    (C) Sì, da quando è entrato in vigore l'Euro.

    (D) Sì, da quando l'Italia ha vinto i mondiali di calcio 2006.

2
Il Matrimonio

Sabato mattina, in vista del matrimonio al quale ero stata invitata per la sera stessa, sono andata a riprendere il vestito nuovo che avevo lasciato dalla sarta . Purtroppo la sarta non c'era ma lei aveva lasciato il mio vestito a sua madre: anche questa donna faceva la sarta molti anni fa ma quando ho visto che portava degli occhiali che sembravano due posaceneri di vetro, mi sono chiesta come avesse fatto ad aggiustarmi il vestito. Comunque il mio vestito era pronto e mi andava a pennello.

Dopo poche ore ci siamo ritrovati in una piccola chiesina di campagna, immersa tra le dolci colline. Era modesta ed austera con un semplice crocefisso di legno, ma ravvivata dai canti e dagli addobbi floreali, freschi e vivaci.

Dopo la cerimonia gli sposi ci hanno accolto in uno spettacolare agriturismo, dove abbiamo consumato un sontuoso aperitivo a bordo piscina. Abbiamo cenato in una delle grandi sale a volta all'interno della struttura. Eravamo un centinaio di invitati e questa cena luculliana si è svolta all'insegna del calore: l'aria condizionata era pressochè inadeguata e mentre mangiavamo a fatica, ci sventagliavamo con i menu. Sudavo così tanto che il mio appetito se n'era praticamente andato. Pur madida di sudore e quasi inappetente mi sono riservata energie sufficienti per godermi una bella fetta di torta nuziale a sette piani.

36. Quanti erano gli ospiti a queste nozze?

    (A) 100.

    (B) 300.

    (C) Poco più di una decina.

    (D) Solo la famiglia.

37. Perchè la narratrice temeva che la sarta non fosse in grado di fare un buon lavoro al vestito?

    (A) Perchè era anziana e soffriva di artrosi alle mani.

    (B) Perchè era anziana e sembrava troppo debole.

    (C) Perchè era anziana e incredibilmente miope.

    (D) Perchè era anziana e non poteva trovare nessun pennello.

38. Com'erano l'aperitivo e la cena?

    (A) Parchi.

    (B) Abbondanti.

    (C) Appena sufficienti.

    (D) Trascurabili.

39. Com'era la chiesa?

    (A) Piccola, raccolta e semplice.

    (B) Maestosa e solenne.

    (C) Barocca ed eccessiva.

    (D) Bramantesca ed equilibrata.

40. Qual è stato l'unico neo della serata?

   (A) Faceva caldissimo.

   (B) I camerieri erano scortesi.

   (C) L'aria condizionata congelava gli ospiti.

   (D) L'intonaco della volta cedeva, cadendo sui tavoli.

41. Com'era fatta la torta?

   (A) Di bignè.

   (B) Di marzapane.

   (C) Alta sette piani.

   (D) A forma di due fedi matrimoniali.

3
I Pattini

Quando ero piccola, avevo pattini a rotelle regolabili. Si attaccavano con due cinghie di cuoio ai piedi calzati. Si tiravano alle due estremità e si avvitavano con una chiave speciale. Tutti i bambini portavano la loro chiave su una cordicella attorno al collo, tanto era importante. Se i piedi del bambino fossero cresciuti, lui avrebbe potuto comunque aprire di nuovo i suoi pattini. Erano pesanti e ingombranti ma io ci volavo su. Li ho portati per anni.

Non ho mai saputo che fine avessero fatto i miei pattini ma mia madre mi ha telefonato l'altro ieri con una notizia sorprendente. Mentre gli operai stavano mettendo una nuova moquette a casa sua, cioè nella casa dove io sono cresciuta, uno di loro ha trovato la mia vecchia chiave. Lui l'aveva scoperta, ancora legata alla sua cordicella, esattamente come la portavo, mentre stava togliendo la vecchia moquette. La conservo ancora oggi nel mio portagioie. Qualche volta, me la metto attorno al collo, chiudo gli occhi e ridivento bambina.

42. Chi racconta questa storia?

   (A) Una ragazza adolescente.

   (B) Una persona già adulta.

   (C) Una bambina della scuola media.

   (D) Una persona molto anziana.

43. Perché i bambino portavano i bambini la chiave attorno al collo?

    (A) Per non perderla.

    (B) Per seguire la moda.

    (C) La portavano come medaglietta.

    (D) Per aprire la porta della casa quando non c'era la mamma.

44. Dove sono i pattini oggi?

    (A) Sua madre li ha buttati.

    (B) Sono sempre nella soffitta della casa.

    (C) Li ha dati ai nipoti.

    (D) La narratrice non lo sa.

45. Come era la chiave quando è venuta alla luce?

    (A) Era tutta arrugginita.

    (B) Era torta e distorta.

    (C) Era come sempre.

    (D) Era schiacciata.

4

Emma strega i big della moda – Deborah Ameri
OGGI, n° 30, 25 luglio 2007

Londra, luglio A furia di indossare abiti Chanel sul tappeto rosso delle *première* e durante tutte le interviste televisive, Emma Watson, Hermione sullo schermo, ha convinto la *maison* francese. È lei il nuovo, freschissimo, volto della *griffe*. L'amica di Harry Potter non ha neppure avuto bisogno della bacchetta magica. L'eleganza innata, le doti da attrice e modella e quel suo volto dolce e sensuale hanno conquistato non solo il pubblico, ma anche l'industria della moda. Emma è stata messa sotto contratto dalla Storm, una delle agenzie di modelle più famose, che rappresenta anche Kate Moss. Da lì a firmare un accordo con Chanel è stato un passo.

La Watson, 17 anni e già una solida carriera sul set, diventerà il volto della *maison* per tre milioni di euro e un accesso illimitato alla collezione di abiti. [...]

Al *David Letterman Show*, in Usa, ha scioccato un po' tutti con la sua sincerità: "Via, siamo onesti. Ho guadagnato abbastanza soldi da ritirarmi e non lavorare più per tutta la vita" se n'è uscita. "Ma io non voglio farlo, me ne guardo bene."

Per poco si è temuto che Emma volesse rinunciare agli ultimi due film. Così aveva minacciato, facendo tremare i fan del maghetto. Ma alla fine ha firmato il contratto per continuare a essere Hermione Granger.

"È stata una decisione difficile dire di nuovo sì a Harry Potter." Ha confessato. "Quando ho fatto la prima audizione avevo 10 anni, ero convinta che non mi avrebbero mai presa e comunque non potevo sapere che mi sarebbe toccata questa ondata di celebrità improvvisa. Essere sempre al centro dell'attenzione e la mancanza di libertà sono le due condizioni che mi hanno fatto pensare molto prima di accettare iI nuovo contratto. Ma almeno per i prossimi 3 o 4 anni la mia vita sarà così. Poi vedremo."

46.   Come è diventata celebre Emma Watson?

   (A)   Come modella.

   (B)   Sul tappeto rosso.

   (C)   Sullo schermo.

   (D)   Come agente della Storm.

47.   Che cosa ha scioccato un po' gli spettatori al *David Letterman Show*?

   (A)   La sua risposta ingenua e candida sui soldi suoi.

   (B)   La sua eleganza innata.

   (C)   Il volto freschissimo.

   (D)   Il suo ruolo di icona.

48.   Perché esitava a firmare il contratto per i due ultimi film?

   (A)   Perché guadagnerebbe meno del collega Daniel Radcliffe.

   (B)   Perché sapeva che la libertà le sarebbe mancata molto.

   (C)   Perché voleva firmare con Chanel.

   (D)   Perché era stufa di vivere sul set.

49. Che cosa farà per Chanel?

    (A) Sarà il volto della loro *griffe*, cioè dei loro prodotti.

    (B) Disegnerà abiti.

    (C) Lavorerà come consulente.

    (D) Giudicherà la nuova linea.

50. Che specie di agenzia è Storm?

    (A) È un'agenzia francese di pubblicità.

    (B) È un'agenzia di attori e attrici.

    (C) È un'agenzia di modelle.

    (D) È una gran casa di moda.

SECTION II: Free Response

Part A: Writing

Fill in a Verb

> **DIRECTIONS:** In each sentence a verb has been omitted and replaced by a line. Supply the missing verb form on the blank to the right. There you will see the infinitive form of the verb you are to use. Read the whole paragraph before choosing your answer. Spelling, agreement, and accent marks must all be accurate for your answer to be correct.

1.

Cinzia _1_ la porta per vedere se il suo quotidiano _2_ . Le _3_ leggerlo ogni mattina mentre _4_ il suo caffè. Non era ancora arrivato! Delusa, _5_ la porta e _6_ sulla poltrona davanti alla finestra, i piedi alzati, per _7_ la sua tradizione mattinale.

2.

_8_ Francesca _9_ il seguente messaggio sulla sua segretaria telefonica: "Salve Francé, sono io, Daniele. _10_ , se tu _11_ libera domani sera, vorrei venire a _12_ verso le 18. Danno l'ultimo film di Pupi Avati all'Odeon e _13_ che ti piacerebbe." _14_ appena _15_ ."

1. _____ (aprire)
2. _____ (arrivare)
3. _____ (piacere)
4. _____ (bere)
5. _____ (chiudere)
6. _____ (sedersi)
7. _____ (aspettare)
8. _____ (rincasare)
9. _____ (trovare)
10. _____ (sentire)
11. _____ (essere)
12. _____ (prendere + ti)
13. _____ (credere)
14. _____ (richiamare + mi)
15. _____ (potere)

Fill in a Word

> **DIRECTIONS:** In each sentence a single word has been omitted and replaced by a line. Write your answer, **ONE** single Italian word on the line to the right. Make sure the word is correct in form, as well as in meaning and in context. None of your answers will be verbs.
>
> Please note that a response such as *fino a* (or *di cui*) will be considered two words, not one. For full credit you must spell each word correctly and include any necessary accent marks or apostrophes.

Claudia fa __1__ festa per __2__ 8 settembre e ci invita __3__. __4__ divertiremo __5__ lei e __6__ andremo __7__ vedere i fuochi d'artificio insieme. Ognuno deve portare __8__ __9__ mangiare. Verrà anche suo fratello di __10__ ti ho già parlato. Sta facendo il servizio militare __11__ ha tre giorni di permesso.

__12__ aver visto __13__ spettacolo, tutti verranno da noi __14__ un brindisi prima __15__ lasciarsi.

1. _____
2. _____
3. _____
4. _____
5. _____
6. _____
7. _____
8. _____
9. _____
10. _____
11. _____
12. _____
13. _____
14. _____
15. _____

General Essay

DIRECTIONS: Write a composition in Italian of about 150 words on the topic below. Your essay must be organized and coherent. It must demonstrate your mastery of verb tenses and grammar. It must illustrate a good command of vocabulary. Plan before you begin. Check your work carefully for accents, spelling and agreement. You have 30 minutes.

Note: Essays are evaluated on organization and clarity, range and choice of appropriate vocabulary, grammatical accuracy and spelling.

Com'è la tua camera da letto?

Part B: Cultural Essay

> **<u>DIRECTIONS</u>:** Write a composition in Italian of about 150 words on the topic below. You must demonstrate the depth of your cultural knowledge in an organized and coherent essay. Showcase your mastery of verb tenses and grammar; evidence a good command of vocabulary. Plan before you begin. Check your work carefully for accents, spelling and agreement. You have 30 minutes.

Note: The student's knowledge of culture determines 80% of his or her score on this essay. The remaining 20% is based on organization, clarity, range and choice of appropriate vocabulary, grammatical accuracy and spelling.

Se tu fossi invitato ad un ballo in maschera veneziano a Carnevale, cosa indosseresti? Descrivi il tuo costume.

Part C: Speaking—Narration

[*From the Editor:* On the actual AP exam there will be one series of six pictures for you to record your two-minute response. For this pre-exam practice section, six complete sets of pictures are included for extra practice. Please time yourself, allowing two minutes to study the pictures and two minutes to record your response on your recording device.]

DIRECTIONS: You will have two minutes to look at and think about a series of six pictures found on the following pages. You are to narrate a story suggested by the picture sequence. You may take notes in the test booklet insert if you like. Your notes will not be graded. You will then have two minutes to record your response. Comment on each picture and use all of the time allotted. You will be scored on your level of fluency, your ability to narrate, grammatical accuracy, vocabulary range and pronunciation. The completeness of your response will also be taken into consideration.

1 il gatto

DIRECTIONS: The following pictures present a story. Pretend you are speaking to a friend and narrate a complete story suggested by the pictures. Your story should contain a beginning, a middle, and an end.

2 sabato mattina

3 il colpo di sole

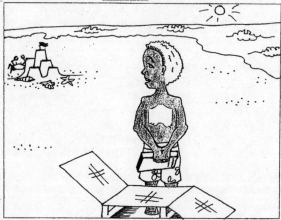

4 il professore

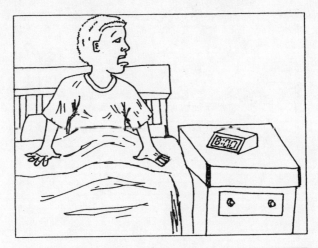

5 la grassottella

6 le caramelle

Speaking—Conversation

CD 1, Track Number 2

DIRECTIONS: You are now asked to participate in a simulated conversation in Italian. The questions you will hear are not printed for you to read. You must rely solely on what you hear. You will hear each question twice, followed by a tone. Once you have heard the tone you will have 20 seconds to record your response to the question in Italian. A second tone signals that 20 seconds have elapsed. Stop talking, even if you haven't finished what you were saying. Don't worry if you have been cut off. Listen immediately for the next question. Do not, at any time, stop the recorder until you are instructed to do so.

You will be evaluated on your ability to answer each question completely and promptly. You will be scored on fluency and the appropriateness of your answer. Your score will be lowered if your answer is too short. Use every second allotted. It is better to be cut off than to stop speaking too soon.

You will hear a total of six questions. The first question is for practice only. Try to answer it. It will not be recorded or scored but will give you a good idea of the type of questions to follow. They will all be related to one theme, alluded to in the practice question. You will record your responses to the next five questions.

Pre-Exam Practice

AP Italian Language and Culture

Answer Key

SECTION I: Multiple Choice

Part A: Listening

1.	(C)	11.	(C)	21.	(D)
2.	(A)	12.	(A)	22.	(A)
3.	(B)	13.	(C)	23.	(B)
4.	(B)	14.	(D)	24.	(C)
5.	(A)	15.	(A)	25.	(B)
6.	(C)	16.	(C)	26.	(B)
7.	(B)	17.	(C)	27.	(C)
8.	(C)	18.	(D)	28.	(D)
9.	(B)	19.	(B)	29.	(A)
10.	(B)	20.	(A)	30.	(C)

Part B: Reading

31.	(D)	38.	(B)	45.	(C)
32.	(C)	39.	(A)	46.	(C)
33.	(D)	40.	(A)	47.	(A)
34.	(B)	41.	(C)	48.	(B)
35.	(A)	42.	(B)	49.	(A)
36.	(A)	43.	(A)	50.	(C)
37.	(C)	44.	(D)		

SECTION II: Free Response

Part A: Writing

Fill in a Verb

1. ha aperto
2. era arrivato
3. piaceva
4. bevendo
5. ha chiuso
6. si è seduta
7. aspettare
8. rincasando
9. ha trovato
10. senti
11. sei
12. prenderti
13. credo
14. richiamami
15. potrai

Fill in a Word

1. una
2. l'
3. tutti
4. ci
5. da
6. poi, allora
7. a
8. qualcosa
9. da
10. cui
11. ma, e
12. dopo
13. lo
14. per
15. di

Pre-Exam Practice

AP Italian Language and Culture

Detailed Explanations of Answers

Section I: Multiple Choice
Part A: Listening

1

1. **(C)** No, Danneggiano la pelle.
   No, tanning lamps damage the skin.

2. **(A)** Invecchiano la pelle.
   The UV rays age the skin prematurely.

3. **(B)** Espore la pelle gradualmente, pian piano.
   The safest and best way to accustom the skin to the summer sun is to expose it very gradually, a little bit at a time.

4. **(B)** Filtri solari protettori.
   Protective sun-screens are advised.

2

5. **(A)** Sono fra i giocattoli.
   They're in the toy department. They're not looking for sunscreens, they're not in the do-it-yourself aisle, and they are certainly not in appliances.

6. **(C)**   A una ragazzina, forse la loro figlia.

They'll give it to a little girl named Maia for her birthday in June. Maybe she's their daughter.

7. **(B)**   Prende la tintarella.

The little doll gets a tan when exposed to the sun.

8. **(C)**   Nc sono affascinati tutti e due.

They are both equally intrigued.

9. **(B)**   Prende colore se rimane sull'asciugamano.

She tans if she's in contact with her special little beach towel.

10. **(B)**   Sì, totalmente!

They've never heard of or seen such a doll before. They think it's really cute and that Maia will be crazy about it.

3

11. **(C)**   Si ricordano con tenerezza questo periodo della loro vita.

They cherish their memories of that time in their lives. They speak fondly of being parents. They were not fed up with parenthood, nor was it bothersome. Their recall of parenthood is quite vivid.

12. **(A)**   La nostalgia.

Besides genuine good will towards their new neighbors, the couple is definitely feeling nostalgic about their early years as parents.

13. **(C)**   Una giovane coppia la cui donna è incinta.

It's a young couple and the wife is pregnant.

14. **(B)**   Credono che siano gentili, giovani e senza esperienza.

They like their new neighbors very much, and think of them as young and inexperienced, having no idea of what lies ahead.

15. **(A)**   Lui, verniciare la vecchia culla, lei, fare a ferri scarpette.

He'll repaint their old crib for them, she'll knit some baby booties.

4

16. **(C)**   non vogliono perdere il volo.

It's obvious that they don't want to miss their flight.

17. **(C)**   Per essere sicuri di avere abbastanza tempo prima del volo.

They'll be leaving very early because their flight is at 10 am, and they want to allow themselves enough time to get there, check in, and go through customs and boarding.

18. **(D)**   No, si sentirà assai sollevato di arrivare in anticipio.

No, he's not annoyed at having to leave at 4:30 am. He says he'll actually be relieved to get there well ahead of time.

19. **(B)**   Il traffico, i bagagli e tutti i controlli prima del volo.

She mentions the possiblilty of a traffic jam on the way, the luggage check-in and customs before their flight.

20. **(A)**   In macchina.

They're going by car. Once they've decided on their departure plan he begins to load the trunk and says he'll fill the tank that evening.

5

21. **(D)**   Sì, spesso.

He is hesitant to tell her how he got the black and blue mark because he's afraid she'll tease him. His reaction suggests that she may tease him often.

22. **(A)**   Sulla fronte, fra gli occhi.

It's on his forehead, right between the eyes.

23. **(B)**   Perché era coperto di tante foglie.

He couldn't see the rake on the ground because it was covered up under so many leaves.

24. **(C)**   L'ha detto scherzando.

He's joking when he asks if she thinks the bruise brings out the blue of his eyes.

25. **(B)**   Nel giardino, sotto gli alberi.

He was working in the yard, under the trees, not in the study, not on the stairs, and not in the lock-up garage.

6

26. **(B)**   Non sa neppure cominiciare.

He doesn't even know where (how) to begin.

27. **(C)**   Crede che sia facilmente realizzabile.

She thinks it's quite doable and knows just how to go about it.

28. **(D)**   Vuotarlo interamente.

The first thing to do is to empty the closet completely.

29. **(A)**   È riconoscente e ottimistà.

He's grateful and hopeful that the task will go quickly if they do it together.

30. **(C)**   Perché vogliono ridurre la quantità di cose conservate.

The last pile (the things he will keep) shouldn't be higher than the other three stacks as they're trying to reduce the number of things he'll keep in the closet.

Part B: Reading

1

31. Perchè gli sportelli devono rimanere chiusi?

    (D) A causa della scomparsa dei libri.

    The book closet will remain locked from now on due to the disappearance of so many reference books.

32. Chi è incaricato di tenere le chiavi?

    (C) L'una o l'altra dipendente della scuola.

    Either Federica or Giulia, one or other of the office staff.

33. Cosa succede d'ora in avanti se manca un libro?

    (D) Chi non avrà restituito le chiavi verrà considerato responsabile.

    Should another book go missing, whoever has not returned the keys (after requesting them from a staff member) will be held responsible.

34. Come deve fare uno studente che ha bisogno di un libro?

    (B) Deve chiedere al suo insegnante.

    If a student wants to borrow a book, he should ask his teacher (to get it for him).

35. È stato sempre così?

    (A) No, prima gli sportelli erano sempre aperti a chiunque.

    No, before the doors were always open to everyone.

2

36. Quanti erano gli ospiti a queste nozze?

    (A) 100.

    There were one hundred guests.

37. Perchè la narratrice temeva che la sarta non fosse in grado di fare un buon lavoro al vestito?

(C)   Perchè era anziana e incredibilmente miope.

The elderly woman (a retired seamstress) wore glasses as thick as ashtray bottoms, and appeared to be incredibly near-sighted.

38. Com'erano l'aperitivo e la cena?

(B)   Abbondanti.

The appetizers are described as *sumptuous*, and the dinner as *lavish*. There was plenty of food.

39. Com'era la chiesa?

(A)   Piccola, raccolta e semplice.

The church was very small, cozy and quite plain.

40. Qual è stato l'unico neo della serata?

(A)   Faceva caldissimo.

The only thing that marred the beautiful evening was the oppressive heat.

41. Com'era fatta la torta?

(C)   Alta sette piani.

The wedding cake had seven layers.

3

42. Chi racconta questa storia?

(B)   Una persona già adulta.

An adult, a grown woman, is telling this story.

43. Perché i bambini portavano i bambini la chiave attorno al collo?

(A)   Per non perderla.

It was worn around the neck so as not to lose it. With his skate key, a child could loosen, tighten and adjust his skates to fit, no matter what shoes he was wearing and no matter how big his foot was.

44. Dove sono i pattini oggi?

    (D) La narratrice non lo sa.

    She says she never knew what happened to her skates. She doesn't know.

45. Come era la chiave quando veniva alla luce?

    (C) Era come sempre.

    It was just the same as always, still attached to its little cord.

4

46. Come è diventata celebre Emma Watson?

    (C) Sullo schermo.

    On the screen. She became famous as an actress.

47. Che cosa ha scioccato un po' al gli spettatori *David Letterman Show*?

    (A) La sua risposta ingenua e candida sui soldi suoi.

    Her guileless admission was that she had already earned enough money never to have to work again for the rest of her life.

48. Perché esitava a firmare il contratto per i due ultimi film?

    (B) Perché sapeva che la libertà le sarebbe mancata molto.

    She was wary of signing the contract for the last two films because she knew that (being in the spotlight again) she would miss her personal freedom very much.

49. Che cosa farà per Chanel?

    (A) Sarà il volto della loro *griffe*, cioè dei loro prodotti.

    She (her face) will represent their label, that is, all of their products.

50. Che specie di agenzia è Storm?

    (C) È un'agenzia di modelle.

    Storm is a top English modeling agency.

Section II

Part A: Writing

Fill in a Verb

1

1. + 2.   Cinzia <u>ha aperto</u> la porta per vedere se il suo quotidiano <u>era arrivato</u>.

Cynthia opened the door to see if her daily paper had arrived.

The *passato prossimo* expresses an action whose completion is easy to visualize within the confines of the sentence. Use the *trapassato* (had arrived) for an action which was to have taken place prior to the opening of the door.

3. + 4.   Le <u>piaceva</u> leggerlo ogni mattina mentre <u>bevendo</u> il suo caffè.

She liked to read it every morning while drinking her coffee.

Ogni mattina is a clue to use the imperfect for this habitual action. Place a present participle after *mentre* to create a simultaneous activity.

5. 6. + 7.   Non era ancora arrivato! Delusa, <u>ha chiuso</u> la porta e <u>si è seduta</u> sulla sua poltrona davanti alla finestra, i piedi alzati, per <u>aspettare</u> la sua tradizione mattinale.

It hadn't arrived yet! Disappointed, she closed the door and sat down in the arm chair in front of the window, with her feet up, to wait for her morning tradition (to begin).

The completion of the first two verbs is easy to visualize. She closed the door. She sat down. *Chiudere* is conjugated with *avere* because it is transitive, that is, capable of accepting a direct object: the door. *Sedersi*, a reflexive verb, is conjugated with *essere*. The preposition *per* signals that an infinitive is to follow.

2

8. + 9.   <u>Rincasando</u>, Francesca <u>ha trovato</u> il seguente messaggio sulla sua segretaria telefonica: "Salve Francé, sono io, Daniele."

On coming home Francesca found this message on her answering machine: "Hi Franny, it's me Dan."

The present participle makes the equivalent of the English gerund *coming home.* Use the *passato prossimo* for the simple completed action *she found.*

10. 11. + 12.   "<u>Senti</u>, se sei libera domani sera, vorrei venire a <u>prenderti</u> verso le 18.

"Listen, if you're free tomorrow night, I'd like to come pick you up around six o'clock."

Make a familiar command. Since Daniele calls her Francé, they know each other well. Use the present tense for *essere*, just as you would in English. *If you are free...* Always use an infinitive form after a modal verb such as *volere.*

13.   Danno l'ultimo film di Pupi Avati all'Odeon e <u>credo</u> che ti piacerebbe."

They're showing Pupi Avati's latest film at the Odeon and I think you you'd like it.

Use the *present* to say *I think, I believe.*

14. + 15.   <u>Richiamami</u> appena <u>potrai</u>."

Call me back as soon as you can.

Another familiar command. Notice the use of the future after *appena* here.

Fill in a Word

1

1. 2. + 3. Claudia fa <u>una</u> festa per <u>l</u>'otto settembre e <u>ci</u> invita tuttti.

*Claudia is having **a** party for September 8ᵗʰ and she's inviting all of **us**.* (There are often huge fireworks on September 8ᵗʰ in honor of the Virgin Mary.)

The indefinite article *una* completes the phrase nicely. The usual *il* for dates is replaced here by *l'* since *otto* begins with a vowel. An open space in front of the verb *invita* suggests the need for a pronoun object. Here we use *ci* for us.

4. 5. 6. + 7. <u>Ci</u> divertiremo <u>da</u> lei e <u>poi/allora</u> andremo a vedere i fuochi d'artificio insieme.

*We'll have a good time **at her house and then** we'll go to see the fireworks together.*

Divertirsi requires a reflexive pronoun (here it's *ci*) in front of the verb form. *Da + lei* create *at her place. Andare* requires *a* before an infinitive.

8. + 9. Ognuno deve portare <u>qualcosa</u> <u>da</u> mangiare.

Everyone is supposed to bring something to eat.

The indefinite pronoun *qualcosa* (something) needs the preposition *da* in front of the infinitive.

10. Verrà anche suo fratello di <u>cui</u> ti ho già parlato.

Her brother is coming too, the one I've already told you about.

11. Sta facendo il servizio militare <u>ma/e</u> ha tre giorni di permesso.

*He's doing his military service **but (and)** has three days' leave.*

12. 13. 14. + 15.   <u>Dopo</u> aver visto <u>lo</u> spettacolo, tutti verranno da noi <u>per</u> un brindisi prima <u>di</u> lasciarsi.

After having seen the show, everybody will come back to our place for a drink (a toast) before going home. (before leaving)

Dopo provides *after*. Did you remember to use the special article *lo* in front of *spettacolo*? (s+consonant) *Prima* requires *di* in front of an infinitive.

Sample Essay Answer in Response to General Essay Question

Read the following essay to see how a student might have answered this question.

Com'è la tua camera da letto?

Io condivido la mia camera da letto con mia sorella. È piccola ma comoda. Abbiamo ciascuna un letto singolo. C'è una vecchia poltrona raccolta in cui mi piace leggere o guardare la TV. Ci sono due piccole scrivanie dove facciamo i compiti e andiamo su internet.

Ci sono tre finestre luminose che danno sul giardino. C'è un armadio, una cassettiera e un bel tappeto persiano sul pavimento. Le pareti sono bianche ma i copriletti e il tappeto sono a fiori dai colori rosa, blu e verde pastello. Abbiamo tantissimi scaffali zeppi di libri, CD e DVD.

La mia sveglia non è sul comodino perchè mi addormenterei di nuovo se potessi spegnerla senza dovermi alzare. Ho dovuto metterla dall'altro lato della camera, lontano dal letto. Così sono costretta ad alzarmi completamente per farla smettere.

Mi piace stare nella mia camera; lì dentro mi sento a mio agio. È il mio rifugio. Lì, mi rinfresco, mi ricarico e sogno il futuro.

Part B: Culture

Sample Essay Answer
in Response to Cultural Essay Question

Read the following essay to see how a student might have answered this question.

Se tu fossi invitato ad un ballo in maschera veneziano a Carnevale, cosa indosseresti? Descrivi il tuo costume.

Se andassi al ballo in maschera inviterei un'amica ed andremmo in coppia con costumi ben assortiti. Io mi metterei la maschera bianchissima che portavano i medici durante la pesta bubonica. Copra solo tre quarti della faccia e ha un naso lunghissimo per tenere sali e piante erbacei protettrici. Avrei un magnifico capello tricorno, con piume, e un mantello lungo e nerissimo.

Anche la mia compagna sarebbe vestita di nero e bianco. Avrebbe una maschera bianca con una lacrima di nero lucente sul viso e le labbra rossissime. Porterebbe ganti lunghissimi e terrebbe in mano un enorme vantaglio di piume e lustrini. Sulla testa porterebbe una parrucca altissima con perle e piume nere.

Insieme faremmo galleggiare sul Canal Grande e getteremmo coriandoli neri e piccoli gioielli di strass ai nostri ammiratori sui ponti e sulle rive. Andremmo piano piano per permettere agli spettatori di fotografarci e di meravigliarsi, chiedendosi chi potrebbe essere questa spendida coppia.

Part C: Speaking

Speaking—Narration

1 – il Gatto

Here is how a student might have narrated these sketches:

1. C'è un gatto su un albero. È in equilibrio su un alto rame. Ci è salito per cacciare gli uccellini.

2. La sua padroncina, una bambina, capisce il guaio in cui si sta cacciando ancora prima di lui.

3. L'uccellino vola via e adesso il gatto non sa come scendere.

4. Un pompiere, forse avvertito dalla bambina, sale sulla scala per prendere il gatto.

5. Lui scende la scala con il gatto in mano, sano e salvo.

6. Il pompiere se ne va, si allontana sulla grande autobotte. Il gatto è salvo e la bambina tira un sospiro di sollievo.

   Penso che la bambina avesse più paura del gatto perchè si era resa conto del pericolo. Lei ha capito che il suo gatto non poteva scendere da solo, per questo ha chiamato un adulto. È stata molto responsabile.

   Ha scoperto di essere capace di affontare un pericolo. Ha mostrato sangue freddo e ha potuto risolvere il problema. Queste sono lezioni molto utili, succeda quel che succeda. Spero che imparerà a badare di più al suo gatto.

2 – sabato mattina

Here is how a student might have commented on the sketches:

1. È un sabato mattina di giugno. Un ragazzo sta per uscire di casa. Sotto il braccio tiene un pallone da calcio. Sua madre sta lavando i piatti in cucina.

2. La sua camera sembra essere in completo disordine. Sua madre pretende che lui metta tutto a posto prima di uscire.

3. Sale le scale controvoglia. Deve fare quello che sua madre gli ha detto.

4. Adesso si vede il gran disordine della sua camera. Il letto non è fatto e tutte le sue cose sono buttate in giro senza cura. Anche il quadro è di traverso.

5. Ormai la sua camera è in perfetto ordine. Sua madre ne sarà contenta. Credo che in ogni casa tutti i membri della famiglia debbano contribuire ai lavori domestici. Soprattutto se tutti e due i genitori lavorano. Mia madre, ad esempio, è infermiera. Io prendo fuori la pattumiera e prendo cura del nostro cane. Papà cucina e le mie sorelle apparecchiano la tavola.

6. Adesso il ragazzo è finalmente libero. Ha finito di fare le faccende. Gioca a calcio, sorridente. Secondo me, i figli dovrebbero fare piccole faccende a casa senza esserne pagati. Se ricevono qualche soldo settimanale tanto meglio; è l'idea di pagarli che non mi piace. Preferisco che facciano le loro piccole faccende come membri di una squadra, la famiglia.

3 – il Colpo di sole

Here is how a student might have spoken about the sketches:

1. Un ragazzo sta per passare un pomeriggio in spiaggia. Porta con sè una sedia pieghevole e un libro. Fa bel tempo. Credo che stia cercando un posticino per sedersi.

2. Si siede al sole. Comincia a leggere. Dietro di lui si vedono due bambini mentre cominciano a costruire un castello di sabbia.

3. Si addormenta con il libro aperto sul petto.

4. Il tempo passa. I bambini hanno fatto molti progressi con il castello. Senza accorgersene, il ragazzo comincia a prendere colore.

5. I bambini se ne sono andati, il castello finito. Il ragazzo si è svegliato. Adesso è in piedi, sorpreso e confuso. Ha sul petto il segno bianco del libro. Che strana tintarella!

6. Il ragazzo se ne va, tutto bruciato e senza dubbio, con molta sete. Si era seduto proprio sotto il sole. Avrebbe dovuto portare un ombrellone. Non ha messo neanche la crema prottetrice. Si è addormentato senza nemmeno fare attenzione al tempo passato a contatto con il sole. Non aveva neppure una bibita fresca. È molto facile disidratarsi quando si è in spiaggia se non si beve niente. Sarebbe meglio stare sulla battigia con qualcun'altro. Un amico avrebbe potuto svegliarlo prima, così da evitare il colpo di sole. È consigliato non entrare mai in acqua da soli.

4 – il Professore

Here is how a student might comment on the sketches:

1. Un giovane uomo se sveglia alle otto. Ha l'aria sorpresa ma preoccupata. Arriverà sicuramente in ritardo al lavoro.

2. Si veste in fretta. Non se ne parla né di doccia né di barba stamattina, tantomeno della colazione. Sono già le otto passate.

3. Si precipita verso la porta dando una rapida occhiata al suo orologio. Ha in mano una valigietta e porta la cravatta. Si sta velocemente avviando al lavoro.

4. Si vede un'aula. I bambini, senza un adulto che li guardi, fanno quello che vogliono. Il professore non è ancora arrivato. Lanciano aerei di carta, disegnano sulla lavagna, fanno la verticale.

   Anche i migliori studenti possono fare stupidaggini quando il professore non c'è. Secondo me, il loro comportamento è del tutto normale. Almeno, nessuno si è fatto male, e non ci sono stati danne in classe. Se ci fosse stato un incidente, ne sarebbe stato responsabile il loro giovane professore.

5. Il professore entra nell'aula. Gli alumni sono seduti come se nulla fosse successo. I pochi minuti di libertà sono finiti.

6. La lezione riprende come normale, ma perchè non si è potuto svegliare, questo professore? Si sarà svegliato e poi riaddormentato? Vive da solo? Una madre, una moglie o un coinquilino avrebbe potuto svegliarlo di nuovo. Forse è andato a letto troppo tardi e non ha dormito abbastanza. Può darsi che abbia sbagliato giorno, credendo che fosse un sabato o una domenica. Ha corso molti rischi lasciando i suoi alunni così senza sorveglianza.

5 – la grassottella

Here is how a student might have narrated the sketches:

1. Nel primo disegno vediamo una ragazza avvolta in un asciugamano. Sta per pesarsi ma sembra esitare davanti al piatto della bilancia. Sebbene sia giovane e bella, sembra un po' paffuta. È il due gennaio. Può darsi che abbia mangiato troppo durante le feste natalizie e di Capodanno.

2. Poi si pesa e forse si trova più grassa di quanto avrebbe pensato.

3. Decide di dimagrire e rinuncia alle caramelle, alla torta, ai biscotti ed al gelato. Sarà faticoso ma sembra risoluta a mettersi a dieta.

3. Eccola a febbraio a mangiare carote e a bere acqua.

4. Si sta allenando sul serio. Corre giornalmente.

5. Adesso è marzo. Sono trascorsi due mesi. La vediamo di nuovo snella e sottile.

6. Sorride perchè è riuscita a perdere chili. Si mette il piccolo costume da bagno che le sta benissimo.

   Molta gente cerca di mettersi a dieta. All'inizio ci si dedicano tutti. Cominciare è semplice. *Rimanere* a dieta, ecco il problema. Come rinunciare a un pezzettino di pane, come privarsi della pasta? Un attimo di debolezza e ci siamo ricaduti. Cediamo e poi diventiamo delusi. Stare a dieta è faticoso e arduo. Ci sono molti che provano e pochi che riescono.

   Per riuscire in qualsiasi obbiettivo, bisogna tenere duro, cosa che non è semplice. Ci vogliono la pazienza, la concentrazione, e la determinazione.

6 – le caramelle

Here is how a student might have narrated the sketches:

1. Si vede una bambina davanti a delle caramelle. La scatola aperta ha la forma di un cuore, come i regali per la festa di San Valentino.

2. Va pazza per le caramelle alla ciliegia. Ma nella scatola sono miste e non sa quelle sono, come trovare le sue amate ciliegie?

3. Deve averne provate tante ma senza successo. Per trovare le sue peferite ne ha mangiate molte, lasciandole a metà.

4. Finalemente! Ha trovato quella che cercava. Assapora tutto il gusto speciale della ciliegia.

5. La sorella maggiore la scopre mentre gusta la ciliegia. Vede tutte le caramelle a metà. Il suo regalo distrutto! Non sembra avere l'aria contenta.

    Credo che si tratti di un regalo destinato alla sorella maggiore. Forse l'aveva aperto e prima che potesse assaggiarne una, era stata interrotta, probabilmente dal telefono.

6. La sorella maggiore non è affatto contenta ma non credo che la piccola debba essere punita. Una scatola intera di caramelle non sorvegliate è una tentazione troppo forte per una bambina. Lei è mossa dalla curiosità, e non dalla cattiveria. Spero che la sorella possa perdonarla.

Practice Exams

AP Italian Language and Culture

Practice Exam 1

AP Italian Language and Culture

Practice Exam 1

AP Italian Language and Culture

Answer Sheet

SECTION I: Multiple Choice

Part A: Listening

1. (A) (B) (C) (D)   11. (A) (B) (C) (D)   21. (A) (B) (C) (D)
2. (A) (B) (C) (D)   12. (A) (B) (C) (D)   22. (A) (B) (C) (D)
3. (A) (B) (C) (D)   13. (A) (B) (C) (D)   23. (A) (B) (C) (D)
4. (A) (B) (C) (D)   14. (A) (B) (C) (D)   24. (A) (B) (C) (D)
5. (A) (B) (C) (D)   15. (A) (B) (C) (D)   25. (A) (B) (C) (D)
6. (A) (B) (C) (D)   16. (A) (B) (C) (D)   26. (A) (B) (C) (D)
7. (A) (B) (C) (D)   17. (A) (B) (C) (D)   27. (A) (B) (C) (D)
8. (A) (B) (C) (D)   18. (A) (B) (C) (D)   28. (A) (B) (C) (D)
9. (A) (B) (C) (D)   19. (A) (B) (C) (D)   29. (A) (B) (C) (D)
10. (A) (B) (C) (D)   20. (A) (B) (C) (D)   30. (A) (B) (C) (D)

Part B: Reading

31. (A) (B) (C) (D)   38. (A) (B) (C) (D)   45. (A) (B) (C) (D)
32. (A) (B) (C) (D)   39. (A) (B) (C) (D)   46. (A) (B) (C) (D)
33. (A) (B) (C) (D)   40. (A) (B) (C) (D)   47. (A) (B) (C) (D)
34. (A) (B) (C) (D)   41. (A) (B) (C) (D)   48. (A) (B) (C) (D)
35. (A) (B) (C) (D)   42. (A) (B) (C) (D)   49. (A) (B) (C) (D)
36. (A) (B) (C) (D)   43. (A) (B) (C) (D)   50. (A) (B) (C) (D)
37. (A) (B) (C) (D)   44. (A) (B) (C) (D)

Practice Exam 1

AP Italian Language and Culture

Total Test Time—3 hours

SECTION I: Multiple Choice

Time—1 hour and 20 minutes

Part A: Listening

> **DIRECTIONS:** You will now listen to several selections. For each selection you will have time to read over the questions printed in your booklet. Then you will hear the selection. You may take notes in your exam booklet as you listen. Your notes will not be graded. After listening to the selection, you will have time to answer the questions. Blacken the corresponding oval on your answer sheet.

CD 1, Track Number 3

1
La Crociera

1. Perchè si preoccupa la ragazza?

    (A) Teme il mal di mare.

    (B) Ha paura di essere ristretta in uno spazio limitato.

    (C) Crede che la gente non sia della sua età.

    (D) Pensa che avrà nostalgia di casa.

2. Che cosa vedrà secondo te durante questa crociera?

    (A) I paesi scandinavi.

    (B) Le isole caraibiche.

    (C) Trieste e Venezia.

    (D) La Sicilia e la Grecia.

3. Quanto durerà la crociera?

    (A) una settimana.

    (B) qualche giorno.

    (C) fino a Ferragosto.

    (D) una quindicina di giorni.

4. Che ne pensa il ragazzo?

    (A) Non piacerebbe neanche a lui fare questa crociera.

    (B) Crede che lei abbia fortuna.

    (C) Crede che abbia ragione di preoccuparsi.

    (D) Crede che le crociere siano per i vecchi.

2
Il Prestito

5. Presterà a Sofia il suo abito rosa oppure no?

    (A) Sicuramente sì.

    (B) Le presterà piuttosto il celeste.

    (C) No, perchè l' indosserà alle nozze.

    (D) No, perchè ha le maniche lunghe.

6. Cosa farà Sofia prima di restituire l'abito?

    (A) Lo tingerà di celeste.

    (B) Toglierà i bottoni.

    (C) Rifarà l'orlo.

    (D) Lo manderà al lavasecco.

7.   Perché esitava in principio?

    (A) Aveva intenzione di indossarlo per il matrimonio di Fabiola.

    (B) È il suo abito preferito.

    (C) Teme che Sofia non ne prenda cura.

    (D) È un abito firmato.

8.   Cosa metterà la narratrice alle nozze di Fabiola?

    (A) Un accappatoio celeste.

    (B) Un vestito da sposa.

    (C) Un abito blu chiaro con le maniche.

    (D) Un velo azzurro.

3
Cosa mangiamo?

9.   Perchè non vogliono usare il forno?

    (A) Perchè il gas non funziona.

    (B) Perchè c'è un gran calore.

    (C) Perchè preferiscono usare il microonde.

    (D) Perchè non hanno tempo.

10.   Che cosa mangeranno a fine pasto?

    (A) Formaggio.

    (B) Frutta fresca.

    (C) Tiramisù.

    (D) Panna cotta ai lamponi.

11. Che cosa preferirebbe mangiare il signore?

    (A) ogni tipo di arrosto.

    (B) Spezzatino di cinghiale.

    (C) La sua solita insalata.

    (D) Fegato con cipolle.

12. Come berrano il vino?

    (A) Freddo.

    (B) A temperatura ambiente.

    (C) Spumeggiante.

    (D) Riscaldato.

4
Un Weekend all'ombra

13. Perchè la donna non vuole andare in spiaggia?

    (A) Ha preso un paio di chili e esita a mettersi in costume.

    (B) Si annoia in spiaggia.

    (C) Vuole evitare il sole.

    (D) Non le piacciono i luoghi affollati.

14. Che cosa suggerisce di fare l'uomo al posto di andare in spiaggia?

    (A) Un giro in bicicletta.

    (B) Una merenda in canoa.

    (C) Di andare al largo in motoscafo.

    (D) Una scampagnata in un luogo fresco.

15. Chi hanno deciso di invitare?

    (A) I loro vicini che vedono spesso.

    (B) Parenti svizzeri.

(C) Amici gentili che non hanno visto da molto tempo.

(D) I suoceri.

16. Che cosa va a cercare l'uomo allora?

(A) La pattumiera.

(B) Il loro cestino da picnic.

(C) Crema solare.

(D) La sua bicicletta.

5
L'Autogrill

17. Perchè si lamenta l'automobilista?

(A) Ha mal di testa.

(B) Ha perso gli occhiali da sole.

(C) Vuole mangiare qualcosa e rilassare il collo irrigidito.

(D) Ha dimenticato il compleanno di Daria.

18. Che intende la donna quando dice di fare "una sosta"?

(A) Vuole fare una pausa, una fermata.

(B) Cerca un parcheggio.

(C) Vuole controllare il parabrezza.

(D) Chiede un autista privato

19. Ha la patente la donna?

(A) No, non ancora.

(B) Soltanto provvisoria.

(C) Sì, certo.

(D) No, affatto.

6
L'Acquacotta

20. Che cos'è l'Acquacotta?

    (A) È una fonduta di formaggi diversi.

    (B) È una specie di polenta.

    (C) È una minestra di verdure e uova.

    (D) È un dolce freddo.

21. Che tipo di pane ci vuole?

    (A) Fette di pane stagionate e tostate.

    (B) Fette di pane fresche.

    (C) Fette di pane frittate.

    (D) Pane grattugiato.

22. Che tipo di teglia è suggerita?

    (A) Una padella.

    (B) Una pentola.

    (C) Una teglia di acciaio.

    (D) Un tegame di terracotta.

23. Quali ingredienti si aggiungono proprio alla fine?

    (A) Tre cipolle rosse.

    (B) Tre pomodori maturi.

    (C) Tre pepperoni tagliuzzati.

    (D) Tre uova appena sbattute.

24. Come si serve l'Acquacotta?

    (A) Si serve in bicchieri.

    (B) Si serve sui piatti.

    (C) Si serve in scodelle.

    (D) Si serve in una coppa di vetro.

7
La Smart Car

25. Com'è la Smart?

    (A) Ha sedili pieghevoli.

    (B) È piccola ma comoda.

    (C) È lussuosa e ampia.

    (D) È una berlina con quattro posti.

26. Com'è da maneggiare la Smart?

    (A) Facile e divertente.

    (B) È lenta perché è tanto piccola.

    (C) Parcheggiare è un po' arduo.

    (D) Non è molto equilibrata.

27. Quali sono le caratteristiche di una macchina convertibile?

    (A) Ha un tetto rigido e fisso.

    (B) Ha un tetto pieghevole generalmente di cuoio o stoffa.

    (C) Ha solo tre ruote.

    (D) Ha il volante alla destra.

28. È prodotta da Fiat la Smart?

    (A) No, è giapponese.

    (B) No, è da Maserati.

    (C) No, è tedesca.

    (D) Sì, esce appena.

29. Come reagisce il ragazzo all'acquisto di questa macchina?

    (A) Con interessa e entusiasmo.

    (B) Con indifferenza fredda.

    (C) È molto distaccato.

    (D) È tanto geloso che non dice quasi niente.

30. Che ha letto il ragazzo riguardo alla consumazione di benzina?

    (A) Ha letto che il prezzo della benzina andava sempre in su.

    (B) Ha letto che consumava più di un furgone.

    (C) Ha letto che il serbatoio era in avanti.

    (D) Ha letto che consumava poco.

Part B: Reading

DIRECTIONS: Read the following passages with care. Each segment is followed by a series of questions or statements to be completed. Choose the best answer, according to what you have read, from the four choices provided. Blacken the corresponding oval on your answer sheet.

1
La Maglietta Timberland

Oggi sono uscita di casa per comprare un regalo al mio fidanzato. Il suo compleanno è imminente e io ho pensato che era meglio sbrigarsi perchè avevo poche ore di tempo. I negozi di solito chiudono alle 13 e io dovevo tornare al lavoro alle 15. È sempre difficile trovare qualcosa da regalargli perchè ha dei gusti molto particolari. Quest'anno ho scelto per lui qualcosa di piuttosto banale ma diverso dal solito: una polo della Timberland a righe viola, gialle e bianche per dare una sferzata di colore dal momento in cui lui indossa sempre gli stessi spenti colori, cioè il nero, il grigio, il blu.

Quando stasera è rientrato dal lavoro gli ho fatto trovare la maglietta tutta incartata, con un bel fiocco giallo. Avevo paura che non gli piacesse ma ha avuto una reazione inaspettata: appena l'ha vista gli è piaciuta e l'ha messa subito. Ho fatto proprio bene perchè quei colori gli donano sul serio.

31. Perchè ha scelto quei colori vivaci per il suo fidanzato?

    (A) Perchè lui impazzisce per questi colori sgargianti.

    (B) Perchè la maglietta della Timberland era in saldo.

    (C) Perchè di solito mette colori secondo lei scuri e noiosi.

    (D) Perchè lui la voleva.

32. Che tipo di maglietta ha comprato?

    (A) A quadretti.

    (B) A rombi.

    (C) In tinta unita.

    (D) A righe colorate.

33. Quando l'ha comprata?

    (A) Un paio di mesi prima.

    (B) Lo stesso giorno del compleanno.

    (C) Due giorni dopo il compleanno.

    (D) L'ha fatto fare su misura sei mesi prima.

34. Quanto gli è piaciuta?

    (A) Affatto.

    (B) Solo un pò.

    (C) Tantissimo.

    (D) Meno di quello dell'anno scorso.

35. Di che colore è la maglietta della Timberland?

    (A) Viola, bianca e gialla.

    (B) Fucsia.

    (C) Nera, grigia e blu.

    (D) Azzurra.

2
Un Sorriso

Un sorriso non costa nulla, ma vuole dire molto. Arricchisce coloro ai quali esso è rivolto, senza impoverire coloro che lo offrono. Ha la durata di un attimo, ma spesso il suo ricordo non svanisce più.

Nessuno è tanto ricco e tanto potente da poterne fare a meno, e nessuno è talmente arido da non trarre da esso almeno un po' di carica. Un sorriso porta gioia in casa, crea simpatia nei rapporti di lavoro ed è la parola d'ordine dell'amicizia. Dà un attimo di riposo a chi è affaticato, coraggio agli sfiduciati, è un raggio di sole per gli afflitti ed il più naturale rimedio contro la noia.

E tuttavia non lo si può comperare, prendere a prestito o rubare, giacchè non c'è nessuno che abbia più bisogno di un sorriso di colui il quale non ne ha più da regalare.

36. Che prezzo ha un sorriso?

    (A) Ha un costo variabile, dipende da chi lo fa.

    (B) È gratis.

    (C) È troppo costoso per la maggior parte della gente.

    (D) Occorre pagarlo sempre in contanti.

37. Quali sono i vantaggi che derivano dal sorridere?

    (A) Rallegra chi lo riceve e non costa niente.

    (B) Fa uscire il sole da dietro le nuvole.

    (C) Rende i denti più bianchi.

    (D) Ci fa essere più potenti.

38. Chi non è capace di sorridere?

    (A) Gli afflitti.

    (B) Nessuno.

    (C) Gli sfiduciati.

    (D) I potenti.

39. Il sorriso è un valido aiuto naturale per cosa?

    (A) È efficace contro gli starnuti.

    (B) È un sollievo contro la noia.

    (C) È utile contro il mal di testa.

    (D) È efficace per ridurre l'appetito.

40. Chi ha più bisogno di un sorriso?

    (A) La persona che non ha più sorrisi da offrire.

    (B) La persona che ruba.

    (C) Quella che compra.

    (D) Quella che prende in prestito qualcosa.

3
West Chester

La mia cittadina ha appena festeggiato i suoi 200 anni. Paragonata ad altre cittadine americane, la mia è piuttosto vecchia. La maggior parte delle nostre case risale all'Ottocento. Queste sono fatte di mattoni rossi. È difficile camminare sui nostri pavimenti di mattoni rossi a causa della loro superficie non omogenea. Durante l'inverno diventano scivolosi ma amo davvero il loro aspetto. Ci sono bei campi tutt'intorno. La campagna è verdissima e collinare.

In autunno si possono cogliere mele; pesche e fragole in estate. C'è un piccolo centro storico molto vivace, pieno di piccolo botteghe, di antiquari, e di buoni ristoranti. La considero il migliore dei mondi possibili. Quelli che ci abitano hanno New York, Washington e Filadelfia a portata di mano. Ci sono montagne a nord e l'oceano a est.

Lai mia famiglia ci abita da più di 40 anni. Tre generazioni si sono già succedute. Adesso mio fratello e sua moglie aspettano il loro primo figlio. Quindi comincerà la prossima generazione.

41. Dove si trova questa cittadina?

    (A) Sulla costa occidentale degli Stati Uniti.

    (B) In Cornovaglia.

    (C) Negli Stati Uniti, a est.

    (D) Nei sobborghi di Houston.

42. La narratrice è …

    (A) inglese.

    (B) statunitense.

    (C) italiana.

    (D) europea.

43. La narratrice crede che la sua cittadina sia …

    (A) poco degna di nota.

    (B) importantissima.

(C)   troppo lontana dai centri metropolitani.

(D)   ben situata.

44.   Come sono i marciapiedi?

(A)   Di ardesia grigia del secolo scorso.

(B)   Perfettamente lisci e uguali.

(C)   Scomodi per camminare, soprattutto quando gela.

(D)   Acciottolati.

45.   La maggior parte delle case risale …

(A)   al diciannovesimo secolo.

(B)   alla seconda guerra mondiale.

(C)   ai tempi degli esploratori.

(D)   al diciottesimo secolo.

4

Tuscan Sun Festival—Ermanno Romanelli
August 4, 2007, Il Cittadino Oggi, CORRIERE NATIONALE

CORTONA: Sofia Loren è l'ospite d'onore e la prima del lungo elenco di stelle che, grazie al "Tuscan Sun Festival", illumineranno il cielo di Cortona, da questa sera sino al 16 agosto. Con il concerto inaugurale diretto dal figlio della star, il maestro Carlo Ponti Jr., in onore del padre, Cortona si trasforma infatti in un affascinante teatro diffuso, uno straordinario palco all'aria aperta, fra piazza Signorelli, il Teatro Signorelli, la chiesa di San Francesco e antichi palazzi del centro storico.

Mai come per questa quinta edizione del "Tuscan Sun Festival" i numeri e gli aggettivi si sprecano, all'insegna di un gigantismo che coinvolge gli interpreti più rappresentativi della grande musica classica, molti in data unica per l'Italia. […]

A fare del Sun Fesitval una "copia" del già glorioso festival di Spoleto (ma una copia rivista e corretta in meglio, e rilanciata in alto), provvedono dibattiti, mostre d'arte, fotografia, conversazioni letterarie, cinema, enogastronomia,yoga e proposte per il wellness.

46. Da quanti anni ha luogo questo festival?

    (A) Quest'anno c'è l'inaugurazione.

    (B) Da quindici anni.

    (C) Da cinque anni.

    (D) Da dieci anni.

47. Dove ha luogo questo Festival di musica già famoso?

    (A) A Cortona.

    (B) A Spoleto.

    (C) A Volterra.

    (D) A Siena.

48. Questo Festival a Cortona è ....

    (A) un programma autunnale.

    (B) un concerto primaverile.

    (C) una presentazione invernale.

    (D) uno spettacolo estivo.

49. Per quanti giorni durerà il Festival?

    (A) Dal 4 al 16 agosto.

    (B) Dal 16 alla fine agosto.

    (C) Per tutto il mese di agosto.

    (D) Avrà luogo solo una sera.

50. Paragonato *al festival già famoso* di un'altra città rinomata, com'è quello di Cortona, secondo lo scrittore?

    (A) Non vale la pena.

    (B) È meno glorioso.

    (C) È una copia corretta in meglio.

    (D) È una copia esatta.

SECTION II: Free Response

Time–1 hour and 25 minutes

Part A: Writing

Fill in a Verb

> **DIRECTIONS:** In each sentence a verb has been omitted and replaced by a line. Supply the missing verb form on the blank to the right. There you will see the infinitive form of the verb you are to use. Read the whole paragraph before choosing your answer. Spelling, agreement, and accent marks must all be accurate for your answer to be correct.

All'éta di cinque anni la piccola Giulia _1_ una principessa magica. Il cambiamento _2_ subito, dall'oggi al domani. Tuttavia, _3_ necessario andare molte volte al Mercatone Uno per realizzare il suo abito reale. Ogni giorno _4_ allora vestita da principessa magica. _5_ sempre il suo abito con i lustrini e la mantellina assortita, la sua corona di carta d'alluminio e la bacchetta di plastica rosa.

Le commesse le _6_ spesso la riverenza, sorridendo. il signor Ricci, il fornaio, la _7_ sempre con brio e un piccolo cornetto farcito di frutta. Il pasticciere, il signor Catagna, le _8_ una caramella quotidiana che _9_ su un piccolo vassoio di vero argento.

1. _____ (diventare)

2. _____ (capitare)

3. _____ (stare)

4. _____ (uscire)

5. _____ (esigere)

6. _____ (fare)

7. _____ (salutare)

8. _____ (riservare)

9. _____ (offrire)

(Continued)

Qualche volta, la piccola sovrana doveva __10__ la bacchetta fra i denti per potere __11__ teneramente tra le dita paffute una margheritina offerta dalla Signora Crespi (la fioraia), mentre teneva dall'altra manina quella materna.

Un bel giorno il regno di Giulia __12__ in maniera infame. Quando la mamma __13__ i suoi soliti abiti di principessa, Giulia le __14__, "Mamma, non voglio più indossare questi stracci sciocchi ovunque io __15__! Preferisco mettere la mia salopette."

10. _____ (mettere)

11. _____ (impugnare)

12. _____ (concludersi)

13. _____ (stendere)

14. _____ (dire)

15. _____ (andare)

Fill in a Word

DIRECTIONS: In each sentence a single word has been omitted and replaced by a line. Write your answer, **ONE** single Italian word on the line to the right. Make sure the word is correct in form, as well as in meaning and in context. None of your answers will be verbs.

Please note that a response such as *fino a* (or *di cui*) will be considered two words, not one. For full credit you must spell each word correctly and include any necessary accent marks or apostrophes.

Da __1__ Gina ha festeggiato i suoi diciotto anni, non pensa __2__ altro __3__ ottenere la patente di guida. Ogni domenica guida con __4__ padre e cerca di parcheggiare la macchina. Papà ha molta pazienza. Gina fa costanti progressi. Crede di poter prendere la patente __5__ un mese.

Se riesce al primo tenativo, Gina __6__ sarà __7__ contenta. Sarebbe inoltre qualcosa di __8__ potrebbe essere orgogliosa. Se non riesce al primo colpo, continuerà a praticare __9__ a quando non raggiungerà il suo obiettivo. Per il momento, studia il suo manuale e sogna __10__ sua realizzazione.

1. _____

2. _____

3. _____

4. _____

5. _____

6. _____

7. _____

8. _____

9. _____

10. _____

General Essay

DIRECTIONS: Write a composition in Italian of about 150 words, on the topic below. Your essay must be organized and coherent. It must demonstrate your mastery of verb tenses and grammar. It must illustrate a good command of vocabulary. Plan before you begin. Check your work carefully for accents, spelling and agreement. You have 30 minutes.

Note: Essays are evaluated on organization and clarity, range and choice of appropriate vocabulary, grammatical accuracy and spelling.

Che cosa vorresti fare nella vita?

Part B: Cultural Essay

> **DIRECTIONS:** Write a composition in Italian of about 150 words on the topic below. You must demonstrate the depth of your cultural knowledge in an organized and coherent essay. Showcase your mastery of verb tenses and grammar; evidence a good command of vocabulary. Plan before you begin. Check your work carefully for accents, spelling and agreement. You have 30 minutes.

Note: The student's knowledge of culture determines 80% of his or her score on this essay. The remaining 20% is based on organization, clarity, range and choice of appropriate vocabulary, grammatical accuracy and spelling.

Se potessi vedere soltanto tre capolavori dell'arte italiana, che cosa vedresti, e perchè? Dove andresti a cercarli?

Part C: Speaking—Narration

CD 1, Track Number 4

DIRECTIONS: You will have two minutes to look at and think about a series of pictures found on the following pages. You are to narrate a story suggested by the picture sequence. You may take notes in the test booklet insert if you like. Your notes will not be graded. You will then have two minutes to record your response. Comment on each picture and use all of the time allotted. You will be scored on your level of fluency, your ability to narrate, grammatical accuracy, vocabulary range and pronunciation. The completeness of your response will also be taken into consideration. Start your recorder when told to do so.

DIRECTIONS: The following pictures present a story. Pretend you are speaking to a friend and narrate a complete story suggested by the pictures. Your story should contain a beginning, a middle, and an end.

il ballo di fine anno

Speaking—Conversation

CD 1, Track Number 5

DIRECTIONS: You are now asked to participate in a simulated conversation in Italian. The questions you will hear are not printed for you to read. You must rely solely on what you hear. You will hear each question twice, followed by a tone. Once you have heard the tone you will have 20 seconds to record your response to the question in Italian. A second tone signals that 20 seconds have elapsed. Stop talking, even if you haven't finished what you were saying. Don't worry if you have been cut off. Listen immediately for the next question. Do not, at any time, stop the recorder until you are instructed to do so.

You will be evaluated on your ability to answer each question completely and promptly. You will be scored on fluency and the appropriateness of your answer. Your score will be lowered if your answer is too short. Use every second allotted. It is better to be cut off than to stop speaking too soon.

You will hear a total of six questions. The first question is for practice only. Try to answer it. It will not be recorded or scored but will give you a good idea of the type of questions to follow. They will all be related to one theme, alluded to in the practice question. You will record your responses to the next five questions.

Practice Exam 1

AP Italian Language and Culture

Answer Key

SECTION I: Multiple Choice

Part A: Listening

1.	(C)	11.	(C)	21.	(A)
2.	(D)	12.	(A)	22.	(D)
3.	(A)	13.	(C)	23.	(D)
4.	(B)	14.	(D)	24.	(C)
5.	(A)	15.	(C)	25.	(B)
6.	(D)	16.	(B)	26.	(A)
7.	(A)	17.	(C)	27.	(B)
8.	(C)	18.	(A)	28.	(C)
9.	(B)	19.	(C)	29.	(A)
10.	(B)	20.	(C)	30.	(D)

Part B: Reading

31.	(C)	38.	(B)	45.	(A)
32.	(D)	39.	(B)	46.	(C)
33.	(B)	40.	(A)	47.	(A)
34.	(C)	41.	(C)	48.	(D)
35.	(A)	42.	(B)	49.	(A)
36.	(B)	43.	(D)	50.	(C)
37.	(A)	44.	(C)		

SECTION II: Free Response

Part A: Writing

Fill in a Verb

1. è diventata
2. è capitato
3. è stato
4. usciva
5. esegiva
6. facevano
7. salutava
8. riservava
9. offriva
10. mettere
11. impugnare
12. si è concluso
13. ha steso
14. ha detto
15. vada

Fill in a Word

1. quando
2. a (ad)
3. che
4. suo
5. entro, tra, in
6. ne
7. molto, tanto
8. cui
9. fino
10. la

Practice Exam 1

AP Italian Language and Culture

Detailed Explanations of Answers

Section I: Multiple Choice
Part A: Listening

1

1. **(C)** Crede che la gente non sia della sua éta.
   She's afraid she'll be bored if there aren't any other young people.

2. **(D)** La Sicilia e la Grecia
   She tells us that she will be taking a Mediterranean cruise.

3. **(A)** Una settimana.
   She states that her cruise will last seven days.

4. **(B)** Crede che lei abbia fortuna.
   He thinks she's lucky and reassures her that there will be lots of people her own age. He also says there will be so much to do.

2

5. **(A)** Sicuramente sì.
   The speaker tells her husband that Sofia wants to borrow her pink dress, the one he likes so much. He says that as long as she returns it, he sees no problem. Eventually, she agrees with her husband.

6. **(D)** Lo manderà al lavasecco.
Sofia will have it dry cleaned before returning it.

7. **(A)** Aveva intenzione di indossarlo per il matrimonio di Fabiola.
She was planning on wearing it to Fabiola's upcoming wedding.

8. **(C)** Un abito blu chiaro con le maniche.
She has agreed to lend her pink dress to Sofia and will wear her light blue dress with sleeves so she won't be too cold in the air-conditioning.

3

9. **(B)** Perché c'è un gran calore.
They don't want to use the oven because it's so hot. The woman will prepare a light, cool salad.

10. **(B)** Frutta fresca.
Fresh fruit is the correct answer as they will have watermelon.

11. **(C)** La sua solita insalata.
As they discuss what to eat on this hot night he mentions that he really likes the mixed salad of tuna and hard-boiled eggs she makes once in a while.

12. **(A)** Freddo.
They'll have a chilled white wine.

4

13. **(C)** Vuole evitare il sole.
When he suggests they go to the beach for the weekend, she asks if they couldn't plan something else. She's already had a bad sunburn this summer and she's worried about her skin. She wants to avoid the sun.

14. **(D)** Una scampagnata in un luogo fresco.
He suggests an outing, a picnic, under the trees in the woods.

15. **(C)**   amici gentili che non hanno visto da molto tempo

They decide to invite their good friends Eleonora and Alessandro whom they haven't seen in a long time.

16. **(B)**   Il loro cestino da picnic.

He goes to find their picnic basket for her.

5

17. **(C)**   Vuole mangiare qualcosa e rilassare il collo irrigidito.

The driver complains that he's hungry and that his neck hurts. He suggests they look for a rest stop. She agrees.

18. **(A)**   Vuole fare una pausa, una fermata.

A *sosta* is a stop. She wants him to take a break.

19. **(C)**   Sì, certo.

Yes, we can assume that she has her license as she offers to drive so that he can nap after their rest stop.

6

20. **(C)**   È una minestra di verdure e uova.

Acquacotta is a rustic vegetable soup of onions, green peppers, celery, tomatoes and beaten eggs served hot over crusty toasted bread with a drizzle of olive oil. It's a specialty of Tuscany.

21. **(A)**   Fette di pane stagionate e tostate.

The bread slices need to be hard in order to withstand the hot soup. They should be a few days old, toasted or grilled.

22. **(D)**   Un tegame di terracotta.

A *terracotta* (ceramic clay pottery) pan is recommended.

23. **(D)**   Tre uova appena sbattute.

Three barely beaten eggs are the very last ingredients.

24. **(C)**   Si serve in scodelle.

Like any hot soup, *acquacotta* is served in bowls.

7

25. **(B)**   È piccola ma comoda.

The *Smart Car* is little but comfortable. It's certainly not a luxury car as it can only seat two people.

26. **(A)**   Facile e divertente.

It's easy to handle and fun to drive. He calls it *scattante,* very peppy, zippy, responsive.

27. **(B)**   Ha un tetto pieghevole generalmente di cuoio o stoffa.

A convertible has a folding roof, usually made of leather or fabric.

28. **(C)**   No, è tedesca.

The *Smart Car* is not produced by *Fiat.* It's a German product.

29. **(A)**   Con interessa e entusiasmo.

He is genuinely interested in her new car, and very enthusiastic about her choice.

30. **(D)**   Ha letto che consumava poco.

He's read that it doesn't use much gas, an important factor in Italy where gas is extremely expensive.

Part B: Reading

1
La Maglietta Timberland

31. Perchè ha scelto quei colori vivaci per il suo fidanzato?

    (C) Perchè di solito mette colori secondo lei scuri e noiosi.

    She buys him the brightly colored shirt because she thinks the colors he usually wears are dark and boring. Rule out that he was crazy for the loud colors. It wasn't on sale, and he didn't *want* it as he didn't even know about it.

32. Che tipo di maglietta ha comprato?

    (D) A righe colorate.

    She bought a shirt with colored stripes. It wasn't checkered, argyle, or solid colored.

33. Quando l'ha comprata?

    (B) Lo stesso giorno del compleanno

    She bought it on the very day of his birthday. She did not buy it a couple of months before or two days after his birthday. She didn't have it custom-made six months ahead.

34. Quanto gli è piaciuta?

    (C) Tantissimo.

    He really liked it, so much so that he put it right on and wore it immediately.

35. Di che colore è la maglietta della Timberland?

    (A) Viola, bianca e giallo.

    The shirt is purple, white and yellow. It is not fuchsia, nor black, gray and blue. It's not blue like a national team soccer shirt.

2
Un Sorriso

36. Che prezzo ha un sorriso?

   (B)   È gratis. A smile is free.

   It doesn't vary in price depending on who is smiling. It isn't too expensive for most people, and it doesn't always have to be paid for in cash.

37. Quali sono i vantaggi che derivano dal sorridere?

   (A)   Rallegra chi lo riceve e non costa niente.

   It makes the person who receives it happy and it doesn't cost a thing. It doesn't bring the sun out from behind the clouds and it doesn't make teeth brighter, nor does it make us more powerful.

38. Chi non è capace di sorridere?

   (B)   Nessuno.

   No one in incapable of smiling, not the afflicted (the desolate), not the discouraged or disheartened, not the powerful.

39. Il sorriso è un valido aiuto naturale per cosa?

   (B)   È un sollievo contro la noia.

   It's a relief from boredom. It's not effective for sneezes. It doesn't relieve headaches, and it's not an appetite surpressant.

40. Chi ha più bisogno di un sorriso?

   (A)   La persona che non ha più sorrisi da offrire.

   The person who needs a smile the most is the one who has no more smiles to give. It's not the person who steals, not the one who buys, nor the one who borrows.

3
West Chester

41. Dove si trova questa cittadina?

    (C) Negli Stati Uniti, a est.

    The little town is on the East coast, in the U.S., it's not on the West coast, in Cornwall, or in the suburbs of Houston.

42. La narratrice è...

    (B) statunitense.

    She's American, not English, Italian, or European.

43. La narratrice crede che la sua cittadina sia...

    (D) ben situata.

    She thinks it has a great location. She doesn't think it's of little interest. She doesn't think it's overly important, and she doesn't think it's too far from the bigger urban centers.

44. Come sono i marciapiedi?

    (C) Scomodi per camminare, soprattutto quando gela.

    The red brick sidewalks are hard to walk on, especially when it freezes. They're not made of 19th century gray slate, they are not perfectly smooth and even, and they are not cobblestone.

45. La maggior parte delle case risale ...

    (A) al diciannovesimo secolo.

    This is a hard question. Most of the houses date back to the *Ottocento*, which means the 19th century (the 18 *hundreds*) in Italian. They are earlier than World War II, but don't go back to the time of the explorers. Neither were they built in the 18th century (*il diciottesimo secolo*), that is, the 17 *hundreds*.

4
Il Tuscan Sun Festival

46. Da quanti anni ha luogo questo festival?

    (C) da cinque anni.

    This is the fifth year, *la quinta edizione*, of the Tuscan Sun Festival.

47. Dove ha luogo questo Festival di musica già famoso?

    (B) A Spoleto.

    Spoleto is world famous for its yearly arts festival, founded by composer Gian Carlo Menotti in 1957. After his father's death, Menotti and his mother moved to the U.S. where he studied music at the Curtis Institute in Philadelphia. While a student there, he lived in West Chester, Pa., at the home of one of his classmates, the future American composer, Samuel Barber.

48. Questo Festival a Cortona è....

    (D) uno spettacolo estivo.

    The festival takes place every summer.

49. Per quanti giorni durerà il Festival?

    (A) Dal 4 al 16 agosto.

    It will run through the week of August 4th to the 16th.

50. Paragonato al festival già famoso di un'altra città rinomata, com'è quello di Cortona, secondo lo scrittore?

    (C) È una copia corretta in meglio.

    While the author allows that the Cortona festival is a copy of the more famous one in Spoleto, he thinks it's even better.

Section II

Part A: Writing

Fill in a Verb

1. All'éta di cinque anni, la piccola Giulia è <u>diventata</u> una principessa magica.

   Little Julia became a magic princess at the age of five.

   Use the *passato prossimo* for an action whose beginning takes place within the sentence. If the passage were part of a more formal literary text, the *passato remoto* would be used instead.

2. Il cambiamento è <u>capitato</u> subito, dall'oggi al domani.

   The transformation happened quickly, from one day to the next.

   Use the *passato prossimo* for an action whose ending takes place within the sentence.

3. Tuttavia, è <u>stato</u> necessario andare molte volte al Mercatone Uno per realizzare il suo abito reale.

   Nevertheless, it was necessary to make many trips to Mercatone Uno to complete her regal attire.

   Although the trips to Mercatone Uno (like a K-Mart) were repeated, *molte volte*, the goal of putting together her outfit has been accomplished, so we use the *passato prossimo*.

4. Ogni giorno <u>usciva</u> allora vestita da principessa magica.

   And so she went out every day dressed as a magic princess.

   The words *ogni giorno* make clear that this action was repeated many times. Use the *imperfect* for habitual past action.

5. <u>Esigeva</u> sempre il suo abito coi lustrini e la mantellina assortita, la sua corona di carta d'alluminio e la bacchetta di plastica rosa.

   She would always demand her sequined dress with its little matching cape, her aluminum foil crown and her pink plastic wand.

   This sentence further clarifies her repeated behavior. Use the *imperfect*.

6. Le commesse le <u>facevano</u> spesso la riverenza, sorridendo.

   The saleswomen used to (would) curtsey to her, smiling.

   Use the *imperfect*.

7.   Il signor Ricci, il fornaio, la <u>salutava</u> sempre con brio e un piccolo cornetto farcito di frutta.

The baker would always greet her with flair and a little fruit-filled crescent.

Use the *imperfect*.

8. + 9.   Il pasticciere, il signor Castagna, le <u>riservava</u> una caramella quotidiana che <u>offriva</u> su un piccolo vassoio di vero argento.

The confectioner saved a candy for her every day which he offered on a little sterling tray.

Both verbs are in the *imperfect* because Signor Castagna did these actions *daily*. *Quotidiana* is a clue to habitual action!

10. + 11.   Qualche volta la piccola sovrana doveva <u>mettere</u> la sua bacchetta fra i denti, per potere <u>impugnare</u> teneramente tra le dita paffute, una margheritina offerta dalla Signora Crespini (la fioraia), mentre teneva con l'altra manina quella materna.

Sometimes the little sovereign had to carry her wand in between her teeth, so she could grasp with her chubby fingers a daisy offered by the florist, while holding onto her mother with the other hand.

Both verbs appear in the *infinitive* form as each one follows a *modal* verb.

12.   Un bel giorno il regno di Giulia <u>si è concluso</u> in maniera infame.

One day Julia's reign came to an abrupt end.

Use the *passato prossimo* for an action which ends within the sentence. Remember to conjugate all reflexive verbs with *essere*.

13. 14. + 15.   Quando la mamma <u>ha steso</u> i suoi soliti abiti da principessa, Giulia le <u>ha detto</u> "Mamma, non voglio più indossare questi stracci sciocchi ovunque io <u>vada</u>! Preferisco mettere la mia salopette."

When her mother spread out her usual princess outfit, Julia said to her "Mom I don't want to wear these silly rags wherever I go anymore, I'd rather wear my dungarees." (overalls)

Use the *passato prossimo* to express what her mother *did*. Don't be mislead by *soliti*, which refers to her usual attire. Use the *passato prossimo* to express what Giulia *said*. Use the subjunctive after the subordinating conjunction *ovunque*.

Fill in a Word

1. + 2. + 3.   Da <u>quando</u> Gina ha festeggiato i suoi diciotto anni, non pensa a (ad) altro <u>che</u> ottenere la patente di guida.

Since her 18th birthday, Gina can think of nothing but (nothing other than) getting her license.

Quando completes this conjunction meaning *since*. The verb *pensare* requires the preposition **a** when it means *to think of* or *about*. If an opinion were to follow, which is not the case here, *pensare* would require **di**. **Che** completes the expression *altro che*.

4.   Ogni domenica guida con <u>suo</u> padre e cerca di parcheggiare la macchina.

She drives with her father every Sunday and tries to park the car.

Supply a masculine possessor to express *her* father! Possessive adjectives always agree with the thing possessed, not the owner!

5.   Crede di poter prendere la patente <u>entro/ tra / in</u> un mese.

She thinks she'll be able to get her license in a month.

Entro is the preposition of choice when *in* refers to a period of time which has not yet taken place. **Tra** and **in** are also possible.

6. + 7.   Se Gina riesce al primo tentativo, <u>ne</u> sarà <u>molto / tanto</u> contenta.

If Gina passes on the first try, she will be very (so) happy.

The pronoun **ne** stands for the inanimate object of the preposition **di**. *(essere contento di)*. *Molto* functions as an invariable adverb in front of the adjective *contenta*. No agreement!

8.   Sarebbe inoltre qualcosa di <u>cui</u> potrebbe essere orgogliosa.

Furthermore it would be something she could be proud of.

Cui is the only relative pronoun possible here, that is, for an object introduced by **di** *(essere orgoglioso di)*.

9.   Se non riesce al primo colpo, continuerà a praticare <u>fino</u> a quando non raggiungerà il suo obiettivo.

If she doesn't pass on the first try, she'll continue to practice until she reaches her objective.

Fino + **a** creates *until*. The *non* is pleonastic. That means it's just part of the *fino a* construction, without lending a negative meaning. We have no equivalent in English.

10. Per il momento, studia il suo manuale e sogna <u>la</u> sua realizzazione.

For now, she's studying her driver's manual and dreaming about her success.

Sognare (to dream of, about) requires the preposition *di* when followed by a verb. If it's followed by a noun, however, as it is here, no preposition is used. Supply the definite article to complete the feminine singular possessor.

Sample Essay Answer
in Response to General Essay Question

Read the following essay to see how a student might have answered this question.

Che cosa vorresti fare nella vita?

Ho in mente di fare tante cose! Innanzitutto andrò all'università per studiare le lingue straniere. Quando sarò laureato mi piacerebbe viaggiare ovunque nel mondo. Vorrei conoscere soprattutto la Cina e il Giappone. Ho un amico il cui cugino abita in Cina attualmente e insegna l'inglese. Si è sposato con una cinese e si è immerso interamente nella loro cultura.

Uno dei miei fratelli è andato in India dove lavora come missionario. È diventato una specie di tuttofare. Insegna alla gente come irrigare meglio i loro campi, si prende cura dei bimbi ammalati, insegna a leggere a chiunque e aiuta quando un animale partorisce. Se qualcuno costruisce una capanna, c'è lui.

Ogni anno torna a casa nostra per le feste natalizie ma dopo due o tre settimane ha fretta di tornare al suo lavoro lontano, alla sua vocazione.

Ora non so esattamente quello che farò nella mia vita, ma sono sicuro che andrò in un posto lontano dove potrò usare le mie abilità linguistiche e dove potrò scoprire mondi nascosti e sconosciuti.

Part B: Culture

Sample Essay Answer
in Response to Cultural Essay Question

Read the following essay to see how a student might have answered this question.

Se potessi vedere soltanto tre capolavori dell'arte italiana, che cosa vedresti, e perchè? Dove andresti a cercarli?

Se dovessi sceglierne solo tre fra tanti, io andrei prima a Firenze per vedere con i miei occhi la statua di Davide fatta da Michelangelo. L'ho visto molte volte in fotografia e anche quello di bronzo di Donatello che mostra un Davide vincitore con la testa del gigante Golia ai suoi piedi. Mi piacerebbe vedere il Davide di Michelangelo perchè è rappresentato prima del confronto e si legge nello sguardo del giovanotto la tensione, la paura, la sicurezza e il dubbio allo stesso tempo. Dicono che sia gigantesco, tutto scolpito di un marmo bianchissimo di Carrara. Lo vorrei vedere da vicino.

Poi andrei a Firenze, agli Uffizi, per vedere La Nascita di Venere di Sandro Botticelli. Chi non vorrebbe vedere questa tela? La mia professoressa d'italiano ci ha spiegato il mito greco, e com'è nata da una lacrima di suo padre Zeus, caduta nell'oceano. Ecco perchè la vediamo sulla conchiglia. Non ho mai visto una composizione più bella.

Alla fine andrei probabilmente al Louvre, a Parigi, per vedere la Gioconda di Leonardo DaVinci. Peccato che non sia in Italia, ma Leonardo è morto in Francia, e ha legato molti suoi lavori al suo amico François I, il rè francese. Leonardo ha concepito per il suo castello Chambord una magnifica scala a doppia chiocciola.

In Italia le belle opere d'arte si vedono dappertutto, bisogna soltanto aprire gli occhi per goderne, ma se dovessi scegliere soltanto tre capolavori, io vorrei vedere soprattutto questi tre.

Part C: Speaking

Speaking—Narration

Il Ballo Di Fine Anno

Here is how a student might have narrated these sketches:

1. È evidente che il ragazzo si è preso una cotta per la ragazza ma lei non lo sa. Lui non le parla.

2. L'anno scolastico sta per finire. Il ballo si terrà il 10 maggio. Ogni ragazzo che vuole andare dovrà avere il coraggio di chiedere a una ragazza di accompagnarlo. Lei cercherà un vestito da sera indimenticabile e passerà ore con le sue amiche a parlare di acconciatura e accessori.

3. Le due ragazze parlano del grande evento. Quella di sinistra ha già scelto il vestito e sa con chi andrà. Riconosciamo la ragazza a destra, è quella per cui il nostro ragazzo ha una cotta. Anche lei ha trovato il vestito ideale ma non è stata ancora invitata.

4. Ecco di nuovo il ragazzo. Questa volta lei gira la testa verso di lui e lo vede. Lui sembra a disagio vicino a lei ma deve dire qualcosa.

5. Fa appello a tutto il suo coraggio e le fa la domanda. Lei accetta il suo invito. È stato più facile di quanto credesse. Andranno insieme al ballo. Credo che sia normale per un ragazzo giovane e con poca esperienza sentirsi un po' nervoso e a disagio quando una ragazza piace veramente. Esita perchè non ha la minima idea di cosa fare. Sicuramente ha il cuore che batte a mille e le mani sudate, ma è parte della vita. Ci siamo passati tutti

6. Ecco la nostra giovane coppia la sera del loro ballo sognato. Benche questi balli costino troppo per i giovani, i biglietti, lo smoking per lui, l'abito da sera per lei, i fiori, trovare un mezzo di trasporto elegante come una limousine, è, d'altra parte, un'occasione unica che viene solo una volta. È un momento dell'adolescenza che rimarrà impresso per tutta la vita.

Practice Exam 2

AP Italian Language and Culture

Practice Exam 2

AP Italian Language and Culture

Answer Sheet

SECTION I: Multiple Choice

Part A: Listening

1. Ⓐ Ⓑ Ⓒ Ⓓ
2. Ⓐ Ⓑ Ⓒ Ⓓ
3. Ⓐ Ⓑ Ⓒ Ⓓ
4. Ⓐ Ⓑ Ⓒ Ⓓ
5. Ⓐ Ⓑ Ⓒ Ⓓ
6. Ⓐ Ⓑ Ⓒ Ⓓ
7. Ⓐ Ⓑ Ⓒ Ⓓ
8. Ⓐ Ⓑ Ⓒ Ⓓ
9. Ⓐ Ⓑ Ⓒ Ⓓ
10. Ⓐ Ⓑ Ⓒ Ⓓ

11. Ⓐ Ⓑ Ⓒ Ⓓ
12. Ⓐ Ⓑ Ⓒ Ⓓ
13. Ⓐ Ⓑ Ⓒ Ⓓ
14. Ⓐ Ⓑ Ⓒ Ⓓ
15. Ⓐ Ⓑ Ⓒ Ⓓ
16. Ⓐ Ⓑ Ⓒ Ⓓ
17. Ⓐ Ⓑ Ⓒ Ⓓ
18. Ⓐ Ⓑ Ⓒ Ⓓ
19. Ⓐ Ⓑ Ⓒ Ⓓ
20. Ⓐ Ⓑ Ⓒ Ⓓ

21. Ⓐ Ⓑ Ⓒ Ⓓ
22. Ⓐ Ⓑ Ⓒ Ⓓ
23. Ⓐ Ⓑ Ⓒ Ⓓ
24. Ⓐ Ⓑ Ⓒ Ⓓ
25. Ⓐ Ⓑ Ⓒ Ⓓ
26. Ⓐ Ⓑ Ⓒ Ⓓ
27. Ⓐ Ⓑ Ⓒ Ⓓ
28. Ⓐ Ⓑ Ⓒ Ⓓ
29. Ⓐ Ⓑ Ⓒ Ⓓ
30. Ⓐ Ⓑ Ⓒ Ⓓ

Part B: Reading

31. Ⓐ Ⓑ Ⓒ Ⓓ
32. Ⓐ Ⓑ Ⓒ Ⓓ
33. Ⓐ Ⓑ Ⓒ Ⓓ
34. Ⓐ Ⓑ Ⓒ Ⓓ
35. Ⓐ Ⓑ Ⓒ Ⓓ
36. Ⓐ Ⓑ Ⓒ Ⓓ
37. Ⓐ Ⓑ Ⓒ Ⓓ

38. Ⓐ Ⓑ Ⓒ Ⓓ
39. Ⓐ Ⓑ Ⓒ Ⓓ
40. Ⓐ Ⓑ Ⓒ Ⓓ
41. Ⓐ Ⓑ Ⓒ Ⓓ
42. Ⓐ Ⓑ Ⓒ Ⓓ
43. Ⓐ Ⓑ Ⓒ Ⓓ
44. Ⓐ Ⓑ Ⓒ Ⓓ

45. Ⓐ Ⓑ Ⓒ Ⓓ
46. Ⓐ Ⓑ Ⓒ Ⓓ
47. Ⓐ Ⓑ Ⓒ Ⓓ
48. Ⓐ Ⓑ Ⓒ Ⓓ
49. Ⓐ Ⓑ Ⓒ Ⓓ
50. Ⓐ Ⓑ Ⓒ Ⓓ

Practice Exam 2

AP Italian Language and Culture

Total Test Time—3 hours

SECTION I: Multiple Choice

Time—1 hour and 20 minutes

Part A: Listening

> **DIRECTIONS:** You will now listen to several selections. For each selection you will have time to read over the questions printed in your booklet. Then you will hear the selection. You may take notes in your exam booklet as you listen. Your notes will not be graded. After listening to the selection, you will have time to answer the questions. Blacken the corresponding oval on your answer sheet.

CD 2, Track Number 1

1
Il Pozzo magico

1. Perchè la ragazza vuole farsi prestare soldi?

    (A) Per poter andare al cinema con le sue amiche.

    (B) Deve comprare una scheda per il telefonino.

    (C) Ha visto un paio di scarpe in saldo belle da morire.

    (D) Vorrebbe spiccioli.

2. Che cosa vuole sapere il padre dalla ragazza?

   (A) Dove va nel pomeriggio.

   (B) Per quale motivo vuole i soldi.

   (C) Con chi esce.

   (D) Quando torna a casa.

3. Il padre acconsente alla richiesta della ragazza?

   (A) No perchè chiede troppo spesso.

   (B) No perchè è un motivo frivolo.

   (C) Sì, non importa quanto lei chiede.

   (D) Sì ma soltanto una volta.

4. Come le darà i soldi il padre?

   (A) Le scriverà un assegno.

   (B) Le farà inviare un bonifico bancario.

   (C) Le darà i soldi in contanti dopo averli presi al Bancomat.

   (D) La manderà a pescarli dal pozzo.

2
Mirabilandia

5. Le è piaciuta la grande ruota?

   (A) Sì, tanto.

   (B) Sì, un po'.

   (C) No, le dà i giramenti di testa.

   (D) No, perchè non aveva il tempo di salire.

6. Le è piaciuto lo zucchero filato?

   (A) Sì, molto.

   (B) No, l'ha trovato troppo dolce.

(C) Sì, ne ha mangiato a bizzeffe.

(D) No, l'ha trovato troppo gommoso.

7. Che cosa le è piaciuto di più?

(A) Le montagne russe.

(B) La ruota panoramica.

(C) Lo zucchero filato.

(D) La mezz'ora d'attesa.

8. Quanto lungo ha dovuto aspettare la ragazza per entrare?

(A) Un quarto d'ora.

(B) Un'oretta.

(C) Trenta minuti.

(D) Venti minuti.

3
Le Foto digitali

9. Quali sono i vantaggi dei foto digitali?

(A) Si può stampare le sue foto in un'occhiata.

(B) Le foto non si possono mai cancellare.

(C) È difficile ma risparmia tempo.

(D) Si mandano le foto a un sito internet e tornano stampate qualche giorni dopo.

10. Che cosa vuole imparare il ragazzo?

(A) Come diventare fotografo.

(B) Come prendere foto.

(C) Come sviluppare e stampare belle foto.

(D) Come scontornare una foto.

11. Perché viene il ragazzo dopo lavoro?

    (A) Perché è il loro anniversario e vuole prendere foto.

    (B) Perché la ragazza gli spiegherà e gli mostrerà come ha fatto le belle foto a casa.

    (C) Perché vuole rilassarsi dopo il lavoro.

    (D) Perché la ragazza ha bisogno del suo aiuto.

12. Quando tornerà il ragazzo?

    (A) Domani sera.

    (B) La sera stessa.

    (C) L'indomani.

    (D) Quando sarà pensionato.

4
Un Pomeriggio in cucina

13. Cosa preparerà questa donna oggi pomeriggio?

    (A) Una torta alla ciliegia.

    (B) Una crostata con marmellata di ciliegia.

    (C) Albiccoche al forno.

    (D) Un budino alla marmellata di albiccoche.

14. Quando la donna voleva servire questo dolce?

    (A) A cena.

    (B) A pranzo.

    (C) Domani.

    (D) Dopodomani.

15. Perché ha cambiato d'idea?

    (A) Perché suo figlio non ci sarà.

    (B) Perché piace a suo figlio l'idea di mangiarla subito.

    (C) Perché le albicocche sono fresche.

    (D) Perché suo figlio ha chiesto le ciliege.

16. Che cosa vuole sostituire il figlio nella ricetta?

    (A) La marmellata di albicocche.

    (B) La crostata.

    (C) Lo zucchero.

    (D) La pasta frolla.

5
La Fede

17. Perchè la ragazza voleva parlare al Signor Mariani?

    (A) Per chiedergli dove avevano passato la loro luna di miele.

    (B) Per invitarlo alle sue nozze.

    (C) Per dirgli che ammirava tanto la fede che aveva regalato alla sua sposa.

    (D) Per domandargli consigli sul matrimonio.

18. Quanti anni avrebbe la Signora Mariani?

    (A) Almeno settant'anni.

    (B) Avrà passato da poco la trentina.

    (C) Magari quarant'anni.

    (D) Cinquant'anni più o meno.

19. I Mariani hanno goduto una vita coniugale ...

    (A) lunghissima.

    (B) di pochi anni.

    (C) che è durata un decennio.

    (D) che è durata un secolo.

20. Secondo la ragazza, a che cosa servirebbe questa fede dopo la morte dello sposo Mariani?

    (A) Servirebbe da assicurazione.

    (B) Servirebbe da ricordo avuto caro.

    (C) Servirebbe da punto di discussione.

    (D) Servirebbe da gioiello.

6
Liliana

21. Il 27 luglio sarebbe...

    (A) l'onomastico di Liliosa.

    (B) le nozze di Liliosa.

    (C) il funerario di Liliosa.

    (D) la nascita di Santa Elisabetta.

22. Il fiore collegato a Liliana sarebbe...

    (A) il garofano bianco.

    (B) la rosa inglese.

    (C) il giglio.

    (D) la margheritina.

23. Il nome Liliana è di origine…

    (A) tedesca.

    (B) inglese.

    (C) salva.

    (D) nordica.

24. Quanto diffuso in Italia è il nome di Liliana?

    (A) Liliana si è affermata particolarmente in Sardegna.

    (B) Liliana è molto diffusa nelle regioni di tutta Italia.

    (C) Liliana è oggi nome rarissimo.

    (D) Liliana è diffusa soprattutto al Nord e al Centro del Paese.

25. Quanti anni risale l'introdotto del nome Liliana in Italia?

    (A) Benchè vecchia in Inghilterra, Liliana è piuttosto recente in Italia.

    (B) Risale ai tempi etruschi.

    (C) Risale all'Impero Romano.

    (D) Liliana è stata introdotta in Italia poco dopo il Rinascimento.

26. Il nome *Lillian*…

    (A) vuole dire *luglio*.

    (B) è diminuitivo di Margherita.

    (C) è diminuitivo di Elizabeth.

    (D) è diminuitivo di Liliosa.

7
Il Mouse bloccato

27. Che cosa suggerisce la ragazza per riparare il mouse?

(A) Suggerisce di buttarlo via.

(B) Suggerisce di cambiare la pallina.

(C) Suggerisce di controllare la corda.

(D) Suggerisce di pulirlo.

28. Che cose sono utili per riparare un mouse che non reagisce?

(A) Pinzette, cottonfioc e alcool.

(B) Accesso a Internet e un fornitore.

(C) Una corda più lunga e una pallina di ricambio.

(D) Un martello, del nastro adhesivo e due fermagli.

29. Qual'era il problema con il mouse?

(A) Fumava.

(B) La corda si è rotta.

(C) La freccia sullo schermo non andava.

(D) La pallina è andata smarrita.

30. Come erano i consigli della ragazza?

(A) Costosi.

(B) Semplici e efficaci.

(C) Complicati e difficili.

(D) Lunghi e confusi.

Part B: Reading

DIRECTIONS: Read the following passages with care. Each segment is followed by a series of questions or statements to be completed. Choose the best answer, according to what you have read, from the four choices provided. Blacken the corresponding oval on your answer sheet.

1
Magic Bullet

Potete tritare cipolle e aglio senza neanche toccare un coltello, macinare caffè fresco ogni mattina, preparare salse fresche, salse marinate, pranzi completi senza sporcare nemmeno una pentola! Un pesto delizioso fatto in casa in meno di 10 secondi! Formaggio duro grattugiato! È talmente semplice da usare! Per risparmiare tempo in cucina, chiamate ora!

Diciamo che vogliamo fare un frappé per tutta la famiglia ... mettiamo un sacco di gelato, ghiaccio, aggiungiamo latte, fragole fresche, un po' di zucchero.... avvitiamo il coperchio e è pronto da servire in un attimo.

Adesso inseriamo un pezzo di anguria, tre prugne mature, una manciata di spinaci, un po' di broccoli... e in meno di 5 secondi avete una bevanda sana e piena di vitamine... pronto da bere! Il gusto della frutta copre il gusto delle verdure e i bambini non se ne accorgeranno!

Chiamate subito per prenotare il vostro! Potreste spendere centinaia di Euro ma se chiamate adesso riceverete non solo il Magic Bullet con sei bicchieri miscelatori completamente lavabili in lavastoviglie, ma anche sei guarnizioni colorate per riconoscere il proprio bicchiere, un frullatore, una centrifuga, tutte le lame e accessori in omaggio! C'è anche un bel ricettario e un manuale d'uso! E con questa offerta televisiva Italia Vini ha selezionato sei bottiglie di vino per voi! Che ne dite?

31. Perchè dobbiamo comprare questo piccolo elettrodomestico?

   (A) Risparmia tempo e fa qualunque lavoro di cucina.

   (B) Cuoce meglio del forno a microonde.

   (C) Ci permette di togliere il frigorifero dalla cucina.

   (D) Fa il ghiaccio 24 ore su 24.

32. Quale sarebbe il vantaggio di chiamare subito?

    (A) Ne rimangono solo pochi.

    (B) È un prodotto di fine serie.

    (C) Se ci sbrighiamo riceveremo accessori e vini in omaggio.

    (D) È un'offerta che non verrà fatta mai più.

33. A che cosa servono le guarnizioni di colori diversi che si attaccano ai bicchieri?

    (A) A fare i cappuccini.

    (B) Sono 'segnabicchieri' per riconoscere la propria bevanda.

    (C) Per rallegrare la tavola.

    (D) Per prevenire le perdite di liquidi.

34. Come può essere d'aiuto per una mamma in difficoltà col suo bambino che non mangia verdure?

    (A) La mamma può creare una sana bevanda fatta di frutta e verdure senza che il bimbo se ne accorga.

    (B) La mamma può fare un bel frappé di gelato.

    (C) La mamma può eliminare tutte le verdure più salutari.

    (D) La mamma può evitare tutte le vitamine e sali minerali.

35. Come puoi imparare ad ottimizzare l'uso del Magic bullet?

    (A) Attraverso un video incluso nel prezzo.

    (B) Leggendo il manuale d'uso e il ricettario forniti.

    (C) Sperimentando.

    (D) Contattando l'azienda americana che distribuisce il prodotto.

2
Lettera dalla Puglia

Cara Federica,

Ormai sono partita da un paio di giorni e già sento la vostra mancanza: tu, Giacomo e Laura siete i miei migliori amici. Vi penso spesso, visto che questa è la prima vacanza che passiamo lontano. Quante ne abbiamo passate insieme!

Come sono andate le vostre vacanze in Spagna? Le avete sognate così tanto che spero proprio vi siate divertiti. Qualche regalino per me lo avete comprato?

Ti sto scrivendo dal lungomare di Otranto, vicino a me ci sono bambini con la bocca sporca di gelato e gente che passeggia in costume da bagno. Il tempo è meraviglioso, non c'è una nuvola e si sta divinamente; la spiaggia è di una sabbia bianca come quella dei Caraibi. In questi giorni sto scoprendo che la Puglia è davvero spettacolare: prima di arrivare qui ho visitato Alberobello con le sue strane casette, i trulli. Sai cosa sono? Un trullo è una vera e propria abitazione ma la sua forma lo rende estremamente particolare: la base è circolare, l'intonaco è sempre bianco e il tetto sembra un cono gelato grigio rovesciato.

Ho fatto molte foto che posso mostrarti quando tornerò, ma ce n' è una in particolare che mi è venuta benissimo: sembra di guardare la casa in cui potrebbero vivere i sette nani. Baci pugliesi, a tra poco, Cinzia

36. Dov'è Cinzia?

    (A) In Spagna.

    (B) In spiaggia.

    (C) In Trentino Alto Adige.

    (D) In mare aperto.

37. Che cos'è un trullo?

    (A) Una villa faraonica.

    (B) Un casolare.

    (C) Una piccola residenza che si può trovare unicamente in Puglia.

    (D) Un podere con vigne e ulivi.

38. Che forma ha un trullo?

    (A) È rettangolare.

    (B) È quadrata.

    (C) È una torre.

    (D) È cilindrico.

39. Di che colore è un trullo?

    (A) Bianco e grigio.

    (B) Vaniglia e pistacchio.

    (C) Marrone.

    (D) Sempre avana.

40. Di che forma è il tetto di un trullo?

    (A) Conico.

    (B) Cubico.

    (C) Sferico.

    (D) Piramidale.

3
Candida

Dopo aver tolto la sua crostata ai mirtilli dal forno, Mamma l'ha posata vicino alla finestra aperta affinchè si raffreddasse un po'. Le bacche luccicavano al sole e un profumo delicato saliva al naso. Doveva ammettere che aveva fatto davvero una bella crostata . Sodisfatta della sua fatica, è uscita per fare qualche piccola spesa. Tornata a casa dopo un'oretta, ha dato un'occhiata alla sua opera culinaria. Era rimasta solo una crosta vuota! L'autore di questo delitto non aveva lasciato nemmeno una traccia blu, soltanto la crosta scavata! Chi avrebbe potuto rinunciare alla sua rinomata crosta leggera e morbida? Ad un tratto si è messa a ridere. Si è diretta verso il giardino, armata di una brocca d'acqua fresca, la sua scatoletta di ricette e una matita. Candida russava all'ombra della grande quercia. L'enorme barbone bianco aveva l'aria sazia; il muso bluastro faceva ridere. Mamma ha versato l'acqua fresca nella sua scodella sussurrando "Come avrei potuto migliorare la mia crosta?"

41. Che tipo di animale di compagnia è Candida?

    (A) Un gatto.

    (B) Un coniglio bianco.

    (C) Un cane.

    (D) Un pappagallo albino.

42. È arrabbiata la signora?

    (A) Sorpresa e delusa, ma non arrabbiata.

    (B) Sì, furibonda.

    (C) Triste e lacrimosa, ma non arrabbiata.

    (D) Agitata e nervosa, ma non arrabbiata.

43. Perché è un po'offesa nell'orgoglio?

    (A) Perché un barbone al naso azzurro sarebbe imbarazzante.

    (B) Perché è fiera della sua crosta leggera e Candida l'aveva lasciata intatta.

    (C) Perché non è esperta e la crostata era un fiasco.

    (D) Perché ha messo troppi frutti dí bosco.

44. Che cosa faceva Candida dopo essersi mangiata e aver leccato tutte le bacche?

    (A) Dormiva.

    (B) Abbaiava.

    (C) Dimenava la coda.

    (D) Saltava su e giù.

45. Che specie di crostata era?

    (A) Era una crostata di fragole.

    (B) Era una crostata di mele e pesche.

    (C) Era una cryostat di lamponi.

    (D) Era una crostata di mirtilli.

4
Le buone maniere – Valentina D'Urso
Società editrice il Mulino

Nei galatei che si sono succeduti negli ultimi cinque secoli si possono identificare almeno tre principi ai quali le norme si ispirano, tratti dai seguenti ambiti:

1) l'igiene, che comprende la pulizia del corpo, dell'abbigliamento e della casa, così come le regole dell'alimentazione, della sessualità e dei costumi quotidiani;

2) l'estetica, che riguarda propriamente la bellezza dei modi, la qualità del gesto, l'adeguatezza dell'acconciatura, dell'abito e del discorso rispetto al tempo, al luogo, all'età, al genere sessuale di chi è sulla scena;

3) l'etica, cioè l'agire secondo bontà, cercando di rendersi gradevoli agli altri e di rendere nello stesso tempo la vita degli altri più gradevole.

A questi tre ambiti, da cui nascono una gran quantità di regole pratiche di condotta, ne ho aggiunto un quarto, che si è imposto in questi ultimi decenni: l'ecologia.

I principi ecologici—che riguardano essenzialmente il rapporto fra l'uomo e la natura—mettono sopra ogni cosa il benessere dell' ecosistema, cioè l'armonia fra sviluppo delle attività umane e conservazione delle altre specie animali e vegetali.

46. Quali sono i 4 ambiti del galateo, secondo l'autrice?

(A) Il comportamento, il tempo, l'età, e il luogo.

(B) L'igiene, l'estetica, l'etica, e l'ecologia.

(C) L'armonia, la conservazione, la bellezza, e i costumi.

(D) Il benessere, lo sviluppo, la bontà e la condotta.

47. Secondo l'etica dobbiamo cercare di rendere la vita degli altri....

(A) più gradevole.

(B) più pulita.

(C) più bella.

(D) più adeguata.

48. L'adeguatezza dell' acconciatura vuole dire:

(A) Portare guanti bianchi.

(B) Portare i capelli di modo appropriato.

(C)   Selezionare con cura i suoi gioelli.

(D)   Essere piuttosto truccate.

49.   Come dev'essere il rapporto fra l'uomo e la natura?

(A)   Equilibrato fra attività umana e conservazione.

(B)   La natura dev'essere sottomessa ai bisogni umani.

(C)   Non importano le altre specie animali e vegetali.

(D)   Un utilizzo lucroso della natura deve essere in primo piano.

50.   Nella gamma dei galatei quanto è importante la pulizia?

(A)   È al numero uno, è la prima cosa menzionata.

(B)   È facoltativa.

(C)   È gradevole ma non è necessaria.

(D)   Dipende dal luogo, dal tempo, e dall'età.

5
Seta – Alessandro Baricco
Bibliteca Universale Rizzoli

Il giorno dopo, presto, al mattino, Hervé Joncour partì. Nascoste tra i bagali, portava con sé, migliaia di uova di baco, e cioè il futuro di Lavilledieu, e il lavoro per centinaia di persone, e la ricchezza per una decina di loro. Dove la strada curvava a sinistra, nascondendo per sempre dietro il profilo della collina la vista del villaggio, si fermò, senza badare ai due uomini che lo accompagnavano. Scese da cavallo e rimase per un po' sul bordo della strada, con lo sguardo fisso a quelle case, arrampicate sul dorso della collina.

Sei giorni dopo Hervé Joncour si imbarcò, a Takaoka, su una nave di contrabbandieri olandesi che lo portò a Sabirk. Da lì risalì il confine cinese fino al lago Bajkal, attraversò quattromila chilometri di terra siberiana, superò gli Urali, raggiunse Kiev e in treno percorse tutta l'Europa, da est a ovest, fino ad arrivare, dopo tre mesi di viaggio, in Francia. La prima domenica di aprile – in tempo per la Messa grande – giunse alle porte di Lavilledieu. Vide sua moglie Hélène corrergli incontro, e sentì il profumo della sua pelle quando la strinse a sé, e il velluto della sua voce quando gli disse

– Sei tornato.

Dolcemente.

– Sei tornato.

51. Da quale paese venivano i contrabbandieri sulla cui nave si imbarcò a Takaoka?

    (A) Dalla Cina.

    (B) Dall Francia.

    (C) Dai Paesi Bassi.

    (D) Dalla Siberia.

52. Dove ha preso il treno?

    (A) In Ucraina.

    (B) Prima degli Urali.

    (C) A Sabirk.

    (D) Presso il lago Bajkal.

53. Quanto a lungo ha viaggiato?

    (A) Almeno tutto il mese d'aprile.

    (B) Almeno 90 giorni.

    (C) Almeno sei settimane.

    (D) Almeno 40 giorni.

54. Cosa portava con sé, nascoste tra i bagagli?

    (A) Migliaia di essenze per profumi francesi.

    (B) Migliaia di bachi.

    (C) Migliaia di semi.

    (D) Migliaia di uova di baco.

55. Qual'era la sua destinazione finale?

    (A) Kiev.

    (B) Lago Bajkal.

    (C) La Francia.

    (D) L'Olanda.

SECTION II: Free Response
Time–1 hour and 25 minutes

Part A: Writing

Fill in a Verb

> **DIRECTIONS:** In each sentence a verb has been omitted and replaced by a line. Supply the missing verb form on the blank to the right. There you will see the infinitive form of the verb you are to use. Read the whole paragraph before choosing your answer. Spelling, agreement, and accent marks must all be accurate for your answer to be correct.

1.

Chiara ama dormire. Lei è molto indaffarata ma **1** sempre un po' di tempo per fare un pisolino ogni pomeriggio. **2** 30 minuti dopo, i capelli arruffati, una guancia rossa; ma riposata dopo la sua piccola pausa. Lei dice sempre " **3** la prova!" Lei lo consiglia a tutto il mondo. " **4** una volta e vedrete quanto **5** meglio."

1. _____ (prendersi)
2. _____ (scendere)
3. _____ (farsi)
4. _____ (provare + lo)
5. _____ (sentirsi)

(Continued)

2.

" **6** tutti gli esercizi di pagina 50 per domani. Non **7** di consegnare la seconda dei vostri temi giovedì e **8** che l'interrogazione **8** luogo martedì prossimo…. "Mi fa impazzire, il lavoro che si aspetta da noi. L'italiano non è la mia unica materia!" "Sì, è un lavoro enorme ma ho parlato con un suo ex-alunno che studia italiano all'università adesso. Si trova a suo agio in una classe avanzata e difficile. **10** di piagnucolare! Tu ti lamenti in un italiano perfetto. Cos'altro vuoi dell'insegnante?"

6. _____ (finire)

7. _____ (dimenticare)

8. _____ (sapere)

9. _____ (avere)

10. _____ (smettere)

Fill in a Word

DIRECTIONS: In each sentence a single word has been omitted and replaced by a line. Write your answer, **ONE** single Italian word on the line to the right. Make sure the word is correct in form, as well as in meaning and in context. None of your answers will be verbs.

Please note that a response such as *fino a* (or *di cui*) will be considered two words, not one. For full credit you must spell each word correctly and include any necessary accent marks or apostrophes.

L'estate scorsa sono andata a Perugia per migliorare il mio italiano. _1_ di partire ho raccolto tutti i libri di _2_ credevo avere bisogno. Nella mia fretta non ho trovato il mio Zanichelli, il libro di grammatica _3_ consultavo il più spesso. Per fortuna ho potuto comprarmene uno nuovo _4_ arrivata. Sono andata direttamente a Grimanalibri per rimpiazzare il mio fedele Zanichelli. L'ho trovato _5_ problema.

Contenta del mio acquisto, sono andata alla cartoleria per cercare _6_ quaderni quadrettati. _7_ ho scelto qualcuni _8_ copertine vivaci. Mi piace notare le parole _9_ imparo nei questi piccoli taccuini. Tornata nella mia camera d'albergo, mi sono divertita a riempire parecchie pagine _10_ guardavo la TV.

1. _____
2. _____
3. _____
4. _____
5. _____
6. _____
7. _____
8. _____
9. _____
10. _____

General Essay

> **DIRECTIONS:** Write a composition in Italian of about 150 words on the topic below. Your essay must be organized and coherent. It must demonstrate your mastery of verb tenses and grammar. It must illustrate a good command of vocabulary. Plan before you begin. Check your work carefully for accents, spelling and agreement. You have 30 minutes.

Note: Essays are evaluated on organization and clarity, range and choice of appropriate vocabulary, grammatical accuracy and spelling.

Qual'è il tuo passatempo preferito?

Part B: Cultural Essay

DIRECTIONS: Write a composition in Italian of about 150 words on the topic below. You must demonstrate the depth of your cultural knowledge in an organized and coherent essay. Showcase your mastery of verb tenses and grammar; evidence a good command of vocabulary. Plan before you begin. Check your work carefully for accents, spelling and agreement. You have 30 minutes.

Note: The student's knowledge of culture determines 80% of his or her score on this essay. The remaining 20% is based on organization, clarity, range and choice of appropriate vocabulary, grammatical accuracy and spelling.

Quale tradizione italiana t'interessa di più?

Part C: Speaking—Narration

CD 2, Track Number 2

> **DIRECTIONS:** You will have two minutes to look at and think about a series of six pictures found on the following pages. You are to narrate a story suggested by the picture sequence. You may take notes in the test booklet insert if you like. Your notes will not be graded. You will then have two minutes to record your response. Comment on each picture and use all of the time allotted. You will be scored on your level of fluency, your ability to narrate, grammatical accuracy, vocabulary range and pronunciation. The completeness of your response will also be taken into consideration. Start your recorder when told to do so.

DIRECTIONS: The following pictures present a story. Pretend you are speaking to a friend and narrate a complete story suggested by the pictures. Your story should contain a beginning, a middle, and an end.

il cane vagabondo

Speaking—Conversation

CD 2, Track Number 3

DIRECTIONS: You are now asked to participate in a simulated conversation in Italian. The questions you will hear are not printed for you to read. You must rely solely on what you hear. You will hear each question twice, followed by a tone. Once you have heard the tone you will have 20 seconds to record your response to the question in Italian. A second tone signals that 20 seconds have elapsed. Stop talking, even if you haven't finished what you were saying. Don't worry if you have been cut off. Listen immediately for the next question. Do not, at any time, stop the recorder until you are instructed to do so.

You will be evaluated on your ability to answer each question completely and promptly. You will be scored on fluency and the appropriateness of your answer. Your score will be lowered if your answer is too short. Use every second allotted. It is better to be cut off than to stop speaking too soon.

You will hear a total of six questions. The first question is for practice only. Try to answer it. It will not be recorded or scored but will give you a good idea of the type of questions to follow. They will all be related to one theme, alluded to in the practice question. You will record your responses to the next five questions.

Practice Exam 2

AP Italian Language and Culture

SECTION I: Multiple Choice

Part A: Listening

1.	(B)	11.	(B)	21.	(A)
2.	(B)	12.	(B)	22.	(C)
3.	(D)	13.	(B)	23.	(B)
4.	(C)	14.	(A)	24.	(D)
5.	(C)	15.	(B)	25.	(A)
6.	(D)	16.	(A)	26.	(C)
7.	(A)	17.	(C)	27.	(D)
8.	(A)	18.	(A)	28.	(A)
9.	(A)	19.	(A)	29.	(C)
10.	(C)	20.	(B)	30.	(B)

Part B: Reading

31.	(A)	40.	(A)	48.	(B)
32.	(C)	41.	(C)	49.	(A)
33.	(B)	42.	(A)	50.	(A)
34.	(A)	43.	(B)	51.	(C)
35.	(B)	44.	(A)	52.	(A)
36.	(B)	45.	(D)	53.	(B)
37.	(C)	46.	(B)	54.	(D)
38.	(D)	47.	(A)	55.	(C)
39.	(A)				

SECTION II: Free Response

Part A: Writing

Fill in a Verb

1. si prende
2. scende
3. fatevi
4. provatelo
5. vi sentirete

6. finite
7. dimenticate
8. sappiate
9. avrà
10. smetti

Fill in a Word

1. prima
2. cui
3. che
4. appena
5. senza

6. dei
7. ne
8. dalle
9. che
10. mentre

Detailed Explanations of Answers

Section I: Multiple Choice
Part A: Listening

1

1. **(B)** Deve comprare una scheda per il telefonino.

The daughter tells her father she needs 30 Euros and points out that he has his credit card. She needs to recharge her cell phone minutes.

2. **(B)** Per quale motivo vuole i soldi.

He tells her that the ATM is not a magic well. She says it would just be a loan. He does ask her what she needs the money for.

3. **(D)** Sì ma soltanto una volta.

He agrees to give her the money, but just this once.

4. **(C)** Le darà i soldi in contanti dopo averli presi al Bancomat.

He'll give her the cash she needs after he makes a withdrawal at the ATM.

2

5. **(C)** No, le dà i giramenti di testa.

No, the Ferris Wheel makes her dizzy.

6. **(D)**   No, l'ha trovato troppo gommoso.

She did try the cotton candy but didn't really like it, she says she thought it was too sticky.

7. **(A)**   Le montagne russe.

Her favorite attraction at Mirabilandia is the roller coaster.

8. **(A)**   Un quarto d'ora.

She only had to wait in line for a quarter of an hour.

3

9. **(A)**   Si può stampare le sue foto in un'occhiata.

She mentions that you can cancel any photo you don't like and that she printed them via her own computer.

10. **(C)**   Come sviluppare e stampare belle foto.

He's very keen on learning exactly how she was able to develop and print such beautiful pictures so quickly.

11. **(B)**   Perché la ragazza gli spiegherà e gli mostrerà come ha fatto le belle foto a casa.

He's coming over at 8 o'clock because she has offered to show him how easy it is to do.

12. **(B)**   La sera stessa.

He'll be back that same evening, after work.

4

13. **(B)**   Una crostata con marmellata di ciliegia.

She says she feels like making a pie.

14. **(A)**   A cena.

Her plan was to serve the pie at dinner.

15. **(B)**   Perché piace a suo figlio l'idea di mangiarla subito.

Her son wants to eat it as soon as it comes out of the oven, warm and steaming. He's begun to set the table, so she agrees and tells him to make coffee while she puts it in the oven.

16. **(A)**   La marmellata di albicocche.

He wants her to replace the apricot jam with cherry (which he prefers).

5

17. **(C)**   Per dirgli che ammirava tanto la fede che aveva regalato alla sua sposa.

She thinks Signora Mariani's wedding ring is the most beautiful she's ever seen. She wanted to congratulate her husband on his choice of ring but learns that the woman is a widow.

18. **(A)**   Almeno settant'anni.

Mrs. Mariani must be at least seventy if she spent 50 years with her husband before he died.

19. **(A)**   lunghissima.

The couple enjoyed a long marriage. The male speaker says that they lived near his family for over 50 years.

20. **(B)**   Servirebbe da ricordo avuto caro.

She thinks it will be a cherished keepsake of the life they lived together.

6

21. **(A)**   l'onomastico di Liliosa.
July 27th is the feast day of Saint Liliosa.

22. **(C)**   il giglio.
Liliana's flower is, of course, the lily.

23. **(B)**   inglese.

The name is English in origin.

24. **(D)**   Liliana è diffusa soprattutto al Nord e al Centro del Paese.

The name is most popular in the north and central part of the country.

25. **(A)**   Benchè vecchia in Inghilterra, Liliana è piuttosto recente in Italia.

While quite old in England, the introduction of the name *Lillian* is much more recent in Italy.

26. **(C)**   è diminuitivo di Elizabeth.

It's a diminutive of the English name *Elizabeth*.

7

27. **(D)**   Suggerisce di pulirlo.

When the mouse doesn't respond, she suggests cleaning it.

28. **(A)**   Pinzette, cottonfioc e alcool.

To clean a fuzzy mouse she uses tweezers, cotton swabs and rubbing alcohol.

29. **(C)**   La freccia sullo schermo non andava.

The cursor on the screen didn't respond to the clogged-up mouse.

30. **(B)**   Semplici e efficaci.

Her suggestions were easy to follow and they worked.

Part B: Reading

1

31. Perchè dobbiamo comprare questo piccolo elettrodomestico?

(A) Risparmia tempo e fa qualunque lavoro di cucina.

It's a great time saver and does a variety of kitchen tasks. It doesn't cook better than the microwave oven, it doesn't allow us to remove the refrigerator from the kitchen, and it doesn't make ice round the clock.

32. Quale sarebbe il vantaggio di chiamare subito?

(C) Se ci sbrighiamo riceveremo accessori e vini in omaggio.

If we hurry and call right away we'll receive free accessories and an assortment of wines at no additional cost. The advertisement doesn't say there are only a few left, that the product is being discontinued, or that the offer will never be made again.

33. A che cosa servono le guarnizioni di colori diversi che si attaccano ai bicchieri?

(B) Sono 'segnabicchieri' per riconoscere la propria bevanda.

The colored rings distinguish one glass from the next, so that each guest can identify his or her drink. They don't make *cappuccino*, and while they may brighten the table, that is not their purpose. They don't prevent spills or leaks.

34. Come può essere d'aiuto per una mamma in difficoltà col suo bambino che non mangia verdure?

(A) La mamma può creare una sana bevanda fatta di frutta e verdure senza che il bimbo se ne accorga.

She can create a healthy beverage with fruits and vegetables without the child's even realizing (that there are vegetables in it). None of the other answers would help a mother get vegetables into child who doesn't like them: making a beautiful milkshake, eliminating the healthiest vegetables, or avoiding all vitamins and minerals. None are what she had in mind.

35. Come puoi imparare ad ottimizzare l'uso del Magic bullet?

(B) Leggendo il manuale d'uso e il ricettario forniti.

By reading the instruction booklet and recipe collection which are included with the product. There is no video. You are not expected to learn how to use the product by experimenting, and you are not expected to call the American company which distributes the item.

2

36. Dove Cinzia?

    (B) In spiaggia.

    She's writing the letter at the beach (in Puglia). She's not in Spain, Trentino Alto Adige, or on the open sea.

37. Che cos'è un trullo?

    (C) Una piccola residenza che si può trovare unicamente in Puglia.

    It's a little (style of) house that can only be found in Puglia. It's not a villa fit for a Pharaoh; it's not a cottage, or an estate with vineyards and olive trees.

38. Che forma ha un trullo?

    (D) È cilindrico.

    It's cylindrical, not rectangular, square, or a tower.

39. Di che colore è un trullo?

    (A) Bianco e grigio.

    A traditional *trullo* has white walls and a gray roof. It is not vanilla and pistachio, brown, or always tan.

40. Di che forma è il tetto di un trullo?

    (A) Conico.

    The roof of a trullo is shaped like an upside-down cone. It's not shaped like a cube, a sphere, or a pyramid.

3

41. **(C)** Un cane.

    Candida is a huge white poodle.

42. **(A)** Sorpresa e delusa, ma non arrabbiata.

    She's surprised and disappointed that her very fine pie has been ruined, but she's not really angry about it.

43. **(D)**   Perché è fiera della sua crosta leggera e Candida l'aveva lasciata intatta.

Her feelings are hurt as she was proud of her light, flaky crusts. Candida didn't even touch this perfect crust. She left it completely intact after licking it clean of it's filling.

44. **(A)**   Dormiva.

After eating her fill, the dog was sleeping (snoring) under the oak tree in the garden.

45. **(D)**   Era una crostata di mirtilli.

It was a beautiful blueberry pie which had stained the perpetrator's snout blue.

4

46. **(B)**   L'igiene, l'estetica, l'etica, e l'ecologia.

The author delineates four basic ranges of etiquette: hygiene, good taste, ethics and ecology.

47. **(A)**   Più gradevole.

We should strive to make the lives of others more pleasant (agreeable).

48. **(B)**   Portare i capelli di modo appropriato.

We should chose a hairstyle appropriate to age and occasion.

49. **(A)**   Equilibrato fra attività umana e conservazione.

The relationship between man and nature should be balanced between human endeavors and conservation.

50. **(A)**   È al numero uno, è la prima cosa menzionata.

Personal hygiene is the most important tenet of good manners, it's the first thing mentioned, at the top of the list.

5

51. **(C)**   dai Paesi Bassi.

They were from the Netherlands. The ship he boarded in Takaoka belonged to Dutch smugglers.

52. **(A)**   In Ucraina.

He doesn't mention the train until he reaches Kiev, in the Ukraine. From there he travels by train through all of Europe, from east to west, until he reaches his destination.

53. **(B)**   Almeno 90 giorni.

At least 90 days. He traveled for three months from Japan to France, via the Chinese mainland, Siberia, the Ukraine, and all of eastern Europe.

54. **(D)**   Migliaia di uova di baco.

He was traveling with thousands of live silk-worm eggs hidden in his luggage.

55. **(C)**   La Francia.

His final destination was France, to the home of Lavilledieu and his wife Hélène.

Section II

Part A: Writing

Fill in a Verb

1.   Chiara ama dormire. Lei è molto indaffarata ma si prende sempre un po' di tempo per fare un pisolino ogni pomeriggio.

Claire likes to sleep. She's very busy but always takes the time to have a little nap each afternoon.

This is the present tense of the regular verb *prendersi*.

2.   Scende 30 minuti dopo, capelli arruffati, una guancia rossa, ma riposata dopo la sua piccola pausa.

She comes down 30 minutes later, her hair disheveled, one red cheek, but refreshed after her little rest.

Stay with the present tense here.

3.   Lei dice sempre: Fatevi la prova! Lo consiglia a tutto il mondo.

She always says try it out! She recommends it to everyone.

This is an affirmative command. It is Claire telling others, *Try it out yourself!* Did you remember to attach the pronoun to the back of the verb? *Una prova* is a piece of evidence or proof. The expression *farsi la prova* is frequently heard in TV commercials and appears in advertising and on product packaging. It means *test it and prove it to yourself.*

4. + 5.   Provatelo una volta e vedrete quanto vi sentirete meglio.

Try it once and you will see how much better you feel.

Another command form, *Try it once...* Follow with the future of both *vedere* and *sentirsi.*

6.   Finite tutti gli esercizi di pagina 50 per domani!

Finish all of the problems on page 50 for tomorrow!

This is a command form. The teacher is giving instructions. You may have hesitated about which form of the command to choose as the teacher could be speaking to an individual rather than to a group. Reading a little further we come upon the words *i vostri temi*. She is clearly addressing the whole class.

7. 8. + 9.   Non <u>dimenticate</u> di consegnare la seconda versione dei vostri temi giovedì e sappiate che l'interrogazione avrà luogo martedì prossimo....

Don't forget to turn in the second draft of your essays Thursday and know that the oral exam will take place next Tuesday....

Two more commands for *dimenticare* and *sapere*. Use the future tense of *avere* as the oral exam *will take place...*

10.   <u>Smetti</u> di piagnucolare!

Stop whining!

The student has just complained to a classmate about the workload this teacher piles on her pupils. The latter is now speaking back to him so use the familiar form of the command. *Piagnucolare* means to snivel or whine.

Fill in a Word

1. + 2.   L'estate scorsa sono andata a Perugia per migliorare il mio italiano. <u>Prima</u> di partire, ho raccolto tutti i libri di cui credevo avere bisogno.

Last summer I went to Perugia to improve my Italian. Before leaving, I gathered up all of the books I thought I would need.

The context of the sentence suggests the need for the preposition *prima* to specify that these activities took place *before* leaving. We use the relative pronoun *cui* to link *the books* to the verbal expression *avere bisogno di (to need)*. This is the case because *the books* are the object of the preposition *di*.

3.   Nella fretta non ho trovato il mio Zanichelli, il libro di grammatica <u>che</u> consultavo il più spesso.

In the rush I couldn't find my Zanichelli, the grammar book I would most often refer to.

We chose the relative pronoun *che* to connect *the grammar book* to the clause containing the verb *consultare*.

4.   Per fortuna ho potuto comprarmene uno nuovo <u>appena</u> arrivata.

*Happily I was able to buy another one **as soon as** I arrived.*

5. Sono andata direttamente da Grimanalibri per rimpiazzare il mio fedele Zanichelli. L'ho trovato senza problema.

I went straight to Grimanalibri (a book store in Perugia) to replace my trusty Zanichelli. I found it with no problem.

The preposition *senza* expresses *without.*

6. Contenta del mio acquisto sono andata alla cartoleria per cercare dei quaderni quadrettati.

Happy with my purchase, I went to the stationery store to look for some cross-ruled notebooks.

Use the partitive article to express *some* notebooks.

7. + 8.   Ne ho scelti alcuni dalle copertine vivaci.

I chose a few of them with bright covers.

The pronoun *ne* stands for the object of the preposition *di* in a *number expression*. *I chose a few of them*. The preposition *da* contracts with *le* in this common construction to mean *with.*

9. Mi piace annotare le parole che imparo in questi piccoli taccuini.

I like to jot down the words I learn in these little notebooks.

The two clauses connect smoothly with a relative pronoun.

10. Tornata nella mia camera d'albergo, mi sono divertita a riempire parecchie pagine mentre guardavo la TV.

Back in my hotel room I enjoyed filling in several pages while I watched TV.

The preposition *mentre*, gives us *while*, or *at the same time.*

Sample Essay Answer
in Response to General Essay Question

Read the following essay to see how a student might have answered this question.

Qual'è il tuo passatempo preferito?

Mi piace andare su internet. Ci vado spesso quando sono libera. Se avessi più tempo passerei ore e ore sempre su Ebay. Mi piace la caccia all' oggetto desiderato, e poi la vendita all'asta mi fa battere il cuore. Mi commuovo, soprattutto se riesco a vincere. Quando vinco aspetto la consegna del mio piccolo acquisto come un bimbo che aspetta il Natale.

Ho imparato molte cose su Ebay e mi diverto a saltare da un oggetto all' altro. Lo trovo tanto interessante, anche quando non ho soldi da spendere.

Mi piace inviare e ricevere e-mail. Leggo almeno due o tre "giornali" numerici al giorno. Seguo la Borsa e fingo di essere azionista. Cerco di indovinare quali azioni comprare per diventare ricca.

Scelgo libri, CD e film su internet. Ordino regali e posso confrontare molti prodotti e prezzi prima di decidermi. Pago quasi tutte le mie bollette in rete. Non scrivo più assegni. Non uso né francobolli né buste e so ad ogni momento quanti centesimi rimangono nel mio conto bancario.

Part B: Culture

Sample Essay Answer
in Response to Cultural Essay Question

Read the following essay to see how a student might have answered this question.

Quale tradizione italiana t'interessa di più?

Sono colpita dalla Festa della Donna che ha luogo l'8 marzo e che si festeggia quasi dappertutto in Italia dagli anni venti. Ha le sue origini in un brutto disastro a New York nel 1908 quando 129 operaie sono state uccise in un incendio perchè tutte le porte della loro fabbrica tessile erano chiuse a chiave e non potevano uscire. La gran parte delle operaie erano povere immigrate italiane.

Qualche anno dopo, questa data è stata scelta per onorare quelle vittime. Poi è diventato un giorno per manifestazioni, soprattutto per i diritti delle donne e l'uguaglianza. Col passare degli anni è diventata una festa con molta allegria. Le amiche escono insieme, lasciando quella sera, i figli con il marito e i piatti sporchi nell'acquaio. Molte giovani donne non sanno nemmeno quando o come la festa ha avuto origine.

La tradizione vuole che ognuno offra un mazzo di mimose alla donna amata che sia la madre, la moglie, la figlia o l'amica. Questi fiori gialli sono diventati il simbolo della festa. Si scambiano anche piccoli regali e dolci e bevono lo champagne.

L'anno scorso abbiamo fatto cartoline e mazzi di mimose nella mia classe d'italiano. Quest' idea è piaciuta moltissimo a me e alle mie amiche. Abbiamo deciso di festeggiare ormai l'8 marzo secondo la tradizione italiana.

Part C: Speaking

Speaking—Narration

Il Cane Vagabondo

Here is how a student might have narrated these sketches:

1. Due bambini tornano a piedi da scuola. Tutti e due hanno lo zaino pieno di libri. Poco dietro di loro si vede un cane che sembra seguirli.

2. I bambini si fermano. Il cane si avvicina. Non porta il collare ma sembra gentile e in buona salute.

3. È amore a prima vista. Il ragazzo si lasica leccare dal suo nuovo amico. E poi, probabilmente anche lei.

4. I bambini vogliono adottare il cane. Vogliono tenerlo con loro ma devono prima convincere la mamma. Le ci pensa. I bambini la supplicano e il cane aspetta educatamente.

5. La mamma sembra dire di sì. I figli l'abbracciano. Lei sorride, c'è un nuovo membro nella famiglia.

6. Ecco i bambini che portano fuori il nuovo cane.
   Forse hanno promesso di assumersi la responsabilità nella cura del loro nuovo compagno. Loro dovranno dargli da mangiare, portarlo fuori e tenere pulita la sua cuccia.

Gli animali domestici insegnano la pazienza e la tolleranza. Rafforzano i legami familiari. Ci amano per come siamo. Apprezziamo le loro eccentricità, e quando hanno paura, li coccoliamo. Li amiamo, li guardiamo invecchiare e li perdiamo. Tutte le lezioni importanti della vita si possono apprendere anche grazie a loro.

Practice Exam 3

AP Italian Language and Culture

Practice Exam 3

AP Italian Language and Culture

Answer Sheet

SECTION I: Multiple Choice

Part A: Listening

1. Ⓐ Ⓑ Ⓒ Ⓓ
2. Ⓐ Ⓑ Ⓒ Ⓓ
3. Ⓐ Ⓑ Ⓒ Ⓓ
4. Ⓐ Ⓑ Ⓒ Ⓓ
5. Ⓐ Ⓑ Ⓒ Ⓓ
6. Ⓐ Ⓑ Ⓒ Ⓓ
7. Ⓐ Ⓑ Ⓒ Ⓓ
8. Ⓐ Ⓑ Ⓒ Ⓓ
9. Ⓐ Ⓑ Ⓒ Ⓓ
10. Ⓐ Ⓑ Ⓒ Ⓓ

11. Ⓐ Ⓑ Ⓒ Ⓓ
12. Ⓐ Ⓑ Ⓒ Ⓓ
13. Ⓐ Ⓑ Ⓒ Ⓓ
14. Ⓐ Ⓑ Ⓒ Ⓓ
15. Ⓐ Ⓑ Ⓒ Ⓓ
16. Ⓐ Ⓑ Ⓒ Ⓓ
17. Ⓐ Ⓑ Ⓒ Ⓓ
18. Ⓐ Ⓑ Ⓒ Ⓓ
19. Ⓐ Ⓑ Ⓒ Ⓓ
20. Ⓐ Ⓑ Ⓒ Ⓓ

21. Ⓐ Ⓑ Ⓒ Ⓓ
22. Ⓐ Ⓑ Ⓒ Ⓓ
23. Ⓐ Ⓑ Ⓒ Ⓓ
24. Ⓐ Ⓑ Ⓒ Ⓓ
25. Ⓐ Ⓑ Ⓒ Ⓓ
26. Ⓐ Ⓑ Ⓒ Ⓓ
27. Ⓐ Ⓑ Ⓒ Ⓓ
28. Ⓐ Ⓑ Ⓒ Ⓓ
29. Ⓐ Ⓑ Ⓒ Ⓓ
30. Ⓐ Ⓑ Ⓒ Ⓓ

Part B: Reading

31. Ⓐ Ⓑ Ⓒ Ⓓ
32. Ⓐ Ⓑ Ⓒ Ⓓ
33. Ⓐ Ⓑ Ⓒ Ⓓ
34. Ⓐ Ⓑ Ⓒ Ⓓ
35. Ⓐ Ⓑ Ⓒ Ⓓ
36. Ⓐ Ⓑ Ⓒ Ⓓ
37. Ⓐ Ⓑ Ⓒ Ⓓ

38. Ⓐ Ⓑ Ⓒ Ⓓ
39. Ⓐ Ⓑ Ⓒ Ⓓ
40. Ⓐ Ⓑ Ⓒ Ⓓ
41. Ⓐ Ⓑ Ⓒ Ⓓ
42. Ⓐ Ⓑ Ⓒ Ⓓ
43. Ⓐ Ⓑ Ⓒ Ⓓ
44. Ⓐ Ⓑ Ⓒ Ⓓ

45. Ⓐ Ⓑ Ⓒ Ⓓ
46. Ⓐ Ⓑ Ⓒ Ⓓ
47. Ⓐ Ⓑ Ⓒ Ⓓ
48. Ⓐ Ⓑ Ⓒ Ⓓ
49. Ⓐ Ⓑ Ⓒ Ⓓ
50. Ⓐ Ⓑ Ⓒ Ⓓ

Practice Exam 3

AP Italian Language and Culture

Total Test Time—3 hours

SECTION I: Multiple Choice

Time—1 hour and 20 minutes

Part A: Listening

> **DIRECTIONS:** You will now listen to several selections. For each selection you will have time to read over the questions printed in your booklet. Then you will hear the selection. You may take notes in your exam booklet as you listen. Your notes will not be graded. After listening to the selection, you will have time to answer the questions. Blacken the corresponding oval on your answer sheet.

CD 2, Track Number 4

1
Il Naso

1. Che cosa è successo al fratello?

    (A) Si è distorto il naso.

    (B) Ha fatto uno starnuto.

    (C) Si è fatto fare la chirugia plastica.

    (D) Sì è rotto il naso.

2. Come va adesso?

   (A) Meglio ma gli occhi sono sempre nerastri.

   (B) Va di male in peggio.

   (C) Non si sta migliorando.

   (D) È ancora all'ospedale.

3. Dov'è andato il fratello?

   (A) Alla pediatria.

   (B) Al pronto soccorso.

   (C) A vedere il rinologo.

   (D) A vedere il ginecologo.

4. Quale risultato non si predeva?

   (A) Respira meglio adesso che prima.

   (B) È più bello così.

   (C) Rimane col naso bloccato da una settimana.

   (D) Non può sentire profumi.

2
Le Calle

5. Cosa sono le calle?

   (A) Sono uccellini canori.

   (B) Sono fiori.

   (C) Sono barboni nani.

   (D) Sono pillole.

6. Sono difficili da fare crescere?

   (A) Sì, molto.

   (B) Sì, perché muoiano subito.

(C)   Sì, come le orchidee.

(D)   No, vogliono soltanto acqua e nutrienti.

7.   Perché la *Naomi* è apprezzata?

(A)   Per il suo colore ricco e vellutato.

(B)   Per la sua bellezza bianca.

(C)   Per la sua grandezza.

(D)   Perché è tanto adattibile.

8.   La *Naomi* è …

(A)   rarissima.

(B)   quasi nera.

(C)   una nuova varietà.

(D)   la calla più popolare.

3
La Filastrocca

9.   Cos'è una filastrocca?

(A)   È un video per bimbi.

(B)   È un romanzo giallo a gran tiratura.

(C)   È una ninna nanna.

(D)   È una poesiola infantile.

10.   Come si cambia una banana non mangiata da due giorni?

(A)   Si diventa un principe azzurro.

(B)   Si diventa marrone.

(C)   Si cambia in oro filato.

(D)   Si cambia in pietra dura.

11. Quale banana viene comprata nella filastrocca?

    (A) La verde.

    (B) La gialla.

    (C) La rossa.

    (D) Quella marrone.

12. Di che colore è la banana quando sbarca?

    (A) È marrone.

    (B) È gialla.

    (C) È verde.

    (D) È rosso.

4
I Denti del Giudizio

13. Quando si devono togliere i denti del giudizio?

    (A) Quando l'eruzione sarà difficile o impossibile.

    (B) Quando c'è spazio sufficiente perché escano.

    (C) Quando la giovane persona avrà circa 19 anni.

    (D) Non si devono toglierli affatto.

14. Di quanti denti si trattano?

    (A) Il dentista vuole togliere tutti i quattro.

    (B) Il dentista vuole togliere solo quelli inferiori.

    (C) Il dentista ha trovato tre germi malposizionati.

    (D) Il dentista vuole togliere solo i denti di latte.

15. Dovrebbe aspettare la figlia prima di subire l'estrazione?

    (A) No, ha già 15 anni, è il momento giusto.

    (B) Sì, fino all'età di 21 anni.

(C)   Avrebbe dovuto fatto farlo l'anno scorso.

(D)   Sì, per vedere cosa succederà.

16.   Che cosa consulta il dentista per vedere i germi?

(A)   Uno specchio speciale.

(B)   La mascella.

(C)   La radiografia.

(D)   I disegni.

5
Topo Gigio

17.   Chi è Topo Gigio?

(A)   È uno dei sette nani.

(B)   È una creatura del film *La Guerre delle Stelle*.

(C)   È un topo biondo.

(D)   È un extraterrestre.

18.   Quando era popolare?

(A)   Negli anni sessanta.

(B)   Negli anni postbellici.

(C)   Negli anni settanta.

(D)   Negli anni venti.

19.   Che peculiarità aveva Topo Gigio?

(A)   Orecchi enormi.

(B)   Una testa grossa.

(C)   Un naso lunghissimo.

(D)   Una gran pancia.

20. Topo Gigio era ….

    (A) quasi sconosciuto.

    (B) rinomato.

    (C) una marca di scarpe per bimbi.

    (D) un ratto nero.

6
Le Carte

21. Perché non vuole giocare né a schacchi, né a dama lei?

    (A) Perché lui vince sempre.

    (B) Perché non sa giocare.

    (C) Perché non ha tempo.

    (D) Perché sono giochi noiosi.

22. Dov'è la schacchiera?

    (A) Nella camera sua.

    (B) Nel soggiorno.

    (C) Davanti a loro.

    (D) Temporaneamente smarrita.

23. Cosa suggerisce la ragazza invece?

    (A) Una partita a carte.

    (B) Il gioco dell'Oca.

    (C) Un gioco dei dadi.

    (D) Di mettere qualche CD.

24. A che cosa decidono di giocare?

    (A) A Tre Sette.

    (B) A Scopa.

    (C) A Sette Bello.

    (D) A Briscola.

25. Che cosa sarebbe più interessante secondo lui?

    (A) Di giocare al fresco, nel giardino.

    (B) Di giocare con quattro persone invece di due.

    (C) Un gioco degli zeri e ics.

    (D) Un gioco di nascondino.

26. Perché non potranno continuare con la partita?

    (A) Perché si mettono a discutere su chi debba andare di primo.

    (B) Perché mancano carte.

    (C) Perché si fa tardi.

    (D) Perché non sanno le regole.

7
Il Tè

27. Questo prodotto è…

    (A) Una spremuta di limone e pesca.

    (B) Un tè istantaneo.

    (C) Una cioccolata calda.

    (D) Una bevanda senza calorie.

28. Dove lo troveresti?

    (A) All'ufficio postale.

    (B) Alla drogheria.

    (C) Dal pescivendolo.

    (D) Dal fruttivendolo.

29. Ci sono gusti vari?

    (A) Sì, limone, pesca, e tè verde.

    (B) No, c'è soltanto il classico.

    (C) Sì, una trentina di gusti.

    (D) Sì, bacche, tuttti frutti, e caramella.

30. È disponibile senza caffeina?

    (A) No, ma viene *light*.

    (B) Sì, viene deteinato.

    (C) No, ma è pratico e conveniente.

    (D) No, ma viene al *te verde*.

Part B: Reading

> **DIRECTIONS:** Read the following passages with care. Each segment is followed by a series of questions or statements to be completed. Choose the best answer, according to what you have read, from the four choices provided. Blacken the corresponding oval on your answer sheet.

1

Le Mongolfiere

Da alcuni anni a questa parte in Umbria si tiene un festival che richiama centinaia di persone di tutte le età: quello delle mongolfiere. Si svolge i primi di luglio presso Todi, una cittadina che ha il vantaggio di una posizione collinare.

Una mongolfiera è un enorme pallone di nylon tutto colorato. Funziona grazie a gas propellenti che gli consentono di volare in aria, sorvolando la Media valle del Tevere. Salendo sulla cesta attaccata sotto al pallone i passeggeri, sospesi tra cielo e terra, possono godere di un panorama rigoglioso e verdissimo.

Il festival è una specie di esibizione e lo spettatore da terra può avere l'impressione di un grande stormo colorato. Questa è una visione indimenticabile e un'opportunità fotografica irrinunciabile.

31. Dove ha luogo questa manifestazione estiva?

    (A) Lazio.

    (B) Toscana.

    (C) Umbria.

    (D) Tra le colline lombarde.

32. Come vola una mongolfiera?

    (A) Con il carburante aereo.

    (B) Con il gas propellente che produce una fiamma.

    (C) Con la potenza di un motore elettrico.

    (D) Con l'energia eolica.

33. Perché Todi è un luogo ideale per questo tipo di attività?

    (A) Perché è in cima ad una collina.

    (B) Perché è vicino a Perugia.

    (C) Perché c'è il Tevere.

    (D) Perché c'è una brezza.

34. Di che stoffa è fatta la monqolfiera?

    (A) Di lana.

    (B) Di pura seta.

    (C) Di caucciù.

    (D) Di una fibra sintetica e leggera.

35. Dove salgono i passeggeri?

    (A) Sopra il pallone.

    (B) Nella cesta.

    (C) Sopra sedie sospese.

    (D) Dentro il pallone.

2
YOMO

Un gusto fresco e diverso ogni volta, in una ampia gamma di yogurt e frutta, ingredienti genuini e naturali anche per i gusti golosi come caffè, malto e biscotto ai 4 cereali. Solo la semplice bontà di latte italiano selezionato, fermenti lattici vivi e vitali, un po' di zucchero e una pregiata miscela di sapori, per un gusto caldo ed avvolgente. Questo è lo yogurt YOMO.

Non aggiungiamo conservanti né aromatizzanti, né coloranti. Per una colazione buona e sana, per un mini-pranzo leggero e naturale, per una merenda semplice e gustosa, YOMO è la scelta giusta.

36. Che tipo di prodotto è questo?

    (A) Cereali.

    (B) Agrumi.

(C) Verdure.

(D) Caseario.

37. Quali gusti sono disponibili secondo la pubblicità?

(A) C'è una ampia gamma di gusti.

(B) Solo agrumi.

(C) C'è lo yogurt bianco naturale.

(D) Cioccolato.

38. Dove potresti trovare questo prodotto per comprarlo?

(A) In qualsiasi supermercato.

(B) In farmacia.

(C) In ferramenta.

(D) In macelleria.

39. Si tratta di un prodotto sano e *benefico*?

(A) No, perché è grasso.

(B) No, perché è troppo zuccherato.

(C) Sì, perché è interamente naturale.

(D) Sì, perch contiene fiocchi d'avena.

40. Come sono i fermenti lattici?

(A) Vivi.

(B) Congelati.

(C) Sott'olio.

(D) Asciutti.

3

Il Lupettino

"Drea, sii buono e vai a cercare la mia borsa. La troverai appesa sul gancio dietro la porta. Grazie amore mio. Tieni, ecco una moneta di due Euro per il tuo salvadanaio." "Ti voglio bene Mamma, ma non posso prendere questi spiccioli. Sei la mamma e è necessario che un figlio agisca senza interessi, sai?" "Che cosa sento? Sto sognando? Sei davvero mio figlio, lo stesso che mi chiede sempre soldi?" È per i lupetti*, Mamma. Tento di guadagnare la mia targhetta dei buoni proposti. Bisogna che io penso agli altri durante le 24 ore." i lupetti = Cub Scouts

41. Quanti anni avrà questo ragazzo?

    (A) È uno studente liceale.

    (B) È un bambino ai primi passi.

    (C) È un ragazzino di 7 o 8 anni circa.

    (D) È un giovane universitario.

42. Che cos'è un salvadanaio?

    (A) Un posto per tenere abiti sporchi.

    (B) Un conto in banca.

    (C) Un posto in cui mettere piccole monete.

    (D) Un libretto di assegni.

43. Dov'era la borsa della madre?

    (A) Per terra, dietro la porta.

    (B) Su una sedia, dietro la porta.

    (C) Sul gancio dietro la porta.

    (D) Appesa sulla parete.

44. Che cosa offre la mamma al bambino?

    (A) Due Euro in quattro monete da 50 centesimi.

    (B) Un euro e ottanta centesimi.

    (C) Un biglietto.

    (D) Una sola moneta.

45. Come risponde il bambino?

     (A) La mette in tasca.

     (B) La respinge.

     (C) Bacia la mamma, ringraziandola.

     (D) L'afferra con gioia.

4
Vai dove ti porta il cuore – Susanna Tamaro
Biblioteca Universale Rizzoli

Il mio primo incontro con la morte l'ho avuto verso i sei anni. Mio padre possedeva un cane da caccia, Argo; aveva un temperamento mite e affettuoso ed era il mio compagno di giochi preferito. Per pomeriggi interi lo imboccavo con pappine di fango e di erbe, oppure lo costringevo a fare la cliente della parrucchiera, e lui senza ribellarsi girava per il giardino con le orecchie ornate di forcine. Un giorno, però, proprio mentre gli provavo un nuovo tipo di acconciatura, mi sono accorta che sotto la gola c'èra qualcosa di gonfio. Già da alcune settimane non aveva più voglia di correre e di saltare come una volta, se mi mettevo in un angolo a mangiare la merenda, non si piazzava più davanti a sospirare speranzoso.

Una mattina, al ritorno da scuola, non lo trovai ad attendermi al cancello. In principio pensai che fosse andato da qualche parte con mio padre. Ma quando vidi mio padre tranquillamente seduto nello studio e senza Argo ai suoi piedi, mi nacque dentro una grande agitazione. Uscii e urlando a squarciagola lo chiamai per tutto il giardino, tornata dentro per due o tre volte esplorai la casa di cima a fondo. La sera, al momento di dare il bacio obbligatorio della buonanotte, raccogliendo tutto il mio coraggio chiesi a mio padre: "Dov'è Argo?" "Argo", rispose lui [...] "Argo è andato via."

46. Che specie di cane era Argo?

     (A) Era un cane di razza.

     (B) Era un barboncino.

     (C) Era un cane da caccia.

     (D) Era un cane meticcio.

47. Che tipi di giochi faceva la ragazzina con il suo compagno canino?

    (A) Fingeva di cucinare e giocava alla parrucchiera.

    (B) Andava a caccia.

    (C) Giocava con le bambole.

    (D) Giocava a bocce.

48. Come era il temperamento di Argo?

    (A) Scorbutico e difficile.

    (B) Feroce e pericoloso.

    (C) Paziente e tollerante.

    (D) Agitato ed eccitabile.

49. Dove aspettava Argo quando la ragazza tornava di scuola?

    (A) Nello studio, ai piedi del padre.

    (B) Davanti al cancello del giardino.

    (C) Sul letto suo.

    (D) Davanti all'ingresso della casa.

50. Com ha reagito la ragazza quando non trovava Argo?

    (A) È diventata molto triste e agitata.

    (B) È andata ad aspettarlo vicino al cancello.

    (C) Era convinta che Argo fosse andato alla caccia.

    (D) È andata nel giardino per fare pappine di fango.

5
Pinocchio – Carlo Collodi
Biblioteca Universale Rizzoli

Appena che Pinocchio fu entrato nel letto, si addormentò, e principiò a sognare. E sognando gli pareva essere in mezzo a un campo, e questo campo era pieno di arboscelli carichi di grappoli, e questi grappoli erano carichi di zecchini d'oro che, dondolandosi mossi dal vento, facevano *zin,*

zin, zin, quasi volessero dire: "Chi ci vuole, venga a prenderci." Ma quando Pinocchio fu sul più bello, quando cioè allungò la mano per prendere a manciate tutte quelle belle monete e mettersele in tasca, si trovò svegliato all'improvviso da tre violentissimi colpi dati nella porta di camera.

Era l'oste che veniva a dirgli che la mezzanotte era sonata.

"E i miei compagni sono pronti?" gli domandò il burattino.

"Altro che pronti! Son partiti due ore fa."

"Perché mai tanta fretta?"

"Perché il Gatto ha ricevuto un'imbasciata che il suo gattino maggiore, malato di geloni ai piedi, stava in pericolo di vita."

"E la cena l'hanno pagata?"

"Che vi pare?" Quelle lì sono persone troppo educate, perché facciano un affronto simile alla signoria vostra."

"Peccato! Quest'affronto mi avrebbe fatto tanto piacere!" disse Pinocchio grattandosi il capo.

51. Di che cosa sognava il burattino?

   (A) Sognava di un campo dove i soldi crescevano sugli alberi.

   (B) Sognava dei suoi compagni di viaggio, il Gatto e La Volpe.

   (C) Sognava di un campo meraviglioso dove c'erano nascosti zecchini a manciate.

   (D) Sognava che aveva geloni ai piedi.

52. Chi è venuto alla porta e perché?

   (A) Era l'oste per chiedere che il burattino pagasse la cena.

   (B) Era un'ambasciata per scusare il Gatto già partito.

   (C) Era l'oste per dirgli l'ora.

   (D) Era la Volpe che chiedeva qualcosa per la nausea.

53. Che fine hanno fatto i compagni di viaggio?

   (A) Russavano tutti e due nella camera vicina.

   (B) Erano partiti due ore fa, lasciando pagare a Pinocchio la cena e le camere.

   (C) L'aspettavano nel campo dei miracoli.

   (D) Erano andati a pescare triglie.

54. Come crescevano gli zecchini d'oro nel campo sognato?

    (A) Come l'erbaccia, per terra.

    (B) Come le cipolle, con le monete sotto la terra.

    (C) A grappoli, dondolandosi degli arboscelli.

    (D) A grappoli, come l'uva sulla vite.

55. Che rumore facevano gli zecchini d'oro?

    (A) Squillavano forte.

    (B) Tintinnavano, mossi del vento.

    (C) Picchiettavano quando si sono caduti a terra.

    (D) Sussurravano "vattene via."

SECTION II: Free Response

Time–1 hour and 25 minutes

Part A: Writing

Fill in a Verb

> **DIRECTIONS:** In each sentence a verb has been omitted and replaced by a line. Supply the missing verb form on the blank to the right. There you will see the infinitive form of the verb you are to use. Read the whole paragraph before choosing your answer. Spelling, agreement, and accent marks must all be accurate for your answer to be correct.

1.

Trasloco la settimana prossima. La nuova casa non **1** completamente pronta prima della fine del mese, ma occorre che **2** lo stesso. Possiedo una casetta estiva vicino a Orvieto dove **3** aspettare. Così, avrò un intermezzo piacevole fra il trasloco dalla prima casa alla seconda. Vorrei visitare i vigneti intorno e spero che **4** possibile ordinare alcune buone bottiglie per la festa con la quale mia nuora vorrà "sorprendermi." Ovviamente, bisognerà che io **5** molti bicchierini prima di scegliere. Tanto meglio!

1. _____ (essere)

2. _____ (andarsene)

3. _____ (potere)

4. _____ (essere)

5. _____ (assaggiare)

(Continued)

2.

Devo presentare un piccolo resoconto sull'artista Arcimboldo. __6__ da due settimane le sue tele e ho già scritto gran parte della mia presentazione. L'inconveniente è che ho già restituito i libri che usavo e voglio verificare una citazione. Che fare? È semplice. Tu __7__ scaricare il testo digitale al computer. Così __8__ verificare la citazione senza __9__ la tua camera da letto. Ottima idea! Grazie, mi __10__ !

6. _____ (studiare)

7. _____ (dovere)

8. _____ (potere)

9. _____ (lasciare)

10. _____ (salvare)

Fill in a Word

> **DIRECTIONS:** In each sentence a single word has been omitted and replaced by a line. Write your answer, **ONE** single Italian word on the line to the right. Make sure the word is correct in form, as well as in meaning and in context. None of your answers will be verbs.
>
> Please note that a response such as *fino a* (or *di cui*) will be considered two words, not one. For full credit you must spell each word correctly and include any necessary accent marks or apostrophes.

1.

Mamma vuole **1** io sistemi un po' la mia camera **2** letto. Devo pulire tutte le superfici coperte **3** polvere, che però non sarà facile **4** **5** di tutti i ninnoli che dovrò togliere prima. **6** impresa faticosa!

1. _____

2. _____

3. _____

4. _____

5. _____

6. _____

2.

Di **7** i ponti che attraversano l'Arno il Ponte Vecchio è **8** che preferisco. Mi piace vagare per i piccoli negozi **9** un pirata cercando un tesoro nascosto. **10** oro in un solo luogo mi fa battere il cuore più forte. Potrei passare una giornata intera a cercare un solo piccolo ciondolo.

7. _____

8. _____

9. _____

10. _____

General Essay

DIRECTIONS: Write a composition in Italian of about 150 words on the topic below. Your essay must be organized and coherent. It must demonstrate your mastery of verb tenses and grammar. It must illustrate a good command of vocabulary. Plan before you begin. Check your work carefully for accents, spelling and agreement. You have 30 minutes.

Note: Essays are evaluated on organization and clarity, range and choice of appropriate vocabulary, grammatical accuracy and spelling.

Cosa pensi dei tatuaggi? Se ne hai uno, com'è? Se non ne hai affatto, vorresti averne uno?

Part B: Cultural Essay

DIRECTIONS: Write a composition in Italian of about 150 words on the topic below. You must demonstrate the depth of your cultural knowledge in an organized and coherent essay. Showcase your mastery of verb tenses and grammar; evidence a good command of vocabulary. Plan before you begin. Check your work carefully for accents, spelling and agreement. You have 30 minutes.

Note: The student's knowledge of culture determines 80% of his or her score on this essay. The remaining 20% is based on organization, clarity, range and choice of appropriate vocabulary, grammatical accuracy and spelling.

Se potessi viaggiare in Italia, dove andresti e perché?

Part C: Speaking—Narration

CD 2, Track Number 5

DIRECTIONS: You will have two minutes to look at and think about a series of six pictures found on the following pages. You are to narrate a story suggested by the picture sequence. You may take notes in the test booklet insert if you like. Your notes will not be graded. You will then have two minutes to record your response. Comment on each picture and use all of the time allotted. You will be scored on your level of fluency, your ability to narrate, grammatical accuracy, vocabulary range and pronunciation. The completeness of your response will also be taken into consideration. Start your recorder when told to do so.

DIRECTIONS: The following pictures present a story. Pretend you are speaking to a friend and narrate a complete story suggested by the pictures. Your story should contain a beginning, a middle, and an end.

il gelato

Speaking—Conversation

CD 2, Track Number 6

DIRECTIONS: You are now asked to participate in a simulated conversation in Italian. The questions you will hear are not printed for you to read. You must rely solely on what you hear. You will hear each question twice, followed by a tone. Once you have heard the tone you will have 20 seconds to record your response to the question in Italian. A second tone signals that 20 seconds have elapsed. Stop talking, even if you haven't finished what you were saying. Don't worry if you have been cut off. Listen immediately for the next question. Do not, at any time, stop the recorder until you are instructed to do so.

You will be evaluated on your ability to answer each question completely and promptly. You will be scored on fluency and the appropriateness of your answer. Your score will be lowered if your answer is too short. Use every second allotted. It is better to be cut off than to stop speaking too soon.

You will hear a total of six questions. The first question is for practice only. Try to answer it. It will not be recorded or scored but will give you a good idea of the type of questions to follow. They will all be related to one theme, alluded to in the practice question. You will record your responses to the next five questions.

Practice Exam 3

AP Italian Language and Culture

Answer Key

SECTION I: Multiple Choice

Part A: Listening

1.	(D)	11.	(C)	21.	(A)
2.	(A)	12.	(C)	22.	(D)
3.	(C)	13.	(A)	23.	(A)
4.	(A)	14.	(A)	24.	(D)
5.	(B)	15.	(A)	25.	(B)
6.	(D)	16.	(C)	26.	(B)
7.	(A)	17.	(C)	27.	(B)
8.	(B)	18.	(A)	28.	(B)
9.	(D)	19.	(A)	29.	(A)
10.	(C)	20.	(B)	30.	(B)

Part B: Reading

31.	(C)	40.	(A)	48.	(C)
32.	(B)	41.	(C)	49.	(B)
33.	(A)	42.	(C)	50.	(A)
34.	(D)	43.	(C)	51.	(A)
35.	(B)	44.	(D)	52.	(C)
36.	(D)	45.	(B)	53.	(B)
37.	(A)	46.	(C)	54.	(C)
38.	(A)	47.	(A)	55.	(B)
39.	(C)				

SECTION II: Free Response

Part A: Writing

Fill in a Verb

1. sarà
2. me ne vada
3. posso, potrò
4. sia
5. assaggi

6. studio
7. devi, dovrai, dovresti
8. puoi, potrai, potresti
9. lasciare
10. hai salvato/a

Fill in a Word

1. che
2. da
3. di
4. a
5. causa

6. che
7. tutti
8. quello
9. come
10. tanto

Practice Exam 3

AP Italian Language and Culture

Detailed Explanations of Answers

Section I: Multiple Choice
Part A: Listening

1

1. **(D)** Sì è rotto il naso.
   Her brother broke his nose yesterday.

2. **(A)** Meglio ma gli occhi sono sempre nerastri.
   He's better than he was but still has two black eyes.

3. **(C)** A vedere il rinologo.
   He went to an ENT (a rhinologist).

4. **(A)** Respira meglio adesso che prima.
   Oddly enough she reports that he can breathe better (since his nose was reset) than he could before he broke it.

2

5. **(B)** Sono fiori.
   Calla lilies are flowers, not song birds, miniature poodles, or pills.

6. **(D)** No, vogliono soltanto acqua e nutrienti.
   No, they just need water and an occasional feeding (twice a month).

7. **(A)** Per il suo colore ricco e vellutato.
This variety is prized for its deep, rich, velvety (dark purple) color.

8. **(B)** Quasi nera.
The purple is so dark that the *Naomi* seems almost black.

3

9. **(D)** È una poesiola infantile.
A *filastrocca* is a child's nursery rhyme.

10. **(B)** Si diventa marrone.
The banana turns brown if it isn't eaten in a few days.

11. **(B)** La gialla.
The yellow one is bought in the nursery rhyme.

12. **(C)** È verde.
The banana is green when she first sets ashore from Central America.

4

13. **(A)** Quando l'eruzione sarà difficile o impossibile.
Wisdom teeth should be extracted if their eruption will be difficult or impossible.

14. **(A)** Il dentista vuole togliere tutti i quattro.
Based on her X-rays, the dentist thinks all four wisdom teeth should be removed.

15. **(A)** No, ha già 15 anni, è il momento giusto.
No, she's already turned 15, it's just the right time.

16. **(C)** La radiografia.
The dentist relies on the X-Ray to see the position of the roots.

5

17. **(C)**   È un topo biondo.
Topo Gigio is a blond mouse.
He began as a soft puppet on an Italian children's show and eventually became world-famous.

18. **(A)**   Negli anni sessanta.
His heyday was in the sixties.

19. **(A)**   Orecchi enormi.
He had huge, disk-like ears, blond bangs and tiny freckles.

20. **(B)**   rinomato.
Topo Gigio was world-renowed, a famous celebrity.

6

21. **(A)**   Perché lui vince sempre.
She doesn't want to play chess or checkers with him as he always wins at both.

22. **(D)**   temporaneamente smarrita.
She can't remember where she put the chessboard. It's temporarily lost; she can't find it at the moment.

23. **(A)**   Una partite a carte.
She suggests a game of cards instead.

24. **(D)**   A Briscola.
They decide to play *Briscola*, a very popular Italian card game similar to Bridge. The object is to win four-card tricks with a partner. The Italian card deck used for this game and the others mentioned has only 40 cards. Each suit numbers from Ace to seven, with three face cards, Fante (Jack), Cavallo (Horseman), and Rè (King). The fours suits are Bastone, Spada, Denaro, and Coppa.

25. **(B)**   Di giocare con quattro persone invece di due.

He says that *Briscola* is more interesting with four players. With only two players, each will be dealt two hands and will play twice per trick, once as himself and once again, standing in for his partner. He doesn't suggest going outside. He doesn't suggest tic-tac-toe or hide-and-seek.

26. **(B)**   Perché mancano carte.

They won't be able to continue their card game as three cards are missing, the Ace of Coppa (cup, chalice), and the 3 and 5 of Bastone (club, cudgel)

7

27. **(B)**   Un tè istantaneo.
Ristora is an instant tea.

28. **(B)**   Alla drogheria.
Drogheria is a false cognate, it means grocery store, not drugstore.
You could expect to buy this product in any grocery store.

29. **(A)**   Sì, limone, pesca, e tè verde.
Yes, it comes in different flavors, lemon, peach, and green tea.

30. **(B)**   Sì, viene deteinato.
Yes, it comes without caffeine. Italians use *decaffeinato* for decaffeinated coffee, and *deteinato* for decaffeinated tea.

Part B: Reading

1

31. Dove ha luogo questa manifestazione estiva?
    (C) Umbria.
    This summer event takes place in Umbria.

32. Come vola una mongolfiera?
    (B) Con il gas propellente che produce una fiamma.
    The hot air balloon is fired by a gas propellant which emits a *whooshing* sound and produces a flame.

33. Perchè Todi è un luogo ideale per questo tipo di attività?
    (A) Perchè è in cima ad una collina.
    Like so many other towns in Umbria, Todi sits at the very top of a hill, an ideal spot for hot-air ballooning and hang-gliding.

34. Di che stoffa è fatta la mongolfiera?
    (D) Di una fibra sintetica e leggera.
    The colorful balloon is made of a light synthetic fiber, nylon.

35. Dove salgono i passeggeri?
    (B) Nella cesta.
    Passengers ride in the basket which is attached under the balloon.

2

36. Che tipo di prodotto è questo?
    (D) Caseario.
    Yogurt is a dairy product. It's not cereal, citrus or vegetable.

37. Quali gusti sono disponibili secondo la publicità?
    (A) C'è una ampia gamma di gusti.
    There's a wide variety of flavors.

38. Dove potresti trovare questo prodotto per comprarlo?

    (B) In qualsiasi supermercato.

    Yogurt can be found in any supermarket.

39. Si tratta di un prodotto sano e *benefico*?

    (C) Sì, perchè è interamente naturale.

    Yes, it's very healthy and beneficial as it's an entirely natural product.

40. Come sono i fermenti lattici?

    (A) Vivi.

    The yogurt cultures are *live*, not frozen, pickled, or dried.

3

41. Quanti anni avrà questo ragazzo?

    (C) È un ragazzino di 7 o 8 anni circa.

    As a cub scout working on a badge, he would be somewhere between 7 and 8 years old.

42. Che cos' è un salvadanaio?

    (C) Un posto in cui mettere piccole monete.

    A place in which to save small coins. A *salvadanaio* is a piggy bank.

43. Dov'era la borsa della madre?

    (C) Sul gancio dietro la porta.

    Her bag was hanging on a hook behind the door.

44. Che cosa offre la mamma al bambino?

    (D) Una sola moneta.

    She offers him a single coin (a 2 Euro piece) for his piggy bank.

45. Come risponde il bambino?

    (B) La respinge.

    He refuses it, turns it down. He's working on a Good Deeds Badge and must put others before himself for at least 24 hours.

4

46. Che specie di cane era Argo?

    (C) Era un cane da caccia.

    Argo was a hunting dog belonging to the father of the narrator.

47. Che tipi di giochi faceva la ragazzina con il suo compagno canino?

    (A) Fingeva di cucinare e giocava alla parrucchiera.

    She liked to make mud pies and pretend she was a hairdresser.

48. Come era il temperamento di Argo?

    (C) Paziente e tollerante.

    He was very patient and tolerant. He let her feed him mud pies and put bobby-pins on his ears. He was very gentle, not mean, dangerous, or nervous and excitable.

49. Dove aspettava Argo quando la ragazza tornava di scuola?

    (B) Davanti al cancello del giardino.

    He would wait for her every day after school at the garden gate.

50. Come ha reagito la ragazza quando non trovava Argo?

    (A) È diventata molto triste e agitata.

    She became extremely upset and agitated when she couldn't find him. She ran through the house and then outside, calling his name at the top of her lungs, over and over.

5

51. Di che cosa sognava il burattino?

    (A) Sognava di un campo dove i soldi crescevano sugli alberi.

    He was dreaming of a field where money grew on trees.

52. Chi è venuto alla porta e perché?

    (C) Era l'oste per dirgli l'ora.

    It was the innkeeper who told him what time it was (midnight).

53. Che fine hanno fatto i compagni di viaggio?

(B)   Erano partiti due ore fa, lasciando pagare a Pinocchio la cena e le camere.

His traveling companions (remember the Cat and the Fox?) skipped out two hours before the agreed upon wake-up call at midnight, thus leaving Pinocchio to pay for the rooms and an extravagant dinner.

54. Come crescevano gli zecchini d'oro nel campo del sogno?

(C)   A grappoli, dondolandosi degli arboscelli.

The gold coins hung in clusters, dangling from little trees. They didn't grow on the ground like weeds, nor like onions with the coins under earth, and they didn't grow like grape clusters on a vine.

55. Che rumore facevano gli zecchini d'oro?

(B)   Tintinnavano, mossi del vento.

They made a tinkling noise as they were moved by the wind. It sounded like *zin, zin, zin*. They seemed to be saying, "whoever wants us, come and get us."

Section II

Part A: Writing

Fill in a Verb

1. + 2.   Trasloco la settimana prossima. La nuova casa non sarà completamente pronta prima della fine del mese, ma occorre che io <u>me ne vada</u> lo stesso.

I'm moving next week. The new house won't be completely ready until the end of the month, but I have to go just the same.

The future is literal here; the house *will not* be ready. Use the subjunctive after *occorrere*.

3.   Possiedo una casetta estiva vicino a Orvieto dove <u>posso/potrò</u> aspettare. Così, avrò un intermezzo piacevole fra il trasloco dalla prima casa alla seconda.

I own a little summer house near Orvieto where I can (where I'll be able to) wait. This way I'll have a pleasant interlude between moving from the first house to the second.

4.   Vorrei visitare i vigneti intorno e spero che <u>sia</u> possibile ordinare alcune buone bottiglie per la festa con la quale mia nuora vorrà "sorprendermi".

I'd like to visit the surrounding vineyards and I hope it'll be possible to order some good wine for the party my daughter-in-law is going to "surprise" me with.

Use the subjunctive after *sperare che*.

5.   Ovviamente, bisognerà che <u>assaggi</u> molti bicchierini prima di scegliere. Tanto meglio!

Obviously I'll have to taste many little glasses (of wine) before choosing. So much the better!

Use the subjunctive after *bisognare che*. Here it appears in the future tense.

6.   Devo presentare un piccolo resoconto sull'artista *Arcimboldo*. Studio le sue tele da due settimane e ho già scritto gran parte della mia presentazione. L'inconveniente è che ho già restituito i libri che usavo e voglio soltanto verificare una citazione.

I have to present a little report on the artist Arcimboldo. I've been studying his paintings for two weeks and I've already written most of what I'll say. The problem is that I've already returned the books I was using and I just have to check a quotation.

Use the *present tense* with *da due settimane*. The little formula *present tense + da + time element* is used for an action which began in the past and continues into the present.

7.   È semplice. Devi/dovrai/dovresti scaricare il testo digitale al computer.

You have to / you'll have to/ you ought to download the digital text on the computer.

Use the present tense, the future, or the conditional of *dovere* here.

8. + 9.   Così puoi/potrai/potresti verificare la citazione senza lasciare la tua camera da letto.

That way you can / you'll be able to / you could check your quote without leaving your room.

You could answer with either the present, the future or the conditional of *potere* here. Always use the infinitive form of the verb after *senza*.

10.   Ottima idea! Grazie, mi hai salvato/a!

Great idea! Thanks, you've saved me.

Fill in a Word

1. + 2.   Mamma vuole che io sistemi un po' la mia camera da letto.

Mom wants me to straighten up my bedroom.

The verb *volere (to want)* is always followed by the subordinating conjunction (**che** + *subjunctive*) if the next verb is conjugated and not in the infinitive. The preposition **da** enables us to link two nouns into one. Similarly *una tazza **da** caffè,* is a coffee cup, as opposed to *una tazza **di** caffè* (a cup of coffee).

3. 4. + 5.   Devo pulire tutte le superfici coperte <u>di</u> polvere, che però non sarà facile <u>a causa</u> di tutti i ninnoli che dovrò togliere prima.

I've got to clean all the dusty surfaces, which won't be easy because of all the little knick-knacks I'll have to remove first.

The preposition **di** is frequently used after a *past participle* acting as an *adjective*. Here it means *covered with dust*. The preposition **a** combined with **causa**, gives us *because of*.

6.   **Che** impresa faticosa!

What a tiresome, boring undertaking!

The interrogative adjective serves here to make an exclamation in Italian. Note the lack of article in the construction!

7. + 8.   Di <u>tutti</u> i ponti che attraversano l'Arno, il Ponte Vecchio è <u>quello</u> che preferisco.

Of all the bridges that cross the Arno, the Ponte Vecchio is the one I like best.

We know from the context of the sentence that the adjective *all* is needed. *Tutti* agrees with the masculine plural *ponti*. The relative pronoun *che* (which) then links it to the verb *attraversare*. The masculine singular pronoun *quello,* meaning *the one,* links the bridge to the verb which governs it, *preferire*.

9. + 10. Mi piace vagare per i piccoli negozi <u>come</u> un pirata cercando un tesoro nascosto.

<u>Tanto</u> oro in un solo luogo mi fa battere il cuore più forte. Potrei passare una giornata intera a cercare un solo piccolo ciondolo.

*I like to wander from shop to shop **like** a pirate searching for hidden treasure.*

***So much** gold in one single place makes my heart beat faster. I could spend a whole day looking for just one little trinket.*

Sample Essay Answer
in Response to General Essay Question

Read the following essay to see how a student might have answered this question.

Cosa pensi dei tatuaggi? Se ne hai uno, com'è? Se non ne hai affatto, vorresti averne uno?

Conosco molte persone con tatuaggi. Io volevo farmi un filo spilato sul braccio ma i miei genitori mi hanno proibito di farlo. Un'amica mia si è fatta un piccolo sole raggiante sulla caviglia. Si va benissimo. Fra i miei insegnanti quasi la metà hanno tatuaggi! Sono andata in Italia con la mia classe d'italiano durante le vacanze di primavera e ho osservato che molti giovani italiani portano il tatuaggio anche loro, ragazzi e ragazze.

Mia madre vede tutto rosso quando parliamo di questo soggetto. Lei è inflessibile su questo punto. Il no è categorico. Papà dice che dovrò aspettare fino che io sia indipendente di loro. Quando avrò ventun'anni e un reddito mio, quando non abiterò più da loro...

Mio zio, (fratello di mia madre!) si è fatto un tatuaggio sulla mano quando era marinaio. È una grand'aquila con le ali aperte. Quando lo dico alla mamma, mi risponde sempre così "Tuo zio non porterà mai un vestito da sposa!" Mi racconta ad nauseum quanto difficile è togliere un tatuaggio e quanto doloroso. Mi dice che un giorno mi sveglierò una vecchietta e farò ridere la gente con i miei tatuaggi sulle rughe.

Part B: Culture

Sample Essay Answer
in Response to Cultural Essay Question

Read the following essay to see how a student might have answered this question.

Se potessi viaggiare in Italia, dove andresti e perché?

Il mio viaggio sognato sarebbe di seguire l'intera linea costiera della penisola italiana e poi di navigare le coste delle grandi isole della Sicilia e della Sardegna. Io vedrei tutte le belle spiagge, il mare Ligure, il Tirreno, il Mediterraneo, l'Ionio e l'Adriatico.

Comincerei al Nord-Ouest, a Ventimiglia per esempio, e poi scenderei tutta la costa, fermandomi ad ogni porto interessante, fra cui Genoa, Livorno…. Napoli. Dopo esser arrivato a Reggio Calabria, farei le grandi isole prima di salire tutto lo stivale fino a Venezia, la Serenissima, il mio ultimo scalo.

Visiterei Bari, Ancona, Pesaro e Rimini, e non mi sbrigerei mai. Farei la conoscenza di tanti pescatori e mangerei pesci freschissimi e frutta di mare. Di notte dormirei sulla mia piccola barchetta ed ogni giorno scenderei a terra per conoscere la gente e scoprire e grandi porti e piccoli paesi.

L'Italia è dotata da quante coste che questo viaggio non finerebbe quasi mai. La penisola è tanto lungo e stretto che anche quelli che abitano al centro possono raggiungere il mare in meno di due ore. Mi piacerebbe tanto conoscere l'Italia di questo punto di vista marina.

Un viaggio di marinaio farei, così, con il mare sempre al mio destra, e, a sinistra, lato cuore, l'Italia, ciottoli, sabbia, sole e vento.

Part C: Speaking

Speaking—Narration

Il Gelato

Here is how a student might have narrated these sketches:

1. Un signore compra due coni di gelato. Le sue figlie aspettano pazientemente la loro piccola felicità. Le due sorelline non hanno la stessa età. La più alta è probabilmente la maggiore, la più piccola la minore.

2. In questo disegno le due bambine mangiano con gusto i loro gelati. Sembrano avere l'aria molto contenta.

3. Attraversando la strada si vede la più piccola che inciampa e le cade il gelato a terra.

4. Eccola in ginocchio che piange davanti al suo tesoro perso. La poverina era tanto contenta poco prima.

5. La sorella maggiore le offre il suo cono. Il padre sembra contento del gesto generoso e mette la mano sulla spalla della figlia maggiore come a dimostrare la sua approvazione silenziosa. La piccola smette di piangere. Avrà un gelato grazie a sua sorella. La grande reagisce in modo spontaneo. Vede cosa succede a sua sorella e vuole aiutarla. Non riflette affatto. Fa un gesto molto altruista.

6. Credo che i fratelli maggiori debbano sempre servire da esempio ai minori, che li seguono nel bene e nel male. Visto che esercitano una tale influenza sui piccoli, anche senza volerlo, è necessario che mostrino la strada giusta.

Transcripts

AP Italian Language and Culture

Pre-Exam Transcript

AP Italian Language and Culture

SECTION I

Part A: Listening

Get ready for the listening part of the Pre-Exam Practice for the Advanced Placement Italian Language and Culture Pre-Exam.

Directions: You will now listen to several selections. For each selection you will have time to read over the questions printed in your booklet. Then you will hear the selection. You may take notes in your exam booklet as you listen. Your notes will not be graded. After listening to the selection, you will have time to answer the questions. Blacken the corresponding oval on your answer sheet.

Selection 1

W: Vorrei prepare la pelle per l'estate. Sono utili le docce solari o sono dannose per la pelle?

M: Il sole artificiale riflette raggi Uva che invecchiano più precocemente la pelle. Per preparare la pelle è meglio esporsi gradualmente proteggendosi con filtri solari adeguati. Le lampade solari danneggiano la pelle e nuocono alla salute.

Selection 2

W: Marco, vieni a vedere questa bambola che si abbronza! È tanto carina!

M: Non l'aurei mai immaginato! Ma come fa?

W: Non so, ma viene con occhialetti di sole, un bikini e il proprio asciugamano.

M: Fammi vedere. Mmm.. sembra che tutte le parti del corpo prendano la tinarella se hanno contatto con l'asciugamano. C'è anche un ombrellone.

W: Sono sicura che Maia ne andrà pazza. Cosa ne pensi?

M: Prendiamla per il suo compleanno a giugno.

W: Perfetto, così l'avrà durante l'estate e potrà portarla in spiaggia.

Selection 3

W: I nostri nuovi vicini sono tanto simpatici!

M: Hai ragione, sono gentilissimi. Ah, la gioventù! Tante cose li aspettano.

W: Figurati, è incinta di quattro mesi.

M: Meraviglioso! Ti ricordi della nascita di Martino? Eravamo tanto giovani!

W: Ma certo! Me lo ricordo come se fosse ieri. Ma noi avevamo i nostri genitori per aiutarci consigliarci. Quei giovani non hanno nessuno al mondo.

M: Se la caveranno. Io potrei verniciare la vecchia culla, sai?

W: Ed io potrei fare ai ferri qualche scarpetta…cosa pensi di Fulvia come nome feminile?

Selection 4

M: A che ora vuoi partire per l'aeroporto domani mattina?

W: Sai che sia importante arrivare molto in anticipo della partenza.

M: Appunto. Se il volo è per le dieci, tentiamo di arrivare verso le otto.

W: Non basterà! Con tutti i bagagli e controlli ci voranno almeno tre ore di anticipo.

M: Allora, cioè di partire alle cinque di mattina!

W: E se vuoi evitare il traffico intasato anche più presto.

M: D'accordo, sarà un sollievo di esserci di buon'ora. Ce ne andremo alle 4 e mezzo. Carico adesso il bagagliaio e poi farò il pieno stasera.

Selection 5

W: Come hai preso questo livido bluastro sulla fronte? È spaventoso!

M: Non credi che aumenti il blu degli occhi miei?

W: Sii sul serio. Racconta. Fa centro degli occhi, sei tanto scemo così!

M: Non oso dirtelo. Ti divertirai a burlarti di me.

W: Ti giuro, nemmeno una parola beffa. Puoi credermi. Ti do la mia parola.

M: Allora, rastrellavo le foglie. Le avevo messe in mucchi, c'erano tante.. delle foglie fino ai polpacci…

W: Non dire di più. Crollo già. È troppo bello, hai lasciato il rastrello per terra, i punti in aria..

M: Esatto, ma il tuo promesso di non burlarti di me?

W: E poi hai messo il piede…

M: Sì, ammetto che sia un po' ridicolo..

W: Un po'? E così nei cartoni animati!

Selection 6

W: Il tuo armadio sta per scoppiare! È pieno zeppo. Se apri la porta tutta la roba tua cade per terra in una valanga! È tempo di sistemarlo!

M: Sinceramente, è un tale miscuglio che non so davvero cominciare.

W: Ti aiuterò. Anzitutto, sgombriamolo. Dopo, farai quattro mucchi: buttare fuori, vendere, dare, e conservare. E l'ultimo mucchio non può superare gli altri, d'accordo?

M: Benone! Sarà semplice!

W: Mentre stai facendo io pulirò il didentro con l'aspirapolvere. Strofinerò gli scaffali e butterò le grucce storte.

M: Grazie tanto. L'incarico si farà subito a due!

Section II

Part C: Speaking

You will have a conversation with a good cook.

Here is your practice question:

(woman)   Ti piace cucinare?
Ti piace cucinare?
TONE (20 seconds) TONE

You will be scored on the next five questions:

(woman)   numero 1
Di solito chi cucina a casa tua?
Di solito chi cucina a casa tua?
TONE (20 seconds) TONE

(woman)   numero 2
Hai mai preparato un piatto per la tua famiglia?
Hai mai preparato un piatto per la tua famiglia?
TONE (20 seconds) TONE

(woman)   numero 3
Chi apparecchia?
Chi apparecchia?
TONE (20 seconds) TONE

(woman)   numero 4
Chi sparecchia?
Chi sparecchia?
TONE (20 seconds) TONE

(woman)   numero 5
Chi lava i piatti?
Chi lava i piatti?
TONE (20 seconds) TONE

You will have a phone conversation with an Italian film buff.

Here is your practice question:

(man)   Ti piace andare al cinema?
          Ti piace andare al cinema?
          TONE (20 seconds) TONE

You will be scored on the next five questions:

(man)   numero 1
          Ci vai spesso?
          Ci vai spesso?
          TONE (20 seconds) TONE

(man)   numero 2
          Che tipo di film ti piace?
          Che tipo di film ti piace?
          TONE (20 seconds) TONE

(man)   numero 3
          Qual'è il tuo attore preferito e perché?
          Qual'è il tuo attore preferito e perché?
          TONE (20 seconds) TONE

(man)   numero 4
          Hai un'attrice preferita?
          Hai un'attrice preferita?
          TONE (20 seconds) TONE

(man)   numero 5
          Di solito che snack prendi quando guardi il film?
          Di solito che snack prendi quando guardi il film?
          TONE (20 seconds) TONE

You will have a conversation with some Italian musicians.

Here is your practice question:

(woman)   Ti piace la musica?
          Ti piace la musica?
          TONE (20 seconds) TONE

You will be scored on the next five questions:

(woman)   numero 1
          Hai un gruppo o un cantante preferito?
          Hai un gruppo o un cantante preferito?
          TONE (20 seconds) TONE

(man)   numero 2
          Sai suonare uno strumento? Se sì, quale?
          Sai suonare uno strumento? Se sì, quale?
          TONE (20 seconds) TONE

(woman)   numero 3
          Sai cantare?
          Sai cantare?
          TONE (20 seconds) TONE

(woman)   numero 4
          Che genere di musica preferisci?
          Che genere di musica preferisci?
          TONE (20 seconds) TONE

(man)   numero 5
          Hai un I-pod? Se no, ne vorresti uno?
          Hai un I-pod? Se no, ne vorresti uno?
          TONE (20 seconds) TONE

You will have a conversation with an Italian sports fan.

Here is your practice question:

(man)   Ti piace lo sport?
        Ti piace lo sport?
        TONE (20 seconds) TONE

You will be scored on the next five questions:

(man)   numero 1
        Quale sport pratichi?
        Quale sport pratichi?
        TONE (20 seconds) TONE

(man)   numero 2
        Tifi per una squadra in particolare? Se sì, quale e perchè?
        Tifi per una squadra in particolare? Se sì, quale e perchè?
        TONE (20 seconds) TONE

(man)   numero 3
        Guardi mai lo sport in tv?
        Guardi mai lo sport in tv?
        TONE (20 seconds) TONE

(man)   numero 4
        Hai mai visto una partita dal vivo? Ti sei divertito? Raccontalo.
        Hai mai visto una partita dal vivo? Ti sei divertito? Raccontalo.
        TONE (20 seconds) TONE

(man)   numero 5
        Cosa pensi dei compensi milionari degli atleti professionisti al
        giorno d'oggi?
        Cosa pensi dei compensi milionari degli atleti professionisti al
        giorno d'oggi?
        TONE (20 seconds) TONE

You will have a phone conversation with an Italian designer.

Here is your practice question:

(man)   Segui la moda?
              Segui la moda?
              TONE (20 seconds) TONE

You will be scored on the next five questions:

(man)   numero 1
              Spendi molti soldi per vestirti?
              Spendi molti soldi per vestirti?
              TONE (20 seconds) TONE

(man)   numero 2
              Cosa metti per andare a scuola?
              Cosa metti per andare a scuola?
              TONE (20 seconds) TONE

(man)   numero 3
              Cosa porti per sentirti a tuo agio?
              Cosa porti per sentirti a tuo agio?
              TONE (20 seconds) TONE

(man)   numero 4
              Cosa indosseresti per una serata speciale?
              Cosa indosseresti per una serata speciale?
              TONE (20 seconds) TONE

(man)   numero 5
              Quali sono gli accessori indispensabili per te?
              Quali sono gli accessori indispensabili per te?
              TONE (20 seconds) TONE

Exam 1 Transcript

AP Italian Language and Culture

SECTION I

Part A: Listening

Get ready for the listening part of Practice Exam 1 for the Advanced Placement Italian Language and Culture Exam.

> **Directions:** You will now listen to several selections. For each selection you will have time to read over the questions printed in your booklet. Then you will hear the selection. You may take notes in your exam booklet as you listen. Your notes will not be graded. After listening to the selection, you will have time to answer the questions. Blacken the corresponding oval on your answer sheet.

Selection 1

W: I miei genitori partiranno per una crociera e vogliono che io li accompagni, ma sono un po' preoccupata.

M: Che fortuna! Ma perchè ti preoccupi?

W: Ho paura di annoiarmi se non ci saranno altri giovani.

M: Ce ne saranno moltissimi, e poi c'è tanto da fare e da scoprire! Beata te!

W: Spero che tu abbia ragione, la nave è lussuosa, ho visto delle fotografie…

M: Dove andate di preciso?

W: Facciamo una crociera sul Mediterraneo per sette giorni.

Selection 2

W: Sofia vuole che io le presti il mio abito rosa, sai, quello che ti piace tanto.

M: Ah sì? Se te lo restituisce, non vedo qual'è il problema.

W: Hai ragione, e poi lo farà pulire prima di ridarmelo.

M: E allora?

W: Pensavo di metterlo per il matrimonio di Fabiola e Rosario..

M: Non avrai freddo senza maniche nella sala con l'aria condizionata?

W: Probabilmente, dirò di sì a Sofia per il vestito rosa e per me porterò quello celeste.

Selection 3

M: Che si mangia stasera?

W: Visto che fa così caldo, vorrei preparare qualcosa di leggero.

M: Mi piace molto l'insalata mista con uova sode e tonno che prepari ogni tanto.

W: Ci sono anche fagioli sotto aceto. Posso tagliare un bel pomodoro con fette di mozzarella, qualche oliva...

M: Io metterò una bottiglia di vino bianco in fresco.

W: Benone, così non bisognerà accendere il forno.

M: Perfetto! Taglierò il cocomero.

Selection 4

M: E se andassimo in spiaggia questo fine settimana?

W: Non potremmo fare un'altra cosa? Mi sono già scottata quest'estate e devo stare attenta alla pelle.

M: Va bene, ti va di fare un picnic nel bosco sotto gli alberi?

W: Che bello, così almeno non mi brucio e poi dovrebbe essere un luogo piuttosto fresco.

M: Che ne dici di chiamare anche Eleonora e Alessandro? Sono così simpatici!

W: Ottima idea, è così tanto che non li vediamo!

M: Bene, allora vado a cercarti il cestino da picnic.

Selection 5

M: Muoio di fame e mi fa male il collo. Cerchiamo un autogrill.

W: Ottima idea. Facciamo una sosta.

M: Va bene, possiamo mangiare un po' e poi darci il cambio alla guida.

W: Puoi anche fare il pieno mentre scelgo un piccolo regalo per Daria.

M: D'accordo, prendimi anche qualcosa da leggere.

W: Certo caro, Ti sentirai meglio dopo aver mangiato, io guiderò fino a Pesaro.

M: Grazie. Farò un pisolino.

Selection 6

W: Per fare l'Acquacotta tagliuzatte 3 cipolle rosse, un peperone giallo e una costola di sedano. Soffriggete in una teglia con un po' d'olio d'oliva la cipolla, fatela imbiondire un po', quindi unitevi il peperone ed il sedano, la polpa di tre pomodori maturi e fate cuocere lentamente per circa un'ora. Versate poi il tutto in un tegame (meglio se di terracotta) ed aggiungere circa un litro d'acqua. Fate bollire ancora per poco, circa 10 minuti; preparate intanto delle scodelle con delle fette di pane raffermo abbrustolite, coprite con l'acquacotta e con tre uova appena sbattute. Fate riposare un attimo e servite.

Selection 7

W: Ho comprato or ora una macchina nuova. È piccolissima e facile da parcheggiare... sono tanto contenta!

M: Ma guarda, è la Smart Car di Mercedes! Ho letto che era solida e che consumava poco, e....hai scelto la convertibile? Fico!

W: Sapevo che ti sarebbe piaciuta. Ecco le chiavi. Puoi fare un giro di prova.

M: Volentieri! È facile da guidare e scattante!

W: Com'è il sedile secondo te?

M: Comodo!

W: Accoglie tranquillamente due persone.

Section II

Part C: Speaking—Conversation

You will have a conversation with an Italian businesswoman.

Here is your practice question:

(woman)   Che lavoro vorebbe fare dopo la scuola?
Che lavoro vorebbe fare dopo la scuola?
TONE (20 seconds) TONE

You will be scored on the next five questions:

(woman)   numero 1
Perchè vuole intraprendere questa carriera?
Perchè vuole intraprendere questa carriera?
TONE (20 seconds) TONE

(woman)   numero 2
È più importante lo stipendio o la realizzazione personale?
È più importante lo stipendio o la realizzazione personale?
TONE (20 seconds) TONE

(woman)   numero 3
Le piacerebbe lavorare all'estero? Perché sì o no?
Le piacerebbe lavorare all'estero? Perché sì o no?
TONE (20 seconds) TONE

(woman)   numero 4
Cosa sognava di diventare da bambino?
Cosa sognava di diventare da bambino?
TONE (20 seconds) TONE

(woman)   numero 5
Quanti anni ci vorranno, secondo lei, per diventare affermato in questo lavoro?
Quanti anni ci vorranno, secondo lei, per diventare affermato in questo lavoro?
TONE (20 seconds) TONE

Exam 2 Transcript

AP Italian Language and Culture

SECTION I

Part A: Listening

Get ready for the listening part of Practice Exam 2 for the Advanced Placement Italian Language and Culture Exam.

Directions: You will now listen to several selections. For each selection you will have time to read over the questions printed in your booklet. Then you will hear the selection. You may take notes in your exam booklet as you listen. Your notes will not be graded. After listening to the selection, you will have time to answer the questions. Blacken the corresponding oval on your answer sheet.

Selection 1

W: Papà, mi presti la carta di credito? Ho bisogno di 30 Euro.
M: Mia cara, il Bancomat non è un pozzo magico!
W: Dai, per favore! È solo un prestito papà.
M: Che cosa ci devi fare?
W: Dovrei comprare una ricarica per il cellulare.
M: Va bene, ma solo per questa volta.
W: Grazie papà, sei un angelo!

Selection 2

W: Sono andata a Mirabilandia, vicino Ravenna. Che esperienza!
M: Quale attrazione ti è piaciuta di più?
W: La ruota panoramica mi dà le vertigini, però mi piacciono molto le montagne russe!

M: Hai provato lo zucchero filato?
W: Sì, ma lo trovo troppo appiccicoso.
M: Quanto avete aspettato per entrare?
W: Abbiamo dovuto fare una fila di mezz'ora.

Selection 3

W: Guarda queste foto, sono bellissime!
M: Ma come hai fatto a svilupparle così velocemente?
W: Grazie alla mia nuova macchina fotografica digitale che stampa dal computer.
M: Davvero? Puoi farmi vedere come si fa?
W: Non è difficile, basta fare una foto e se non ti piace puoi cancellarla. Stampi solo le foto che preferisci. Se vieni a casa mia ti faccio vedere come si fa.
M: Volentieri, passerò dopo il lavoro.
W: Va be', allora ti aspetto verso le otto.

Selection 4

W: Ho voglia di fare una crostata oggi pomeriggio.
M: Evviva! Ma non metterci la marmellata di albicocche. Preferisco quella di ciliegie.
W: Va bene, vai a cercarmi il barattolo.
M: Ci sarà un buon profumo in cucina fra poco….apparecchio per due?
W: No, è troppo presto, potremmo degustarla a cena.
M: A cena? Ma… ma credevo che potessimo mangiarla subito, uscendo dal forno tutto fumante…
W: Ahimè, d'accordo, puoi prepararci un caffè mentre la metto al forno.

Selection 5

W: Secondo me la fede della signora Mariani è la più bella che io abbia mai visto. Mi piacerebbe fare i complimenti a suo marito per la splendida scelta.

M: Non è possibile. È vedova.

W: Che peccato! Non lo sapevo.

M: Sì, ha perso suo marito due anni fa.

W: Lo conoscevi?

M: Sì certo, hanno abitato vicino a noi per quasi cinquant'anni.

W: Ma almeno ha quella bellissima fede come ricordo della loro vita insieme.

Selection 6

M: *Liliana* è nome introdotto in Italia di recente e affermatosi diffusamente al Nord e al Centro del Paese. È ripreso dall'inglese *Lillian*, diminuitivo di *Elisabeth*, documentato in Inghilterra fin dal sedicesimo secolo, ma popolarmente viene collegato al latino *lilium* (che vuole dire *giglio*). Il Martirologio Romano ricorda una santa di nome *Liliosa* il 27 luglio, mentre Santa Elisabetta viene festeggiata il 10 novembre.

Selection 7

M: Cavolo! Il mouse non risponde. Guarda, il cursore non si muove neanche! Come faccio a connettermi ad Internet per leggere la mia e-mail?

W: È soltanto la polvere. Apri il mouse e togli la pallina. Tu vedrai della lanugine sopra. Qualche volta l'estraggo con le pinzette. Ecco un cottonfioc inumidito di alcool per pulire la pallina. Poi soffia dentro il mouse. Ecco fatto!

M: Si muove! Io temevo che fosse irreparabile! Che consiglio pratico! Grazie!

Section II—Conversation

Part C: Speaking

You will have a conversation with an Italian classmate.

Here is your practice question:

(woman)   Hai un migliore amico o una migliore amica?
          Hai un migliore amico o una migliore amica?
          TONE (20 seconds) TONE

You will be scored on the next five questions:

(woman)   numero 1
          Da quanto tempo vi conoscete?
          Da quanto tempo vi conoscete?
          TONE (20 seconds) TONE

(woman)   numero 2
          Come vi siete conosciuti?
          Come vi siete conosciuti?
          TONE (20 seconds) TONE

(woman)   numero 3
          Com'è il tuo amico o la tua amica?
          Com'è il tuo amico o la tua amica?
          TONE (20 seconds) TONE

(woman)   numero 4
          Vi vedete spesso?
          Vi vedete spesso?
          TONE (20 seconds) TONE

(woman)   numero 5
          Che cosa fate insieme?
          Che cosa fate insieme?
          TONE (20 seconds) TONE

Exam 3 Transcript

AP Italian Language and Culture

SECTION I

Part A: Listening

Get ready for the listening part of Practice Exam 3 for the Advanced Placement Italian Language and Culture Exam.

Directions: You will now listen to several selections. For each selection you will have time to read over the questions printed in your booklet. Then you will hear the selection. You may take notes in your exam booklet as you listen. Your notes will not be graded. After listening to the selection, you will have time to answer the questions. Blacken the corresponding oval on your answer sheet.

Selection 1

M: Mio fratello si è rotto il naso ieri.

W: No, il povero! Come va adesso?

M: Va meglio ma ha gli occhi pesti. Mi è capito la stessa cosa due anni fa.

W: Davvero? Quanto tempo ci vuole per guarire?

M: Grosso modo due o tre mesi, i compressi freddi aiutano molto.

W: È andato all'ospedale?

M: Sì, alla clinica del rinologo. Respira meglio adesso che prima dell'incidente.

Selection 2

W: Le calle richiedono pochissime cure. Basta bagnarle con regolarità in modo da mantenere la terra sempre abbastanza umida e concimarle un paio di volte al mese. Gli amanti di quelle nere possono quindi coltivarle direttamente sul balcone o in giardino. Quale scegliere? La *Naomi* è quella che presente le tonalità porpora più vellutate.

Selection 3

M: Ti ricordo come andava la filastrocca che recitavamo sempre da bambino, quella con le banane?

W: Ma certo! Va così: Banana Verde è appena sbarcata, dal Centro America è arrivata. Banana Gialla l'ho comperata, ed in un cesto l'ho sistemata. Poi per due giorni non l'ho mangiata, Banana Marrone è diventata.

Selection 4

W: Il dentista dice che bisogna togliere i quattro denti del giudizio a mia figlia di 15 anni. Cosa ne pensa? Secondo lui non c'è spazio sufficiente perché escano.

M: In linea generale i denti del giudizio si tolgono quando i germi sono malposizionati e la radiografia mostra che l'eruzione sarà difficile, se non impossibile. Nel caso non sia possibile evitare l'estrazione, l'età migliore per toglierli è proprio intorno ai 15 anni.

Selection 5

W: Nonna mi ha regalato questo topo biondo alle orecchie grandissime che aveva di ragazzina. Com'è buffo! Non ho mai visto per nulla simile.

M: Ma è Topo Gigio! Come non conoscerlo? Non mi sono mai sentito tanto vecchio! Era un topo italiano conosciuto in tutto il mondo. Faceva programmi televisivi, anche all'estero!

W: Non sapevo che fosse tanto rinomato...

M: Era molto popolare nei paesi ispanici, al Giappone e nemmeno negli Stati Uniti dove veniva spesso sullo spettacolo settimanale di Ed Sullivan.

W: Non l'avrei mai saputo....

Selection 6

M: Vuoi giocare a dama o a scacchi?

W: Non mi ricordo dove ho messo la scacchiera, e d'altronde tu vinci sempre e a dama e a scacchi! Giochiamo piuttosto a carte! Briscola o Scopa?

M: D'accordo, Briscola, ma è più interessante da quattro. Smazzo io.

W: Benissimo . . . Cosa c'è?

M: Mancano tre carte, l'asso di Coppa, il tre e il 5 di Bastone.

W: Accidenti!

Selection 7

M: Preparati a casa il tè che vuoi, come vuoi, istantanco. Buono, pratico e conveniente, sceglilo nel gusto classico limone o pesca, al te verde con le sue benefiche proprietà, deteinato per tutta la famiglia e *light* con solo settantadue calorie per litro. *Ristora* e la vita migliora.

Section II

Part C: Speaking— Conversation

You will have a conversation with an Italian travel agent.

Here is your practice question:

(man)   Se Lei potesse viaggiare in tutto il mondo dove andrebbe?
           Se Lei potesse viaggiare in tutto il mondo dove andrebbe?
           TONE (20 seconds) TONE

You will be scored on the next five questions:

(man)   numero 1
           Preferisce i paesi caldi o freddi?
           Preferisce i paesi caldi o freddi?
           TONE (20 seconds) TONE

(man)   numero 2
           Con che mezzo di trasporto vorrebbe andare?
           Con che mezzo di trasporto vorrebbe andare?
           TONE (20 seconds) TONE

(man)   numero 3
           Con chi passerebbe queste vacanze?
           Con chi passerebbe queste vacanze?
           TONE (20 seconds) TONE

(man)   numero 4
           Viaggia spesso?
           Viaggia spesso?
           TONE (20 seconds) TONE

(man)   numero 5
           Pensa che avrebbe nostalgia di casa?
           Pensa che avrebbe nostalgia di casa?
           TONE (20 seconds) TONE